The three-volume *Encyclopedia of Rock* is simply the
best, most comprehensive Rock reference work ever
written. Compiled by an international team of
specialists working under expert editorial control, it
combines hard accurate facts with lively critical
comment. Clearly arranged in alphabetical order the
Encyclopedia is the essential and definitive book for
anyone – from the serious student to the casual fan –
who wants to know more about what lies behind the
music.

This first volume covers the earliest origins of
rock'n'roll and its heyday – for many the Golden Age.
Bill Haley, Buddy Holly, Elvis Presley – all the
strands and influences in the styles of the superstars
are carefully analysed. And how about Tommy
Facenda, Chan Romero and the Kalin Twins?
To find out, read on . . .

The Encyclopedia of Rock
Edited by Phil Hardy and Dave Laing

Consultant Editors:
Charlie Gillett
Greil Marcus
Bill Millar
Greg Shaw

The Encyclopedia of Rock

Volume I
The Age of Rock'n'Roll

Edited by Phil Hardy and Dave Laing

Panther

Granada Publishing Limited
Published in 1976 by Panther Books Ltd
Frogmore, St Albans, Herts AL2 2NF

Copyright © Aquarius Books and Phil Hardy and Dave Laing
This volume first published in
Great Britain by Hanover Books in
cooperation with Panther Books, 1975
Made and printed in Great Britain by
Hazell Watson & Viney Ltd
Aylesbury, Bucks
Set in Linotype Times

Contributors to this volume:

CLIVE ANDERSON
STEPHEN BARNARD
JOHN BROVEN
PETER CARR
JOHN COLLIS
DR ROCK
ADAM FINN
ROB FINNIS
PETE FOWLER
MICHAEL GRAY
PHIL HARDY
MARTIN HAWKINS
GARY HERMAN
IAN HOARE
NORMAN JOPLING
DAVE LAING
DAVID McGILLIVRAY
BILL MILLAR
JONATHAN MORRISH
CLIVE RICHARDSON
TONY RUSSELL
RAY TOPPING
DAVE WALTERS
CLIFF WHITE

This book is dedicated to Mike Leadbitter

ACKNOWLEDGEMENTS

The editors and contributors freely acknowledge the considerable debt they owe to the following:
Bigtown Review, Billboard, Bim Bam Boom, Blues & Soul, Blues Research, Blues Unlimited, Blues World, Boppin' News, Cashbox, Barrett Hansen, *Jazz & Blues, Let It Rock, Living Blues, Melody Maker, New Musical Express, Penniman News, Record Mirror, Rock File, R&B Monthly, R&B Magazine, Rollin' Rock, Rolling Stone, Shout, Soul Bag,* Joel Whitburn and *Who Put the Bomp.*

INTRODUCTION

This is the first of a three-volume Encyclopedia of Rock. It takes the story of the music up to the emergence of the Beatles as international stars in 1963. Volumes 2 and 3 cover the periods from Merseybeat to San Francisco, and from Woodstock to the present day, respectively.

The criteria for inclusion in the Encyclopedia are two-fold. The first is success: artists whose records were very successful in the Hit Parades of America and/or Britain will almost invariably be included. The exceptions are those artists unconnected with rock music, such as Les Baxter and Russ Conway. The second basis for inclusion involves our assessment of historical influence and artistic significance. Here we have drawn heavily on our Consultant Editors and contributors, all acknowledged experts in the field. The length of each entry has been dictated by our estimate of the importance of its subject to rock music as a whole. The people behind the scenes have been as influential as the performers. So here, in many cases for the first time, is recognition of the contribution made by the record-company bosses, record producers, session musicians and songwriters. The Encyclopedia gives due weight to the work of these often neglected figures, and also to musicians from areas of music which border on rock, and which have exerted considerable influence on it. Thus, in addition to an entry on gospel music, there are individual entries on six major gospel artists.

Each volume contains a complete index of every person in the text. This means that many figures who do not have an entry devoted exclusively to them can still be located and cross-references can be followed. References to the main entries will be indicated by bold type.

Because the aim of the Encyclopedia is to provide information and informed comment for the general reader, no discographies are included as such, though in many cases reference is made to an artist's significant recordings. In any case, a definitive discography of all the artists in this volume would fill a book at least as big as this. Leadbitter and Slaven's *Blues Records* provides such information for blues artists, and a comparable work in rock is urgently needed, as interest in the past of the music grows. The only equivalent in rock at present are Joel Whitburn's collection of the *Billboard* charts in America (*Record Research*) and Pete and Annie Fowler's collation of the British charts in *Rock File*. Except where noted, all chart positions noted in the Encyclopedia refer to these charts.

Volume 1

The focal point of this first volume is the classic era of rock'n'roll, from 1955–9. The older musical forms of both the black and the white South, whence it grew, are fully dealt with, as well as the seminal figures who helped to bring it into being – Sam Phillips, Alan Freed as well as performers like Elvis Presley, Chuck Berry and Little Richard. In the entries devoted to record companies, large and small, can be found the details of the battle between the mainly localized labels who pioneered rock and the 'Big Six' establishment companies who attempted to co-opt the new sounds, either by producing watered-down 'cover versions' of rock songs by their own middle-of-the-road performers, or by signing up rock'n'roll singers. Many of the covers were of songs from R&B, whose rhythmic and emotional intensity brought it to the attention of a white teenage audience beginning to assert itself as a distinct social group. The soul music of the Sixties, which also grew out of R&B, is dealt with fully in Volume 2 of this Encyclopedia. By the end of the Fifties, the first phase of rock'n'roll was over, and rock-inflected teenage ballads were dominating the charts. Britain's teenagers were enthusiastic consumers of rock'n'roll, but contributed little to it. Rock in Britain prior to the Beatles was merely an enthusiastic cover version of American music, with occasional inspiration from Lonnie Donegan, Billy Fury and Johnny Kidd.

Although the last few years have seen a welcome re-kindling of general interest in the music of the Fifties, the new audience for rock'n'roll has not been well served by careful re-issues of recordings from that era, apart from randomly released isolated series in particular territories.

This Volume covers a well-defined period, however, many of whose figures have careers which stretch beyond into the Sixties and, in some cases, the Seventies. In these instances, the entry is placed according to the period of that figure's greatest importance. Thus, Elvis Presley is to be found in Volume 1 and his Sun label-mate, Charlie Rich, is dealt with in detail in Volume 3, since the Seventies have seen his emergence as a major performer. In the case of institutions, such as record companies, and of music centres such as Nashville or New York, however, there is a separate entry in each volume.

We will be delighted if the course of events make it necessary to move other artists from this volume to the last volume of future editions, for which corrections and suggestions will be welcomed.

ABC Records was formed in Hollywood in 1956 by Sam Clark – who left in 1960 – as a subsidiary of Paramount Pictures. ABC saw rock'n'roll as a way to quickly establish themselves in the market and brought in Buck Ram as a free-lance A&R man, and employed Don Costa to produce the company's major discovery, Paul Anka. Anka's nine-million seller, 'Diana', set ABC off to a good start and his later, worldwide hits – arranged by Sid Feller, as were those of Lloyd Price and Ray Charles – helped the company to grow. Dick Clark was employed by ABC TV and his help and advice was always on tap – hence the signing of Danny and the Juniors. The arrival of Lloyd Price in 1959, signalled an interest in black music that developed with the signing of Ray Charles in 1960 and the Impressions in 1961. Their chart success compensated in part for the loss of Paul Anka (and the rights to his material) in 1962.

Ewart Abner's career began in 1950 on the staff of Chance Records in Chicago, writing songs and producing acts like the Flamingos and Moonglows. The company never achieved national prominence and folded in 1954, by which time Abner had helped to form Vee Jay Records, where he teamed up with Calvin Carter to write and produce many hits for acts including the Dells and Dee Clark. Abner's forte, however, lay in promotion and marketing. The Falcon subsidiary was formed in 1957 and later changed to 'Abner' to avoid confusion with an existing label. This subsidiary was active up to 1960, by which time Abner had become president of Vee Jay. During the early Sixties, the company was well-represented in the charts with such acts as Gene Chandler and the Four Seasons, but in 1963 Abner was deposed as president and quit. He was reinstated as General Manager in 1965, but despite chart success the company was financially unsound and folded in 1966. Abner then joined Motown as a producer, moving to the West Coast with them and eventually becoming president of the corporation in 1973.

Johnny Ace, born on June 9, 1929, in Memphis, Tennessee, as John Marshall Alexander Jnr., began his career as a pianist with Adolph Duncan's Band. Ace joined the Beale Streeters – whose other members included B. B. King, Bobby Bland and Rosco Gordon in the late Forties – following naval service during the war. His solo debut, the plaintive 'My Song' (Duke), topped the R&B charts in 1952, and subsequent discs – generally sensitive baritone performances of love ballads accompanied by understated small combo support – enjoyed great success. Stylistic parallels include Jesse Belvin, Charles Brown and Nat 'King' Cole, though Ace occasionally recorded jump items in the style of Roy Brown or Amos Milburn. He toured constantly, and was voted 'Most Programmed R&B Artist of 1954' in Cashbox's DJ poll. His life came to an early, tragic end when he shot himself playing Russian roulette backstage at Houston's City Auditorium on Christmas Eve, 1954. A measure of immortality was assured by his posthumous hit, 'Pledging My Love'.

Ace Records, though operating from the small-time atmosphere of the Southern country town of Jackson, Mississippi, became a major independent label in the late Fifties thanks to its active involvement in the fermenting New Orleans R&B scene and using such sessionmen as Lee Allen (tenor) and Red Tyler (baritone). Founded in 1955 by Johnny Vincent, they had an early regional R&B hit with Earl King's 'Those Lonely, Lonely Nights'. Huey 'Piano' Smith took Ace into the Hot Hundred charts in 1957 with 'Rockin' Pneumonia And The Boogie Woogie Flu', followed quickly by 'Don't You Just Know It'. This inspired a succession of hits from Joe Tex, James Booker, Bobby Marchan and Eddie Bo. Vincent then had even bigger success with white rock'n'rollers Jimmy Clanton ('Just A Dream') and Frankie Ford ('Sea Cruise'), and straining for further commercial success, turned Ace into a dire middle-of-the-road pop label. In 1962, Ace merged with Vee Jay, had another massive hit with Jimmy Clanton's 'Venus In Blue Jeans' and then fell apart at the seams – a long way from its New Orleans roots.

Roy Acuff was born on September 15, 1903, at Maynardsville, Tennessee. Acuff's greatest musical influence was during the middle and late Thirties and early Forties when he led a band, the Smokey Mountain Boys, whose sound was echoed by many contemporaries. Featuring a thick-textured fabric of fiddle and steel guitar, it was heard regularly over the *Grand Ole Opry* and elsewhere in Acuff's native Tennessee. The coupling of 'Wabash Cannonball' and 'Freight Train Blues' – the latter the original for Bob Dylan's version – was a hit, but was eclipsed by the fundamentalist 'Great Speckled Bird', and Acuff continued to evoke Southern rurality through railroads and religion. His status encouraged him to run for State governorship – unsuccessfully – and to found, with Fred Rose, the Acuff-Rose music-publishing concern, now a substantial power in country music. He still leads a band whose personnel and style have changed little in three decades, and is one of the few Nashville personalities of consequence who adheres to an uncompromisingly old-time approach.

Faye Adams, a member of Joe Morris's Blues Cavalcade, was signed to Atlantic in New York, where Herb Abramson rehearsed her and the band on 'Shake A Hand'. Soon after Abramson left to do military service and Morris and Adams (born Scruggs) switched to Herald, the label on which 'Shake A Hand' appeared. It topped the R&B charts for many weeks during 1953. A moving plea for brotherly tolerance, it has since been revived by innumerable soul singers. Faye Adams cut over 30 tracks for Herald, including two subsequent R&B No. 1 hits – 'I'll Be True' and 'Hurts Me To My

Heart'. Between 1957 and 1963, she recorded for Imperial, Lido, Warwick, Savoy and Prestige.

Johnny Adams, the most important quality soul singer from New Orleans, scored locally with his early records for Ric, 'Come On' (1960) and 'A Losing Battle' (1962). These initial releases had a more blatantly pop approach than the mainstream New Orleans R&B sounds of the time, but his strong, soulful voice was well able to compete with full orchestras and heavenly choirs. After recording for Watch in 1963, he fell out of favour but was rescued from oblivion in 1969 when he had three successive and classy Hot Hundred hits for SSS International with 'Release Me', 'Reconsider Me' and 'I Can't Be All Bad'. He still works consistently in the New Orleans area and records for Atlantic.

Marie Adams, born in Lyndon, Texas, was a gospel singer before making her first records in 1952. An R&B Top Ten hit, 'I'm Gonna Play The Honky Tonks' (Peacock), led to further blues with the bands of Cherokee Conyer, Johnny Otis and Pluma Davis. In 1957, the nineteen-stone (266 pounds) Marie formed the Three Tons Of Joy with Sadie and Francine McKinley. Their 'Ma She's Making Eyes At Me' on Capitol topped the British charts. A duet with Johnny Otis, 'Bye Bye Baby', was the exciting follow-up. Sweeter pop-blues records followed (on Capitol, Sure-Play and Encore) and in 1972 Marie and the Tons recorded for Vantage and toured Europe with Otis.

Aladdin Records was formed in Los Angeles in 1945 by brothers Eddie and Leo Mesner. It was swept along in the emergent post-war record boom and for a time in the Fifties was recognized as one of the premier R&B labels. With Maxwell Davis as staff producer, early R&B hits were had with Charles Brown's classic 'Drifting Blues', Amos Milburn, Peppermint Harris, Lightnin' Hopkins and the Five Keys. The company hit the national Hot Hundred charts in a big way with the million-selling 'Let The Good Times

Roll' by Shirley and Lee in 1956, and in early 1958 Thurston Harris's 'Little Bitty Pretty One' made the Top Ten. Aladdin never really came to grips with rock'n'roll and was a spent force by 1960. In 1962, the entire catalogue was purchased by Imperial and selected re-issues have since been made.

Lee Allen, whose searing tenor sax solos on countless classic New Orleans R&B sessions of the Fifties made his name, was born in Pittsburgh, Kansas, on July 2, 1926. He started playing in the clubs of New Orleans in the late Forties with Paul Gayten's band, and in between recording sessions he also played with the bands of Fats Domino and Dave Bartholomew. After helping make all those hit records for other artists, he finally had his own hit in 1958 with the R&B instrumental, 'Walking With Mr Lee'. In the early Sixties he moved to the West Coast and still does the occasional recording session and 'live' gig.

Lee Andrews and the Hearts (Roy Calhoun, Butch Curry, Jimmy McAlister and John Young) first recorded for Eddie Heller's Rainbow (1954) and Gotham (1955), owned by Irvin Ballen. Inspired by the Orioles, this Philadelphia group had 1957 hits with 'Long Lonely Nights' (No. 45) and 'Teardrops' (Top Twenty), which Chess purchased from Jocko Henderson's Main-Line label. The following year, 'Try The Impossible' – which United Artists bought from Casino – reached the Top Forty. Later members included Wendell Calhoun, Ted Weems and Gerald Thompson, but the group split up when doo-wop became unfashionable. With and without the Hearts, Lee Andrews has recorded for Gowen, Lost Nite, Parkway, Jordan, Swan, RCA and Crimson. In the Seventies he led new groups, First Born and Congress Alley.

Paul Anka, born on July 30, 1941, in Ottawa, Ontario, entered show business at the early age of 12 as an impersonator. In 1956, under the supervision of Ernie Freeman, he cut his first (unsuccessful) record, 'I Confess', for Modern Records. The following year, while staying in New York with the Rover Boys, who were contracted to ABC, he took their advice and contacted Don Costa who signed him to ABC and produced 'Diana'. That song, the story of his love for a 20-year-old girl – 'I'm so young and you're so old' – only reached No. 2 in the Hot Hundred but went on to sell nine million copies worldwide. It was followed by a string of hits, including the seminal 'Lonely Boy' [from which came the short film of the same title] 'Put Your Head On My Shoulder' (both in 1959) and 'Puppy Love' (1960) – this last supposedly reflecting his admiration for Annette whom he was dating at the time.

Anka was no manufactured idol. Through a mixture of luck and good judgement in the Fifties and early Sixties, he made the middle ground – between the aggression of Presley and the repression of 'good guy' Pat Boone – his own. Anka's market was the girls between 12 and 14 who had few stars they could relate to before the arrival of the Beatles, Monkees and Osmonds. Quite simply, Anka, with his calculatingly honest songs of teenage *angst*, could make 12-year-old girls cry in their beds at night – and it would be his songs that the Osmonds would later revive.

A prolific songwriter, as well as his own hits he wrote 'It Doesn't Matter Anymore' for Buddy Holly before moving on to the mainstream of popular music with 'My Way' for Sinatra and 'She's A Lady' for Tom Jones, among others. Anka was also a shrewd businessman – on leaving ABC for RCA in 1962, he bought back all his ABC masters. By then he had sold 30 million records throughout the world and couldn't have been particularly worried by his declining American chart success. Moreover, his songwriting and various business concerns were going well. In the Sixties, Anka spent most of his time working behind the scenes – for example, he gave Steve Goodman and John Prine their starts in the record industry. However, in 1970, he began to feel the urge to perform again. He quit RCA for Buddah and then UA, for whom in 1974 he wrote and recorded – at Rick

18

Hall's Muscle Shoals studio – the sickly, but very successful, 'You're Having My Baby'. The wheel had come full circle.

Annette, an ever-present in beach party movies from the early Sixties, was born Annette Funicello in Utica, New York on Oct. 22, 1942. Moving to the West Coast, she joined Walt Disney's Mouseketeers in October 1955 and three years later was launched as a singer at the male teenage market by the Disney organisation. Her first record, 'Tall Paul' (on the Disney label, Vista) reached No. 7, and was followed by a series of forgettable hits on Disneyland. The biggest were 'First Name Initial' (No. 20 in 1959), 'O Dio Mio' (No. 10 in 1960) and 'Pineapple Princess' (No. 11 in the same year).

30/6/201

Chet Atkins, born in Lutrell, Tennessee on June 20, 1924, as Chester Burton Atkins, took an early interest in country music and before he left school joined Bill Carlisle and his Dixieland Swingers on WNOX radio in Knoxville, Tennessee. Eventually he moved to Nashville and by the time the town became a really important recording centre in the Fifties, he had established himself as one of its leading musicians.

Recording in Nashville depended then – as it still does – on the skills of a small number of session players .Many of these men are untutored in the formalities of music, although they possess a notation system of their own. Their success rests on their improvisational abilities and a close knowledge of each other's work, refined by playing together weekly as sidemen on the *Grand Ole Opry*, WSM's legendary country music show, and daily on countless recording sessions.

By 1960, Atkins, a guitarist in the Merle Travis tradition, already had a long association with RCA both as performer and producer, and was moving out of the straight country music field. He ran a small jazz-oriented nightclub group of drums, bass, guitarists Grady Martin and Hank Garland, and pianist Floyd Cramer. They threw out the conventional instrumentation, piano and the guitars taking the lines that had formerly belonged to the fiddle and steel guitar. The resulting rhythm had a light, rocking feel and when Atkins took it back into the studio it became known as the Nashville Sound.

As an A&R director with RCA, among his responsibilities was the career of the newly-arrived Elvis Presley whose records he supervised. He was also responsible for much of the Everly Brothers' early work, but is best known for the resuscitation of the ailing body of country music. Hank Locklin, Bobby Bare, Skeeter Davis, Jim Reeves, Don Gibson and John D. Loudermilk all gained important successes with Atkins. He and Floyd Cramer played on most of the records themselves and it is his fluent guitar and Cramer's tinkling right-hand piano that characterises many records of this period. At one time he was the most powerful man in Nashville. He stayed with RCA and has encouraged new singers such as Charley Pride, Waylon Jennings, Dottie West, Connie Smith and Jerry Reed (another graduate Nashville sideman).

But like most of Nashville's defences against musical impurity, Atkins' fabled 'Sound' lived on to become a barrier to progress. The original small group sound was soon lost in a mush of strings and crooning singers that ossified into a musical orthodoxy which Nashville applied to all who recorded there. It's no coincidence that RCA was the last of the major recording companies to give cover credits to sidemen: under RCA's guidance, they were all starting to sound the same. Some singers, notably Waylon Jennings, moved out of the Atkins orbit to experiment on their own but others, like Charley Pride, remained, their later records standing as tedious (though profitable) testimony to Nashville's inherent musical conservatism. Atkins was elected to the Country Music Hall of Fame in 1973.

Atlantic Records was formed in 1947 by Herb Abramson and Ahmet Ertegun with the help of a $10,000 loan from the latter's dentist. At a time when the American music market was dominated by majors like Columbia, RCA and Decca with franchises in the key stores, distribution was a major problem. National distributors didn't think that the music

Atlantic was recording for the customers of the side-street stores – a rough danceable combo blues – would be successful. Ertegun quickly discovered the importance of setting up national distribution and was aided by Stick McGhee's big 1949 hit, 'Drinkin' Wine Spo-De-O-Dee', and in the next few years a consistent string of hits followed by Ruth Brown, the Clovers and Joe Turner.

In 1953 Abramson left and his place was taken by Jerry Wexler. Often, however, at this stage, the majors were being successful with songs – 'Such A Night', 'Tweedle Dee', 'Sh-Boom' and of course 'Shake, Rattle And Roll' – that Atlantic had originally recorded. They used identical arrangements, often the same musicians, but with white singers. In Britain, the situation was even worse as the Atlantic originals were never even released, and it wasn't until 1955 that Decca started to issue Atlantic's material on its London label.

However, the company's growth wasn't to be checked and several factors in the second half of the Fifties ensured its expansion. With the advent of rock'n'roll came the breakdown of all previous distinctions between R&B and pop, between the majors and the 'indies'. In short, the whole industry was radically altered. While rock'n'roll had been a new name for R&B to disguise the fact that the singers were black, it wasn't – as R&B had once been – solely confined to black singers. Moreover, in Jesse Stone, a man intimately acquainted with Southern rhythm and blues records, Atlantic had someone whose arrangements and compositions ('Money Honey' and 'Shake, Rattle And Roll') recreated the bass patterns, rhythms and all-round level of energy for other arrangers to gratefully copy. Atlantic had discovered how to record rock'n'roll successfully.

The arrival in 1956 of the ingenious producing-arranging-writing team of Jerry Leiber and Mike Stoller and the signing of Bobby Darin helped reduce the number of cover versions that had kept Atlantic's records out of the charts. In the following four years – an era renowned for its one-hit wonders – the company (plus the subsidiary Atco) had 84 hits in the Hot Hundred, of which 56 were contributed by five performers – the Coasters (15), La Vern Baker (11) and the Drifters, Clyde McPhatter and Bobby Darin (10).

The pop field was not Atlantic's only concern. In 1956, Ahmet's brother, Nesuhi, moved in to set up the LP department and enlarge the roster of jazz artists – Charlie Mingus, John Coltrane and Ornette Coleman were among those who recorded for the company over the next few years, with the Modern Jazz Quartet easily their most successful jazz artists.

Before the arrival of the Beatles and the industry's next radical change, the company went from strength to strength. The Drifters, Bobby Darin, Solomon Burke, Nino Tempo and April Stevens all had hits at a time when much cornier songs prevailed – an augury of the soul explosion to come. But, above all, the company showed a foresight, integrity and genuine interest in music (like releasing British produced records in America – most successfully with Acker Bilk's 'Stranger On The Shore' – and the signing of a distribution deal with Satellite, later to become Stax) that exemplified their philosophy of providing good material for good singers. It was their broader perspective and refusal to be categorised as a specialist label that ensured their survival.

Sil Austin was born on September 17, 1929, in Dunellon, Florida. A tenor saxophonist, Sylvester Austin worked with jazz bands until he joined Tiny Bradshaw's group with whom he recorded for King in 1952. He left Bradshaw in 1954 and recorded for Jubilee before moving to Mercury in 1956. There, with Mickey Baker on guitar, Doc Bagby on organ, and Panama Francis on drums, he cut a string of consistently popular instrumentals, including 'Slow Walk' (No. 19), 'Birthday Party' (No. 74) and 'Danny Boy' (No. 59). Since leaving Mercury in 1965, he has recorded R&B on Sew City and easy listening ballads with strings on SSS International. Austin is still a prolific album artist.

Frankie Avalon was born Francis Avallone, Sept. 18, 1939. Avalon and his label-mate, Fabian, epitomised the stereotyped American teen-idols who took over American pop in the late Fifties. Avalon began as a trumpet-playing child prodigy, appearing on the Paul Whiteman *Teen Club* TV show in Philadelphia and recording instrumentals for RCA's Vik and 'X' subsidiaries. As he outgrew his novelty appeal, he opened (under the sponsorship of two local businessmen, Bob Marcucci and Peter De Angelis) a youth club called Frankie Avalon's 'Teen And Twenty Club' where Avalon, Fabian and Bobby Rydell would hang out in their pre-fame days.

In 1957, he joined a local group called Rocco and his Saints, then began recording solo for Marcucci and De Angelis' newly-formed Chancellor label and made a brief appearance in the film *Disc Jockey Jamboree*. After two flops, Avalon finally established himself early in 1958 with 'De De Dinah', a pubescent idiot chant which sold a million. He scored again with 'Gingerbread', 'Why', 'Venus' and 'From Bobby Sox To Stockings' before branching out into films – e.g. *The Alamo* – and cabaret. During the early Sixties, his bronzed, clean-cut features graced a series of beach party movies in which he usually co-starred opposite the pneumatic Annette Funicello.

LaVern Baker, born on Nov. 11, 1929, in Chicago, first played in Detroit clubs where, as Little Miss Sharecropper, she is said to have had an enduring influence on Johnnie Ray, before recording unsuccessfully for Columbia and – with Todd Rhodes' orchestra – for King in 1952. The following year, she was snapped up by Atlantic where she remained until 1965. Many of her earliest recordings – 'Tweedle Dee', 'Bop-Ting-A-Ling' (both written by Winfield Scott) and 'Play It Fair' for example – were deliberately pop-slanted with bland, stereotyped, vocal choruses, and hardly stand up today. None the less, her records were ruthlessly covered at the time by white 'name' artists. So much so that she gained useful publicity by writing to her Detroit congressman about the practice.

Her warm, broken-note voice had a sexy, playful quality, and by 1956, she was given the material she deserved. 'Jim

Dandy', 'Jim Dandy Got Married' and 'Voodoo Voodoo' established her as one of the finest female rock'n'rollers of all time while her ballad hits, 'I Cried A Tear' (1958) – her only big hit in the 'pop' charts – and 'I Waited Too Long' (1959) demonstrated the relaxed, gospel feel which earned her a place in the ranks of the first pioneers of soul. 'Tiny Tim', 'Shake A Hand', 'Bumble Bee' (a rockabilly song, replete with twangy guitar), 'You're The Boss' (a duet with the Ravens' bassman, Jimmy Ricks), 'Saved' (a rumbustious neo-gospel Leiber and Stoller composition) and 'See See Rider' kept her (just) in the charts until 1963. Her subsequent records for Brunswick were less successful.

Mickey 'Guitar' Baker, born McHouston Baker in Louisville, Kentucky, on Oct. 15, 1925, originally studied guitar under the tutorship of skilled jazz musician, Rector Bailey. After a trip to Los Angeles, where he was impressed by the alley blues of Pee Wee Crayton, Baker changed his approach and returned to New York where his adaptability let to regular employment as a session musician. Following Ruth Brown's 'Mamma, He Treats Your Daughter Mean' his hard, biting solos graced vast numbers of records for Savoy, OKeh, King, Atlantic and many smaller independents. Throughout the Fifties he accompanied Little Willie John, the Coasters, Nappy Brown and – in brilliant slide guitar fashion – Rollee McGill and Sreamin' Jay Hawkins. With Henry Van Walls (piano), Lloyd Trotman (bass) and Connie Kay (drums), Baker completed Atlantic's best rhythm section. 'Love Is Strange' with Sylvia Vanderpool, as Mickey and Sylvia, is fondly remembered; though his liaison with Kitty Noble (as Mickey and Kitty) was less successful. Baker subsequently moved to France.

Kenny Ball, born in Ilford, Essex, on May 22, 1931, took up the trumpet at 16 and first appeared with Charlie Galbraith, formerly trombonist with Mike Daniels' Delta Jazzmen. Not as much of a traditionalist as some of his contemporaries, he turned professional at 21 and played with the Sid Phillips and Eric Delaney Bands. In 1958, Ball and trombonist John Bennett left the Terry Lightfoot band to form Kenny Ball's Jazzmen with Dave Jones, Vic Pitt, Ron Bowden, Dickie Bishop and Ron Weatherburn. They had five Top Ten hits between February 1961 and February 1962, each progressively 'poppier' than the last – 'Samantha', 'Midnight In Moscow' (also a Top Ten hit in America), 'March Of The Siamese Children', 'Green Leaves Of Summer' and 'Suki Yaki'. They turned to cabaret with the collapse of the trad boom.

Hank Ballard, born on Nov. 18, 1936, in Detroit, Michigan. In 1953 he joined the Royals – Lawson Smith, Norman Thrasher (later replaced by Charles Sutton), Billy Davis (replaced by Arthur Porter) and Henry Booth (replaced on his death by Sonny Woods) – as lead singer. The following year, the group's name was changed to the Midnighters to avoid clashing with the Five Royales – also with King Records – since both groups were becoming successful. In 1954, the Midnighters scored with their now-famous 'Annie' discs – 'Work With Me, Annie', 'Annie Had A Baby' and 'Annie's Aunt Fanny' (Federal). All reached the R&B Top Ten, but were considered too *risqué* for pop exposure. The group recorded steadily over the next four years without spectacular success, then in 1958 they switched from the Federal subsidiary to the main King label – Ballard getting headline billing for the first time – and immediately made the national charts with 'Teardrops On Your Letter'. Its B-side was the original issue of 'The Twist'. 1960 saw the group in the Top Ten with 'Let's Go, Let's Go, Let's Go' and 'Finger Popping Time', a characteristically gritty jump performance featuring the mandatory rasping tenor sax solo. The success of Chubby Checker's version of 'The Twist' led King to re-promote the original, which sold a million.

The next two years brought chart success with mainly dance-aimed songs, but sales were diminishing. Following a period in 'soul limbo', Hank resurfaced in 1968 under the wing of James Brown, touring with his Revue and recording a series of stereotyped funky dance songs. In 1970, he switched briefly and unsuccessfully to Lelan Rogers' Silver Fox label, but soon returned to the Brown fold. Still in search of renewed fame, he signed with Stang Records in 1974.

Chris Barber, born April 17, 1930 in Welwyn Garden City, formed his first band in 1949 with himself on trombone and Dickie Hawdon and Ben Cohen on twin cornets (in the manner of King Oliver's band during the period it featured Louis Armstrong). In 1953, he and clarinettist Monty Sunshine organized a band for Ken Colyer to join on his return from New Orleans. Colyer, whose approach to New Orleans jazz was fundamentalist, dismissed the rhythm section in May, 1954, whereupon Barber and Sunshine resigned. The new Barber band included Pat Halcox on trumpet and Lonnie Donegan on guitar and banjo, with Ron Bowden (later to join Kenny Ball) on drums. It often appeared at Humphrey Lyttelton's club at 100, Oxford Street, London. The band's repertoire included a few 'skiffle' numbers played by Barber (string bass), Donegan (guitar) and Beryl Bryden (washboard).

Donegan left the Barber band in April, 1956, but by this time Barber had added female vocalist Ottilie Patterson, to the band. It became more jazz-oriented but Barber never lost his interest in the blues which skiffle paid homage to. Throughout the early Sixties, Barber's interest in blues developed: he brought American bluesmen to Britain to tour with his band – many for the first time – and became involved in what was to become Britain's annual Folk and Blues Festival. It was through these activities, far more than through his own music, that Barber positively influenced and supported the emergent British R&B movement. The band had one Top Ten hit in 1959 with 'Petite Fleur' and Donegan's 'Rock Island Line' hit was, in fact, by the Barber skiffle group.

Bobby Bare, born April 7, 1935, Ironton, Ohio, reached No. 2 in the charts with 'The All-American Boy', on Fraternity, in 1958 – but Bill Parsons' name was on the label. Boyhood friends, Parsons and Bare made demo tapes for Cherokee, whose owner, Orville Lunsford, leased them to Fraternity. Bare was drafted into the Army two days later and let Parsons take the credit for his narration of 'All-American Boy', which parodied a rock'n'roller's – some said Elvis's – meteoric rise to fame. Bare had previously recorded for Capitol, and when his Army service was over, he cut further records for Valiant, Fraternity, RCA and Mercury where he broke down the barriers between country and pop with many huge hits, like 'Detroit City', '500 Miles Away From Home' and 'Shame On Me'. At present, he is making some headway as a 'progressive' country singer.

Gene Barge came to prominence through Frank Guida, who took him from evangelist 'Daddy' Grace's band in 1960 to become a staff writer/musician with Legrand Records. He co-wrote many of Gary Bonds' hits, including 'Quarter To Three' and 'School Is Out', his raunchy tenor-sax solos contributing to their 'party' atmosphere. When Bonds' hit stream dried up in 1962, Gene featured on Curtis Lee's 'Night At Daddy Gee's' in much the same style. He then joined Chess as staff writer/producer, being responsible for numerous soul and gospel discs from Chicago since the mid-Sixties.

H. B. Barnum claimed to have arranged the Leiber-Stoller produced Robins' classic, 'Riot In Cell Block No. 9' in 1954 as well as the group's many records on Whippet. A utility voice with the group, Barnum went solo and recorded for Fidelity, Eldo – where he made the pop charts with the instrumental 'Lost Love' in 1961 – Imperial and RCA before developing into a jack-of-all-trades. He led a 30-piece band behind rock'n'roll shows at San Francisco's Cow Palace, owned many small labels (Little Star, Prelude, MunRab) and scored for commercials. By the late Sixties, he was a rich man via arrangements for artists on RCA, Sue, Imperial (Irma Thomas) and Capitol (Lou Rawls). With arrangements for Motown stars and the Osmonds, he has emerged into the pop limelight.

Richard Barrett was born in Philadelphia but rose to prominence in the now legendary Brill Building on New York's Broadway, where Roulette Records' Morris Levy bought his song 'Creation Of Love' for $100. His performing career began in Philadelphia with the Angels, who recorded briefly for Gee, and major success followed when his second group, the Valentines, scored hits with 'Tonight Kathleen' (Old Town) and 'Lily Maybelle' (Rama) in 1957. This success heralded the next phase of Barrett's multi-faceted career, as producer. While the Valentines were appearing at the Apollo, Frankie Lymon's Teenagers pestered him into auditioning them, following which George Goldner signed them and Barrett produced their 'Why Do Fools Fall In Love' (Gee). A further discovery was the Chantels, featuring the distinctive voice of Arlene Smith, who hit in 1958 with 'Maybe' (End). He quit the Valentines to concentrate on writing, production and management while still pursuing a limited solo performing career, recording for MGM, Gone, 20th Century Fox, Seville, Atlantic ('Some Other Guy') and Crackerjack. Meanwhile, in his A&R capacity with Goldner's company, Barrett signed such acts as the Isley Brothers, Flamingos and Little Anthony & the Imperials. In 1964, he joined Swan Records in Philadelphia and became mentor to the Three Degrees, who enjoyed a couple of minor hits in 1965/6. After a 1970 hit remake of 'Maybe' on Roulette, in 1972, Barrett and the group signed with Philadelphia International where they have achieved even greater success.

John Barry, who learned his basic arranging skills from a Stan Kenton correspondence course, wielded a prodigious influence over British rock in the late Fifties. Born John Barry Prendergast in York in 1933, he was an arranger for big bands before forming his instrumental group, the John Barry Seven, in 1957. This unit was a staple ingredient of pop shows and package tours for the next five years and, during this time, Barry was also active in other fields, the most significant of which was the launching of Adam Faith's career. Having introduced him to TV – *Drumbeat* – and films – *Beat Girl* – Barry went on to score all his early records. The pizzicato string arrangements (inspired perhaps by middle-period Buddy Holly) later became the basis of the 'new sound' of 1960. Among Barry's other contributions to this movement were the theme tunes to TV's *Juke Box Jury* and radio's *Easy Beat*. In 1962, Barry left his group to concentrate on writing film and TV scores. Best known for his work on the *James Bond* series, he has recently composed a number of jangly TV themes. In 1971, he returned to the charts after a long absence with his music for *The Persuaders*.

Dave Bartholomew, the architect behind Fats Domino's superstardom in the Fifties, was born in Edgard, Louisiana in 1920. The son of Louis Bartholomew, a noted tuba player, he was soon immersed in the New Orleans music scene. The young Bartholomew started to make a name for himself playing trumpet with Fats Pichon's band on the *S.S. President* riverboat as it chugged up the Mississippi to St Paul and back. A spell in the Army halted his rising star temporarily, but on demob in 1946 he formed his first band in New Orleans, playing the lavish balls, fraternity dances and school hops which abounded in the Crescent City. It soon became the city's major orchestra, playing everything from R&B and jazz to popular standards, and he kept it that way by exerting an iron-hard discipline over the top musicians he was attracting.

Bartholomew recorded initially for De Luxe in 1949 and 'Country Boy' sold close on 100,000 copies. Then he met Lew Chudd, of Imperial Records, who was looking for an R&B producer. Bartholomew had all the right qualifications and was hired. He hit the jackpot first time out with '3 × 7 = 21' by Jewel King and, more notably, with 'The Fat Man' by Fats Domino. He worked for Imperial on a freelance basis, and notched up hits for Specialty with Lloyd Price's 'Lawdy Miss Clawdy' and Aladdin with Shirley and Lee's 'I'm

Gone'. However, he was put on a long-term Imperial contract in 1952 when Chudd could see the possibility of Fats Domino becoming a moneyspinner. Besides producing those monumental hits for Domino over the years, from 'Blueberry Hill' on down, Bartholomew was successful with Smiley Lewis's 'I Hear You Knocking', Bobby Mitchell's 'Try Rock'n'Roll', the Spiders' 'You're The One' and Earl King's 'Trick Bag'; he also recorded a host of other classic New Orleans artists – Guitar Slim, Tommy Ridgley, Sugar Boy Crawford, Huey Smith, Frankie Ford and Bobby Charles. He backed these men with members of his band and recorded prolifically in his own right, although his records were to idiosyncratic to sell. But as a producer, Bartholomew had fallen upon a hit formula based on a wholly commercial outlook, with a penchant for simple, almost singalong, melodies dressed up with riffing saxes and exuberant second-line rhythms.

In 1963, Lew Chudd sold Imperial to Liberty and Bartholomew turned down other offers which would have meant leaving New Orleans. He was content just to put a band together for occasional gigs in the city, living off the huge royalties he had amassed as co-writer of most of Domino's hits. Imperial's Man in New Orleans had really made it in the record business, and at the time there weren't many of his race who could say that.

Ralph Bass, a white producer born in New York, has given great service to the cause of R&B. He worked as a violinist in New York society bands before moving into jazz production (Dizzy Gillespie, Charlie Parker, Erroll Garner) and subsequently hustling his way into the burgeoning Los Angeles 'race' market. His first R&B hit, Jack McVea's 'Open The Door Richard' (Black and White) in 1947, led to Savoy where, as the West Coast A&R man, he produced huge hits for Johnny Otis, Little Esther, and the Robins.

Touring the South with the Otis revue was a revelation to Bass; thereafter, he left the sophistication of jazz for a lifelong association with some of the earthiest R&B on record.

30

In the Fifties he masterminded the King subsidiary, Federal, where is productions for the Dominoes, Hank Ballard and the Midnighters, the Five Royales and, later, James Brown and the Famous Flames, monopolised the R&B charts. 'Sixty Minute Man', 'Work With Me, Annie', 'Please, Please, Please' – all these and many more black anthems owed their success to Bass's love for and belief in a rough, raw and gospel-tinged brand of R&B. In 1960, he joined Chess, recording Etta James, Moms Mabley, Ramsey Lewis and the many Chicago blues greats as well as pioneering pop-gospel with the Violinaires. Today, he still prefers mono sound and refuses to work with anything more complicated than four-track recording equipment.

Shirley Bassey, born in Cardiff, Wales, on Jan. 8, 1937, the daughter of a West Indian merchant seaman from Tiger Bay. Her first success in Britain came in 1957 with 'Banana Boat Song' – at the same time as Harry Belafonte's version. She didn't break into the charts again for nearly two years, when a chance appearance on the London Palladium Show helped to break 'As I Love You'. In early 1959, both this and 'Kiss Me Honey, Honey, Kiss Me' were in the Top Ten. Her other chart successes in Britain included 'As Long As He Needs Me' (1960), 'You'll Never Know' (1961), 'Reach For The Stars' (1961), 'What Now, My Love?' (1962), and 'I (Who Have Nothing)' (1963). With the new popularity for groups and renewed emphasis on beat, her chart success declined, although her powerful voice and vibrant personality found a responsive audience in the cabaret field and on TV. A change to United Artists from Columbia (EMI) in 1970 turned her into a steady album seller.

Freddie Bell and the Bell Boys were one of the earliest rock'n'roll combos – closely modelled on Bill Haley and the Comets. Comprising Jack Kane (sax), Frank Brent (bass), Jerry Mayo (trumpet), Russ Contic (piano), Chick Keeney (drums) and Bell (vocals) they appeared with Haley in the first rock movie, *Rock Around The Clock* (1955). The first American rock'n'roll act to visit Britain, they toured with

Tommy Steele in 1956. They had a British hit with the tepid 'Giddy Up A Ding Dong', which reached No. 4 on Mercury's British licensee of the time, Pye Records. They also originated the arrangement of Presley's 'Hound Dog'.

Jesse Belvin, born Dec. 15, 1933, in Texarkana, Arkansas – a singer, composer, pianist whose influence cannot simply be measured by the success of 'Goodnight My Love' (an R&B hit on Modern in 1956) or 'Funny' and 'Guess Who', his Nat 'King' Cole-type pop hits for RCA in 1959. The extent of his prolific activities among the tangled world of West Coast independent labels may never be fully catalogued. After graduating from Big Jay McNeely's band, Belvin became a father-figure to many younger singers and the leader of a Los Angeles group fraternity who sang and practised together. In 1953, he cut an R&B hit, 'Dream Girl' (Specialty) as one half of Jesse and Marvin. The following year, he wrote 'Earth Angel' and legend insists that he wrote many more songs which now have someone else's name on the credits. Until his death in a car crash in 1960 (aged 27) Belvin made numerous solo discs for Specialty. Recorded in Hollywood, Modern, Kent, Knight, Candlelight, Cash, Class, and Jamie. He also doo-wopped his way through a dozen groups including the Cliques (Top Fifty with 'Girl Of My Dreams' in 1956), the Sharptones (Aladdin), Three Dots and A Dash (Imperial) and the Sheiks, whose original 'So Fine' (Federal) was revived by the Fiestas in 1959.

Boyd Bennett was born in Muscle Shoals, Alabama, on Dec. 7, 1924. An insipid cover by the Fontane Sisters outsold his original version of 'Seventeen' in 1955, but Bennett and his primitive five-piece band, the Rockets, still reached many listeners. Wounded in World War II, Bennett was discharged from the Navy and had a weekly TV show in Louisville, Kentucky, before signing with King in 1955. Modelled on Bill Haley's Comets, the Rockets cut over a dozen corny but elemental singles – on which Bennett shared the vocals with Big Moe and, on occasion, Moon Mullican – before switching to Mercury and then small labels like Kernal before drifting into obscurity.

Chuck Berry's significance lies partly in his own stylistic innovations and the vivid articulation of a spirit of rock'n'roll rebellion in his lyrics. And, partly, it lies in the fact that his career uniquely encapsulates the links between the rock'n'rollers of the Fifties and the bands of the Seventies, between blues and pop, between black and white musical cultures. His origins are, in many ways, representative of the black artists primarily responsible for hammering out the musical identity of rock. Born Charles Edward Berry in St Louis, Missouri, on Oct. 18, 1931, he began singing in a church choir at the age of six. He learned the rudiments of guitar while still at high school, and made his debut performance at the school glee club review, playing the Chicago blues standard, 'Confessin' The Blues' – which, he has recalled, was avidly welcomed for what was seen at the time as an almost *risqué* earthiness.

Berry's next move was equally part of a wider pattern: the journey to Chicago itself, following in the steps of the many Southern country blues artists who had subsequently abandoned their intimate, solo approach in favour of the heavily amplified and raucous bar blues style associated with the northern city. One such was Muddy Waters. Berry – an ardent admirer – played with the Waters band in early 1955, and the blues star recommended that he get in touch with Leonard Chess, whose Chess and Checker labels provided the major outlet for black artists in the area. Berry got the audition he wanted and was signed up immediately. His first recording, 'Maybellene', was released in May, 1955. It sold a million in a matter of weeks and reached No. 5 in the national singles charts. 'Maybellene' sprang from a blues environment but the song – written by Berry himself – owed almost as much to country-and-western influences. This was clearly indicated by the oddly foreign hillbilly title, of which Berry once remarked, 'The only Maybellene I ever knew was the name of a cow'. Moreover, the performance itself, with its heavily accentuated backbeat, bore a notable resemblance to the rockabilly style being developed by Sun's white country-rooted artists in Memphis – though the harshness, the heaviness and the whining guitar were pure Chicago. The major rock'n'roll populariser, deejay Alan Freed, was credited as co-writer, and it seems likely that the sound that eventually emerged was inspired in part by a desire to match the commercial success being enjoyed by the new Southern hybrid music. Berry's own remark that 'The dollar dictates what music is written' tends to confirm that impression. This is not to say that the C&W tradition was completely alien to him: he has frequently said that he had listened to a great deal of country music on the radio in St Louis.

There were other major non-blues influences on Berry's approach. He has expressed a lasting affection for popular performers of the Forties – ranging from Frank Sinatra to jazz guitarist Charlie Christian – and has said that he thinks of music as falling into two basic categories – 'swing' and 'sentimental'. Significantly, he has repeatedly cited Nat 'King' Cole as a major influence – one of the first black male balladeers to cross over successfully to a mass audience. But the B side of 'Maybellene' – the slow, reflective 'Wee Wee Hours' revealed that his deepest stylistic roots lay in the blues. And on the next two A sides, 'Thirty Days' and 'No Money Down', this foundation was again very much apparent. Neither record, however, entered the Hot Hundred.

Berry became securely established as a performer with mass appeal only when the blues element in his work had undergone considerable modifications. His fourth single, 'Roll Over Beethoven', reached the Top Thirty in 1956 and pointed the way forward. Over the next two years, he produced his most important music in a string of commercially successful singles. 'School Day' and 'Rock And Roll Music' both achieved Top Ten successes in 1957. The following year saw his biggest seller, 'Sweet Little Sixteen' reach No. 2, while 'Johnny B. Goode' went to No. 8 and 'Carol' also entered the Top Twenty. There were no other major hits in the Fifties, but several of his minor successes exemplified his mature style at its best and most influential. In 1957, there was 'Oh Baby Doll', which failed to get beyond the bottom half of the Hundred. In 1958, 'Beautiful Delilah', 'Sweet Little Rock And Roller', 'Jo Jo Gunne' and 'Run Rudolph Run' all entered the lower reaches of the charts. The story was the same the following year with 'Anthony Boy', 'Almost Grown', 'Little Queenie' and 'Back In The USA', and in 1960 with 'Too Pooped To Pop' and 'Let It Rock'. Berry was a prolific writer, and several of the songs for which he is best remembered were not even released as A sides at the time – such as 'Memphis, Tennessee' and 'Reelin' And Rockin' '.

Berry's style in this period had a number of distinctive features. The bold 'rocking' beat of 'Maybellene' was filled out with 'rolling' rhythms, achieved mainly by swiftly alternating between a handful of chords, particularly the 'blue' sixths and sevenths. His records were also instantly recognizable by the wailing, chiming guitar sound and the fast, cutting, high-pitched solos he used as introductions. The overall impression of speed was strengthened by the machine-gun rhythms of the lyrics; and his vocal style lacked the coarseness generally associated with city blues and rock'n'roll. He articulated the words extremely clearly, a characteristic which probably derived partly from another of his idols, Louis Jordan. By singing in a manner not totally given over to wildness and emotionalism, he allowed room for humour to enter the picture. And because virtually every word could be understood, the lyrics themselves came to have a more essential function than they did with most other rock'n'rollers.

In his lyrics, Berry defined a new audience. He crystallized the meaning of white teenage rock'n'roll in terms of a lifestyle in which the search for physical excitement – especially in the form of dancing, driving and sex – was paramount. If rock'n'roll was implicitly anti-romantic and anti-puritan, Berry made it explicitly so. His songs were celebrations of the pleasures available to the dedicated American consumer, typified by 'Back In The USA', with its richly-detailed references to sizzling hamburgers, drive-ins, skyscrapers and the long freeway. But they were also songs of rebellion. The kids might want to have fun, but there were forces that stood in their way – work and school, parents and the law, old age. 'School Day' spelt it out:

> Hail, hail rock'n'roll!
> Deliver me from the days of old.

Berry became one of the leading rock'n'roll stars, with four film appearances to his credit to prove it: *Rock, Rock, Rock* and *Mr Rock And Roll* in 1957, *Go Johnny Go* in 1959, and his performance at the Newport Jazz Festival in *Jazz On A Summer's Day*. Then, late in 1959, his career was sharply interrupted. He was charged with transporting a minor over a State line for immoral purposes. Accounts of the incident vary, but it appears that he brought an Indian girl from Texas to work as an assistant at his night club in St Louis. The police suspected she was working as a prostitute. At some point, Berry gave her the sack, and she then confessed to the police that she was only fourteen. Local court records say that he was convicted after a series of trials and started a two-year prison sentence in February 1962. Berry has denied this, claiming he was acquitted and that he had, in any case, been led to believe that the girl was over twenty.

Berry's disappearance coincided with a period when rock'n'roll had lost a great deal of its original energy and momentum. When he returned in 1964, the British renaissance was in full spate and he was its major hero. Chuck Berry songs were a key part of the repertoire of almost every British group. The Beatles recorded 'Roll Over Beethoven' and 'Rock And Roll Music', and his influence was clearly apparent in such Lennon-McCartney compositions as 'I Saw Her Standing There' and 'Little Child'. The Rolling Stones' first single was Berry's 'Come On'; their debut album included 'Carol', together with his arrangement of 'Route 66'. They later recorded 'Bye Bye Johnny' and 'Round And Round', and other Berry songs, such as 'Little Queenie' and

'Johnny B. Goode' were highlights of their stage act Berry's enormous impact in Britain can be partly attributed to the fact that his lack of major hits in that country – only 'Sweet Little Sixteen' had reached the Top Twenty – made him acceptable to the many new rock musicians and fans who saw 'commercialism' as the main enemy of worthwhile music. His appeal extended to both the R&B 'purists' and to those who made a cult of relatively obscure Fifties rock'n'roll. At the same time, he had been a chart star in America, so the possibility of good music achieving mass success could never be totally ruled out by his admirers.

His influence was also evident in the work of many American performers in the Sixties. The Beach Boys took the melody and guitar figures of 'Sweet Little Sixteen' and merely adapted the lyrics to a Californian surfing context for their first hit, 'Surfin' USA'. When Bob Dylan adopted a rock style in 1965 with 'Subterranean Homesick Blues', he based the tune, the metric pattern and even the mood of the lyrics on Berry's 'Too Much Monkey Business'.

Berry resumed his own recording career in 1964 with 'Nadine' and 'No Particular Place To Go'. The lyric of 'Nadine' was a re-wording of the car-chase motif of 'Maybellene', but the performance was far more relaxed. The record was a Top Thirty hit in America and also sold well in Britain, where the upsurge of interest in his music had put the re-issued 'Memphis Tennessee'/'Let It Rock' in the Top Ten the previous year. 'No Particular Place To Go' – a song based on 'School Day' but with new lyrics about 'cruising' – was a Top Twenty entry on both sides of the Atlantic. The lyrics of his 1964 material covered much the same ground as those of his early hits, but there was a greater stress on his wit and warmth. This came to the fore in his next release that year, 'You Never Can Tell'. An American Top Twenty hit, it told the story of two rock'n'rollers who get married and settle down, with 'a souped-up Jidney, a cherry-red '53' and 'seven hundred little records, all rockin' rhythm and jazz'. It was followed by the less successful 'Little Marie', a variation on the theme of 'Memphis Tennessee'; and 'The Promised Land', a driving song recalling Woody Guthrie. The only release in 1965 was 'Dear Dad'.

In 1966 Berry left Chess and signed a $50,000 contract with Mercury. He made five albums for the label over the next three years, devoting much of his studio time to drab remakes of Fifties songs. But his reputation as a live performer reached its zenith during these years. His cherry-red Gibson and the crouched gliding shuffle which he called the 'duck walk' and which had earned him the nickname 'Crazy Legs', had become legendary trademarks of his act. In Britain, his tours were remarkable for the way they drew together Fifties rock'n'roll fans and the new generation of Beatles and Stones followers.

He returned to Chess in 1969 and by 1971 had recorded two new albums, *Back Home* and *San Francisco Dues*. The music was more consistently and overtly blues-based than ever before, a mature re-exploration of his roots. It seemed that the pop charts had seen the last of him. However, a tour of Britain early in 1972 reversed all expectations. He was received more ecstatically than ever, and a live recording made at the Lanchester Arts Festival in Coventry gave him not only half of the next album, *London Sessions*, but also the biggest hit of his career, 'My Ding-A-Ling'. He had previously recorded much the same song as 'Mr Tambourine' for Mercury, and it had a history stretching back through various R&B artists to 1950 at least. But the new version, publicised and promoted with maximum efficiency, gave him his first No. 1 in both America and Britain. The mild sexual innuendo of the record apparently broadened his appeal, attracting a younger audience. A live version of 'Reelin' And Rockin' ', emphasising the double-entendre of the lyric, was issued as a follow-up and consolidated this revised image.

His subsequent career continued along the newly established lines. Another blues-oriented album, *Bio*, was produced, while Chess systematically re-issued his early material in the *Golden Decade* series of albums. His stage shows degenerated to a great extent into exercises in showmanship and mindless comedy. Berry's songs, however, continued to be played by new rock bands at the climax of their acts; the Electric Light Orchestra took 'Roll Over Beethoven' into the British Top Ten in 1973, amid a spate of Berry revivals; and after Louisiana performer Johnnie Allen had created a minor stir in 1974 in Britain with his remake of 'The Promised Land', Elvis Presley also covered the number and took it high into the British and American charts the following winter.

Richard Berry, influential singer and composer born in New Orleans in 1935, moved to California in the Forties and began writing songs with Jesse Belvin, subsequently becoming one of the first 'session' singers, a position he retained until the early Sixties. His first single with the Flairs in 1953, 'She Wants To Rock' (on Flair) was produced by Leiber and Stoller who brought Berry into the Robins to guest on 'Riot In Cell Block No. 9', a dramatic vignette which he narrated perfectly. He cut solo sides for Modern and RPM until 1956 when he formed the Pharaohs and made the original version of 'Louie, Louie' (on Flip) which sold a million by the Kingsmen in 1963. Berry made some 30 singles in all – on Paxley, Hasil, K&G, Smash, AMC, Bold Soul and others. But he enjoyed greater success on other people's records, duetting with Etta James on 'Roll With Me Henry' (Modern) and sobbing behind Donald Woods on 'Death Of An Angel' (Flip). In the Seventies, he led a soul band in West Los Angeles and has played piano behind Chuck Higgins for Rollin' Rock.

Big Bopper, born J. P. Richardson on Oct. 29, 1932, in Sabine Pass, Texas, worked part-time as a deejay and compère while still at High School in Beaumont, Texas. In the early Fifties, he was voted No. 1 deejay on KTRM radio station in Beaumont, and adopted the name 'Big Bopper', to match his ebullient personality. His career was interrupted by two years of Army service as a radio instructor, but on discharge he returned to work as the station's programme director and found more time for songwriting. Richardson sent some demos to Pappy Daily, a veteran Houston distributor, who signed him to a recording contract and in 1957–8, he recorded two hillbilly singles under his real name for Mercury. In 1958, Richardson recorded a novelty song titled 'The Purple People Eater Meets The Witchdoctor' under his Big Bopper alias, but it was the flip, 'Chantilly Lace' which registered internationally, reaching the Top Ten in America and the Top Twenty in England. He followed this in December, 1958, with 'The Big Bopper's Wedding' (a Top Thirty record in America) before he died with Buddy Holly and Ritchie Valens in a plane crash on February 3, 1959. Richardson's small legacy of recordings suggests that he was a talented songwriter – he wrote Johnny Preston's 'Running Bear' for example – rather than an artist of any durability.

Big Maybelle, born in 1926, in Jackson, Tennessee, as Mabel Smith, recorded with Christine Chatman's Orchestra in 1944 until her solo debut in 1947 on King Records. A big-voiced blues shouter, 1952 saw her as 'Big Maybelle' with Okeh, and 1953 brought three R&B Top Ten hits including 'Gabbin' Blues'. She moved to Savoy in 1956 and 'Candy' became another R&B hit, but the late Fifties saw a steady output of ballads and jump-blues fail to make further commercial impact. The Sixties brought moves to Brunswick, Scepter, Rojac, Port and Chess, then a return to Rojac in 1966 brought success when 'Don't Pass Me By' and '96 Tears' were R&B hits, the latter giving Maybelle her only national 'pop' hit. Apart from one disc on Brunswick in 1968, she remained with Rojac until her death in January 1972.

Acker Bilk, born in Pensford, Somerset, on Jan. 28, 1929, played the clarinet in a semi-professional band in Bristol before joining Ken Colyer in 1954 – replacing Monty Sunshine. In 1958, Acker, christened Bernard, formed the Paramount Jazz Band – the most representative line-up of which was Colin Smith (trumpet), John Mortimer (trombone), Ron

McKay (drums), Roy James (banjo) and Stan Greig (piano) – and had a British Top Ten hit with 'Summer Set' in 1960. The band's success owed more to their bowler hat and striped waistcoat image – created by 'The Bilk Marketing Board' – than it did to their dedication to traditional jazz. Largely on the strength of Peter Leslie's inventive publicity, they had eight Top Twenty hits, including Bilk's solo outing, 'Stranger On The Shore' – a piece of pure pop that made No. 1 on both the British and American charts in 1962. It was this more than anything else that helped the band move into the lucrative cabaret and TV variety show circuit just as the trad boom was collapsing.

Bill Black links the pre-rock'n'roll sounds of C&W with the Sixties rock and soul sounds of the South. Born in Memphis on September 17, 1926, Black became a string bass session player with Sun, and teamed up with Elvis Presley for five years, playing on all his early hits and appearing in movies like *Loving You*. The insistent bass sound of early Presley was carried over into the Bill Black Combo, formed in 1959, by which time he was using an electric instrument. His combo originated a genre of Memphis instrumentals with top hits like 'Smokie' in 1959, 'White Silver Sand' in 1960 and 'Josephine'. Aided by sax innovator, Ace Cannon, on 'Tuff' in 1962 the Combo backed Gene Simmons' 1964 hit 'Haunted House'. Groups like the Mar-Keys and Booker T and the MGs developed Black's sound further into soul, although the Combo itself has continued despite Black's death in October 1965.

'Bumps' Blackwell was born Robert A. Blackwell on May 23, 1918. He was assistant to Art Rupe at Specialty Records, Hollywood, in 1955 when Rupe sent him to New Orleans to record Little Richard. 'Bumps' arranged and produced Richard's sessions, also co-writing such hits as 'Good Golly Miss Molly' and 'Rip It Up'. In 1956, he recorded Sam Cooke's first solo tracks and Rupe gave him the tapes plus Cooke's contract in lieu of royalties – he went to Keen

41

Records and million-seller 'You Send Me' was the result. In 1961, he produced the black music spectacular *Portraits In Bronze* in Hollywood, but latterly worked as personal manager to Little Richard.

Otis Blackwell, a singer-pianist who was also one of the Fifties' premier songwriters, was born in 1931. He began by winning an Apollo Theater talent contest before moving to Joe Davis Records in 1953. His first record, 'Daddy Rollin' Stone' became a cult classic when revived by Derek Martin and the Who. After many more city blues on Jay-Dee, Blackwell recorded rock'n'roll for RCA and Groove and when these did not sell he began writing songs for other artists with immediate success. He built his simple but catchy and bluesy compositions around a familiar catchphrase. 'Don't Be Cruel', 'All Shook Up', 'Return To Sender', 'One Broken Heart For Sale' (for Elvis Presley), 'Great Balls Of Fire', 'Breathless' (for Jerry Lee Lewis), 'Hey Little Girl' (for Dee Clark), 'Fever' (for Little Willie John) and 'Handy Man' (for Jimmy Jones) were some of the biggest and best. With the demise of hard rock'n'roll, Blackwell gave up writing but continued to record R&B, appearing on Gale, Atlantic, Date, MGM, Cub and – in 1971 – Epic.

Billy Bland was born in Wilmington, North Carolina, on April 5, 1932. An ex-ballroom dancer, Bland recorded for Old Town in 1955, making two excellent blues, 'Chicken In The Basket' and 'Chicken Hop' (with Sonny Terry on harp). He hit the Top Ten with an atypically bouncy pop song, 'Let The Little Girl Dance' in 1960. Old Town, with which he remained until the mid-Sixties, issued a large number of extremely varied singles, including three smaller chart entries – 'Born To Be Loved', 'Harmony' and 'My Heart's On Fire'. His excellent version of Bobby Bland's 'Little Boy Blue' should be in any representative collection of deep soul.

Bobby Bland, one of the leading figures in modern blues, was born Robert Calvin Bland in Rosemark, Tennessee on January 27, 1930. He was raised in Memphis, and by the late

Forties had joined the Beale Streeters, a loose assemblage of young talent which included B.B. King, Rosco Gordon, Johnny Ace and Junior Parker. Bland's singing style came straight from the Southwest – deft, swinging, articulate, with a unique dusty blues feeling. In 1954 he made a guest appearance at a Houston talent show which gained the attention of Don Robey, president of Duke Records. Robey quickly signed him to a recording contract, and April 1955 saw the release of 'It's My Life, Baby', his first R&B chart success. This was followed by 'I Smell Trouble', 'Little Boy Blue' and 'Farther Up The Road', which reached the national Hot Hundred in 1957 and stayed there for a remarkable 21 weeks.

Once established, Bland took to the road, touring the well-worn circuit of one-night stands, concerts, dances and theatres such as Harlem's Apollo and the Regal in Chicago. With him went a band so strongly identified with Bland that it has earned its own legend. Led by tenorist Bill Harvey and trumpeter-arranger Joe Scott – whose importance as Bland's longtime musical director cannot be overstated – it was driving and bluesy, loose and loping, with a jump and bite reminiscent of the exciting big bebop bands of the Forties. There was also the stunning lead guitar of Wayne Bennett, who is present on most of Bland's hits. The songs Bland performed were mostly written by Scott and others, under the alias 'Deadric Malone'. The material and arrangements were impeccable, thus ensuring a consistent stream of R&B chart successes. His early Sixties hits included 'Cry, Cry, Cry', 'I Pity The Fool', 'Call On Me', 'Ain't Nothing You Can Do' and 'Two Steps From The Blues'.

As the Sixties progressed, Bland began to experiment with modern soul styles, his songs occasionally sounding almost Motown in their presentation. Producer Andre Williams took over from Joe Scott, although Bland still maintained a regular output of persuasive, bluesy records between his more pop-oriented hits. In 1972, the vast ABC/Dunhill record complex gobbled up Duke and belatedly turned the white rock market onto Bland. Dunhill teamed him up with producer Steve Barri who was then working with the Four Tops. His *California Album* is well into a rock framework, but one which hasn't eroded Bland's gospel roots. Naturally there are songs by 'Deadric Malone', but they nestle alongside compositions by Gerry Goffin and Leon Russell. The album sold phenomenally well and paved the way for the subsequent *Dreamer* set, again produced by Barri. Both albums make a perfect balance of the old blues style, today's sound, tomorrow's image building.

Bo Diddley's 'jungle-rhythm' blues-based music remains a key factor in the origin and development of rock. So much so, that his exuberant vocals and above all his often purposely-distorted guitar work have earned him rock legend status in the Seventies. Born Ellas McDaniel on December 30, 1928, in McComb, Mississippi, he switched from violin to playing guitar in Chicago's Maxwell Street market, a spawning ground for many of today's leading blues figures. In July 1955, he successfully auditioned for Checker, a subsidiary of Chess Records. That same year he wrote and recorded his famous self-dedication, 'Bo Diddley' – a nickname he acquired as a boxer in his youth. The song was a major hit, and stands as one of the greatest R&B records ever made.

From then on he continued to score regular hits, his vocal and writing style often revealing a debt to R&B singer Louis Jordan, whose recordings during the Forties – generally containing witty lyrics – were popular with both black and white audiences. Diddley recorded all his songs in the Chess studios in Chicago, usually accompanied by Jerome Green (maraccas), Otis Spann (piano), Billy Boy Arnold (harmonica) and Frank Kirkland (drums), while his half-sister, known as 'The Duchess', was sometimes featured on rhythm guitar. (Incidentally, Diddley and stablemate Chuck Berry sometimes sat in on each other's sessions – Bo plays rhythm guitar on Berry's 'Memphis Tennessee' and 'Sweet Little Rock And Roller'.) Diddley's unique sound – raw vocals and a heavily amplified guitar underscored by a pounding 'jungle beat' – has been copied and used by a variety of artists. Buddy Holly covered 'Bo Diddley' while Johnny Otis emulated the Diddley sound on 'Willie And The Hand Jive'. It was even rumoured that Elvis Presley copied Diddley's stage antics wholesale when he first came to New York in 1956. But it was the British R&B boom of the early Sixties that really brought Bo Diddley's name into prominence.

The Rolling Stones' original stage act featured such Diddley numbers as 'Mona', 'Diddley Daddy', 'Pretty Thing', 'Hey Bo Diddley', 'Road Runner', 'Bring It To Jerome', 'Cops and Robbers', 'Nursery Rhyme' and – not surprisingly – 'Bo Diddley'. Other British groups who revived Diddley compositions include the Who, Yardbirds, Manfred Mann, Downliners Sect, Johnny Kidd and The Pirates and the Zephyrs, who reached No. 27 in the British charts with 'I Can Tell'. One band, the Pretty Things, was even named after a Diddley song. Running through the Bo Diddley catalougue, 'Who Do You Love' stands out as the song which has received more cover versions than any other. The list is headed up by the Doors, Tom Rush, Ronnie Hawkins, Quicksilver Messenger Service, Juicy Lucy and Bob Seger. Diddley's influence is just as prevalent today; his songs are featured regularly by British pub rock bands like Chilli Willi and The Red Hot Peppers, Dr Feelgood and the Michigan Flyers. Diddley has returned to prominence in recent years by touring America and Europe with various rock revival shows. He can be seen to good effect in the D. A. Pennebaker film *Keep On Rockin'*.

Bobbettes was the name taken by Jannie and Emma Pought, Heather Dixon, Helen Gathers and Laura Webb – all aged between 12 and 14 and attending school in New York – when they wrote a song about their principal in 1957. They went to Atlantic Records and sang 'Mr Lee' to bemused executives who, impressed by the immediacy of the tune – a jump ditty with hiccough-y chorus and incredible growled lead voice – recorded it and scored a Top Ten hit. Subsequent Atlantic discs failed to equal this, and their next hit was 'I Shot Mr Lee'

(Triple X) in 1960. They also recorded for Gone, Jubilee and Diamond.

Johnny Bond came to prominence in 1937 as supporting actor to Gene Autry and other 'cowboy' stars. Bond was later successful in several musical styles and is important as one of the first professional C&W songwriters. Born June 1, 1915, in Enville, Oklahoma, he recorded for Okeh and Columbia in the Fifties and first encountered rock through country-boogie tunes like those of the early Bill Haley. In 1962, he began recording in the C&W 'hot-rod' style with 'Hot Rod Lincoln' on Republic. Pop-country tunes like 'Ten Little Bottles' followed and he has successfully recorded for Starday, 20th Century Fox and Capitol.

Gary U.S. Bonds was born Gary Anderson in Jacksonville, Florida, June 6, 1939. He moved with his parents to Norfolk, Virginia as a child and began singing in church choirs. In 1952, he formed his own high school group, the Turks, and then went solo. In 1960, he met local record shop owner Frank Guida and recorded 'New Orleans' for Guida's newly-formed Legrand label, reaching the Top Twenty in both Britain and America early in 1961. His follow-up, 'Not Me', flopped completely but his third record, 'Quarter To Three' went to No. 1 in America and reached England's Top Ten. Bonds then had a series of consecutive American hits including 'School Is Out', 'School Is In' and 'Twist, Twist Señora', all featuring distinctive riffs and a muzzy, boisterous semi-live effect created by crude phasing and tape-echo techniques. In an era of tinny, thin-sounding records, Bonds' records proved revolutionary and had a great influence on Britain's burgeoning R&B beat group scene. However, Bonds' sound palled through repetition and he turned to song-writing with Swamp Dogg, recording and performing only occasionally.

Boogie Woogie is essentially a piano idiom, in which blues are played with a prominent eight-to-the-bar left-hand bass supporting right-hand improvisations. The style probably took shape as a club and dance-hall music, and was developed at house parties and similar gatherings during the Twenties and Thirties. The earliest record, in every sense, of the style was Pine Top Smith's 1928 performance 'Pine Top's Boogie Woogie', but examples were soon added by players like Meade Lux Lewis (especially his famous 'Honky Tonk Train Blues'), Albert Ammons, Pete Johnson (often in accompaniments to the blues-shouter Joe Turner) and many other blues pianists, such as the obscure but seminal Lee Green, Cripple Clarence Lofton, Montana Taylor and Romeo Nelson, all working around Chicago.

Ammons, Lewis and Johnson were among the most creative of these musicians, and it was appropriate that in the boogie woogie craze of the Forties the three men should form a group and make a number of deft and exciting solo, duet and trio recordings. Another player to attain a reputation at that time was the Chicago-born Jimmy Yancey, an altogether individual player with a spare and restrained style far removed from the hard-driving attack favoured by most of his peers. After World War II a more brittle and showy kind of boogie woogie found wide favour, as played by musicians like Freddie Slack, and this was distantly echoed in the technically crude but well-received records of Merrill F. Moore and other performers on the fringe of rockabilly. Following the hit recording of 'Guitar Boogie' by country guitarist Arthur Smith, and the guitar duet stylings of hillbilly artists like the Delmore Brothers, there was a great fashion for boogie-woogie guitar, and Jimmy Yancey's bass figures appeared in the Delmores' 'Blues Stay Away From Me' and many contemporary recordings, mostly based on Avery Parrish's piano solo 'After Hours'.

With the death of the creators and chief transmitters of boogie woogie, the idiom as a purely pianistic form passed to younger musicians who attempted, with varying success, to re-enact the documented originals. At present, both in America and Europe, there is lively patronage of boogie woogie piano-playing; meanwhile the general lessons of the form have been incorporated into rock music in many ways,

and are implicit in the manner, if rarely explicit in the repertoire, of innumerable bands.

James Booker, who once declared, 'Between the penitentiary, the crazyhouse and the music business, I never had a
chance!', was born in New Orleans on Dec. 17, 1939, to a
family with a long musical heritage, and was known as a
child genius on piano. After recording for Imperial and Ace
while still in his teens, he had a No. 43 national hit record in
1960 as Little Booker with the frolicking R&B organ instrumental, 'Gonzo' on Peacock. He was much in demand for
recording sessions in New Orleans in the early Sixties but
then sank from sight. It was another ten years before he
began to do justice to his undoubted talents by playing with
such rock luminaries as Dr John and the Doobie Brothers.

Pat Boone was born Charles Eugene Pat Boone on June 1,
1934, in Jacksonville, Florida. Next to Elvis Presley, he was
the most successful singer of the era, with dozens of hit
singles stretching from 1955 to the early Sixties. He was
popular simply because he was the total opposite of Presley
in every respect. Where Elvis was sensual, menacing and
intense, Boone was the decent, All-American Boy (with a
neat and pretty wife and four kids) who refused to kiss the
leading ladies in his films. His records represented the successful domestication of the predominantly black sound of
rock'n'roll, his polite tenor transforming it into an acceptable sound for the children of Middle America.

Boone moved to Nashville as a child, where his early years
found him singing C&W for Republic Records – he married
C&W star Red Foley's daughter Shirley – and studying for
his degree in English and Speech. In 1955 he was signed to
Dot Records by the astute Randy Wood, who turned Boone
into the king of the cover versions. In 1955–6 he recorded
somewhat embarrassed versions of 'Ain't That A Shame',
'Tutti Frutti' and 'Long Tall Sally'. All were big hits.

At this point, Boone was a fully-fledged teenage idol as
well as a Columbia University student and a permanent

member of the Arthur Godfrey Show. On record he graduated to insipid romantic ballads, while screen roles in *Bernadine* and *April Love* made him the No. 3 Box Office Attraction of 1957.

Pat Boone's hits of 1957 to 1962 – records like 'Love Letters In The Sand', 'April Love' (1957), 'If Dreams Came True' and 'Sugar Moon' (1958) – had only tenuous connections with rock. They represented the essence of the Pat Boone sound, a lush crooning style in the Bing Crosby tradition. The only exceptions were his two solitary Top Ten records after 1958 the powerfully arranged death ditty 'Moody River' (1961) and the latin-flavoured 'Speedy Gonzales' (1962).

Part of the Boone legacy is *Twixt Twelve And Twenty*, a manual for good, wholesome, teenage living. The contents are entirely in character – get your hair cut, don't go to parties without a chaperone, don't rebel against authority because they know best. For many teenagers caught between the raucous rebellion of authentic rock'n'roll and parental hostility, the Boone compromise came as a welcome relief. Few, however, shared his fundamentalist Christianity which has grown stronger over the years with the result that his occasional performances are now mostly in a religious context.

Earl Bostic, born on April 25, 1913, in Tulsa, Oklahoma, played clarinet and tenor sax in his school band. He attended university in Omaha and New Orleans, studying harmony and theory. In New Orleans, he joined Fate Marable's band before migrating to New York where he played with Don Redman and Cab Calloway, then fronted his own nine-piece combo on alto with Majestic Records in 1945. He moved to Gotham Records, then to King in 1949, where he recorded his 1951 million-seller, 'Flamingo'. Bostic subsequently recorded many hundreds of tracks for King in his biting, swinging alto style up to his death from a heart-attack in 1965.

Alex Bradford, from Bessemer, Alabama, grew up under the influence of the local Blue Jay Quartet, and even sang popular blues while in the Army. In the Fifties, he formed his Bradford Specials, an early all-male group in the gospel rather than gospel quartet tradition, noted for their flamboyant stage appearance and presentation, and a million-selling version of his composition, 'Too Close To Heaven'. He received worldwide acclaim travelling with Marion Williams in the gospel song play, *Black Nativity* from 1962, and furthered his Broadway reputation recently in 'Don't Bother Me, I Can't Cope'.

Tiny Bradshaw led one of the popular R&B dance bands of the late Forties and early Fifties. Besides his own solo hits for Cincinnati-based King records, he was also a regular accompanist for that label, working with top R&B names like Roy Brown. Born Myron 'Tiny' Bradshaw in Youngstown, Ohio in 1905, he began his musical career as a singer with various New York jazz outfits before forming his own big band in 1934. Towards the close of the Forties he moved into the R&B field and signed with King. During the next few years he had a number of hit records, usually characterized by a firm jump rhythm against a growling sax solo (e.g. 'Soft'). A contemporary of Lucky Millinder, Earl Bostic and Bill Doggett, Bradshaw toured America coast-to-coast, playing ballrooms and night clubs. He finally based himself in Chicago, until he suffered two strokes that forced his retirement in the late Fifties. He died in Cincinnati, Ohio, in January 1959. Buddy Holly once cited him as a favourite artist and his song 'The Train Kept A' Rollin'' has been much revived.

British Pop, during 1955, pretended to be aloof from the shame of rock'n'roll, and on the face of it she was. Dickie Valentine, Ruby Murray, trumpeter Eddie Calvert and the Stargazers topped the polls, and only the entry of 'Rock Around The Clock' into the British charts blemished the façade.

But, in 1956, resistance cracked and Britain entered the rock race in the only way she knew how: by studying and copying the American model. Consequently, Britain's first rock'n'roll band were Tony Crombie (a jazz drummer) and The Rockets, *doppelgängers* of Bill Haley and The Comets, and by the end of the year, Britain's rock contingent consisted of Crombie, the Dallas Boys, Lonnie Donegan and a blond version of Elvis Presley named Tommy Steele. In 1957, reinforcements began to arrive and first on the scene were lisping balladeer Russ Hamilton, bluegrass singer Johnny Duncan (a genuine American), fast-singing Don Lang, *6.5 Special* discovery Jim Dale, and former child wonders, the King Brothers. Failures included Terry Mayne, Tommy Steele's brother Colin Hicks, and the Lanza-inspired Toni Dalli, while the briefly popular Terry Dene was better known for his unhappy relationship with the Army. The discovery of 13-year-old Laurie London, who went on to become the first Briton to top the American hit parade, resulted in an invasion of singing children including Sandra Alfred and kilted Jackie Dennis, who had a big hit with 'La Dee Dah'. Gimmicks also assisted blue-rinsed Larry Page, Olympic swimmer Peter Elliott, Frankie Vaughan's sister-in-law Joyce Shock, and one of the better rock'n'rollers, Wee Willie Harris.

A little glory came to a well-behaved trio, the Mudlarks, and to the stars of TV's *Oh Boy!*, many of whom (Vince Eager, Billy Fury, Johnny Gentle, Duffy Power, Dickie Pride and Marty Wilde) had been re-christened by the first entrepreneur of British pop, Larry Parnes. Others making good on TV included Mike Preston, South African organist Cherry Wainer, former Los Angeles heavy Vince Taylor and, in 1959, a family of Italians, Little Tony and His Brothers. 1959 sounded the death knell for the golden age of rock'n'roll. The year's most popular arrival, Joe Brown, had some personality. Other newcomers – Craig Douglas, Rikki Price, Gerry Dorsey (who re-emerged in the Seventies as Engelbert Humperdinck), Michael Cox – hadn't. In 1960 flashes-in-the-pan included Emile Ford and growling Tommy Bruce. Johnny Kidd was a lone hard rocker, unrepresentative of popular taste: the top male singer was Cliff

Richard, the top female, Shirley Bassey, and the top group, the King Brothers.

Nice tunes prevailed in 1961 with trad jazz the dominant force and bland songsters like Eden Kane and 14-year-old Helen Shapiro making headway. Actors Jess Conrad, John Leyton and Hayley Mills looked chartwards – Leyton with great success. The Allisons and the Brook Brothers were more than vaguely reminiscent of the Everlys; Mark Wynter covered everything in sight; and among the one-hit wonders were Ricky Valance, Mike Berry and Shane Fenton. In 1962, during the calm before the storm, Frank Ifield and Jimmy Justice warbled and looked smart, while instrumentalists thrived and an influx of 'teenage' girls (Susan Maughan, Julie Grant etc.) tried to grab a piece of Miss Shapiro's action. Their stock in trade was, as always, the cover version. But the end of this practice was nigh.

Big Bill Broonzy was of the first generation of recorded bluesmen – he was born in Scott, Mississippi, in 1893 – but stylistically he made every transition possible in his lifetime. The last ten years before his death in 1958 were spent chiefly in introducing the blues from concert and club platforms to Americans and Europeans who believed, and were encouraged by fashion and Broonzy's patrons to believe, that he represented uniquely the rural workman/blues-singer. His many records of that period, mostly European-made, accorded with this image – which had little to do with the forceful Chicago band blues that had been Broonzy's chosen and mastered idiom throughout the Thirties and Forties. From early on a supremely accomplished guitarist, he was also an astute composer and clear, expressive singer, besides being a reliable accompanist. His personality lent much distinction even to his last phase, but his stature as a creative blues musician was established by the earlier work.

Buster Brown, born on Aug. 11, 1914, in Criss, Georgia, sang and played harmonica locally before recording for Bobby Robinson in New York City in 1959. In a powerful and intensely rhythmic style reminiscent of Sonny Terry, Brown reached the Top Forty with the much-imitated 'Fannie Mae', on Fire, in 1960. Smaller hits included 'Is You Is Or Is You Ain't My Baby' and 'Sugar Babe' (covered in Britain by Jimmy Powell) in 1962. Brown has also recorded for Serock, Gwenn, Checker, Nocturn and Astroscope.

Charles Brown, born in Texas City, Texas, in 1920, joined guitarist Johnny Moore's Three Blazers as a singer/pianist during the early Forties. Records under Moore's name for Exclusive, including 'Drifting Blues' (an historic session on which Johnny Otis played drums) and 'Merry Christmas, Baby', monopolized the R&B charts from 1946 to 1948. Los Angeles blues enjoyed national popularity at that time, and Brown led the field. His records with Moore were followed by seven Top Ten hits under his own name. His was a cool, late night, almost cocktail blues style. Sophisticated, relaxed and reflective, it had an indelible influence on many West Coast performers. In addition, most of Brown's hits for Aladdin – 'Get Yourself Another Fool', 'Trouble Blues', 'My Baby's Gone', 'Black Night' and the Leiber and Stoller composition 'Hard Times' – have become blues standards. His popularity waned in 1953, but he came back with a pop hit in 1961, 'Please Come Home For Christmas', on King. He has also recorded for Ace, Mainstream and Jewel. His mentor, Johnny Moore died in 1968 at the age of 62.

Clarence 'Gatemouth' Brown, probably *the* Texas blues guitarist during the early Fifties, became one of Duke/Peacock's biggest selling artists. Born on April 18, 1924 in Orange, Texas, he cut his first sides in 1947 for the Los Angeles-based Aladdin label, accompanied by the Maxwell Davis orchestra. He moved to Houston in late 1949 and was discovered by Don Robey, who signed him to Peacock. Among his hits are the intense 'Dirty Work At The Crossroads' and 'Ain't That Dandy', with backing by the Bill Harvey band. His guitar solos are near legendary in blues circles, and have inspired countless young musicians. In addition to

53

his singing and guitar playing, Gatemouth is accomplished on the harmonica and fiddle. He is now making a regular living playing at various blues festivals.

Joe Brown, born Joseph Roger Brown in Swarby, Lincolnshire, on May 13, 1941, moved to Plaistow, East London at the age of two. He joined a skiffle group, the Spacemen, in 1956. Discovered by Jack Good at an audition in Southend in 1959, Good used him as a backing musician on his TV follow-up to *Oh Boy!*, *Boy Meets Girl*. With his blond crewcut and easy stage presence, he seemed a natural for a solo spot and he began doing instrumentals but soon graduated to singing *and* playing and a name billing. Brown released a number of records between 1959 and 1962, starting with 'People Gotta Talk' and 'Darktown Strutters Ball' (on which the Spacemen became the Bruvvers). It wasn't until 'Picture Of You' was released in the summer of 1962 that he had his first hit, to be followed by 'It Only Took A Minute' at the end of the year and 'That's What Love Will Do' in 1963. He quickly moved on to films which consolidated his image as lovable Cockney 'sparrer' – in particular one of the better British pop films, *What A Crazy World* (1963). During the latter part of the Sixties, he turned more and more to acting and has since made an unspectacular comeback with the countryish Brown's Home Brew.

Maxine Brown, ex-beauty queen with a voice to match, was born in Kingstree, South Carolina. She sang with sundry gospel groups (the Royaltones, the Manhattans) around New York before hitting the Top Thirty in 1961 with a couple of sweet, self-composed, soul ballads, 'All In My Mind' and 'Funny' on Nomar, both of which were produced by the label's owner, Tony Bruno. She subsequently had fine chart entries on ABC and Wand – including the powerful Brunos production, 'Ask Me', 'It's Gonna Be Alright' and 'Oh No, Not My Baby', later revived by Manfred Mann – before going into decline on Epic, Commonwealth United and Avco.

Nappy Brown, based in Newark, New Jersey, became the Savoy label's star attraction with over 25 singles between 1954 and 1961. Several of his giant R&B hits – 'Don't Be Angry', 'Pitter Patter' (both 1955), 'Little By Little' (1957), 'It Don't Hurt No More' (1958), and 'Cried Like A Baby' (1959) – also reached the pop charts. His slower ballads were exceptionally soulful, and included 'The Right Time', 'I'm Getting Lonesome' and 'It's Really You' – on which Brown wailed, screamed and barked like a dog. After a long spell in prison, he returned to recording in 1969 – with Elephant – and more recently has cut gospel sides for Jewel with the Bell Jubilee Singers.

Roy Brown, born in New Orleans on Sept. 10, 1925, is best remembered for his pioneering vocal style. In 1948 he recorded 'Good Rockin' Tonight' for De Luxe and turned the national spotlight on New Orleans. The song was also successfully covered by Wynonie Harris – on King – and in later years by Elvis Presley – on Sun. Brown quickly made a name for himself singing in local clubs and concert halls. In 1950 he had topped the R&B charts with 'Hard Luck Blues', and thereafter every Roy Brown record turned 'gold' – 'Boogie At Midnight', 'Love Don't Love Nobody', 'Long About Sundown' and 'Big Town'. In 1952 he moved to King, but suffering a decline in popularity, he signed with Imperial in 1956. Teamed with Dave Bartholomew's band, Brown hit the charts again with a cover of Buddy Knox's 'Party Doll', then – in 1957 – with 'Let The Four Winds Blow'. But by this time the rock'n'roll craze was at its peak, and Brown's success couldn't last. Apart from a few sporadic releases, he was virtually forgotten until 1970 when Johnny Otis brought him back for a guest appearance at the Monterey festival. Many artists have been inspired by Brown's gospel-tinged vocals and he is today acknowledged by such names as B.B. King, Bobby Bland, Little Richard, Jackie Wilson and James Brown.

Ruth Brown, easily the most prolific female R&B singer of the Fifties, was born on Jan. 30, 1928, in Portsmouth, Virginia. Called 'Miss Rhythm', itself an indication of her singing style, her output of some 87 sides released by Atlantic between 1949 and 1962 established her as the label's top-selling artist of the decade, even surpassing the recorded totals of Ray Charles, LaVern Baker, Clyde McPhatter and the Drifters. Her first R&B No. 1 seller was 'Teardrops From My Eyes', released in 1950. Other chart-topping hits included 'Mama, He Treats Your Daughter Mean', '5-10-15 Hours', 'Oh What A Dream' and 'Lucky Lips'. In 1956, she was voted by deejays in a *Cash Box* poll the 'most programmed female vocalist in the R&B field'. Ruth was also a vital part of the pop music scene, and made numerous appearances at Alan Freed rock'n'roll extravaganzas. She is now out of 'retirement', touring clubs and recording new material for the Cobblestone label.

The Browns comprised two sisters and a brother from Pine Bluff, Arkansas. Jim Ed was born on March 1, 1934, Maxine on April 27, 1932 and Bonnie on June 7, 1936. Appearances on the *Louisiana Hayride* led to an RCA recording contract and a lachrymose version of Edith Piaf's French hit, 'Les Trois Cloches'. 'The Three Bells' topped the charts for four weeks in 1959. Later records included a version of the Harry Belafonte hit, 'Scarlet Ribbons'. During the Sixties, Jim Ed Brown established himself as a country singer, still with RCA.

Felice and Boudleaux Bryant wrote a string of hits for the Everly Brothers in the late Fifties. Boudleaux Bryant, born in 1920 in Shellman, Georgia, from a part-Indian background, spent his youth as a violinist in settings, ranging writing in 1948 with his newly-wed wife, Felice born in Milwaukee in 1925. Their first hit was 'Country Boy', originally recorded by hillbilly artist Jimmy Dickens but also covered by numerous others. In the early Fifties, Mitch Miller, an A&R man at American Columbia, made a habit of covering

C&W hits for the national pop market and the Bryants' 'covered' song successes at this time included 'Have A Good Time' (Tony Bennett), 'Hey Joe' (first recorded by C&W singer Carl Smith but covered by Frankie Lane who made it an international hit) and 'Willie Can' recorded in Britain by Alma Cogan.

The Bryants moved to Nashville in 1950 and were among the few people working there solely as songwriters; the other writers were usually also recording artists. In 1957, Archie Bleyer of the New York Cadence label introduced his new C&W signings, the Everly Brothers, to the Bryants who wrote 'Bye Bye Love' for the duo. 'Bye Bye Love' sold a million and from then on, the Bryants were commissioned to provide further material for the Everlys and they wrote either one or both sides of the duo's next five singles, including 'Wake Up Little Susie', 'Problems', 'Bird Dog', 'All I Have To Do Is Dream' and 'Poor Jenny' – all million-sellers. In 1958, they wrote 'Raining In My Heart' for Buddy Holly, which became a posthumous hit for him in 1959 as the 'B' side of 'It Doesn't Matter Anymore'. In 1960, the Bryants wrote Bob Luman's million-seller 'Let's Think About Living', but then their success in the pop market began to dwindle as the New York publishing houses took a firm hold on pop music.

Buchanan and Goodman made the Top Ten in 1956 with 'The Flying Saucer', featuring excerpts from R&B records of the time – for example, Smiley Lewis' 'I Hear You Knocking' and the Penguins' 'Earth Angel' – which greatly aided the sale of the original versions. The combination of two paranoia-inducing fads, rock'n'roll and flying saucers, was certain to arouse teenage enthusiasm. 'Flying Saucer The 2nd' made to Top Twenty the following year, and the duo – Bill Buchanan (born 1935) and Dickie Goodman (born 1934) – recorded other novelty items for Luniverse, Comic and PDQ before splitting up. Buchanan recorded on his own and with other partners on Novel, Gone, and United Artists, while Goodman continued to make the pop charts with a series of spoofs on TV programmes, including 'The Touchables In Brooklyn' (on Mark X in 1961), 'Ben Crazy' (Diamond, in 1962), 'Batman And His Grandmother' (Red Bird, 1966) and 'On Campus' (Cotique, 1969).

Dorsey Burnette's varied career began as string bass player in brother Johnny's Rock'n'Roll Trio – the third member was Paul Burlison – which recorded for Coral between 1956–8. They appeared on national TV and in the movie *Rock, Rock, Rock* and recorded as the Texans for Infinity. Born in Memphis on Dec. 28, 1932 he became a boxer, then an employee at Crown Electric with Elvis Presley, and eventually a successful singer and composer. His rich, deep voice scored on rockers like 'Bertha Lou' for Cee Jam, but major success came in 1960 with ballads 'Tall Oak Tree' and 'Big Rock Candy Mountain', recorded in Hollywood for Era. Currently a successful C&W singer, Burnette has also written many hit songs for Rick Nelson, Jerry Lee Lewis and numerous C&W artists.

Johnny Burnette, born March 25, 1934, in Memphis, Tennessee, attended the same school as Elvis Presley and in 1953 worked at the Memphis electrical firm where Presley drove a truck. His early career was filled with incident. First, he tried boxing, following in his older brother Dorsey's footsteps. But after a period as a lightweight, he decided to roam the South, working as a deckhand on a Mississippi river barge. He then made his way to California but was unable to find a job and hitched the 2,000 miles back to Memphis in late 1955. After singing for a month in St. Louis, Burnette persuaded his brother (who played bass) and a family friend Paul Burlison (a guitarist) to form a rockabilly trio as Elvis had done with Scotty Moore and Bill Black. Sam Phillips at the local Sun label rejected them as being too Presleyish, but the trio drove to New York where they won Arthur Godfrey's *Amateur Hour* show three times in succession. Singing with Decca–Coral, the Johnny Burnette Trio recorded their first single, 'Tear It Up' on May 7, 1956. Between 1956–7, they appeared on the Steve Allen TV show, toured with Gene Vincent, mimed in the film *Rock, Rock, Rock* and made three more singles for Coral. None were hits, and in the summer of 1957, Johnny and Dorsey headed for California where they wrote songs for Imperial's Ricky Nelson and Roy Brown. They also recorded 'Bertha Lou' for a small local label, but their vocals were erased when Coral objected to the duo's breach of contract.

In the autumn of 1958, Johnny joined Liberty's newly-formed Freedom subsidiary, recording three singles in 1958–9. He was transferred to Liberty in 1960, and under the supervision of whizz-kid producer Snuff Garrett, recorded five consecutive American hits including 'Dreamin', 'Little Boy Sad' and 'You're Sixteen'. He enjoyed two years as a teen idol but by 1963, following moves to Capitol and Chancellor, his fortunes had waned. He recorded for Sahara in 1964 before forming his own Magic Lamp label. He died in a boating accident while fishing on August 14, 1964.

James Burton, like Roy Buchanan and Al Casey, was one of the group of influential rockabilly guitarists who survived through to the present with session work, and thus played a major part in the West Coast country-rock scene of the Sixties and Seventies. He first appeared as a guitarist in Shreveport, Louisiana, and recorded with Dale Hawkins whose 'Suzie Q' on Checker was a rock'n'roll hit in 1957. The heavy, deliberate, and – for its time – very inventive guitar work enabled Burton to gain work on the West Coast and he soon joined the band of the young Ricky Nelson. Burton's 'Sun-style' electric lead picking was an important factor in the success of Nelson's discs, and the solos on 'Waitin' In School', 'Believe What You Say' and 'Bucket's Got A Hole In It' were definitive statements of the Carl Perkins, Scotty Moore guitar school. Burton remained with Nelson into the Sixties and has guested on guitar with successive waves of post-Byrds country-rockers, including the new-style Everly Brothers, Mike Nesmith, Delaney and Bonnie and Gram Parsons. He cut a solo album for A & M. In 1969, he backed

Dale Hawkins on a comeback album and, more importantly, he has fought to play against an ever-swelling choral and orchestral section behind Elvis ever since Presley staged his second coming on the concert circuit.

Jerry Butler was born in Sunflower, Mississippi, on Dec. 8, 1939. His family moved to Chicago in 1942. Jerry's early activities in various church choirs and gospel groups paved the way for his current status as one of America's top black vocal stylists of the past 15 years. He met Curtis Mayfield in the Traveling Souls Spiritualist Church Choir and, together with three ex-Roosters from Tennessee, formed Jerry Butler and the Impressions. They wrote 'For Your Precious Love' which became a Top Ten Tune of 1958, and later that year Butler quit to go solo and cut a string of Vee Jay smashes which often crossed over to white markets: 'He Will Break Your Heart', 'Need To Belong' (both written with Curtis Mayfield), 'Moon River' (by Henry Mancini and Johnny Mercer who publicly thanked Jerry for his help in making it 'Song Of The Year' 1961), and 'Make It Easy On Yourself' (by Bacharach and David). His cool on-stage delivery earned him 'The Iceman' tag – though the soubriquet also stems from Butler's one-time ambition to be a chef and ice sculptor. His activities widened when he received his own award for the 'Let It Be Me' duet with Betty Everett in 1964.

He entered the field of producing and publishing and wrote songs for Count Basie, Jackie Wilson and Otis Redding ('I've Been Loving You Too Long'). When Vee Jay folded (after grossing $20 million during their last year of operations) he joined Mercury, went pop for 'Mr. Dream Merchant' and then teamed up with unknown Kenny Gamble and Leon Huff. The classic results included the gold 'Only The Strong Survive' and two smash albums *The Iceman Cometh* and *Ice On Ice*. Gamble-Huff quit Mercury in 1970 and Jerry floundered with his ill-fated labels Fountain and Memphis, but made a personal comeback when he teamed with Brenda Lee Eager for the gold 'Ain't Understanding Mellow'. He now runs the Butler Music Workshop on Chicago's South Side, cultivating new writers, producers and performers.

Jerry Byrne is a contemporary of the young New Orleans rock'n'rollers, Bobby Charles, Frankie Ford and Mac Rebennack. Byrne's claim to fame rests on just one record, 'Lights Out'. Recorded for Specialty in 1958 by producer Harold Battiste when Byrne was a 17-year-old (white) high school student, the record sold only in the South. It is now recognised as a rock'n'roll classic, with its ferocious rhythm and Art Neville's pounding piano solo. Because it sold in only moderate quantities, Byrne continued to play hops and dances around New Orleans, showing a strong Ray Charles influence. Then, in the words of Rebennack (Dr John): 'Jerry got into some trouble and had to go off-the-set for a while.'

Cadence Records was formed in New York in 1953 by Archie Bleyer, and is best known for the seven Nashville-based million-sellers by the Everly Brothers, including 'Bye Bye Love' in 1957 and 'Wake Up Little Susie' in 1958. Bleyer himself hit with the novelty 'The Rockin' Ghost' and Johnny Tillotson scored with 'Poetry In Motion'. Heavier rock sounds like Link Wray's original 'Rumble' appeared, too, while Cadence also fielded several ballad singers headlined by Andy Williams and 'Butterfly'. Williams and the Everly Brothers left in 1960 and partly as a result, Cadence ceased operations in 1961, and Bleyer sold the masters to Williams.

The Cadets, comprising Aaron Collins, Willie Davis, Ted Taylor, Dub Jones and Lloyd McCraw, were a group with a double identity. As the Cadets they covered rock'n'roll songs for Modern, and as the Jacks cut ballads and jump tunes for RPM. They covered a host of hits (e.g. 'Heartbreak Hotel', 'Church Bells May Ring') but failed to improve on the original until their version of the Jayhawks' comic 'Stranded In The Jungle', with its exotic, nocturnal sounds and Jones' sour narration, made the Top Twenty in 1956.

On the Jacks' 1955 hit, 'Why Don't You Write Me' (a cover of the Feathers) the lead was taken by Davis who, with Collins, joined the Flairs. Jones moved on to the Coasters and Taylor became an admired soul singer. Aaron Collins' sisters, Betty and Rosie, formed the Teen Queens of 'Eddie My Love' fame.

The Cadillacs' first line-up – Earl Carroll (born 1937), Bobby Phillips (1935), Lavern Drake (1938), Gus Willingham (1937) and John Clark (1937) – appeared in 1954, when they started their recording career with Josie. Their slow ballads are favoured by present-day devotees, but the group themselves preferred a faster, harder style consistent with the most choreographed of all rock'n'roll stage acts. 'Speedoo' (No. 30 in 1955), a perfect crystallization of the up-tempo East Coast group sound, was a private joke – 'Some folks call me Speedoo but my real name is Mr Earl' – while 'Peekaboo' (Top Thirty in 1958) was inspired by the Coasters. Carroll's voice was light, happy and tuneful. He was one of the best group singers, inspiring many other street-corner groups, black and white. While their manager, Esther Navarro, often took the credit, much of the Cadillacs' material was written by Carroll and other members: his replacement as lead singer, Bobby Spencer, wrote 'My Boy Lillipop' by Barbie Gaye – the original of Millie Small's British hit. Carroll joined the Coasters in 1961, but the Cadillacs carried on to record for Smash, Capitol, Mercury and Polydor.

Cajun Music, which comes out of the sweaty swamplands of South West Louisiana, is one of the last bastions of indigenous American folk music. It has flourished in splendid isolation from the American way of life but not for much longer, because its lilting serenity and innocent charm are universal qualities which are being absorbed with benefit into mainstream rock and pop. However, the vocals, which are sung in local French patois, will ensure that change will not be too violent, although significantly English lyrics are becoming more prevalent.

The roots of the music date back to 1604 when the first settlers from France arrived in the Canadian province of Arcadia. Following the war between Britain and France, the Arcadians (now 'Cajuns') were forced to leave Canada in the mid-18th century and, sailing down the Eastern Seaboard, finally settled in the hostile and virtually unpopulated Louisiana swamplands. The music, like all folk forms, has undergone much change in the last fifty years. For example, the accordion was the prominent instrument in the Twenties but by the Thirties, with the hillbilly influence strong, the fiddle took over. Today both instruments are featured equally, and more recently there has been a noticeable influx of Negro music traditions (when played by black musicians the form is known as 'Zydeco'). But this has not allowed its basic functions to alter, as a dance music consisting mainly of waltzes and two-steps played at Fais do-do's every Saturday night.

Joe Falcon was the early pre-war Cajun recording star, along with Joe Werner and the Hackberry Ramblers. Harry Choates's 'Jole Blonde', the Cajuns' 'national anthem', and Nathan Abshire's 'Pine Grove Blues' were massive hits in the Forties and big names in the Fifties were Iry Le June, Aldus Roger and Lawrence Walker. Cajun's biggest ever commercial success came in 1961 when Cleveland Crochet's classic 'Sugar Bee' with Jay Stutes (Goldband) broke into the lower reaches of the Hot Hundred. There is a loyal local record market which has been readily supplied by George Khoury (Lyric), Lee Lavergne (Lanor), Jay Miller (Kajun), Carol Rachou (La Louisianne), Eddie Shuler (Goldband) and biggest of all Floyd Soileau (Jin & Swallow).

Cameo–Parkway Records, formed in 1956 by two Philadelphian songwriters, Kal Mann and Bernie Lowe, achieved an unparalleled run of success in the early Sixties with a series of dance records based on the phenomenally successful 'Twist'. While working in New York's Tin Pan Alley, Mann and Lowe wrote 'Butterfly' and rather than sell the song to a name artist, they decided to launch their own 'Cameo' label and had a local singer, Charlie Gracie, record the song. Both Gracie's version and a cover rendition by Andy Williams became hits, as did Gracie's follow-up, 'Fabulous', in 1957.

Although Gracie soon faded, Cameo were able to take advantage of Philadelphia's burgeoning record scene which centred around Dick Clark's *American Bandstand*, a TV rock show which attracted a huge national audience and became, in effect, the industry's sole criterion for assessing a record's potential. Cameo struck up a good working relationship with Dick Clark (who chose all the acts and records) and the label geared its entire output towards the show. In 1957, Cameo scored with 'Silhouette' by the Rays (leased from the XYZ label) and John Zacherle's ghoulish 'Dinner With Drac' as well as smaller hits by the Applejacks, Timmie Rogers and Bernie Lowe's Orchestra.

Cameo had yet to establish an identifiable image and recorded virtually anyone and anything which sounded vaguely commercial. In 1959, they signed Bobby Rydell, a 17-year-old Philadelphian who quickly blossomed into America's foremost teenage idol with a colossal run of totally dispensable hits, including 'Volare', 'Kissin' Time', 'Wild One' and 'Forget Him'. Also in 1959, the label signed one Ernest Evans, who had plucked chickens in a shop patronised by Kal Mann, and renamed him Chubby Checker. After one flop, one moderate hit ('The Class' on which Checker mimicked Elvis, the Coasters, Fats Domino and the Chipmunks), then two more flops, Checker recorded 'The Twist', an undistinguished dance-disc which zoomed to No. 1 in America in August, 1960. He followed up with several more dance hits – 'The Hucklebuck', 'Pony Time' (a No. 1) and 'Dance The Mess Around' – before recording 'Let's Twist Again' which re-focused attention on 'The Twist' and sparked off the biggest dance craze in years. His original 'Twist' disc was re-released and reached No. 1 in America for the second time in November, 1961. Cameo demonstrated an unmatched flair for exploitation by cashing in shamelessly with more dance discs, including Checker's 'Limbo Rock', 'Slow Twistin'', 'The Fly', the Orlons' 'Wah-Watusi' and 'South

Street', and Dee-Dee Sharp's 'Mashed Potato Time' – all big American hits.

By 1963, however, the formula had grown stale and Mann and Lowe sold their label to retire as extremely rich young men. Their timing, as always, was exemplary – by 1964, Cameo's hits had dried up and although Bunny Sigler and the Mysterins had huge hits in 1965–6, the label folded in 1968. Allen Klein, once the firm's accountant, now owns the assets.

Jo Ann Campbell, born on July 20, 1938, in Jacksonville, Florida, was ex-drum majorette and dancer who recorded unsuccessfully for Eldorado and Gone before her first minor hit, 'Kookie Little Paradise', on ABC in 1960. Jo Ann moved to Cameo-Parkway and made an answer to Claude King's pop-country hit, 'Wolverton Mountain', entitled 'I'm The Girl From Wolverton Mountain' (1962). She married songwriter Troy Seals with whom she had a minor hit with 'I Found A Love, Oh What A Love' (Atlantic, 1964).

Freddy Cannon, born Freddy Picariello in Lynn, Massachusetts, on Dec. 4, 1940, found success mainly through frequent appearances on Dick Clark's *American Bandstand*. Previously, Boston deejay Jack McDermott had put him in touch with Bob Crewe and Frank Slay of Swan Records, with whom Cannon enjoyed an unbroken string of 18 hits beginning with 'Tallahassie Lassie' (co-written by his mother) in 1959. 'Way Down Yonder In New Orleans' and 'Palisades Park' also made the Top Ten. Crewe, Slay and the studio musicians sat around for hours trying to make the records simpler, but the combination of brassy horns and Cannon's sore throat vocals – he must have taken singing lessons from Fabian – has not stood the test of time. 'Buzz Buzz A Diddle It,' with a powerful Diddley-style guitar intro from Kenny Paulson (who added the glitter to 'Tallahassie Lassie') rates as his finest hour. He also had Top Twenty hits with 'Abigail Beecher' and 'Action' on Warner Brothers in

1965–6. Cannon subsequently recorded for Sire, We Make Rock'n'Roll Records and Metromedia, with scant success.

Capitol Records was founded in the Spring of 1942 by record shop owner, Glenn Wallichs (of 'Wallich's Music City'), film producer Buddy DeSylva and songwriter Johnny Mercer on the basis that Wallichs would handle the business aspects, and Mercer the musical scores, while DeSylva looked after the finances. The war years were not auspicious for the formation of a new record company due to an existing shellac shortage and a recording ban imposed by the American musicians' union, but with DeSylva investing more money in the concern, Capitol survived to sign a young black jazz pianist-vocalist named Nat 'King' Cole in 1943. By 1950, Cole had stepped into the front ranks of record personalities with hits such as 'Nature Boy', 'Mona Lisa' and 'Too Young' and accounted for a quarter of the label's turnover. During the early Fifties, Capitol consolidated its position with such pre-rock acts as Les Paul and Mary Ford, Frank Sinatra and the orchestras of Les Baxter and Nelson Riddle.

In 1948, the label also activated a successful C&W division by signing the popular Tex Ritter and staff producer Ken Nelson quickly developed an outstanding country roster, including Tennessee Ernie Ford, Jean Sheppard, Faron Young, Hank Thompson and Merle Travis, who all registered hits in the hillbilly market. In 1954, Capitol announced a $20 million turnover and the following year, EMI in Britain bought Capitol for £8½ million.

Ken Nelson also masterminded Capitol's entry into rock'n'roll by signing Gene Vincent, whose 'Be-Bop-A-Lula' sold a million in 1956. Other Capitol rock acts at this time included Esquerita, Tommy Sands, Merrill Moore and Johnny Otis, but the label's success in this field was extremely limited due to its condescending attitude towards the idiom – a reaction after the fabulous success of the post-war years. Then, in 1961, a young staff producer named N. K. Venet signed the popular Lettermen vocal group and in 1962 he contracted the Beach Boys, who quickly went on to become foremost American act of the mid-Sixties. The acquisition in 1964 of the Beatles, Peter and Gordon and other British rock acts consolidated Capitol's position in the rock field and precipitated a boom period. In the C&W market, Buck Owens, Merle Haggard and Sonny James all became major acts.

During the late Sixties, Capitol were slow in catering for hard rock audiences, but quickly made amends by signing Joe South, Steve Miller, the Band and Grand Funk Railroad – the latter accounting for ten million records sales in three years (1971–3).

The Carter Family, the most influential singing group in rural American music, was composed of A. P. Carter (1891–1960), his wife Sara (born 1898) and her cousin Maybelle (born 1909), all from southern Virginia. The trio performed locally during the Twenties but achieved fame throughout the South after their first recordings (Victor, 1927). In contrast with contemporary fiddle bands and solo singers, they defined the style of the family harmony group, employing two and three-part vocal arrangements of traditional ballads, lyric songs and hymns. Their instrumental accompaniments – two guitars, or guitar and autoharp – lent prominence to Maybelle Carter's innovative fashion of melody-line guitar-playing.

Recording regularly throughout the Thirties, the family touched upon most idioms of Southern song and devised some of their own. A. P. Carter was an astute song-collector, obtaining material from both white and black informants and channelling it into a stream of commercial records, which in turn became a legacy for later artists. Songs associated with the Carters are current today among many bluegrass and C&W artists. 'Wildwood Flower' has become a test-piece for country guitarists, while 'Keep On The Sunny Side', 'Worried Man Blues', 'Will The Circle Be Unbroken' and a score more have permanent places in the idiom.

The original trio disbanded in 1943, and the numerous Carter children provided the wherewithal for two distinct groups. One of these still performs, headed by Maybelle and including her daughter June, wife of Johnny Cash. The recordings of the original family, made between 1927 and 1941, have been extensively reissued.

The Cascades, a vocal quintet from San Diego, California – John Gummoe, Eddie Snyder, Dave Stevens, Dave Wilson and Dave Zabo – scored a Top Three hit on Valiant with 'Rhythm Of The Rain' in 1963. A clean-cut bunch of skin-diving mountaineers, the group specialized in soft, pretty, summery sounds and their smooth harmonies remained in the American charts right into the Seventies. Lesser hits included 'The Last Leaf' (Valiant), 'For Your Sweet Love' (on RCA in 1964) and 'Maybe The Rain Will Fall' (on Uni in 1969).

Al Casey's band, the Arizona Hayriders, originally backed local rockabillies – Jimmy Johnson, Don Cole, Jimmy Spellman – but he first received national attention as the guitarist responsible for the fascinating rhythm behind Sanford Clark's hit, 'The Fool', in 1956. Casey subsequently joined Duane Eddy's Rebels, playing lead on the occasional early hit – for example, 'Ramrod' – for which Eddy received the kudos. 'Jivin' Around', a Top Thirty R&B hit in 1962, and 'Surfin' Hootenanny', a Top Fifty pop hit in 1963, on Stacy, were among the best of his fast and gritty instrumental sides.

The Champs, a largely instrumental rock'n'roll combo, were Chuck 'Tequila' Rio (tenor sax), Dave Burgess and Dale Norris (guitars), Dean Beard (piano), Van Norman (bass) and Gene Alden (drums). They were West Coast sessionmen who made eight hits on Joe Johnson's Challenge label between 1958 and 1962. The first, 'Tequila', reached No. 1 and stayed on the charts for 19 weeks. The other brash and gutty hits included 'El Rancho Rock', 'Chariot Rock', 'Too Much Tequila' and 'Limbo Rock'. Rio and Alden left to be replaced by Jimmy Seals and Dash Crofts (later to become

Seals and Crofts), while Burgess and Beard made solo rock'n'roll records of considerable distinction.

Bruce Channel was born in Jacksonville, Texas on Nov. 28, 1940. At 17 Channel was a regular on the *Louisiana Hayride*, and made a series of unsuccessful country-rock records (for King and others) before cutting 'Hey Baby', which reached No. 1 in 1962. Originally, only 200 copies had been pressed by the producer, Major Bill Smith, for release on LeCam, but demand soared and Smash bought the master. It was a seminal white blues disc, heavily played on R&B stations before television appearances revealed that Channel wasn't black. His unvarnished vocal and Delbert McClinton's harmonica accompaniment impressed the Beatles, with whom Channel shared the bill at a Liverpool concert in 1962. 'Love Me Do' was said to have owed a lot to Channel's sound. An astute performer, he came back with hits every now and then, including a Dixieland rocker, 'Going Back To Louisiana' (LeCam, 1964), 'Mr Bus Driver' and 'Keep On' (Mala, 1968).

The Chantels – Rene Minus (born 1943), Lois Harris (1940), Sonia Goring (1940), Jackie Landry (1940) and lead singer Arlene Smith (1941) – became the premier girl group of the mid-Fifties, with a handful of choral hits – 'He's Gone', 'Maybe', 'Every Night' and 'I Love You So' – on George Goldner's End label. Produced by Richie Barrett, they were innovatory records, doomy and inspirational with lashings of echo over which Arlene, then 15, sang with exceptional power and clarity. The group returned to the charts in 1961–3 with 'Look In My Eyes' and 'Well I Told You' (an answer to Ray Charles' 'Hit The Road Jack') on Carlton and 'Eternally' on Ludix. While Barrett switched his attentions to the Three Degrees, the Chantels recorded for Verve and RCA without success. Arlene, who doubled as a housewife in the Bronx, also made some sides for Spectorious and Big Top.

Chubby Checker, born on Oct. 5, 1941, in Philadelphia, was working in a chicken market when his boss, impressed by his singing, contacted Kal Mann, a staff-writer with the local Parkway label, who signed him to a long-term contract in 1959. Ernest Evans then became Chubby Checker and his first disc 'The Class' was quite successful, but a later disc changed the course of pop history. 'The Twist' had been the flipside of a Hank Ballard and the Midnighters hit in 1959: it seems that Dick Clark called in Checker as a replacement when Ballard didn't show for rehearsals of his *American Bandstand* TV show and recorded the song to accompany his appearance (in fact, Clark's wife created his stagename, remarking that he resembled a young Fats Domino – hence Chubby Checker!). 'The Twist' was a No. 1 hit (twice) and Checker went on to capitalize by recording nebulous dance songs – 'Pony Time', 'Let's Twist Again', 'The Fly', etc. – over the next six years, most achieving chart status but few creating any musical landmarks, being largely nasal tenor chants accompanied by somewhat tuneless vocal choruses and stereotyped rhythm/saxophone bandtracks. It was obviously what the public wanted, however, since he had no less than 31 chart entries up to Parkway's demise in 1968, regularly featuring on TV and movies demonstrating his dances. He made a brief comeback on Buddah in 1969, and a disastrous foray into 'reggae' and 'Progressive' sounds on Chalmac in 1971, but has since settled into a comfortable niche on rock'n'roll revival shows, featuring in the movie *Let The Good Times Roll*.

Clifton Chenier, born on a farm near Opelousas, Louisiana, on June 25, 1925, is the foremost exponent of 'Zydeco', the little-known equivalent of Cajun music found among the French-speaking blacks of the Louisiana and Texas Gulf Coasts. His blues accordion playing and funky English/French patois vocals have long enjoyed considerable local appeal. Since the mid-Fifties he has recorded for numerous labels, including Elko, Part, Specialty, Checker and Zynn.

Prolific sessions for Arhoolie, with his older brother, Cleveland, on washboard, have met with universal acclaim by blues enthusiasts throughout the Sixties.

Chess Records, perhaps the supreme blues and R&B label, has been responsible for dozens of classic recordings and some of the biggest hits in the field of popular black music. It has also, by sheer virtue of its artistic roster, influenced and shaped – either directly or indirectly – the entire white rock movement from the early Sixties on.

The company was formed by Leonard and Phil Chess, Jewish immigrants from Poland who settled in Chicago in 1928. They worked their way into the liquor business and by the Forties owned a string of bars on the Southside of Chicago. From there they purchased a night-club, the Macomba, which featured names like Billy Eckstine and Gene Ammons. The popularity of these artists with the black clientele was quickly appreciated by Leonard Chess, as was the lack of local recording facilities for the newer names who appeared at the club. Satisfied that a demand existed, the Chess brothers started Aristocrat records in 1947 and hit lucky when blues pianist Sunnyland Slim hustled a recording date, bringing with him a Mississippi-born singer/guitarist named Muddy Waters, who was recorded as an afterthought. One of Muddy's songs, 'I Can't Be Satisfied', was released and became an immediate hit as thousands of disillusioned black migrants identified with his lyrical invitation to return 'back down South, 'cos I just can't be satisfied and I just can't keep from cryin''. He followed it with 'You're Gonna Miss Me' and 'Screamin' And Cryin'' and within three years Leonard Chess had become a major producer in black music and Muddy the biggest name in blues.

In June, 1950, the Chess label was launched and Aristocrat slipped into history. The first Chess single was by tenorist Gene Ammons, and led to releases by Howlin' Wolf, Elmore James, Rosco Gordon and Willie Dixon, who subsequently acted as musical adviser, arranger, producer and session bassist for the Chess brothers. Three years later, the

71

Checker subsidiary label introduced Little Walter, Lowell Fulson, Little Milton and the Flamingos.

While Phil stayed in Chicago taking care of business, Leonard made innumerable trips down South, selling records from the back of his car as well as making contacts. From Sam Phillips he bought the rights to Jackie Brenston's 1951 recording of 'Rocket 88' (with Ike Turner on piano), which is often cited as the first rock'n'roll record. Leonard Chess appreciated the importance of the deejay as an advertising asset and was one of the first associates of Alan 'Moondog' Freed, who greatly helped spread Chess sales and ultimately caused the label to expand its horizons. Perhaps the greatest years for Chess were 1954–5 when records by Muddy, Wolf, Walter, John Lee Hooker, Sonny Boy Williamson, Eddie Boyd, Willie Mabon, Jimmy Rogers and the Moonglows continually dominated the R&B Top Ten. Soon after, Chuck Berry and Bo Diddley came to Chess, pushing the name into the national charts with a constant stream of hits. Both artists still record prolifically for the label.

As the Fifties progressed, Chess and its subsidiaries, Checker and Argo, looked more towards the rock'n'roll and soul market, signing up such acts as the Dells, Jimmy McCracklin, Dale Hawkins, Clarence 'Frogman' Henry, Etta James, Johnny and Joe, the Monotones, Ramsey Lewis and Bobby Charles. By the late Fifties Chess had dropped all their blues acts with the exception of Muddy, Wolf, Sonny Boy, Walter, Otis Rush and Buddy Guy, going into the Sixties with Sugar Pie Desanto's 'Soulful Dress', Koko Taylor's 'Wang Dang Doodle' and Fontella Bass's 'Rescue Me'. Since then the company's hit-makers have been the Dells on Cadet. On October 16, 1969 Leonard Chess died and the Chess organization was bought out by GRT, America's second largest tape corporation. Phil left to run a radio station and Marshall Chess, Leonard's son, went to work for the Rolling Stones. Little remains today of the Chess Chicago operation, and the studios are reduced to an editing room (2120 South Michigan Avenue). The head office subsequently moved back to New York, comprising Chess and the subsidiary Janus, Checker, Cadet, GRT, Westbound and Concept. Chuck Berry's early Seventies hit 'My Ding-A-CLing' revitalised the company, now totally impersonalized but back in the top league with artists as diverse as Solomon Burke and Baker-Gurvitz Army.

Chicago Blues were a phenomenon of the late Forties and early Fifties, blossoming from an amalgam of Southern regional blues styles. Its sound is characterized by heavily amplified guitars, piano, bass, drums and usually harmonica and is best exemplified by the Muddy Waters band, considered the finest ever to emerge from that city.

The style reached its creative peak in 1954–5, when Chicago blues records dominated the national R&B Top Ten. A handful of key names can be cited as having made a real and innovative contribution to the pure strain of Chicago blues. Sonny Boy Williamson No. 1 (John Lee) was the first bluesman to score a major impact on the Chicago scene of the Forties. His records for RCA Victor paved the way for the group ensemble sound of later years. The most commercially successful artist to perform in the style was undoubtedly Little Walter, often regarded as simply Muddy Waters' harp player. He did, in fact, sell more records than any other Chicago blues artist, Waters included. Walter was a total innovator and his revolutionary harmonica sound – deeply rooted in jazz – remains unsurpassed. His Top Ten R&B hits like 'Juke' and 'Last Night' – cut for Chess in the early Fifties – mark the pinnacle of Chicago blues. Another Waters' sideman, guitarist Jimmy Rogers, must share credit for his contribution to the music. His solo records, usually with the Waters band in attendance, are again brilliant examples of the undiluted Chicago blues sound. Nor can Jimmy Reed's stature in the 'Windy City' be overlooked. Between the years 1955–61 he was continually on the charts with a succession of hit singles for Vee Jay including 'Honest I Do' and 'Bright Lights, Big City'. Today the Chicago blues style is kept on by Junior Wells, Carey Bell and a host of lesser known bluesmen still active in the clubs and bars of South Side Chicago. The influence of Chicago blues on today's rock musicians – whether direct or indirect – has been enormous. For instance, the Rolling Stones based their early sound and line-up on that of the Muddy Waters band.

The Chiffons, a successful black female vocal group, were contemporaries of other early-Sixties pop-oriented acts like the Crystals (produced by Phil Spector) and the Cookies (produced by Goffin-King). The Chiffons were produced by Bright Tunes Productions Inc. of Brooklyn, who were essentially Margo/Margo/Medress/Siegel of Tokens fame. The group comprised Judy Craig (born 1946), Barbara Lee (May 16, 1947), Patricia Bennet (April 7, 1947) and Sylvia Peterson (Sept. 30, 1946), plus resident guitarist Butch Mann (from Ruby and the Romantics, later with the Drifters). Their first record was 'Tonight's The Night' on Big Deal in 1960, then came a string of hits on Laurie, including, 'He's So Fine' (their only No. 1, in 1963, written by their manager, Ronald Mack, and later acknowledged to have been the source of George Harrison's 'My Sweet Lord'), 'One Fine Day', 'Sweet Talking Guy' (a re-issue Top Ten in Britain in 1972), 'A Love So Fine' and 'I Have a Boyfriend'. They also recorded as the Four Pennies, under which name they made the American Hot Hundred. The group still perform in the New York area.

The Chipmunks were the creation of David Seville (real name Ross Bagdassarian) born on Jan. 27, 1919, in Fresno, California. Seville started out as an actor and then as a song-writer for, among others, Rosemary Clooney ('Come On-A My House'), Johnnie Ray ('What's The Use') and Sammy Davis ('Red Grapes'). He produced the Chipmunks by use of a complex multi-tracking technique and based their names (Simon, Theodore and Alvin) on those of Liberty record company executives. He hit on a winning formula with their first record, 'The Chipmunk Song', one of the most success-ful Christmas songs yet, selling over $3\frac{1}{2}$ million copies.

Other records included 'Witch Doctor', 'Alvin's Harmonica' and 'Ragtime Cowboy Joe', the last two of which were Top Twenty hits in 1959. Seville's films include *Rear Window*, (the composer) *The Deep Six* and *The Devil's Hairpin* and he played the Pin Ball Maniac in his cousin William Saroyan's *The Time Of Your Life*. He died in Jan. 1972.

The Chordettes bridged the gap between Fifties pop and the rock'n'roll era, and consisted originally of four girls from Sheboygan, Wisconsin – Dorothy Schwarz, Jinny Osborne, Janet Ertel and Carol Bushman. Before they came to notice via the Arthur Godfrey show, Dorothy and Jinny were replaced by Lynn Evans and Margie Needham. Following the Godfrey appearance, they were signed to Cadence by Archie Bleyer, and their first record, 'Mr Sandman', was at No. 1 for seven weeks in 1954. They appeared frequently in the charts until the early Sixties with records like 'Eddie My Love', 'Lay Down Your Arms' (covered in Britain by the matronly Anne Shelton), 'Lollipop' (a British hit for the Mudlarks in 1958), 'A Girl's Work Is Never Done', 'Born To Be With You' and 'Never On Sunday'.

The Chords, of whom *Billboard* wrote in April, 1954, 'Playful bounce and tasty restrained styling will appeal to customers in both R&B and pop markets', made a trailblazing contribution to rock'n'roll with 'Sh-Boom'. Covered by the Crewcuts, parodied by Stan Freberg – 'stuff some old rags in your mouth and take it again from the top' – and revived by Sha Na Na, the song is universally famous. But the Chords, who became the Chordcats, could never repeat its success despite further records for the Atlantic subsidiary, Cat. Claude and Earl Feaster (or Feister), Jimmy Keyes, Floyd McRae, James Edwards and Bobby Spencer were among the personnel.

Jimmy Clanton, born in Baton Rouge, Louisiana on Sept. 2, 1940, discovered by New Orleans studio engineer, Cosimo Matassa, and signed by Ace Records in 1958. His second record, 'Just A Dream', a wistful R&B ballad, shot up the charts to No. 4, earning a gold record on the way. His record company quickly saw the potential of making the good-looking high school kid into an all-American teen-idol and so the R&B content of his records was quietly extinguished in favour of a commercial-pop approach. This scheme paid hefty dividends for a while with a series of hit records, culminating in another million-seller, 'Venus In Blue Jeans' in 1962. After this it was all downhill; his time as teen-fodder was up.

Dee Clark, born in Blythville, Arkansas on July 11, 1938, as Delecta Clark, moved to Chicago, where he sang in gospel groups prior to recording with the Hambone Kids for Okeh in 1952. He subsequently joined the Kool Gents, who recorded for Vee Jay. Recognising Clark's ability to imitate either Little Richard or Clyde McPhatter, the company signed him as a solo artist. A string of discs on Falcon, Abner and the parent label, Vee Jay, followed, including hits with 'Nobody But You', 'Just Keep It Up', 'Hey Little Girl' (all Top Thirty in 1958–9), 'How About That', 'Your Friends' and 'Raindrops' (No. 2 in 1961). Skilfully produced and memorably tuneful, they were among the best black pop records of their era. Clark also recorded for Constellation, Columbia, Wand and Liberty, and helped to write 'You Can't Sit Down' while on tour with Phil Upchurch.

Dick Clark, born in Mount Vernon, New York in 1929, graduated from radio announcer to host of Philadelphia's top TV show *Bandstand* in 1956. Clark's perceptive choice of music (solid rock and pop) and programme format (stomping Philly High School regulars) interested the giant ABC network. In 1957, it was dubbed *American Bandstand* and went national and the daily 90-minute show began to draw up to a million fan letters weekly. Clark single-handedly established Frankie Avalon, Fabian and Connie Francis among others, and began other ventures including the weekly *Dick Clark Show*, a syndicated newspaper column, working as a tour emcee and the ill-fated *World Of Talent*. When the payola crisis hit rock in early 1960, he was called 'the single most influential person' in the popular music industry and made to divest himself of some business interests after the Congressional probe. Despite that, ABC kept on the show and the sponsors continued their support. Clark made more movies throughout the Sixties on everything from high-school dropouts to acid casualties, moved to Hollywood for *Where The Action's At* and swung into the Seventies with *In Concert* and, briefly, *Soul Unlimited*.

Sanford Clark was born in 1933 in Oklahoma. His parents moved to Phoenix, Arizona, soon after his birth. After serving three years in the US Air Force, he began singing C&W on radio and TV shows in the Phoenix area. In 1956 he met Lee Hazlewood, a Phoenix deejay, and recorded Hazlewood's rockabilly song 'The Fool' with Al Casey's group providing the backing – for a small local label. The master was promptly purchased by Dot in Hollywood who turned it into a major hit in August that year, but Clark was unable to follow it up despite several more Dot releases. In 1959, he made a short comeback on Jamie with 'Run Boy Run' and 'Son Of A Gun' (both written and produced by Hazlewood) and subsequently recorded, without success, for Warner Brothers, Ramco and LHI. He still sings part-time in the Phoenix area.

The Cleftones – Charlie James (born 1940), Berman Patterson (1938), Warren Corbin (1939), William McClain (1938) and lead singer Herbie Cox (1939) – were students from Jamaica High, New York, when they first recorded for Gee in 1956. Hits followed with Patterson's 'You Baby You' and Cox's 'Little Girl Of Mine'. Returning from the limbo to which most black groups were consigned by the rise of rock'n'roll, the Cleftones re-entered the charts in 1961–2, with 'Heart And Soul' (Top Twenty), 'I Love You For Sentimental Reasons', and 'Lover Come Back To Me'. Under the guidance of Henry Glover, and with new members including Pat Span and Gene Pearson, these revitalised standards were an ideal showcase for Cox's soulful rasp. The group also recorded for Rama, Roulette and Ware.

Jack Clement, born Jack Henderson Clement in Memphis in 1932, is one of the most colourful characters on the Nashville scene. His career began in Washington, in 1950, in a bluegrass duo called Buzz and Jack, at which time Clement began to master the guitar, mandolin, bass, steel guitar and drums, enabling him to become a sessionman and eventually a record producer in Memphis during the rockabilly boom of the Fifties. He has recorded country material for Sheraton, Sun and RCA and has a distinguished, if unsuccessful, country vocal style. His 'Ten Years' was a minor success for Sun in 1958.

As a writer and producer, he has contributed much to country-influenced rock. He was responsible for commercializing the Johnny Cash sound with his own songs 'Ballad Of A Teenage Queen' and 'Guess Things Happen That Way', and for Dickey Lee's Hallway recordings. His production work began in 1955 with Fernwood in Memphis and continued with Sun and his own label. Summer, until in 1960 he moved to the Hallway label in Beaumont. In 1966, he launched the first commercially successful black country artist, Charley Pride, with 'Just Between Yon And Me' on RCA and produced seven years of sustained top country hits. He has also a considerable reputation as an unpredictable joker and has written many comedy songs, such as the Johnny Cash hits 'Everyone Loves A Nut' and 'The One On The Right Is On The Left'. Currently, he works as a freelance producer in Nashville, controlling sessions varying from the traditional Doc and Merle Watson to the modern Area Code 615. He owns Jack Music and a movie company.

Patsy Cline, born in Winchester, Virginia in 1932, as Virginia Hensley, first made her name in New York – unusual for a country singer – when she won the Arthur Godfrey Talent Scouts television show in 1957 with 'Walking Before Midnight'. It was an immediate million-seller and the first of a string of hits. The form that she made her own was the heartbreak ballad. Ben Hecht, who wrote 'Walking Before Midnight' described her as the one person who could 'cry on both sides of the microphone'. It was this unique quality in her voice that allowed her to dominate the modern 'weepie' genre with songs like 'She's Got You', 'Faded On Your Mind', 'Faded Love' and 'I Fall To Pieces'. By the time she recorded this last song she was the undisputed top female country singer in America. That was in 1963, the year she died, with Hawkshaw Hawkins and Cowboy Copas, in a plane crash. Her legend survives, and in 1973 she was elected to the Country Music Hall of Fame.

The Clovers began as a trio – Harold Lucas, Thomas Woods and Billy Shelton – in 1946 at school in Washington. John Bailey was soon added, and in the late Forties Matthew McQuator replaced Woods. Harold Winley then replaced Shelton and, in 1949, guitarist Bill Harris joined the throng. In 1950 they were introduced to Lou Krefetz who became their manager and had them record for Rainbow; the disc didn't sell and Krefetz placed them with Atlantic, where their first two discs, Ahmet Ertegun's 'Don't You Know I Love You' and 'Fool Fool Fool', were No. 1 R&B hits during 1951. Both raw beat ballads, they sold 250,000 and 500,000 respectively – massive quantities in their limited market. In 1952, Bailey was drafted and replaced by Billy Mitchell, who was retained when Bailey returned after Army service, making a sextet.

Enjoying a string of 17 R&B hits up to 1956, they varied their style between harmonic ballads ('Blue Velvet') and novelty jump items ('Nip Sip'). Their magic ran out by 1957 when they left Atlantic for Poplar, making a couple of undistinguished singles and an LP subsequently issued by United Artists, whom they joined in 1958. The next year saw their biggest hit, 'Love Potion No. 9', in their novelty 'jump' style. But after brief outings on Port and Atlantic, the sextet split in 1961, different factions subsequently recording for Winley, Porwin, Brunswick, Tiger and Josie. A Clovers group led by Lucas still plays revival shows. Harris is a respected jazz guitarist.

The Coasters were created in 1955 from the nucleus of a Los Angeles based group, the Robins. They were the agents through which Leiber and Stoller marketed some of the most entertaining songs of the Fifties. Founder member Bobby Nunn had led the Robins through numerous West Coast labels, recorded with Johnny Otis on Savoy, and had a hit with Little Esther Phillips, 'Double Crossing Blues' (1950), before teaming with Leiber and Stoller on RCA in 1953. When the writing and producing duo formed their own label, Spark, a year later, they scored several local hits with the Robins, notably 'Riot In Cell Block No. 9' (featuring Richard Berry), 'Framed' (Nunn), 'The Hatchet Man' (Nunn), and 'Smokey Joe's Café' (Carl Gardner). Eight cuts from this period were later included on the first Coasters' album and have subsequently been regarded as Coasters' recordings.

Attracted by the success of 'Smokey Joe's Café', Atlantic signed them to their subsidiary label, Atco, retaining Leiber and Stoller as the creative force behind the group. Gardner and Nunn, with newcomers Billy Guy and Leon Hughes (also from California), were renamed the Coasters and achieved widespread popularity with their first releases 'Down In Mexico' and 'One Kiss Leads To Another' (1956), followed more emphatically by 'Searchin'/'Young Blood' (1957) – a Top Ten pop hit. After three less successful outings, Nunn and Hughes were replaced by Will 'Dub' Jones and Cornel Gunter who, with Guy and Gardner, formed the quartet that recorded all the other famous Coasters' hits: 'Yakety Yak' (1958) – their only No. 1 – 'Charlie Brown', 'Along Came Jones', 'Poison Ivy' (1959), and 'Little Egypt' (1961). The arrangement of these records used the differing character of each singer's voice to full effect around a catchy guitar figure (often Mickey Baker) or a fruity sax break (King Curtis). The production, particularly on the Robins' and early Coasters' releases, was far superior to any contemporary group efforts; and the lyrics, humorous cameos each neatly deriding an aspect of teenage and/or black ghetto life, were more adventurous than most other popular songs. In short, they were a unique series of statements influencing many other groups (the Cadillacs, the Olympics, the Hollywood Argyles) and yet never bettered. Hilarious stage routines worked out for each song ensured that they were as entertaining in person as on record. Apart from the hits, other sides – 'My Baby Comes To Me' (1957), 'The Shadow Knows' (1958), 'I'm A Hog For You' (1959), and 'Shopping For Clothes' (1960) – were equally fine examples of the partnership.

In 1961 Earl 'Speedoo' Carroll from the Cadillacs replaced Gunter and the group continued on Atco until 1966, without Leiber and Stoller. Despite a couple of good releases – 'T'ain't Nothin' To Me' (recorded live at The Apollo in 1963) and 'Let's Go Get Stoned' (1965) – the Coasters' audiences dwindled. On Date in the late Sixties (reissued on King in the Seventies) Leiber and Stoller attempted to revive the Coasters' career. Although the best of these recordings, 'Down Home Girl' and 'D. W. Washburn', were as good as the Fifties hits, they were ignored by a new generation of record buyers.

Eddie Cochran was born Eddie Ray Cochran in Oklahoma City on Oct. 3, 1938, the youngest of five children. Soon after his birth, the family moved north to Albert Lea, Minnesota, where they remained until he was 11. In 1949, they moved again to California, land of post-war opportunity, and settled in the Bell Gardens area where Eddie took up the guitar in earnest. In 1953, he met Connie 'Guybo' Smith who later became his bassist.

In 1954, Cochran began his professional career as back-up guitarist behind an obscure hillbilly singer, Hank Cochran. Though unrelated, Hank did resemble Eddie and before long they hit the road as the Cochran Brothers, one of many hillbilly duos playing local fairs and dances in the South-West. In 1955, they recorded two straight hillbilly singles for the small Ekko label in Hollywood ('Guilty Conscience' and 'Mr Fiddle') but switched to rock'n'roll late in 1955 after seeing Elvis Presley (then still on Sun) in a Dallas stage show. Augmented by a heavy-handed drummer and an excitable pianist, the Cochrans cut 'Tired And Sleepy' and 'Fool's Paradise', progressing in one step from acoustic hillbilly to frantic country-based rock, the spirit of which had now caught Eddie's fancy.

In 1956, Hank and Eddie split up and Eddie teamed up with Jerry Capehart, a songwriter who secured a deal with American Music, a Hollywood music publishing company, and Eddie recorded 'Skinny Jim' for their small Crest label. Using 'Skinny Jim' as a demo, Capehart, by now Cochran's manager and confidant, secured Eddie a contract with Liberty who in turn found him a part in the forthcoming movie, *The Girl Can't Help It*. Although Cochran sang '20 Flight Rock' in the film, his first Liberty release was 'Sittin' In The Balcony', a smoochie 'rockaballad' which reached No. 18 in America in May, 1957. Despite this flying start, however, Cochran had problems finding a follow-up and had to wait until September, 1958, for his next big hit – 'Summertime Blues', a million-seller and one of the classics of rock'n'roll.

Although contracted to Liberty, Cochran spent a great deal of time in the studio surrounded by musician friends and singers under the auspices of American Music and the fruits of these jam sessions were often released on obscure American Music subsidiaries such as Silver Capehart, Crest and Zephyr as by the Kelly Four (Cochran's backing group), Jewel and Eddie and others.

After 'Summertime Blues' came 'C'mon Everybody', 'Weekend', 'Somethin' Else' and 'Cherished Memories' – all much bigger hits in Britain where, like Gene Vincent, he was more popular than in America. Cochran appeared in two other films, *Untamed Youth* (1957) and *Go Johnny Go* (1959). Finally, in 1960, he was booked to tour England with his close friend, Gene Vincent. He was ecstatically received both on stage and TV (*Boy Meets Girl*) and made his final appearance at the Bristol Hippodrome on April 16, 1960. The following day, the car in which he was travelling to London Airport skidded and crashed into a lamp standard. Cochran was killed and passengers, Gene Vincent and Shari Sheeley (Cochran's fiancée), were badly injured. Ironically, his British chart hit at the time was 'Three Steps To Heaven'.

When Cochran died at 21, he was only beginning to realize ambitions which went far beyond the scope of most of his contemporaries, in terms of studio activity. He was not merely a singer and a talented guitarist and songwriter, he was also an arranger and an A&R man. Moreover, considering him only as a singer-songwriter, if some of his records seem a little too slick now, the wit of his running commentary on teenage life, seen from within, puts him only a couple of notches below Chuck Berry.

Nat 'King' Cole, a pioneer of the sophisticated West Coast nightclub style of singing and playing that was later picked up by Charles Brown, Floyd Dixon, Ivory Joe Hunter and a host of others, remains the only black performer in this style to attain lasting acceptance by a mass white audience.

Born Marc 17, 1917, in Montgomery, Alabama, he first attracted attention as an Earl Hines influenced pianist in his brother's band in Chicago. By 1939, he had formed his own trio with Oscar Moore on guitar and Wesley Prince on bass and was playing regularly in Hollywood night spots. *Downbeat* jazz magazine voted the Nat Cole Trio the Top Small Combo between 1944–7, while Moore topped the guitarists section between 1945–8. During the mid-Forties, Cole started to make a series of recordings for the then newly-formed Capitol label which ultimately brought him fame as a highly polished, commercial singer. In 1948, he scored his first Gold disc for 'Nature Boy', then a year later he received a second for 'Mona Lisa' and a third in 1951 for 'Too Young'. All three songs were successfully covered in later years by Bobby Darin, Conway Twitty and Donny Osmond, respectively.

By 1953, Cole was a huge name, knocking Billy Eckstine

from the Top Male Vocalist slot in the annual *Downbeat* poll. In 1957, he cut perhaps his best remembered hit, 'When I Fall In Love' and was given his own national TV series but abandoned the project that same year, complaining that the attitude of advertising agencies had resulted in his failure to find a regular sponsor (a year earlier Cole had been physically attacked by a gang of Southern racialists while performing on-stage to a predominantly white audience of 3,000 in Birmingham, Alabama).

In August 1962 Cole again broke into the national charts with 'Let There Be Love', followed two months later by the million-seller 'Ramblin' Rose' and the subsequent hit 'Those Lazy, Hazy Days Of Summer'. Although these later recordings were performed in a pedestrian singalong style, they proved Cole's staying power over two decades. He died on February 14, 1966.

Columbia Records (CBS) was formed in 1887 as the Columbia Phonograph Company to market wax cylinders and recording machines. In 1890, the company introduced the first pre-recorded cylinders and the record industry was born. Yet, while the company has always been at the fore in technical advances in recording and merchandising – including the introduction of the long-playing record in 1947 and the first major company subscription club in 1955, the Columbia Record Club, the Fifties saw Columbia, under the direction of Mitch Miller, who replaced Mannie Sachs as head of Columbia's A&R department in 1950, attempt to bury its head in the sand as far as rock'n'roll was concerned.

One reason for this was its undeniable success in the early Fifties, when Frankie Laine, Rosemary Clooney, Guy Mitchell, Doris Day, Johnnie Ray and Jo Stafford marched up the singles charts, almost in rotation, with few other artists even getting a look in, while Mitch Miller and his gang persuaded America to 'Sing Along With Mitch' on numerous very successful albums. Indeed, Columbia's only failure in these years was the loss of Frank Sinatra to Capitol in 1950. (Sinatra had objected to the regimentation of Columbia's

A&R department.) Thus Columbia wasn't worried by the arrival of rock'n'roll, because it wasn't 'good' music; and anyway, Columbia had the pop and country charts sewn up.

Where other companies were looking for R&B songs for their artists to cover, Miller, with writers pounding on his door all the time, could afford to give 'Singing The Blues' to Guy Mitchell for the pop market, and to Marty Robbins for the C&W market, and get both to No. 1 in 1956 – and then do the same thing again with 'Knee Deep In The Blues', only a little less successfully next year. Moreover, in contrast to the country singers of other labels, who by 1957 were becoming interested in rock'n'roll, Columbia's were kept on the straight and narrow by Miller whose notion of C&W was of a country (or folk) inflected pop song. None the less, Miller bid for Presley in 1955 when he announced he was leaving Sun for a bigger company, and a couple of Columbia's country singers, notably Ronnie Self and Sid King and the Five Strings, were allowed to cut some of the best rockabilly of the late Fifties.

Similarly, where most other labels' black artists were heavily R&B influenced, Columbia's Johnny Mathis – in the Fifties, certainly – was a remarkably successful singer of sweet, smooth ballads. The only part of Columbia's empire to come to terms with rock before the mid-Sixties was the autonomous subsidiary, Okeh, with the Treniers, Chuck Willis and Titus Turner among others. Johnnie Ray, whose 'Cry' sold a million in 1951, was originally issued on Okeh and sold remarkably well in the R&B market. Later, in 1956, Okeh produced arguably the most bizarre piece of rock'n'roll recorded in Screamin' Jay Hawkins' 'I Put A Spell On You'.

Perry Como, born in Canonsburg, Pennsylvania, on May 18, 1912, has proved the most durable of the second generation of crooners who came to prominence in the early Forties. His hits stretch from 'Till The End Of Time' (1945) up to the present day. He sang from 1934 to 1937 with Freddie Carlone's band in the Midwest, and then joined the Ted

Weems Orchestra. After the war, he signed to RCA Victor and gained widespread popularity through radio and television appearances. He weathered the storm of rock'n'roll by successfully covering songs, like 'Kokomo', and recording catchy singalong numbers such as 'Hot Diggity', 'Catch A Falling Star' and 'Delaware'. During the Sixties and Seventies he has returned to smooth, somnolent crooning and achieved bigger hits than ever with well-made ballads like 'It's Impossible' and 'For The Good Times.'

Bobby Comstock was born on Dec. 28, 1943 at Ithica, New York, the home town of his group, the Counts – Gus Eframson (guitar), Chuck Ciaschi (bass) and Dale Sherwood (drums). Snappy purveyors of blues-rock, they made the charts with 'Tennessee Waltz' (on Blaze in 1959), 'Jambalaya' (on Atlantic in 1960) and 'Let's Stomp' (Lawn in 1963). Comstock's greatest record was an edgy, cavernous revival of Bo Diddley's 'I'm A Man' (a Feldman-Goldstein-Gottehrer production). It was not a hit, but rock'n'roll revival shows kept him and the band busy right into the Seventies, when they were the backing band for acts appearing in the movie *Let The Good Times Roll.*

Cookie and His Cupcakes were a tremendously popular Louisiana group in the late Fifties and early Sixties as they toured constantly throughout the South, distilling their distinctive brand of swamp-pop. Led by Huey Thierry and Shelton Dunaway, they recorded prolifically for the tiny Khoury label of Lake Charles, and hit the Top 100 at No. 47 in 1959 with the archetypal Louisiana ballad, 'Mathilda', which was leased to Judd; they also brushed the charts in 1962 with 'Got You On My Mind' on Chess. Like so many similar acts, they never really survived the onslaught of the British groups on America in the mid-Sixties.

Cover Versions are, strictly speaking, either a version issued to compete with the original, or a carbon copy issued to capitalize on th eoriginal, often in another market. Rock'n'roll, largely music spawned in the urban black ghettos of the late Forties, finally reached middle America through the agency of Bill Haley and Elvis Presley. The former wrote much of his material but nevertheless achieved national fame with 'Shake, Rattle And Roll', a number recorded earlier in 1954 by Joe Turner on Atlantic, which Haley severely edited in order to remove the explicitly sexual references in the original. Presley cut hundreds of black R&B tunes, but in his own inimitable style and invariably after a gap of some years. Often accused of covering Arthur Crudup, it must be emphasized that Presley's epoch-making 'That's All Right' on Sun in 1954 came nearly seven years after the bluesman's original. One might just as well deny Ray Charles access to a country standard like 'Your Cheatin' Heart'.

The real offenders were those whites with no feeling for R&B, but a good ear for commercial possibilities. Those undercutting black performers included Pat Boone, the Crewcuts, the Diamonds, the Fontane Sisters, the Four Lads, Georgia Gibbs, the McGuire Sisters, Kay Starr, and Gale Storm. The righteous Pat Boone rushed out lucrative covers for Dot of Fats Domino's 'Ain't That A Shame' and Little Richard's 'Long Tall Sally' in 1955 and 1956. The Crewcuts (Mercury) battened on the Penguins' 'Earth Angel' (Dootone) in 1955 but fortunately the latter still went gold. In 1954, the Crewcuts had notched a million with 'Sh-Boom' which nevertheless still sold well for its originators, the Chords, on Cat. Georgia Gibbs built her career by recording, and subsequently diluting, R&B originals. Like Haley, she readily changed the lyrics of the songs she copied in order to avoid sexual references. 'Roll With Me Henry', a hit in the R&B market for Etta James under the title of 'Wallflower' on Modern, became 'Dance With Me Henry' when performed by a white woman for a white audience. Etta James' version sold 400,000 – Georgia Gibbs sold a million.

Not all cover versions cross racial boundaries, however. In cut-throat competition, Presley covered Carl Perkins' 'Blue Suede Shoes' and raced him up the charts. The same process happens with black singers – Little Richard recorded Eddie

Bocage's 'I'm Wise' as 'Slippin' And Slidin'' in 1956. Similarly, sometimes covers cross national boundaries. Indeed, in the Fifties and early Sixties, British rock'n'roll – with a few notable exceptions – consisted almost entirely of covers of American hits, white and black. The careers of Marty Wilde, Tommy Steele, Billy Fury and Craig Douglas and many others were liberally dosed with (usually inferior) versions of American hits – a practice that was greatly aided in the early Fifties by the fact that a significant amount of American R&B and rock'n'roll weren't issued in Britain. Even Mersey Beat and the British R&B movement depended heavily on unoriginal material, though with a radical change of emphasis: songs were revived by the British groups, rather than merely covered by them.

In the fiercely chaotic world of reggae, covers (often uncredited) are a frequent occurrence. Thus Jamaican reggae fans preferred their own Lorna Bennett with 'Breakfast In Bed' in 1973, rather than the black American, Baby Washington, whose number it was. Generally, however, it was the reggae song that was covered. In 1974, Eric Clapton scored internationally with 'I Shot The Sheriff'. Very few Anglo-American rock devotees realised – or cared – that the song was written and recorded earlier that year by reggae star, Bob Marley, of the Wailers.

While the 'progressive' music of the Sixties saw few cover versions, the charts in almost any week of the early Seventies looked strangely familiar to those of the Fifties, with a few bizarre changes thrown in for good measure. Thus, in 1975, soul star Betty Wright enjoyed success with 'Shoorah, Shoorah' in both America and Britain at the expense of Frankie Miller who had failed to register with it at the end of 1974. But, then, he cut it for Allen Toussaint in New Orleans long after Chris Kenner's original version.

A contrast of the British and American charts of 1974 showed a similar situation. In Britain, Paper Lace and Leo Sayer were racing up the charts with 'Billy Don't Be A Hero' and 'The Show Must Go On', while in America cover versions of their songs, by Bo Donaldson and the Heywoods and Three Dog Night (surely *the* cover version merchants of the Seventies – in 1975 they had a hit with 'Brickyard Blues', another song off the Frankie Miller album that produced 'Shoorah, Shoorah') were doing precisely the same thing. It was as though the wheel had come full circle.

Floyd Cramer, born in Shreveport, Louisiana, on Nov. 27, 1933, came to public attention playing piano as a sideman on the *Louisiana Hayride* radio show in the early Fifties. Chet Atkins brought him to Nashville in 1955 and he quickly became one of the top session players there and an RCA Victor stalwart, backing artists as diverse as Jim Reeves and Elvis Presley.

If Atkins masterminded the 'Nashville Sound', it was Cramer's 'slipnote' style of playing that characterised it. This technique he describes as a whole-tone slur, and he likens it to Maybelle Carter's distinctive guitar style. It's a right-hand device used at the treble end of the keyboard with the intended note hit precisely on the beat as the last of a triplet. Every other piano player in town quickly mastered the trick and, as the 'Nashville Sound' flagged into stereotype through the Sixties, it became a mechanical feature of almost every successful country record. Cramer continues to work in Nashville as a session player and as a recording artist in his own right with some 20, mostly mediocre, albums to his credit. But, his single, 'Last Date', which sold a million copies in 1960, is the definitive statement of the 'Nashville Sound' and it still sounds as fresh and imaginative as the day it was made.

Johnny Crawford came from a theatre family. Born in Los Angeles in 1946, he began a television career as a Disney Mouseketeer, moving to the ABC-TV series, *Rifleman* in 1960. Bob Keene of Del-Fi Records saw his potential as a ballad-cum-novelty singer, and Crawford had eight hits on the label between 1961 and 1964. Most were particularly cloying examples of the high school 'soda-pop' genre. Songs like 'Cindy's Birthday', 'Your Nose Is Gonna Grow' and

'Rumours' owed their success to Crawford's cutesy good looks and the black arranger, Fred Smith.

The Crests were a racially mixed but otherwise archetypal East Coast vocal group, led by Johnny Maestro (born John Mastrangelo in New York on May 7, 1939). His light and youthful voice took them into the charts ten times between 1957 and 1960. Early records for Joyce were followed by a No. 2 on Coed with 'Sixteen Candles', a slow ballad of great charm. Equally melodic hits included 'The Angels Listened In', 'Step By Step' and 'Trouble In Paradise'. Among the original members of the Crests were Harold Torres, Tommy Gough and Jay Carter, but later personnel changes were intricate, with Eddie Wright, Chuck Foote and Leonard Alexander singing on later records. Maestro's later solo career included one Top Twenty hit ('Model Girl' in 1961). He joined the Brooklyn Bridge as lead singer in 1968.

The Crewcuts were formed in Cleveland, Ohio, as the Canadaires and then changed their name to highlight the members' newly adopted hairstyle. Managed by Fred Strauss, the Crewcuts consisted of Johnny and Ray Perkins, Rudy Maugeri, and Pat Barrett, all born in Canada. Their hits included 'Kokomo', 'Sh-Boom' and 'Earth Angel' in 1955, all diluted copies of R&B originals. On their only visit to Britain, the *New Musical Express* described their music as 'rhythm and barber shop harmony'.

Bob Crewe, a greatly respected record producer of long standing, was born in Bellville, New Jersey in 1931. A male model, an interior decorator and a singer at various times in his career, he met Frank Slay Jnr., a Texan who needed a demo singer for his songs, in 1953; later that year Crewe made his first record (co-written by Slay) for BBS, a small Philadelphia label. Between 1954 and 1956, Crewe recorded unsuccessfully for Jubilee and Spotlight. Then in 1956, again with Slay, Crewe began independently producing records of their songs by Charlie and Ray (for Herald) and the Rays (for Chess), and in 1957 they activated their own label, XYZ. They were at the time among the few independent producers in America with Leiber and Stoller and Lee Hazlewood.

In 1957, their composition, 'Silhouettes' by the Rays – originally on XYZ but leased to Cameo – sold a million and Slay and Crewe quickly notched up other hits, including 'La Dee Dah' by Billy and Lillie and 'Tallahassie Lassie' by Freddy Cannon (both for Swan). After co-producing several more Cannon hits, including 'Way Down Yonder In New Orleans' in 1959, Slay and Crewe parted company. Slay became a producer for Swan while Crewe attempted unsuccessfully to break into films as an actor. He recorded his first hit for Warwick in 1961, 'The Wiffenpoof Song'.

Returning to production in 1962, he produced the Four Seasons, initially for Gone ('Bermuda') then for Vee Jay where they scored immediately with 'Sherry', a 1962 million-seller. Between 1962 and 1968, Crewe produced the group's unbroken run of hits, most of which he wrote with group-member Bob Gaudio.

During the mid-Sixties, Crewe formed New Voice records and had million-sellers with 'Walkin' My Cat Named Dog' by Norma Tanega and 'Jenny Take A Ride' by Mitch Ryder and the Detroit Wheels, as well as smaller hits by Eddie Rambeau and Ryder. He had a Top Twenty hit in 1966 with the instrumental 'Music To Watch Girls To'. In 1969, he formed the Crewe label and registered with pop singer Oliver. A quieter period followed in the early Seventies, but Crewe made a solid comeback in 1974 with his productions for Disco Tex and the Sex-O-lettes and Frankie Valli.

The Crickets, originally Buddy Holly's group, separated from him in 1958 but continued recording, mostly in Los Angeles. They remained with Coral until 1961, releasing several unsuccessful singles, and then switched to Liberty. Throughout numerous personnel changes, the backbone of the group remained drummer Jerry Allison and singer/guitarist Sonny Curtis.

In 1962, they toured Britain with Bobby Vee and cut an album with him containing several authentic sounding versions of rock'n'roll standards. Although neglected by American record buyers, the group had two British hits at this time – 'Please Don't Ever Change' (a Goffin-King song) and Curtis's 'My Little Girl'. The arrival of the Beatles left the Crickets, like so many others, stranded, and they officially disbanded in March 1965. Curtis and Allison concentrated on songwriting and session work in Los Angeles. They played on Eric Clapton's 1970 solo album, and it was possibly the interest caused by this that led to the revival of the Crickets soon after. The new band, which includes two Englishmen, Ric Grech (bass) and Albert Lee (guitar), has made three albums on Mercury (two in Britain). The production of the albums is by Bob Montgomery, Buddy Holly's partner in his first-ever recordings.

The Crows were one of the first groups to move outside the R&B market, and their record, 'Gee', is often credited with the inauguration of the rock'n'roll era. From Harlem, Sonny Norton (lead), Bill Davis (baritone and occasional lead), Harold Major and Mark Jackson (tenors) and Gerald Hamilton (bass) recorded for George Goldner's Rama label. Probably it was Goldner who instructed the group to sweeten their delivery in order to increase their exposure on white radio stations. The ploy certainly worked: in April 1954, the Bill Davis composition made the Top Twenty. Although the group's other records for Rama and Tico failed to please, 'Gee' – still one of America's favourite oldies – became the name of yet another of Goldner's labels. The flip of 'Gee', 'I Love You So' was subsequently successfully revived by the Chantels and made the Top Fifty in 1958. By then, however, the Crows had disbanded, and Hamilton and Morton have since died.

Arthur 'Big Boy' Crudup, born in Forest, Mississippi, in 1905, enjoyed wide success in the Forties, recording a series of blues that reached not only their primary market but a substantial number of those whites who were to become both the musicians and the audience of rockabilly. 'Rock Me Mama', 'That's All Right' and 'My Baby Left Me' (all on Victor, 1942–50) were taken up by singers from Elvis Presley on down – an acknowledgement less of Crudup's sparse instrumental sound than of his piercing vocal attack and his musically suggestive reworkings of traditional blues themes. Rediscovered in the late Sixties, he cut some more albums in a virtually unaltered style and appeared before many American and European audiences. He died in 1973.

Johnny Cymbal. One of the commonest tricks employed to capture the listener's immediate attention in the Fifties, was to bring the bass singer into far greater prominence than usual and make a feature of his 'bom, bom' vocal phrases. In 1963, Johnny Cymbal, from Cleveland, Ohio, wrote and performed his tribute to these little known heroes of rock'n' roll, 'Hey Mr. Bassman', which reached the Top Twenty on Kapp. The bass part, the core of the record, was taken by Ronald Bright – an ex-member of the Valentines and Cadillacs, now currently with the Coasters – who had previously put the bomp in Barry Mann's 'Who Put The Bomp' in 1961. After a couple of less successful follow-ups, 'Teenage Heaven' and 'Dum Dum De Dum', Cymbal left Kapp. In 1968, under the name Derek, he had a Top Ten hit with 'Cinnamon' and then a smaller hit with 'Back Door Man' the following year. Currently, he is working as a producer.

Dale and Grace were two young Louisiana kids – Dale Houston and Grace Broussard – who achieved the ultimate in high school dreams whe ntheir staryy-eyed version of Don & Dewey's R&B hit, 'I'm Leaving It All Up To You', shot up the charts all the way to No. 1 in the fall of 1963 (the song was a British hit again in 1974 for Marie and Donny Osmond). Recorded by Sam Montel for his Montel label out of Bâton Rouge, the duo (both born in 1944) had a lot of the soulful feel of Louisiana swamp-pop music and enjoyed a big follow-up hit with 'Stop And Think It Over', which got to No. 8. Dale Houston also recorded prolifically in his own right and had a Southern hit with 'I'm The One' in 1961.

Danny and the Juniors were formed as a street corner group in Philadelphia late in 1957 – Danny Rapp, lead singer (born 1941); Dave White, first tenor (1940), later replaced by Bill Carlucci; Frank Maffe, second tenor (1940) and Joe Terranova, baritone (1941). They were taken by singer friend, Johnny Madara, to his vocal coach, Artie Singer, who had just formed a small label, Singular. White, Madara and Singer co-wrote 'Do The Bop' for the group but on Dick Clark's recommendation, they changed the lyrics and title to 'At The Hop' before recording it. The record sold 7,000 copies locally on Singular before ABC-Paramount bought the master and turned it into an international million-seller. They followed that up with Dave White's similar sounding 'Rock'n'Roll Is Here To Stay', which got to No. 19 in 1958, before commencing upon a string of boring dance records on Swan and Guyden – 'Twistin' USA', 'Doin' The Continental Walk', etc. – each of which gained progressively lower chart places. They disbanded in 1963.

Bobby Darin, born Waldo Robert Cassotto on May 14, 1936 in Philadelphia, blew with the wind. You can listen to the records he made throughout his career and sense the directions the music was taking. Not that you will discover anything about Bobby Darin, because in a musical sense he had no independent existence – he was, instead, a series of identities, a collection of counterfeits, Melville's Confidence Man returning as the rock'n'roll trickster.

After an unsuccessful year at Decca, covering Donegan's 'Rock Island Line', and recording atrocities such as 'Blue-Eyed Mermaid', Darin moved to Atco in 1956. There he began his proper career as a young rocker, blasting out of the Atlantic stable with 'Splish Splash', 'Queen Of The Hop' and 'Plain Jane' – the songs shot up the US charts through sheer force and energy. Not that the records were bad – as a writer and performer Darin was always a superb craftsman and these early records, despite the now fashionable put-downs, stand the test of time more than adequately. Atlantic did not deal with fools. Darin, though, was never satisfied, and he turned his hand to writing an all-time rock classic using the perennial C/Am/F/G7 chord changes. Of all the hundreds of hit songs that have used this sequence, his adaptation of 'Dream Lover' must rank alongside 'All I Have To Do Is Dream' as one of the very best. It was his biggest smash hit, in 1960.

It was after 'Dream Lover' that Darin first switched roles, and he emerged overnight – with his record 'Mack the Knife' – as a finger clicking hipster, a Sinatra in embryo. This particular phase, however, lasted not much more than a year for in the meantime he had discovered Ray Charles and responded to his love for his music by writing a song better suited to Charles than anything he was recording at that time. 'You're The Reason I'm Living' was a smash hit for Darin in 1962, on Capitol, the label he had moved to as a replacement for Sinatra.

He had rung the changes many times – even starting what looked like becoming a respectable film acting career – but the British Beat Invasion in the mid-Sixties left him stranded. Darin was only able to pick up the pieces of his career in the late Sixties after the new breed of singer-songwriters had emerged in the wake of Dylan. However, Darin himself could not write that sort of material and his only real success – which coincided with his return to Atlantic in 1966 – was a version of Tim Hardin's 'If I Were A Carpenter'. Another reason for the ups and downs of his career was his ill-health. On Dec. 20, 1973 he died of a heart attack.

James Darren, born James Ercolani on Oct. 3, 1936, in Philadelphia, took drama lessons after graduating and won a contract with Columbia Pictures. One of the Philadelphia school of good-looking Italian boys (Fabian, Avalon etc.) his first record on Colpix was the title song from the movie *Gidget*. 'Goodbye Cruel World' was his first hit, reaching No. 3 in America and No. 15 in Britain, where it was released on Pye. Its success was due mainly to a gimmicky fairground organ sound, though the following year (1962), Darren growled his way through two more Top Twenty records, 'Her Royal Majesty' and 'Conscience'. In 1967, he re-surfaced on Warner Bros with the minor hit, 'All'.

Maxwell Davis was an important figure in black music for nearly 20 years, as saxophone player, A&R man and arranger. Born in Independence, Kansas, on Jan. 14, 1916, he moved to Los Angeles in 1937 and played tenor with the bands of Fletcher Henderson and Happy Johnson. From 1948 to 1954 he was effectively A&R chief for Aladdin, and later for Federal and Modern. Davis wrote for, directed and played on innumerable R&B sessions, including many by Percy Mayfield, Amos Milburn, B. B. King and Etta James. His extremely adaptable sax playing was also heard on jazz and rock'n'roll records for Capitol, notably those of Ray Anthony and Ella Mae Morse. He was perhaps the most influential behind-the-scenes presence of West Coast R&B. Davis died in 1967. His last hit was Lowell Fulsom's 'Tramp', which he arranged.

Skeeter Davis, born in Dry Ridge, Kentucky on Dec. 30, 1931, as Mary Frances Penick, formed the Davis Sisters with schoolmate Betty Jack Davis in 1953. Later that year, after a No. 1 country record – a version of 'I Forget More Than You'll Ever Know' – Betty Jack died on the road returning from a show. She stopped performing until Chet Atkins persuaded her back five years later. In 1959, she hit with 'Set Him Free' and then she made her best couple of singles – both answer songs – 'Last Date', a vocal version of Floyd Cramer's hit and 'I'm Falling Too', a response to Hank Locklin's 'Please Help Me I'm Falling'. Skeeter Davis has never enjoyed an easy relationship with the Nashville establishment. Her Gold record, 'The End Of The World' – a 1963 No. 2 in the pop charts – was dismissed as a rock tune and in 1974 she was barred from the stage of the *Grand Ole Opry* after using it for an attack on the Nashville police department for their harassment of the religious sect with which she is associated.

Bobby Day was born Robert Byrd in Fort Worth, Texas in 1934. As a child, he moved to Los Angeles, where he appeared in Johnny Otis's Barrelhouse Club. In 1957, he wrote and recorded 'Little Bitty Pretty One', but a cover version by Thurston Harris outsold his own. Among eleven other singles for the Class label, 'Rockin' Robin' was the most successful, reaching No. 2 in 1958. Lesser hits included 'Over And Over', 'Bluebird, Buzzard and Oriole' and 'Gotta New Girl'.

Day's distinctive baritone also appeared on discs for Rendezvous, RCA and Sureshot, and as lead vocal for the Day Birds (on Jama). He also sang with the Hollywood Flames, whose novelty rock'n'roll records (notably 'Buzz Buzz Buzz' which made the Top Twenty in 1957) were more successful than their many beautiful ballads. Bobby Day's songs have been revived by various artists in the Sixties and Seventies, the most successful being the Dave Clark Five and the Jackson Five.

Jimmy Dean came to international fame in 1961 through his semi-recitation, 'Big Bad John', which established him as a pop-country entertainer. In America, he had already starred in a syndicated CBS TV show, and he gained another series with ABC in the mid-Sixties. Born in Plainview, Texas, on August 10, 1928, Dean began in country music on radio WLS Washington in 1951 with his Texas Wildcats and became known in 1953 for the hit 'Bumming Around'. C&W hits for Columbia and RCA have been maintained ever since and he has successfully straddled the pop–country fence with his television appearances.

Death Discs only carried an old tradition into a new medium. Death, in the form of the murder ballads that were hawked through the streets of London in the eighteenth century, has some claim to be seen as the cornerstone upon which Tin Pan Alley was built.

By the early twentieth century, when Tin Pan Alley had established itself as the source of popular songs, death was no longer considered a fit subject. Thus in the Twenties, Thirties and Forties, death only appeared in the 'folk musics of the day', notably the blues and country music – the first million-selling country record was Vernon Dalhart's 'Wreck Of The Old '97' in 1924. In the blues, death was treated as a fact of life and hence generally appeared in either a comical guise, 'Stack O'Lee', or at the most it was treated bitterly, 'Frankie And Johnnie'; but never tragically as it was in country music (and popular music when it made its rare appearances) – 'Wreck On The Highway', 'Put My Little Shoes Away', 'The Death of Little Kathy Fiscus', etc.

Hence it was not surprising that what was probably the first death record of the rock'n'roll era, the Kingston Trio's 'Tom Dooley' in 1958, was a dilution of an old folk song. Not surprisingly, it (and the discs that followed) was attacked by assorted clergymen and parent-teacher groups as being corrupt and depraved. Later that year, there was David McEnery's 'New Star Tonight' (dealing with the death of Presley's mother) and in 1959 came Ruby Wright's 'Three Stars' (later recorded by Eddie Cochran) about the deaths of Holly, Valens and the Big Bopper. While the latter is fondly remembered to this day, songs of this kind – which include Mike Berry's 'Tribute To Buddy Holly' (Britain, 1961), tributes to Johnny Ace (e.g. the Ravens' 'Salute To Johnny Ace' and the Five Wings' 'Johnny's Still Singing', both in 1955) and later records such as the Righteous Brothers' 'Rock And Roll Heaven' in 1974 – belong more to the commemorative tradition than the rock'n'roll death song proper.

The classic death songs of the Fifties and early Sixties were simply translations of the minor traumas of teenage life through the application of excessive doses of romanticism into *the* trauma – 'Endless Sleep' (Jody Reynolds, 1958); 'Teen Angel' (Mark Dinning, 1959); 'Tell Laura I Love Her' (Ray Peterson, 1959) which brought the reply 'Tell Tommy I Miss Him' from Marilyn Michaels – 'Running Bear' (Johnny Preston, 1960); 'Ebony Eyes' (the Everly Brothers,

1961); 'Leah' (Roy Orbison, 1962), 'Give Us Your Blessing' (Ray Peterson, 1963); 'Leader Of The Pack' (the Shangri-Las, 1964); 'Dead Man's Curve' (Jan and Dean, 1964) and 'Last Kiss' (Frank J. Wilson and the Cavaliers, 1964). The period saw other death discs – 'The Three Bells' (the Browns, 1959), Marty Robbins' gunfighter ballads ('El Paso' and 'Big Iron' in 1959 and 1960, respectively), Jimmy Dean's 'Big Bad John' (1961) and 'Steel Man' (1961) and even Abner Jay's 'The Thresher,' about the missing submarine, in 1963 – but their origins lay outside the world of rock'n'roll.

The emergence of the Beatles saw a decline in the genre. A few death records were made, such as 'I Can Never Go Home Anymore' by the Shangri-Las in 1966, Jimmy Cross' 'I Want My Baby Back' in 1965 and the Goodee's 'Condition Red' in 1968, but in the changed world of rock that followed the arrival of the Beatles, Stones and Dylan, death was no longer the comfortable subject it had been earlier. The death of Hendrix and the threatening prescience of the real world in rock closed the door to the innocent world in which Ebony Eyes and Laura lived – and died.

American Decca (MCA). Decca was a British company whose American subsidiary was launched in New York in 1934 by Jack Kapp. It quickly built up a mainstream popular reputation with artists such as Bing Crosby and, later, Sammy Davis Jnr. Much attention was paid to jazz and, later, R&B – the Inkspots, the Mills Brothers, Ella Fitzgerald and Louis Jordan all being highly successful.

The first major to set up an office in Nashville, Decca picked up several of the best C&W artists, including Webb Pierce, Ernest Tubb and Red Foley. This enterprising attitude led to the surprising acquisition of Bill Haley and his Comets from the Philadelphia label, Essex, in 1954. The wisdom of this move was soon demonstrated when Haley became the sensation of the nation with the release of 'Rock Around The Clock', produced by Milt Gabler who had previously supervised Louis Jordan's recordings. The following year, country-boogie pianist Roy Hall was signed and several fine rock'n'roll singles resulted. Decca also recorded rock'n' roll with Johnny Carroll, Webb Pierce, Jackie Lee Cochran, Eddie Fontaine, whose 'Cool It Baby' was a regional hit and, of course, Brenda Lee. The others were not commercially successful, and Decca transferred the rest of its rock activities to its subsidiary label, Coral. With Bob Thiele in charge of A&R, it had been formed in 1949 (originally as Decca's R&B label) and was re-activated late in 1956.

Both labels featured products from Norman Petty's studios in Clovis – Coral with Buddy Holly and Peanuts Wilson, and Brunswick with the Crickets. Memphis rockabilly was represented by the Johnny Burnette Trio and Billy Riley, but the most successful artist, with Haley and Holly, was Jackie Wilson whose R&B rockers, like the Dick Jacobs-arranged 'Reet Petite', were followed by a string of more soulful R&B hits.

In the Sixties, the American Decca organization was merged into the new MCA set up, but by then its concentration on rock had more or less ceased.

Decca (Britain). The Decca Record Company was started in 1929 and rapidly moved to the forefront of the British record industry, sharing the traditional honours as leading company in the British market with EMI. An American subsidiary was formed in 1934, which has since become part of the Music Corporation of America. Under the chairmanship of Edward Lewis, Decca made some remarkable advances in electronics, particularly in the radar field, but also introduced high fidelity recording techniques in 1944 (*ffrr* – full frequency range recording) and the LP record into Britain in 1950. At the end of the Forties, the newly formed American Capitol entered into a licensing arrangement with British Decca, which lasted until 1954. Decca's most important deals, however, were with RCA and Atlantic – both made in 1957. RCA titles came out under their own name and included Presley's records from 'Teddy Bear' onwards in the summer of 1957. The Atlantic titles came out under the Decca London, and then London American, label.

The London label covered releases from many American companies, including titles by Fats Domino, Duane Eddy, Chuck Berry, Roy Orbison, Bobby Vee, the Crystals, the Ronettes, the Ventures, Slim Whitman, Larry Williams, Del Shannon, Rick Nelson, Little Richard, Jerry Lee Lewis, the Everly Brothers and Pat Boone. Not surprisingly, with such a roster, the London-American label was considered *the* label by both R&B and rock'n'roll British collectors until well into the Sixties when the American record companies it represented began to set up their own British organizations.

Earlier, in 1956, Decca had picked up Tommy Steele and seemed set to tie up the British rock'n'roll market since they already had Haley and Buddy Holly and the Crickets. However, with the exception of Billy Fury, their later British signings were not very successful, though the strength of the American artists they released continued to give them a large share of the market. Possibly because their success was founded on America, the company felt secure enough for A&R man Mike Smith to reject the Beatles in 1962. A year later, aware by now of the way the tide was flowing, they did something to correct that mistake by signing the Rolling Stones.

Joey Dee and the Starlighters gyrated to the top of the American charts and into the British Top Twenty in 1961 with 'Peppermint Twist' on Roulette (EMI's Columbia label in Britain). Written by Dee and producer Henry Glover, the song was an undistinguished paean of praise to the Peppermint Lounge, a small New York night-club which had attracted the city's socialites.

Dee was born in Passaic, New Jersey on June 11, 1940. With the Starlighters – Carlton Latimor (organ), Willie Davis (drums), Larry Vernieri and David Brigati (singers/dancers) – he appeared in a couple of Twist-flicks and managed to stay on the charts until 1963 with other dance records for Roulette. His weak, rather anonymous voice could hardly do justice to such frenetic neo-gospel tunes as 'Hey Let's Twist' (Top Twenty), 'Shout' (No. 6) and 'Hot Pastrami With

Mashed Potatoes' (No. 36), but he excelled on the attractive Johnny Nash ballad 'What Kind Of Love Is This' (Top Twenty), and his two black musicians were a joy to watch on stage. The Starlighters proved to be a breeding-ground of talent. Three members of the Young Rascals (Felix Cavaliere, Gene Cornish and Brigati's brother Eddie) were in the 1963 line-up, and Jimi Hendrix is said to have played briefly with the group in 1966.

The Del-Vikings were an integrated vocal group from a Pittsburgh USAF base. The original line-up of Clarence Quick, Corinthian Jackson, Dave Lerchey, Norman Wright and Gus Backus first recorded for Luniverse in 1956. The following year, with new member Kripps Johnson, they had two memorable Top Ten hits with 'Come Go With Me' and 'Whispering Bells', which were leased to Dot by the small Fee-Bee label.

Members of the Dell-Vikings tended to form splinter groups whose personnel changed rapidly, but the Dell-Vikings changed the spelling and moved on to Mercury (where 'Cool Shake' made the Top Fifty), ABC-Paramount, United Artists, Alpine and Gateway. Backus became a cabaret artist in Germany while Chuck Jackson, another important member, became a successful soul balladeer in the Sixties.

The Diamonds were prominent at a time when adult castigation of rock'n'roll was rife, and among the prime perpetrators of diluted, 'acceptable' cover-versions of R&B hits. Canadians Dave Somerville and Mike Douglas and Californians John Felton and Evan Fisher in the five years from 1956 to 1961 achieved some 16 hits, ten of which were 'covers' of R&B discs which, as exemplified by the biggest hit, the Gladiolas' 'Little Darlin' ', employed semi-parodic arrangements of the originals. Significantly, the demise of 'doo-wop' style black groups at the turn of the Sixties also saw the end of the Diamonds' run of success.

Dick and Deedee were one of many cleancut teenage couples to enjoy brief chart success in America. Dick (St John), born in 1944, had originally recorded for Liberty, but with no success. He then called on school friend Deedee Sperling (born 1945) – they both came from Santa Monica, California – to record his song called 'The Mountain's High' which climbed to No. 2 in the Hot Hundred. A remarkable record, its tremulous harmonies sounded as if they had been recorded in a garage. The duo alternated between touring and studying at school during the record's success in 1961. Their follow-up releases ('Tell Me', 'Young And In Love') never sold as well, though they enjoyed a brief comeback in 1964 with 'Thou Shalt Not Steal'.

Dion and the Belmonts. Dion was born Dion Di Mucci on July 18, 1939, in the Bronx, New York, and started singing at the age of five (his father was a singer and his mother an actress). He made his first professional appearance on Paul Whiteman's *Teen Club* TV show in Philadelphia in 1954. By 1957 he had formed his own street-corner group, Dion and the Timberlanes and recorded one unsuccessful single, 'The Chosen Few' for the Mohawk label in New York. In 1958, he formed a new group featuring Fred Milano (second tenor), Angelo D'Aleo (first tenor) and Carlo Mastrangelo (baritone) and named them the Belmonts after the main Bronx thoroughfare where they lived.

They signed with the newly-formed Laurie label and made one unsuccessful single before recording 'I Wonder Why', an inane but engaging vocal workout which reached No. 22 in America. The group followed up with two more American hits, 'No-one Knows' and 'Don't Pity Me' before securing a worldwide hit with the now classic 'Teenager In Love'. That same year, D'Aleo was conscripted and the group continued as a trio, notching up more hits with 'Where Or When' (No. 3 in America), and 'When You Wish Upon A Star'. They were, by this time, the most popular young white vocal group in America.

Late in 1960, Dion was persuaded by his management to

break with the Belmonts and pursue a solo career. The Belmonts joined another label, Sabina, and achieved moderate American success in 1961–3 with 'Tell Me Why' (No. 18) and 'Come On Little Angel' (No. 25) but it was Dion who went on to major stardom. Initially he scored with 'Lonely Teenager' in November 1960, a fairly typical 'rockaballad' which reached the Top Twenty in America. But his next two releases flopped and it seemed as if his solo career had lost its impetus. Then he stormed back late in 1961 with a newly-adopted style which, in effect, could be described as early punk-rock. 'Runaround Sue' reached No. 1 as did the sequel, 'The Wanderer' and from then on Dion appeared to be commercially infallible. His next four records – 'Lovers Who Wander', 'Sandy', 'Little Diane' and 'Love Came To Me' – all reached the American Top Ten.

Late in 1962, Dion moved to CBS but did not let the label's then middle-of-the-road orientation affect his music. Rather than adapt a cabaret image like so many of his contemporaries, he grew funkier. Four more hits followed – 'Ruby Baby' (No. 2), 'Donna The Prima Donna', 'Drip Drop' and 'This Little Girl' – before his sudden fall from popularity early in 1964. This has been attributed to American Beatlemania, which obviously had some bearing. But, in fact, he suffered from a serious narcotics problem (despite his ostensibly boy-next-door image) and spent most of 1964–5 in seclusion. During this time he released a series of R&B numbers – 'Johnny B. Goode', 'Chicago Blues', 'Hoochie Koochie Man' and 'Spoonful' – long before they became fashionable in American pop circles. They met with little success despite their excellence.

In 1967, Dion re-emerged to re-unite with the Belmonts and released two excellent singles ('Mr Movin' Man' and 'Berimbau') and an album on ABC, but met with little success; in 1969, however, he achieved a meteoric comeback (ironically on his old label, Laurie) with 'Abraham, Martin and John' which reached No. 2 in America and heralded the new 'folkie' and introspective Dion. This new Dion was not that new in fact. As early as 1963, he had recorded simple folk songs on the B-sides of his CBS hits and, it is said, wished to pursue a career similar to fellow CBS act, Bob Dylan, but was dissuaded by his management. He signed with Warner Brothers in 1970, and since then has recorded a series of albums as a singer-songwriter and is currently recording under Phil Spector, who considers him one of rock's greatest talents.

The Dixie Hummingbirds, founded by James L. Davis in Greenville, South Carolina in 1928, gained national prominence recording for Apollo and Gotham in the Forties. Their gospel harmonies were built round the rollicking deep bass of William Bobo and versatile lead of Ira Tucker. Their innovative, frenzied showmanship established the stage precedent for the James Browns of soul. With the addition of alternate lead, James Walker and brilliant bluesy guitarist, Howard Carroll, in the Fifties, they have maintained a twenty-year string of hits for Peacock, including 'In The Morning' and 'Bedside Of A Neighbor'.

Floyd Dixon. A West Coast R&B singer and pianist who recorded extensively in the late Forties and early Fifties, Dixon was a protégé of the influential Charles Brown. He first recorded in 1947 for the Supreme label of Los Angeles, switching to the Biharis' Modern label in 1949 where he scored with 'Dallas Blues'. His lazy, dragged-out vocals and tinkling piano followed the tradition set by Nat 'King' Cole and Charles Brown. Around 1950, Dixon signed to Aladdin, teaming up with Johnny Moore's Three Blazers which initially featured Brown on lead vocals. Sixteen sides were cut before Dixon went solo, this time working with arranger Maxwell Davis. After hitting the charts with 'Tired, Broke And Busted' and 'Call Operator 210', his popularity began to slacken off. In 1953, he signed to Specialty, then in 1958 to Chess and several smaller labels – but without too much success. Dixon just couldn't adjust to the influx of rock'n'roll and the changing public taste in R&B. He is today in retirement, still on America's West Coast.

Willie Dixon, born in Vicksburg, Mississippi on April 1, 1915, made a contribution to postwar urban blues which stands as a major and energising force that subsequently laid the basic foundations for the popular music of today. In his combined roles as composer-producer-studio bassist-A&R man for Chess records in the Fifties and Sixties, he was responsible for hit recordings by Muddy Waters, Chuck Berry, Bo Diddley, Howlin' Wolf, Little Walter, Sonny Boy Williamson, Buddy Guy, Otis Rush and others. His compositions include 'Hoochie Coochie Man', 'My Babe', 'Spoonful', 'You Shook Me', 'Whole Lotta Love', 'I Just Want To Make Love To You', 'Little Red Rooster' and 'Seventh Son'. Dixon's songs have been recorded by such contemporary rock artists as the Rolling Stones, Led Zeppelin, Ten Years After, Jeff Beck, Savoy Brown, the Animals and the Spencer Davis Group.

Dr Feelgood was the pseudonym adopted in 1962 by Atlanta bluesman, Willie Perryman, who had recorded prolifically as Piano Red for RCA/Groove between 1950 and 1958. In that period his best-selling R&B records – 'Rockin' With Red', 'Red's Boogie', 'Wrong Yo Yo' and others – were characterised by gruff, good-humoured singing and a rumbustious piano style. 'Yo Yo' had previously been recorded in 1930 by his brother Rufus Perryman (alias Speckled Red). Piano Red also recorded for Jax, Checker and Arhoolie. Emerging as Dr Feelgood and the Interns, Willie Perryman made the pop charts with two exuberant rockers, 'Dr Feelgood' and another version of 'Right String But The Wrong Yo Yo', on Okeh. The flip of the first, 'Mr Moonlight', sung by Roy Lee Johnson, was later recorded by the Beatles.

Bill Doggett, born in Philadelphia, became a pianist in Jimmy Gorham's Band in 1935, and the band's leader in 1938. He soon relinquished the position to Lucky Millinder, though remaining with the band until 1949 when he succeeded Bill Davis in Louis Jordan's Tympani 5. In 1952 he began fronting his own combo, recording prolifically for

King over some nine years, the peak of which came in 1956 with 'Honky Tonk', a jogging instrumental featuring Clifford Scott's sax and Billy Butler's deft guitar. A succession of smaller hits followed before Doggett moved to Warner in 1961. He has subsequently recorded for Columbia, Sue, ABC and Roulette.

Fats Domino, born Antoine Domino in New Orleans, on Feb. 26, 1928, has been playing piano publicly since he was ten. His first engagement was at the Hideaway Club where bassist Billy Diamond's band dubbed him 'Fats'. Lew Chudd, president of Hollywood Imperial, seeking New Orleans talent, signed him up in 1948.

Domino worked a rich cultural heritage. For over two hundred years New Orleans has proved a unique meeting point for Spanish, French, West African, Creole, Protestant American, and Caribbean influences. 'Hey La Bas', from Domino's first session, unconsciously assimilates African and Catholic elements. The majority of slaves brought into New Orleans came from Dahomey and were practitioners of 'vodun' or 'voodoo'. Legba, the omniscient god of cross-roads, luck and fertility, became identified with St Peter, the keeper of the keys. African ritual was preserved because Catholic Orleans preferred to defuse by absorption rather than engage in a theological war of attrition. Papa Legba underwent a transition to Limba, Laba, and finally to 'Hey La Bas'.

Another example is the instrumental 'Second Line Jump', made in 1952. Repetitious to a fault, it nevertheless storms along defying anyone to stay seated. But title and repetitions imply more. Jazz may have been nurtured in the clubs and brothels of Storyville, but it was not born there. It began in a thousand places. Just one of them was the 'second line' in a funeral parade back from the cemetery, characterized by lively 2/4 music and ecstatic dancing.

A final example of the fusions in New Orleans music is the custom of 'lining out'. The call-and-response pattern, obvious in gospel and soul, and imitated instrumentally in blues and jazz, represents a wedding of African chant and British psalmody where lines from the preacher were repeated by an illiterate congregation.

Nor did Domino spring from some personal artistic limbo. Piano-playing contemporaries working New Orleans included Salvador Doucette, Amos Milburn, Little Richard, Roy Byrd (Professor Longhair), Leon T. Gross (Archibald), Joseph Pleasant (Smilin' Joe), S. Q. Reeder (Esquerita) and Eddie Bocage (Eddie Bo). The prime influence, though, was an outsider, boogie pianist Albert Ammons who died the year of Fats' recording debut. Ammons' trilling right hand, played off against the rolling anchor of the left, fits Fats perfectly.

Fats Domino sold a million with his first release, 'The Fat Man', the second number he cut on Dec. 10, 1949. An ebullient eight bar blues, it has a relatively long piano introduction before he broke into that familiar 'wah wah' vocal approximation of a harp. On the flip was the first song from that first session, 'Detroit City Blues', a powerful side opening with the inimitable Domino right hand, then the horns and Domino shouting the blues in sudden excitement. With Frank Fields' remorseless bass and the endless sax riffs, the die was cast.

Domino worked closely with trumpeter and bandleader, Dave Bartholomew, writing and arranging with great success for the first six years. Bartholomew found Domino's approach difficult – allegedly the Fat Man couldn't or wouldn't keep time – but the hits kept coming. There was always something to hold attention. 'Little Bee' (Imperial 5065) is a most attractive performance with a stinging, buzzing little guitar figure from Ernest McLean, substantial piano, and memorable lyrics –

'She's 42 in the hip, 31 in the bust
She's got big fine legs
And she knows how to strut her stuff!'

Fats proved deceptively varied. 'Hideaway Blues' (Imperial 5077), yet another from the debut session, employs a similar opening gambit to 'Detroit City Blues' and there is the repetition of sound and structure usual in his work. That it does not become monotonous is a tribute to the charm of this music, and there are often moments of leavening humour – the sly reference to 'catch a body coming through the rye', for example. Recorded in December 1951 but not released until March the following year was Fats' second Gold disc, the bland 'Goin' Home' (Imperial 5180) and there were several releases before Fats came up with a *bona fide* classic in 'Mardi Gras In New Orleans'. Cut in October, 1952, it is virtually a cover of the Professor Longhair song replete with what Jelly Roll Morton would have termed the 'Latin tinge'. It's a great number, atypical for Fats, employing rhumbalero rhythms and faultlessly executed. Coupled with 'Going To The River', it sold a million in 1953. This latter song exhibits a new assertiveness with just a suggestion of ossification, twelve bar slickness, that points to the greater simplifications of the rock'n'roll era.

From 1955 to 1960 Fats was at his commercial peak, although some would argue a decline in artistry. Despite riotous acclaim coast-to-coast, there were decided lapses in the quality of recorded output – for example, the appalling 'I'm In The Mood For Love' which only sold because it was slapped on the reverse of 'I'm Walkin' ', a considerable rocker. That was in February, 1957. But the first real smash came with 'Ain't That A Shame' in April, 1955. Cornelius Coleman drums up a storm, while Walter Nelson's guitar chops along underneath. From then on the hits came thick and fast – the melancholy 'Blueberry Hill', recorded in Los Angeles and released in September 1956; 'Blue Monday' cut in New Orleans a year earlier but held over; 'Whole Lotta Lovin' ' in 1958; 'I'm Ready' in 1959; and a slow slide into straight pop culminating in the string-laden 'Walking To New Orleans' in 1960. This was the last Gold disc from the man who ranks third in global sales after Presley and The Beatles.

Much of his success rested on a relaxed command of a characteristic New Orleans sound, slightly lugubrious, rolling with effortless charm. It also depended on the long service and high calibre of sessionmen like Jimmie Davis, Frank Fields (bass), Ernest McLean, Roy Montrell, Walter Nelson, Harrison Verrett (guitar), Wendell Duconge (alto), Buddy Hagans, Herb Hardesty (tenor), Cornelius Coleman and Earl Palmer (drums). And, on some rock'n'roll sides such as 'The Big Beat' in 1957, Fats was replaced at piano by Allen Toussaint, James Booker, or Edward Frank. Fats also played on Imperial sessions for Smiley Lewis, Lloyd Price, and Joe Turner. His songs have been recorded by the Band, Chuck Berry, Pat Boone, Johnny Burnette, Bobby Charles, Ronnie Hawkins, Buddy Holly, Jerry Lee Lewis, Rick Nelson, Elvis Presley, Little Richard, Warren Storm, and Larry Williams. His influence in the growth of Jamaican ska and reggae is undeniable.

He went to ABC in Nashville in 1963 and, although he never recovered his former glory, much of the material was agreeable, especially 'There Goes My Heart Again' and 'Sally Was A Good Old Girl'. His last, modest success came with a version of the Beatles' 'Lady Madonna' released in 1968 on Reprise. He has also recorded for Broadmoor and Atlantic. In the right setting, he could surprise us yet.

The Dominoes were recruited by New York composer, pianist and singing coach, Billy Ward from among his best students in 1950. They were Clyde McPhatter, James Van Loan (tenors), Joe Lamount (baritone) and Bill Brown (bass). Brown sang lead on 'Sixty Minute Man', the bestselling R&B disc of 1951, while McPhatter wailed 'Have Mercy Baby', an R&B No. 1 the following year. Producer Ralph Bass rang the changes from jump blues to highly emotive churchy ballads, all on Federal. With a succession of lead singers, including Jackie Wilson and Gene Mumford, the Dominoes also recorded for King, Jubilee, Decca, Liberty ('Stardust' and 'Deep Purple' were two of the group's symphonic black pop hits in 1957) and Melbourne.

Don and Dewey, both born in Los Angeles in 1938, never enjoyed chart success themselves, but their songs were big sellers when revived by the Olympics ('Big Boy Pete'), the Premiers ('Farmer John'), Dale and Grace and Donny and Marie Osmond ('I'm Leaving It Up To You'). Don 'Sugarcane' Harris and Dewey Terry had formed a duo in 1955 after singing with the Squires. Records for Spot and Shade led to a contract with Specialty, where records like 'Jungle Hop', 'Koko Joe' and 'Justine' adhered to the fast and frantic rock'n'roll formula common to many of Art Rupe's post-Little Richard signings. After further discs for Rush and Highland, each concentrated on his own career. Terry recorded for Tumbleweed, while Harris played blues violin with Johnny Otis, Frank Zappa and John Myall.

Don and Juan had a No. 7 hit with 'What's Your Name' on Big Top in 1961. The tight harmonies of Roland 'Don' Trone and Claude 'Juan' Johnson led to rumours that Johnson had double-tracked and found a performing partner only when the disc began to sell. After a smaller hit with 'Magic Wand', the duo recorded unsuccessfully for Mala and Twirl between 1963 and 1966. Johnson, who had previously sung with a New York group, the Genies ('Who's That Knockin'' was a hit on Shad) came out of retirement with a new 'Don' for the revival shows of the early Seventies.

Lonnie Donegan, born Tony Donegan on April 29, 1931, was Britain's first superstar during the Fifties. As a youth, he was immersed in folk music and at 17 he bought his first guitar and made his first appearance with a jazz band before being called up for National Service in 1949. He played drums with the Wolverines Jazz Band in the Army and, on discharge, played banjo with Ken Colyer's band where he was first exposed to the 'skiffle' style. In 1951, Donegan formed his own group and after appearing on the same bill as his idol, Lonnie Johnson, at the Royal Festival Hall, he changed his name to 'Lonnie'. By 1953, he had joined Chris Barber's band on banjo and in 1954 he recorded 'Rock Island Line' in a skiffle style as part of Barber's *New Orleans Joys* album.

Released as a single in 1956, 'Rock Island Line' unexpectedly reached the charts and caused a sensation with its then wild and undisciplined sound. It went on to become one of the first British records to reach the American Top Twenty. Within months, the sales of guitars shot up as hundreds of skiffle groups were formed throughout the country. Leaving Barber's band to go solo in 1956, Donegan scored again with 'Lost John' (No. 2 in Britain) and from then on registered an incredible 24 consecutive hits (a figure topped only by Cliff Richard) including 'Cumberland Gap', 'Dixie Darling', 'Putting On The Style', 'Battle Of New Orleans', 'My Old Man's A Dustman' and 'Pick A Bale Of Cotton'.

Branching out into comedy and variety early in his career, Donegan developed an act which stood him in good stead for the rest of his career, though it did detract from what 'authenticity' he had. His run of hits terminated abruptly in 1963 with Beatlemania, but he still performs in cabaret. He is the man who struck the first immortal chords for Britain's rock empire in the Fifties.

Ral Donner. Born in Chicago on Feb. 10, 1943, Ralph Stuart Donner first recorded in 1958 for Scottie. Moving to New York, he signed with Gone and reached the Top Twenty with 'The Girl Of My Best Friend' (a song from Presley's *Elvis Is Back* album) in 1961. As Presley became more of a Neapolitan balladeer than a rock'n'roller, Donner continued to sing in the manner to which early Elvis fans had been accustomed. His heavily stylized, hot-potato-in-the-mouth vocals smouldered through a string of blistering soul ballads. They included 'You Don't Know What You've Got' (No. 4), 'Please Don't Go', 'She's Everything' (another Top Twenty hit) and 'What A Sad Way To Love Someone'. Donner recorded also for Tau (1960), Reprise (the fine 'I Got Burned' in 1963), Fontana (1965), Red Bird (1966), Rising Sons (where he was produced by Billy 'I Can Help' Swan in 1968), Mid Eagle, M. J. (1971) and Chicago Fire, Sunlight (1972).

Doo-Wop was the term applied to the singing style of American R&B vocal groups of the Fifties, originating from the fact that the harmony support to lead vocals was often derived from simple phrases like 'doo wop'. Such groups, generally four or five strong, usually consisted of a tenor or baritone lead singer supported by a second tenor, baritone and bass voices and were thus, basically, musically self-supporting. In fact, many recorded initially with minimal instrumental accompaniment, partly to avoid detracting from intricate vocal harmonies and partly for economics.

The style is also known as 'street-corner music', since some groups actually rehearsed on the street corners of their neighbourhood, singing 'acappella' (without instruments; literally 'as in chapel'), though often preferring the acoustic qualities of subways or hallways. Doo-wop music had its roots in the late Thirties when the Inkspots climbed to world fame featuring Bill Kenny's high tenor lead and Hoppy Jones' bass voice, while the 'jubilee' (multi-voice harmony lead) and 'quartet' (solo lead with harmony support) styles of gospel groups were the inspiration behind the immediate postwar 'race' market success of earliest doo-wop performers the Orioles (Natural Records), led by the cool and clear tenor of Sonny Til, and the Ravens (National) featuring Jimmy Ricks' bass lead. Coincidentally, these names were precursors of a vast number of 'bird' groups to record durng the Fifties – Larks, Crows, Penguins, Flamingos, etc. The Orioles were also the first group to gain 'mass-market' acceptance when 'Crying In The Chapel' became a national pop hit in 1953. The song's pop success was due to the relative sophistication of the Orioles' delivery which, in contrast to that of the earthier R&B hits of the time, did not immediately give away their colour.

The following year, 1954, was perhaps the turning-point for acceptance of doo-wop (and R&B in general) with the Crows' 'Gee', the Chords' 'Sh-Boom' and the Penguins' 'Earth Angel' selling in huge quantities 'across the board', paving the way for the subsequent success and popularity of the Platters, Coasters, Drifters, Moonglows, etc. during the rock'n'roll heyday of the mid- and late Fifties. This, in turn, inspired the literally hundreds of similar groups in doo-wop hotbeds like New York and Philadelphia in the East, and Los Angeles in the West, many of which had national hits.

The essence of doo-wop was simplicity, and passing years saw arrangers become more ambitious until vocal harmonies became engulfed in string and brass sections of studio orchestras. The last vestiges of the style are evident *circa* 1962, leading into the era of soul vocal groups where the Bluenotes, Four Tops, Isley Brothers, etc. now perpetuate the lead/harmony format over the sophistication of complex orchestral arrangements.

Doo-Wop, White. The white doo-wop bonanza gathered momentum in the late Fifties, reached epidemic proportions in 1961 and faded in 1963 when, following the British invasion, America's white youth gave up singing *per se*. By 1958, early copycats the Crewcuts and the Diamonds had given way to white groups whose love of black harmony brought an honest authenticity to their performances. Most of these pioneers – Slades, Aquatones, Mellokings, Capris, Dion and the Belmonts, Skyliners – came from the cities of the North-East where European immigration was greatest and where the vocal tradition ran deepest. The first exponents (not in fact 'white' by American WASP standards) sprang from the lower status minority groups – Italians, Puerto Ricans, Poles and Spaniards, etc. Ignoring the candid language of black R&B, their original songs expressed love in Puritan terms, much like the Osmonds today.

This immature strain led to a series of hugely popular lullabies by the Mystics ('Hushabye') and the Elegants ('Little Star'). Others revived Tin Pan Alley standards – the Chimes ('Once In A While'), the Demensions ('Over The Rainbow'), Vito and the Salutations ('Unchained Melody') – as well as dusty R&B hits. The Earls ('Remember Then'), Nino and the Ebbtides ('Juke Box Saturday Night') and the Devotions ('Rip Van Winkle') contributed to this fierce blast of *déjà vu*. Apart from using bass/falsetto onomatopoeia in weird and diverting ways, many of the lead singers – Jimmy

114

Beaumont (Skyliners), Lenny Cocco (Chimes), Dion (Belmonts) and Larry Chance (Earls) – were among the finest of their generation. Rangy, piquant, mobile, they had a purity of tone which often escaped the black singers they idolised.

Despite the increasing segregation of R&B radio playlists, most white doo-woppers made the R&B charts because R&B radio stations couldn't tell what colour they really were. That's probably the best tribute that can be paid.

Dot Records, formed in 1950 by Randy Wood in Gallatin, Tennessee (near Nashville) blossomed within five years into a major concern with acts such as Pat Boone, Billy Vaughn and the Hilltoppers plus one-hit-wonders like Robin Luke, the Shields and the Dell-Vikings.

Leaving the US Airforce in 1945, Wood opened a neighbourhood appliance shop and started stocking a few records as a customer service. The record sideline quickly took over, and by 1950 'Randy's Record Store' boasted the largest mail-order catalogue in the South. Having bought a small local radio station to advertise his business, Wood began producing records after hours in the station's studio, releasing them on his newly-formed Dot label. He had hits with honky-tonk pianist Johnny Maddox and various R&B and hillbilly acts, including the Griffin Brothers, Margie Day and Mac Wiseman.

In 1952, 'Trying' by a white vocal quartet, the Hilltoppers, made the national Top Ten and in 1955 Dot signed Pat Boone who rapidly became a Fifties superstar, initially through covering R&B hits for the white masses ('Tutti Frutti', 'Long Tall Sally', 'Ain't That A Shame') and later by adopting a mawkish crooning style on million-sellers like 'It's Too Soon To Know' and 'Love Letters In The Sand'.

Moving from Gallatin to Hollywood in 1956, Dot became one of the first independent labels to license masters from smaller companies and although many of these records fell by the wayside, a significant proportion became hits, including such classics as 'The Fool' by Sanford Clark, 'You

Cheated' by the Shields and Robin Luke's 'Susie Darlin' '.

By 1963, Pat Boone's fortunes had waned considerably but Dot scored with three huge instrumental hits, 'Wipeout' (Surfaris), 'Pipeline' (Chantays) and 'Boss' by the Rumblers which, again, had all been leased from small labels. In 1965, Wood sold Dot to Gulf and Western, the film combine responsible for Paramount, and started Ranwood Records.

The Dovells had a series of eight raucous dance craze hits on Cameo-Parkway between 1961 and 1964. Beginning with 'Bristol Stomp' (No. 2), and moving on through 'Bristol Twistin' Annie', 'Hully Gully Baby', a vocal version of 'You Can't Sit Down' (No. 3) and 'Betty In Bermudas', they petered out with the arrival of the British groups. A white quintet from Philadelphia, their lead singer, Len Barry (born Dec. 6, 1942), went on to success as a solo artist, unlike the other members – Arnie Satin (baritone, born May 11, 1943), Jerry Summers (first tenor, Dec. 29, 1942), Mike Dennis (June 3, 1943), and Danny Brooks (bass, April 1, 1942). On their albums, the Dovells frequently sang in the style of the black doo-wop groups they idolized, but as Barry said later, 'Sometimes we were great, sometimes we stank.'

Big Al Downing, a talented R&B vocalist and writer, has recorded since 1956 in the rock'n'roll, R&B, soul and even C&W idioms Downing recorded first for East West, Whiterock, Challenge, Columbia and Carlton. Rockers like 'Down On The Farm' incorporated the best of rockabilly guitar styles and usually had a solid New Orleans sound. 'Just Around The Corner' and 'Georgia Slop' were especially fine. Soul duets with Little Esther for Lenox were followed by 'Cornbread Row' and 'Soul Medley' recorded in 1968–9 for Silver Fox in Nashville. Recently he has had some disco hits for Janus.

The Drifters are not just one group, but a corporate identity for several different groups permutated over two decades from more than 40 individuals. The Drifters were formed in

116

1953 around lead singer Clyde McPhatter and signed to Atlantic. The first six Drifters' records ('Money Honey', 'Such A Night', 'Honey Love', 'Someday', 'White Christmas', 'Whatcha Gonna Do') were all Top Ten R&B hits. Their strength lay in an exciting blend of gospel phrasing and 'bird-group' harmony, a technique already successful for the Five Royales and originally introduced to the Drifters by McPhatter from his previous group, the Dominoes. His influence was so strong that when he left the Drifters for a solo career, their popularity immediately waned.

Without McPhatter's distinctive lead, they were unable to find an identity strong enough to satisfy the young rock'n'roll audiences beginning to dictate the market. Using five lead singers (David Baughn, Johnny Moore, Bill Pinkney, Gerhart Thrasher, Bobby Hendricks) in three years, they tried a variety of styles from Platters-type ballads to stomping rockers until the group was disbanded in 1958. Their most popular recordings from this period, 'Ruby Baby' (led by Moore) and 'Drip Drop' (featuring Hendricks) were Jerry Leiber-Mike Stoller songs, the writer-producers who sparked off a seven-year run of hits with a new set of Drifters in 1959. This line-up (Ben E. King, Charlie Thomas, Doc Green, Elsbeary Hobbs) had been recording unsuccessfully in New York as The Crowns. Signed by manager George Treadwell to replace the sacked personnel, and teamed with Leiber and Stoller at Atlantic, their first recording as the Drifters, 'There Goes My Baby', was a smash hit in both the R&B and pop charts. The startling, almost experimental, arrangements of the song, involving strings, tympani, and Latin rhythms made the Drifters a top name again, this time with a multi-racial audience. Their following releases ('Dance With Me', 'This Magic Moment', 'Lonely Winds') were equally popular, climaxing with their most famous hit, 'Save The Last Dance For Me', in October, 1960.

By the time the record reached No. 1, King had left the group to be replaced by Rudy Lewis from the Clara Ward Singers. For the next three years, Lewis was the only distinctive voice to be heard on Drifters' recordings. The production techniques first tried in 1959 had been perfected into a glossy formula, blending the rest of the group with a female quartet (Dionne and Dee Dee Warwick, Cissy Houston and Doris Troy) and submerging them all in fancy orchestration. Arrangers Spector, Bacharach, Bert Berns and Garry Sherman each in turn added their ideas to the mixture. The songs were provided by Gerry Goffin and Carole King, Barry Mann and Cynthia Weil, Bacharach and Hal David). The results made the Drifters the most consistently successful pop-orientated black act until Motown took over the market in the mid-Sixties. Of the dozen hits at this time, 'Sweets For My Sweet' and 'When My Little Girl Is Smiling' are the best examples of their pure pop style, while 'Please Stay' and 'Let The Music Play' give a truer indication of Lewis's vocal talent. But it was 'Up On The Roof' and 'On Broadway' that were their best sellers, two good songs that took a deeper look at city life than previous pop records had cared to. This theme was repeated, less successfully, in 'Rat Race' and then, after Lewis's death in 1964, diluted to an endless romantic fantasy.

After six years' absence, Johnny Moore had rejoined the group in 1963, just in time to record their last major hit before leading them slowly to near oblivion. The Drifters' string of hits had been achieved in the few years when the tastes of black and white audiences were more closely aligned than at any other period. As British groups began invading the pop market, black record buyers turned to the rawer soul singers and Motown captured the remaining middle ground. The Drifters and their contemporaries (like the Shirelles and Phil Spector's groups) were gradually squeezed out of the charts. 'Under The Broadwalk' (led by Moore) coupled with 'I Don't Want To Go On Without You' (Charlie Thomas) was a superb double-sided hit in August, 1964, and for three more years they survived, scoring progressively lower entries with following instalments of the same story – 'I've Got Sand In My Shoes', 'Saturday Night At The Movies', 'At The Club', 'Come On Over To

My Place', 'I'll Take You Where The Music's Playing'. By 1968, however, they were a spent force, left with inferior material by the record company and relegated to performing in supper-clubs and lounges.

Shortly after the expiration of their Atlantic contract in 1972, British Atlantic started to hit with re-issues of their old records. Taking advantage of the renewed interest, the Drifters signed to Bell Records and were teamed with British pop veterans Roger Cook, Roger Greenaway and Tony Macaulay who gave them Top Ten hits with 'Like Sister And Brother' in 1973, and two new episodes of their Sixties saga, 'Kissin' In The Back Row Of The Movies', 'Down On The Beach Tonight', in 1974. At the same time, back in America another set of Drifters re-formed around Charlie Thomas and they, too, attempted to recreate the old magic with 'A Midsummer Night In Harlem' (Musicor).

From a raw rhythm and blues group to a middle-of-the-road pop act the Drifters, in one form or another, have survived all the changes of post-war entertainment. With such a flexible arrangement, the name will probably still be around in another 20 years.

Duke/Peacock Records. A key R&B record label of the post-war years, Don Robey's Houston-based company was responsible for the emergence of Bobby Bland, Junior Parker, Johnny Ace, Rosco Gordon and a host of other R&B and gospel acts.

The company was formed by Robey, who in the mid-Forties owned a large night-club in Houston called the Bronze Peacock which attracted a black clientele. Most of the popular black performers were booked into the club and it was T-Bone Walker who, in 1947, suggested that Robey catch the performance of San Antonio singer-guitarist Clarence 'Gatemouth' Brown. The industrious Robey was so impressed with Brown that he became his manager and, after several unsuccessful deals with local recording companies, decided to start a record concern of his own. So, in 1949, Robey issued 'Mary Is Fine' by Gatemouth Brown on the Peacock label. It was an instant local hit, and from then on Robey never looked back.

On August 2, 1952, he took over the Duke label, which was owned by Memphis deejay James Mattis. At the same time, Johnny Ace was making his debut on the label, and was soon to become a very big name with hits like 'Angel' and 'The Clock'. Ace went on to become one of Duke's top-selling stars with 'Pledging My Love', but died young in ridiculous circumstances. The following year, 1953, saw Duke/Peacock's most significant contribution to rock'n'roll. It was Leiber and Stoller's 'Hound Dog', recorded by Willie 'Big Mama' Thornton accompanied by the Johnny Otis band. Big Mama's powerhouse vocal and a piercing, high-register guitar solo anticipated Elvis Presley's multi-million selling version of the same song three years later.

In 1954, Robey negotiated a deal with Sam Phillips to bring Little Junior Parker to Duke. The harmonica-playing blues singer had already scored a few hits on Sun, but was to really establish himself via Robey's guiding hand. A year later Duke made its biggest-ever signing in Bobby Bland, a huge name on today's contemporary blues scene. Robey discovered him in a local talent show and subsequently nurtured his career right through into the Seventies. Bland's string of R&B hits is near endless and includes several national chart entries. Other artists signed by Robey during the Fifties included Jimmy McCracklin, Earl Forrest, Larry Davis, Fention Robinson and Norman Fox and the Rob Roys (who had a chart hit in 1957 with 'Tell Me Why').

A healthy amount of gospel material has also been issued on Peacock over the years. The artist roster is substantial and includes the Dixie Hummingbirds, Spirit Of Memphis Quartet, Mighty Clouds Of Joy, Sensational Nightingales and Inez Andrews and the Andrewettes (on the subsidiary Songbird label). In all, there are over 120 gospel albums in the catalogue.

The continued success of Duke/Peacock and its prestigious position with R&B record buyers can be attributed in part to Robey's total supervision of the recording sessions, his insistence on using only top arrangers, producers and accompanying musicians such as Johnny Otis, trumpeter Joe Scott, tenorist Bill Harvey, guitarists Wayne Bennett and Pat Hare, pianist, James Booker and drummer Sonny Freeman. Harvey's band – usually with arrangements and production by Scott – can be heard on most of the hits by Bland, Parker and Brown, while James Booker played on the Davis and Robinson sessions. The ubiquitous Johnny Otis band provided back-up for Johnny Ace and several other acts.

Duke/Peacock's standing as a major independent label ended abruptly in 1972 when it was purchased by the vast ABC/Dunhill record group. Since then Bobby Bland has become an important figure in the rock world, no doubt helped along by Dunhill's vastly superior coast-to-coast distribution outlets. Don Robey died in 1975.

Johnny Duncan, born in 1931 in Oliver Springs, Tennessee, was a member of a gospel quartet until the age of 16 when he took up the guitar and went on to join Bill Monroe's Blue Grass Boys. He joined the Army and in 1953 was stationed in Britain where he married a British girl later that year. Returning to Britain after his discharge, he replaced Lonnie Donegan as the skiffle singer in Chris Barber's Jazz Band. In 1956, he left to form his own Blue Grass Boys – Denny Wright, electric guitar; Johnny Bell, bass and Lennie Hastings, drums. In 1957, the group had a No. 2 hit on the British charts with 'Last Train To San Fernando', the success of which had a lot to do with Duncan's 'authentic' American whine. Further records failed and in the early Sixties he returned to America and joined Columbia, with whom he has had a string of minor country hits since 1967.

Champion Jack Dupree. A boxer during the Depression (hence the 'Champion' tag), Dupree was born in New Orleans on July 4, 1910. The supreme barrelhouse pianist, he recorded for Okeh from 1940, cutting many superb blues in an exuberant rough-house style. Moving to New York in 1944, he recorded for numerous labels including Joe Davis,

Apollo, Continental and King, for whom he reached the R&B Top Ten in 1955 with 'Walking The Blues'. A later Atlantic session which produced the album *Blues From The Gutter* was critically acclaimed. Now a British resident (Halifax, Yorkshire), his recent records have been aimed at the white blues collector but earlier sides, particularly 'Junker Blues', had a seminal influence on Fats Domino.

Snooks Eaglin, in the late Fifties, was playing two kinds of gigs in New Orleans (where he was born in 1936): R&B dates with a small band and singing, with acoustic guitar, on the streets. The former led to some unremembered singles for Imperial; the latter to a brief but, at any rate in Europe, keenly observed career as folk blues-singer. His highly eclectic repertoire and playing style – both accurately documented on his Folkways album – aroused both discussion and imitation, at a time when too few objects of comparison were available on blues records. There followed a long silence, broken by a 1971 Sonet album which showed Eaglin to have absorbed, very characteristically, music such as José Feliciano's and Sly Stone's.

Duane Eddy was born on April 28, 1938, in Corning, New York, and his family moved West to Phoenix, Arizona, in 1951. At five, Eddy took up the guitar and after leaving Coolidge High School at 16, he played local dances before meeting guitarist Al Casey in 1955. He sat in with Casey's combo and began studying under jazz guitarist Jim Wybele. In 1957, Lee Hazlewood, a Phoenix deejay, and his partner, Lester Sill, signed Eddy and leased the recording to the Jamie label and made 'Movin'n'Groovin'' featuring Eddy and his 'twangy' guitar as one of the Rebels, a sax/guitar group comprised of Al Casey, Larry Knecntel and Steve Douglas. At this point, Eddy and Hazlewood stumbled across the 'twangy' sound by playing the melody on the bottom instead of the top strings and feeding it through a combination of echoes. This sound was epitomized on

Eddy's next record 'Rebel-Rouser' (co-written with Hazlewood) which sold a million in the summer of 1958.

Eddy followed up with more hits including 'Ramrod', 'Cannonball' and 'Peter Gunn' and by 1960 was one of the highest paid pop instrumentalists, although much of his success can be attributed to Hazlewood's superb production. He was especially popular in Britain where he had nine consecutive Top Ten hits and was voted No. 1 Pop Personality by the *New Musical Express* in 1960.

In 1961, Eddy and Hazlewood parted company and Eddy began producing himself, with disappointing results – 'The Avenger', a self-produced final single for Jamie flopped totally late that year. In 1962, he joined RCA and made a modest comeback with 'Deep In The Heart Of Texas' and 'The Ballad Of Palladin' before re-uniting with Hazlewood and recording 'Dance With The Guitar Man', which featured vocals by a girl session group specially christened the Rebellettes. 'Guitar Man', co-written with Hazlewood, reached the Top Ten in both Britain and America but apart from the follow-up, 'Boss Guitar', early in 1963, Eddy never again achieved another hit despite many more releases on RCA. He signed with Colpix in 1967 and recorded the atrocious *Duane Does Dylan* and *Duane A Go Go* albums with no success.

Eddy still visits Britain periodically where he maintains a strong following in rock'n'roll circles. Currently working as a producer for MCA in Hollywood, he was temporarily rescued from oblivion as a recording artist in 1975 by the British chart success of 'Play Me Like You Play Your Guitar', written and produced by Tony Macaulay.

Tommy Edwards, originally a composer, was born in Richmond, Virginia, on Feb. 17, 1922. He wrote 'That Chick's Too Young To Fry' for Louis Jordan. He first recorded 'It's All In The Game' (whose melody was composed by a former US Vice-President in 1912) in 1951, but only on its re-release with a heavier backing was it a hit. In 1958, it went to No. 1 on MGM. The song has since been recorded as a 'beat-ballad' by many singers. Edwards himself died on Oct. 22, 1969.

EMI Limited, now the registered name of the group of companies built up around the original Electrical and Musical Industries, was formed in 1931 by a merger of the Gramophone Company and the Columbia Graphophone Company. The Gramophone Company had earlier swallowed the Marconiphone Company which, in turn, had swallowed His Master's Voice. The companies' main activities covered the production and development of radio receivers and record players, but as with all early gramophone producing companies, EMI quickly realized that the best way to increase demand for playing and receiving equipment was to make and sell recorded music for playing and receiving. EMI rapidly became the market leader in the field and since the Fifties has maintained a constant 20 per cent proportion of the world market in records.

During the Fifties, EMI marketed three British labels – His Master's Voice, Columbia and Parlophone, as well as distributing a number of other independent and semi-independent British labels and being involved in licensing and distribution deals with American labels such as MGM and Mercury. In 1954, the British company bought a controlling investment in the American Capitol label. This followed on the termination of a licensing deal with American Columbia (CBS). CBS subsequently went with the new Philips British subsidiary. In 1957 RCA moved from EMI to Decca, taking Presley and Perry Como with it.

A catalogue deal with Roulette Records, of New York, led to EMI's issuing Frankie Lymon's 'Why Do Fools Fall In Love' in Britain and a deal between EMI and ABC Records, of New York, gave EMI a string of phenomenal Paul Anka hits, starting with 'Diana' in 1957. By this time, EMI's own three labels were being run by a triumvirate of enormously successful label managers: Norman Newell at HMV, Norrie Paramor at Columbia, and George Martin at Parlophone. The group had found a new chairman in 1954 in Joseph

Lockwood and towards the end of the Fifties it became clear that EMI, having achieved a very strong position in its native British market, would try for a big push into America.

While the British market was no longer wholly dominated by American performers, it did not necessarily follow that the American market was prepared to be dominated by British performers. EMI's attempts to break into America, notably with Cliff Richard in 1960, were marked failures, until, in 1964, Capitol took up its option to release the Beatles' fifth single, 'I Want To Hold Your Hand'. George Martin's signing of the Beatles to Parlophone had been on his own initiative and marked the end of the days when Columbia had been EMI's major label with a string of American performers and thinly disguised British derivatives. With Capitol behind the Beatles in America from 1964 on, the way was open for EMI to expand its markets and to diversify its own interests.

Esquerita was one of a number of singers who tried to outscream and shout Little Richard in the late Fifties. A series of records on Capitol in 1958 included 'Oh Baby' and 'Rockin' The Joint', but made no impact whatsoever. Esquerita went home to New Orleans and enjoyed some local success under his real name Eskew Reeder with an organ instrumental of the Jim Lowe hit, 'Green Door', on Minit in 1962. He also recorded for Okeh and Instant, and although something of a legend among rock'n'roll collectors, his reputation in New Orleans was slight.

The Essex were a quintet comprising Marines Walter Vickers (from New Brunswick, NJ), Rodney Taylor (Gary, Indiana), Billie Hill (Princeton, NJ), Rudolph Johnson (New York) plus Anita Humes (Harrisburg, Pa.). Vickers and Taylor formed the group at the Pacific Okinawa base, adding Hill, Johnson and finally Humes upon their return to Camp Lejeune, North Carolina. They auditioned for Roulette while on leave, and the staccato delivery of 'Easier Said Than Done' was an immediate 1963 million seller. A Walking Miracle' was a Top Twenty hit, but success was short-lived.

The Everly Brothers. Although the roots of rock'n'roll are usually traced to black R&B, in retrospect the total picture of rock in the Fifties can be seen to owe as much to white country music. The 'landmark' artists Haley, Presley and Holly added black influences to their country heritage; the Everly Brothers, however, were simply the most successful hillbilly act ever.

Don (born Feb. 1, 1937) and Phil (Jan. 19, 1939) came from a country-music family; their parents, Ike and Margaret, were hillbilly performers with their own Kentucky radio show; as soon as Don and Phil could stand in front of a microphone it became a family act. In 1956 Ike persuaded Chet Atkins in Nashville to take an interest in them, and they cut their first single, 'Keep A Lovin' Me', for Columbia in the same year. They switched to Archie Bleyer's Cadence label in 1957 and the hits started coming. By this time, the family had moved to Tennessee, and the brothers met songwriter Boudleaux Bryant. Bryant, writing either alone or with his wife Felice, was to provide many of their hits, which were recorded in Nashville. The Bryant songs were archetypal teenage love ballads whose frequently lachrymose tone perfectly suited the keening, plaintive harmonies of the Everlys.

The first hit (May 1957) was 'Bye Bye Love', followed the same year by 'Wake Up Little Susie'. The brothers' association with the Cadence label continued until 1960, producing sixteen Hot Hundred entries – of which nine made the Top Ten – including 'Bird Dog', 'Problems' and 'When Will I Be Loved'. The records were melodramatic and forceful, with the Brothers' harmonies soaring above impressive rock arrangements. The act then signed with the new Warner Brothers label, and had an immediate No. 1 in both America and Britain with 'Cathy's Clown'. The big hits continued until 1962, including 'So Sad', 'Walk Right Back', 'Ebony Eyes' and 'Crying In The Rain'.

126

Like all established American acts, the Everly Brothers felt the impact of the 'British invasion', but continued to have the occasional success until 'Bowling Green' (1967). Their biggest mid-Sixties British hit was 'Price Of Love' (1965). The relationship between the two brothers began to deteriorate, however, and from being indistinguishable halves of a harmony act, they became two distinct personalities: Phil lighter and pop-oriented, Don darker and brooding.

They continued to record, and in 1968 produced a classic album aptly titled *Roots*: country songs interleaved with tape excerpts from the old Everly radio show. A friendship with John Sebastian resulted in the 1972 album *Stories We Could Tell*, backed by a host of superstars, and later the same year they returned to their old mentor Chet Atkins for the final Everly Brothers record *Pass The Chicken And Listen*. Since then they have pursued solo careers, Phil most actively. In their youthful prime the Everlys made some of the most exciting pop records of the late Fifties, in the area where C&W met 'teen-appeal'.

Excello Records was formed in Nashville, Tennessee, in 1952 by record man Ernie Young as an outlet for blues and R&B recordings so that the parent label, Nashboro, could concentrate exclusively on the gospel market. The first releases were poor in quality and did not sell until Arthur Gunter clicked in 1954 with 'Baby Let's Play House' (later recorded by Elvis Presley). This inspired Young to expand his blues activities and in 1955 he set up a long-term deal with Jay Miller of Crowley, Louisiana, which led to hit R&B recordings with Slim Harpo ('I'm A King Bee', 'Rainin' In My Heart', 'Baby Scratch My Back') and a remarkably consistent output of Southern downhome blues by Lightnin' Slim, Lonesome Sundown, Lazy Lester and many more. Ernie Young had national hits with the original versions of 'Little Darlin'' by the Gladiolas in 1957 and 'Oh Julie' by the Crescendos on the Nasco affiliate in 1958.

For over a decade Excello was a prime source of authentic R&B, but when Ernie Young retired in 1966 the new management adopted a far more commercial approach, specializing particularly in soul music.

Shelley Fabares, born on Jan. 19, 1944, in Santa Monica, California, started as a dancer and actress, appearing in *Rock Pretty Baby*, before achieving public recognition on TV's *The Donna Reed Show* in the late Fifties. From here it was only a short step to a record contract with Stu Phillips' Colpix label (formed as a subsidiary of Columbia Pictures) where she immediately hit with the embarrassingly cute and wistful Lee Pockriss and Lyn Duddy song 'Johnny Angel', a No. 1 in 1962. A year later, her record career was over. She had pursued the 'Johnny Angel' theme relentlessly but with declining success on 'Johnny Loves Me', 'The Things We Did Last Summer' and 'Ronnie, Call Me When You Get A Chance'. Later in 1963, she retired to marriage with Lou Adler.

Fabian, born on Feb. 6, 1943 in Pennsylvania – also the home town of Frankie Avalon, with whom he shared both manager and record label – his real name was Fabiano Forte Bonaparte. It was said that he was 'discovered' walking down the street by a talent scout impressed by his Italianate profile. If Stan Freberg's character, Clyde Ankle, was a satire on any one figure, it was Fabian. His record company (Chancellor) released five singles in 1959 in the hope that he might catch on as another Elvis Presley. These included 'I'm A Man', 'Turn Me Loose', 'Tiger', 'Come On And Get Me' and 'Hound Dog Man'. All figured in the Hot Hundred although, in Britain, his contrived image never caught on in the same way. His films included *Hound Dog Man* (1959), *North To Alaska* (1960) and *Fireball 500* (1966).

Tommy 'Bubba' Facenda, born on Nov. 10, 1939 in Portsmouth, Virginia, was a classmate of Gene Vincent and in 1957 he joined Vincent's group, the Bluecaps, as a background singer and dancer. Leaving Vincent in 1968, he pur-

128

sued a modest solo career, recording one single for Nasco in Nashville, before meeting Portsmouth record shop owner Frank Guida, for whom he cut 'High School USA', a novelty rock'n'roll song which was mastered in 28 different versions – one for each distributor – each listing the important High Schools in the distributor's area. Leased to Atlantic, the song made No. 28 on the Hot Hundred late in 1959, but Facenda only managed one follow-up before being drafted into the Army. On his discharge in 1962, he joined the Portsmouth Fire Brigade where he still works today.

Adam Faith, born Terry Nelhams in Acton, London, on June 23, 1940, was second only to Cliff Richard as Britain's teenage idol in the early Sixties. His first ambition was to be a film editor and after school he worked as a messenger boy at Rank Screen Services. But caught up in the skiffle craze, he became vocalist with the Worried Men, a group formed by workmates at Rank, until after a year, Jack Good, the scholarly ombudsman of English rock'n'roll, suggested that Nelhams go solo as Adam Faith.

He left his job, appeared on *6.5 Special* twice, went on the road four times and cut two flops for HMV in 1958. Losing heart, he returned to Rank where he worked as an assistant cutter. Early in 1959, after a year's absence from showbiz, John Barry recommended Faith for a residency on a forthcoming TV rock series, *Drumbeat* and after a successful audition, Faith stayed with the show for the whole of its 22-week run. He also recorded another flop, 'Runk Bunk' for Top Rank and appeared in the teen-movie *Beat Girl*.

On *Drumbeat*, he met songwriter Johnny Worth, a member of the Raindrops, who offered Faith his composition 'What Do You Want?'. Recorded at EMI in late 1959 with John Barry providing unique pizzicato string backing over which Faith hiccoughed the lyrics, 'What Do You Want?' became the biggest British hit of 1960, finally establishing the singer. He followed up with a series of huge hits including 'Poor Me' (another No. 1), 'Someone Else's Baby', 'Lonely Pup' and 'Who Am I', all in the same little-boy-lost style.

Though not technically a singer, Faith's contrived enunciation and emasculated vocal style aroused a protective feeling among the era's girl fans; while visually, he was quite chic for the period, eschewing greasy forelocks for a French college boy haircut.

Abandoning his recording career in 1965, he went into repertory and for two years he toured the provinces in obscurity. In 1971, he was widely acclaimed for his portrayal of the loser villain 'Budgie' in the TV series of the same name and many thought he stole the limelight from co-star David Essex in the film *Stardust*. Currently he manages singer Leo Sayer and has attempted a comeback with the album *I Survived* in 1974.

The Falcons, whose 'You're So Fine' (Unart) reached the Top Twenty in 1959 was one of the first obviously soulful records. Originally recorded for a Detroit label, Flick, it featured pungent guitar work and a heartbreakingly sad lead vocal from Joe Stubbs, the brother of the Four Tops' Levi. The rest of the group – Mack Rice, Lance Finnie, Eddie Floyd and Willie Schofield – harmonised in deliciously dusty fashion. With a new lead singer (Wilson Pickett), the group returned to the charts on Lupine in 1962 with 'I Found A Love'. It was their last hit, but the Falcons' recording career had stretched from Mercury in 1956 (when Floyd sang lead), through Savoy, Falcon, Chess, United Artists, Atlantic, Big Wheel and others in the Sixties. Stubbs joined the Contours, while Floyd, Rice and Pickett became solo soul singers of varying distinction.

Charlie Feathers, a vocalist and guitarist from backwoods Mississippi, was born on June 12, 1932, in Hollow Springs. He has never had anything resembling a hit record. His importance to rock is his contribution to the C&W/R&W mélange known as 'rockabilly'. Many artistically successful recordings, mostly made in Memphis, for Flip, Sun, Meteor, King, Hi (unissued), Kay, Walmay, Memphis, Holiday Inn, Pinewood, Barrelhouse, Rollin' Rock and backings for others on Kay, Hi, Royaltone and Shelby County all display his unique rhythmical influence on the sound that spawned Elvis Presley. His band has retained the original rockabilly style and was filmed by the BBC in 1972. ⊃ 1998

The Fireballs came from Raton, New Mexico, with the exception of pianist Jimmy Gilmer, a native of Illinois. Guitarist George Tomsco, bass-player Stan Lark, drummer Eric Budd and Gilmer formed the group in 1959. They were managed by Norman Petty, who used the Fireballs to overdub various Holly demo tracks in the early Sixties. As the Fireballs, the band had four American hits in the years 1959–61, starting with 'Torquay'; they re-appeared in 1968–9 with three more successes. The 1961 hit, 'Quite A Party', also scored in Britain. As Jimmy Gilmer and the Fireballs they had an American No. 1 in 1963 with 'Sugar Shack', following this with two minor hits.

Toni Fisher came from Los Angeles and was only seven when she joined the Marco Juvenile Revue on CBS networked TV and appeared in programmes like the *Hollywood Showcase* and *Mail Call*. She had one big hit, the Latin-avoured 'The Big Hurt' in 1959 which reached No. 3 and was one of the first records to employ phasing. None of her later records ('How Deep Is The Ocean', 'West Of The Wall') enjoyed significant success.

The Five Blind Boys (of Mississippi), also known as the Jackson Harmoneers, are a popular acappella gospel group founded by Lloyd Woodard in Piney Woods near Jackson, Mississippi. In the Fifties, they became famous for the wailing lead vocals of Archie Brownlee, and his characteristic breaking into occasional ecstatic screams can be heard on most of their records, including the 1951 hit for Peacock, 'Our Father'. Their emotional laments to 'mother' made them one of the most popular groups on the gospel circuit, and after Brownlee's death in 1960, Roscoe Robinson and later Big Henry Johnson carried on the role.

The Five Keys, an ex-gospel group from Newport News, Virginia, topped the R&B charts in 1951 with 'Glory Of Love' on Aladdin, which featured the cool and mannered lead tenor of Rudy West. When the group moved to Capitol, Maryland Pierce sang lead for a while – 'Ling Ting Tong' and 'Close Your Eyes' – until West returned from the Army to sing on 'Out Of Sight, Out Of Mind' and 'Wisdom Of A Fool', both of which made the Top Forty in 1956. Bernie West, Ripley Ingram, Dickie Smith and his replacement, Ramon Loper, were among the most important personnel of a group that continued to record well into the Seventies with many less successful records on, among others, King, Segway and Bim Bam Boom.

The Five Royales, originally a gospel group known as the Royal Sons Quintet from Winston, Salem, switched over to R&B for two No. 1 R&B hits, 'Baby Don't Do It' and 'Help Me Somebody' on Apollo in 1953. The lead, Johnny Tanner, had a stout earthy voice which retained the fierce conviction characteristic of post-war gospel quartet singing. Subsequent records for King, including 'Think' and the original 'Dedicated To The One I Love' – Hot Hundred entries in 1957 and 1961 respectively – were equally gritty. The group, which included Lowman Pauling, Obediah Carter, Otto Jeffries and Johnny Moore, also recorded for Home of The Blues, ABC, Todd, Vee Jay and Smash.

The Five Satins. Lead singer Fred Parris formed the Scarlets on Red Robin in 1953 and the Five Satins on Standard in 1956. 'In The Still Of The Night' written by Parris and cut in the basement of a New Haven church, was bought from Standard by Ember, the label on which it made the Top Thirty in 1956 and the Hot Hundred in 1960 and 1961. They say the song hangs in the air over New York City; certainly it's one of the most beautiful R&B ballads ever made. Parris, Al Denby, Jim Freeman and ⸏ ¹ Martin were responsible for the weird but thrilling harmony, while Jessie Murphy played piano. Other sits included 'To The Aisle' – on which Bill

Baker sang lead – and 'I'll Be Seeing You', which the group revived acappella in the film *Let The Good Times Roll*. The group also recorded for First, Cub, Chancellor, Warner Bros, Roulette and Mama Sadie.

The Flamingos, formed in Chicago in 1952 by Zeke and Jake Carey, Johnny Carter, Solly McElroy and Paul Wilson, their first discs appeared on Chance in the following year. The Flamingos' unusually broad influences – from gospel to the Four Freshmen – equipped them well to survive the radical changes to overtake black group singing during their twenty-year history. The Fats Washington ballad 'I'll Be Home' (covered by Pat Boone) made the R&B Top Ten in 1956, and they subsequently made the pop charts with a string of equally romantic tunes on End. They icluded 'Lover Never Say Goodbye', 'I Only Have Eyes For You' (No. 11 in 1959), 'Love Walked In', 'I Was Such A Fool', 'Nobody Loves Me Like You' (No. 30 in 1960) and 'Time Was'. Later hits in the soul vein included 'Boogaloo Party' (on Philips in 1966), 'Dealin' ' (Julma in 1969) and 'Buffalo Soldier' (Polydor in 1970). The Flamingos also recorded for Parrot, Decca and, in 1972, Ronze. Johnny Pearson, Terry Johnson, Nate Nelson (who joined the Platters), Tommy Hunt (a Sixties soul star), Doug McClure and Larry Clinton were among later personnel, while Johnny Carter joined the Dells.

The Flairs/Flares. Cornelius Gunter, Richard Berry, Thomas Fox, Obadiah Jessie and Beverley Thompson formed the Flairs in Los Angeles in 1953. Their first disc, on the Flair subsidiary of Modern, was the Leiber and Stoller production, 'She Wants To Rock', one of a number of regional hits the group had. By 1961, they changed the spelling to 'Flares' and enjoyed a well-deserved national hit with 'Footstompin' ' on Felsted. Despite other popular records on Press, the fresh personnel – Aaron Collins, Willie Davis, George Hollis and Thomas Miller – disintegrated around 1964. Gunter and Jessie joined the Coasters, while Berry's influence remained strong on California's group culture.

The Fleetwoods, formed in 1958 at Olympia High School, Washington, with Gary Troxel (born Nov. 28, 1939), Barbara Ellis (Feb. 20, 1940) and Gretchen Christopher (Feb. 29, 1940), first called themselves Two Girls and a Guy, before changing their name to the Fleetwoods. Their first record, the self-penned 'Come Softly To Me' was a smash No. 1 in the spring of 1959 on Liberty/Dolton, as was their second, and best, the De Wayne Blackwell composition, 'Mr. Blue'. However, their gentle, close harmony sound soon fell out of favour and they had their last Top Ten hit with a revival of Thomas Wayne's 'Tragedy' in 1961.

Emile Ford. British rock was pure white until 1959 when a shy West Indian, Emile Ford, rocketed in and out of favour. Born Emile Sweetnam in Nassau in 1937, he was discovered playing in London coffee bars and decked out with a repertoire similar to Fats Domino's (swinging standards). He had a backing group, the Checkmates (originally comprising his brother George, John Cuffley and Ken Street), and their first record, 'What Do You Want To Make Those Eyes At Me For?', was a million seller. Follow-ups, however, made little impression, and Ford's career was over in less than a year. After dabbling in record production he moved to the Continent and still turns up occasionally on rock'n'roll revival shows.

Frankie Ford, born in 1941 in Gretna, Louisiana, rose to fame when his second record, 'Sea Cruise', was a Top Twenty hit in 1959 on the Ace label. It is now recognised as a New Orleans rock'n'roll classic, but the hit was obtained at the expense of Huey 'Piano' Smith, whose original vocal tracks were wiped off in favour of Ford's – the same thing happened with the follow-up 'Alimony'. In 1960 Ford had a small hit with a cover version of Joe Jones's 'You Talk Too Much' on Imperial but a spell in the Army in 1962 effectively ended his career as a recording star. He has recorded on and off without much success since then, and now plays standards with great poise for the milling throng of tourists in his own nightclub in New Orleans' French Quarter.

Tennessee Ernie Ford, born Ernest Jennings Ford in Bristol, Tennessee on Feb. 13, 1919, worked as a disc jockey before joining Capitol's roster of country singers in the early Fifties. He was never comfortable as a pure country performer – he had scandalised the purists by recording 'I'll Never Be Free' and 'Nobody's Business' with Kay Starr early in his career – and when he hit gold in 1955, it was with a semi-rock record, 'Sixteen Tons'. One of the fastest selling records in history, 'Sixteen Tons' allowed Ford to make his final break with the country music establishment. CBS gave him his own television show and he slipped quickly into the mainstream of American showbusiness. When he retired, still successful, in the early Sixties, he had accumulated some 20 albums of songs, the most popular of which were his religious collections. He died in 1974.

The Four Preps consisted of Bruce Belland and Marvin Inabett (lead tenors), Ed Cobb (bass) and Glenn Larson (baritone). Their arranger-producer Lincoln Mayorga stayed ostage. They first sang together in the Hollywood High School Choir and made their debut with Ricky Nelson, at Hamilton High School, Los Angeles. Clean cut, but with a sense of humour and an early influence on the Beach Boys, they had a Gold record with '26 Miles' in 1958 and 'Big Man', with its distinctive piona, played by Mayorga, was a Top Five hit on both sides of the Atlantic. Their live act included jump numbers, ballads, novelty songs and even vocal impressions.

Connie Francis. Born Constance Franconero on Dec. 12, 1938, she sold vast quantities of records in the years after rock'n'roll and before the Beatles. She graduated from the *Arthur Godfrey Talent Show* at 11, but not from New York University where she abandoned her studies in favour of a musical career.

She sang on Marvin Rainwater's MGM hit 'Majesty Of Love' in 1957, but her own records were at first unsuccessful. Then, a revival of the standard, 'Who's Sorry Now', became a hit in 1958. For the following five years Connie Francis was never out of the charts, having 25 hits in that time. The songs were well split between bouncy novelty sub-rock numbers ('Lipstick On Your Collar', 'Stupid Cupid') and throbbing ballads ('Everybody's Somebody's Fool', 'Don't Break The Heart That Loves You'). Many of the latter were dusty old hits from the pre-war era. 'Who's Sorry Now' was composed in 1923, and 'Among My Souvenirs' and 'Together' in 1928. They were generally more successful than the uptempo songs.

The arrival of the Beatles brought her career as a singles artist to a close. Resourcefully, she turned to a middle-of-the-road audience, for whom she purveyed albums of Jewish, Italian, Country, and Latin American songs in her powerful but undirected singing style. She had nevertheless been the most important female singer of the post rock'n'roll era, and would remain so until the late Sixties.

Stan Freberg. Rock music has always contained a strain of novelty records, and among them have been discs parodying the music itself. The earliest, and still the best, were made during the Fifties by Stan Freberg, who was born on August 7, 1926. He began on radio in the late Forties, doing impersonations, and was soon in demand as a voice for cartoon films. His first record was 'John And Marsha' a satire on soap operas, for Capitol in 1950.

The arrival of rock'n'roll provided him with a whole new area in which to exercise his satirical talent. He delighted in parodying the stylized recordings of both black and white performers, and he had a keen eye for the machinations of the get-rich-quick merchants in the music business. Among his hits were hilarious versions of Presley's 'Heartbreak Hotel', Donegan's skiffle version of 'Rock Island Line' and the Platters' 'The Great Pretender'. He picked upon the most identifiable feature of the original – Presley's vocal echo,

Donegan's spoken introduction in an acquired drawl, and the doo-wop vocals and constant piano figure behind the Platters. Those features, in fact, which the established musical world might have thought the most facile elements of the new music. The overall impression, however, is not one of distaste but of the creative brilliance of the satire. Freberg had, in any case, already parodied that pillar of the previous musical order, Johnnie Ray, and also Southern attitudes in 'Yellow Rose Of Texas', plus the slick sleuth genre in 'St. George And The Dragonet'. With 'Banana Boat' he returned to the 'making of a record theme' utilized on the rock parodies. As an extension of this, he came up with his own comment on one of the realities of rock with 'The Old Payola Roll Blues', which followed the late Fifties' bribery investigations and featured teenage idol 'Clyde Ankle'.

Alan Freed, the Pied Piper of rock'n'roll was born on Dec. 15, 1922, in Johnstown, Philadelphia. At high school in Salem, Ohio, Freed organised a jazz band, the Sultans Of Swing. He started work in radio in 1942, successively holding jobs as a programme director and sportscaster with WKST, WKBN and WAKR in Ohio and Philadelphia. He moved to WJW in Cleveland in 1951.

Encouraged by a local record store owner, Leo Mintz, Freed began to play R&B records on a show which he called *Moondog's Rock'n'Roll Party*. White, of Welsh-Lithuanian descent, he chose the new name to avoid the racial stigma he thought inherent in existing names like 'rhythm & blues' and 'race music'. Rock'n'roll would probably have gained large-scale acceptance without Freed, but he was the catalyst. Throughout his radio show he would thump out the beat on a telephone book and his enthusiasm, as charismatic as the records he played, built up vast listening figures. His first stage-show, in March 1952, was cancelled when 30,000 kids tried to get into the 10,000 capacity Cleveland Arena. Freed was surprised to find that a substantial minority of the disappointed audience was white.

In Sept. 1954, Freed moved to New York, where he hosted

Rock'n'Roll Party over WINS. The following January, he assembled a package show at St Nicholas Arena with a host of groups, virtually all black. By now the audiences were 70 per cent white. He had become a household name by 1957, the year in which he appeared in three films (*Rock Around The Clock; Rock, Rock, Rock* and *Don't Knock The Rock*). He also shared composing credits on many rock'n'roll hits – by Chuck Berry, the Moonglows and others – and very often songwriters were only too pleased to give him a cut in return for continued airplay. Freed, of course, did accept payola but he could not be bribed to play a record he didn't like. He thought black music was honest and refused to play the myriad insipid white cover versions of R&B originals. Those who did, he accused of racialism. His outspoken defence of black music incurred the wrath of the music business establishment. Although charges of anarchy and incitement to riot after a Boston concert were dismissed in 1958, Freed was made a scapegoat for his part in the payola scandals. In 1962 he pleaded guilty to accepting bribes and received a suspended prison sentence and a fine.

Attempts to revive his career were unsuccessful and he died in a Palm Springs hospital on Jan. 20, 1965. 'He had suffered the most', said *Cashbox*, 'and was perhaps singled out for alleged wrongs that had become a business way of life for many others'. Today, most people – not least the performers he helped – recognize his major contribution to the advancement of black music.

Bobby Freeman was born in San Francisco on June 13, 1940. A black pianist and singer, Freeman sang with a local group, the Romancers, on Dootone at the age of 14. As a solo singer, he had a number of spectacular rock'n'roll hits for Josie, beginning with the self-penned and often revived 'Do You Wanna Dance' a No. 5 in 1958. 'Betty Lou Got A New Pair Of Shoes' (Top Forty) and the less successful 'Shame On You Miss Johnson' were equally torrid. Dance-craze items like 'Shimmy Shimmy' (Top Forty on King) and the Sly Stone-produced 'C'mon And Swim' (Top Five in 1964)

138

kept Freeman in the public eye until the Seventies, when he turned towards soul on Double-Shot.

Jerry Fuller, a singer with a country-tinged voice, recorded for Challenge from 1959 with little success, only 'Betty My Angel' and 'Tennessee Waltz' making any real impact on the charts. He is more important as a songwriter and producer for Ricky Nelson and, later, for Gary Puckett and the Union Gap. For Nelson he wrote 'Travelling Man', 'It's A Young Worlfld' and 'It's Up To You'. He wrote and produced Puckett's 'Over You' and 'Young Girl', which had a new lease of life in the British charts in 1974.

Jesse Fuller was born in Jonesboro, Georgia, in 1896, into the generation of itinerant blues songsters whose era his style still evokes. His metier is the one-man-band: he plays 12-string guitar, harmonica, kazoo, hi-hat and fotdella (an instrument of his own devising, a sort of pedal-operated string bass). To this he adapted a repertoire of blues, good-time songs and spirituals, which made him, especially in the early days of blues appreciation, popular as a club and folk-festival act. 'San Francisco Bay Blues' was much copied in the early Sixties, but after its vogue little attention was paid to its creator, and he has been out of the public eye for virtually a decade. His several albums for Good Time Jazz are representative.

Lowell Fulson, born in Tulsa, Oklahoma, in 1921, a singer-guitarist who is one of the chief exponents of West Coast dance-hall blues. Early work with Texas Alexander led to many discs on a prolific number of labels, beginning with those owned by Bob Geddins and Jack Lauderdale in Oakland, California, in 1946. His R&B hits included 'Come Back Baby' for Downbeat in 1949 and 'Every Day I Have The Blues', 'Blue Shadows' (a No. 1) and 'Lonely Christmas' for Swingtime in 1950–51. 'Reconsider Baby', now a blues standard, heralded Fulson's move to Checker in 1954. He finally made the pop charts on Kent with 'Black Night', 'Tramp'

(No. 52 in 1967) and 'Make A Little Love'. His guitar improvisations were submerged among the brass arrangements of Maxwell Davis, but few bluesmen made the pop charts with such minimal stylistic change.

Harvey Fuqua – born on July 27, 1929, in Louisville, Kentucky – began his musical career when he moved to Cleveland in 1951 and helped form the Moonglows, who recorded prolifically and successfully for Chance and Chess until 1959, their best-known hits being 'Ten Commandments of Love', featuring Harvey's bass lead vocal, and 'Sincerely'. When they split in 1959, Fuqua recruited the Marquees (including Marvin Gaye) to record with Chess – as the Moonglows – for a while before becoming A&R director at Chess in 1960, taking Gaye with him to the subsidiary Anna label. At this time he recorded some successful duets with Etta James, issued on Chess, then married Anna label owner, Gwen Cordy. Breaking with Chess, Fuqua formed the Harvey and Tri-Phi labels, subsequently incorporating into the Motown organisation, with whom he worked as writer/producer until 1969, when he began his own production company, channelled through RCA, and has achieved success with the Nitelighters, New Birth, and revived Moonglows.

Billy Fury (born Ronald Wycherly on April 17, 1941 in Liverpool) was perhaps the most talented of the adolescent Britons who aped American rock'n'roll in the late Fifties. He was discovered in the classic manner – late in 1958, while working on the Mersey tugboats, he had written a couple of songs, and when one of the marathon rock shows promoted by impresario Larry Parnes came to Birkenhead, he talked his way into Marty Wilde's dressing room in the hope of interesting the star in his songs. The end result was that Parnes gave Ronald a new name and a spot on the rest of the tour.

Fury's first hit, 'Maybe Tomorrow', followed in April, 1959. After a few misses he returned to the charts in 1960 with two of his own numbers, 'Colette' and 'That's Love', and produced one of the classic rock'n'roll albums in *The Sound of Fury*. It was almost authentic rockabilly throughout, and yet Fury had written all of the songs and the lead guitarist was Cockney Joe Brown.

Fury then turned to the common pattern, of covering American hits and big ballads, 'Halfway To Paradise', 'Jealousy' and 'I'll Never Find Another You', and when his chart reign ended in 1965 he had been in the British Top Twenty 19 times. By this time, he had made the switch to Northern clubs and cabaret for a living, a circuit which he still plays today.

Ill-health has dogged Fury's career, and his dream remains to leave showbusiness and found a bird sanctuary. But *The Sound of Fury* and his almost unprecedented chart run put him among the British pop greats. In what was almost a reprise of his classic style, Fury played the role of the rock'n'roll singer in the acclaimed movie, *That'll Be The Day*, in 1973.

Milt Gabler, in the late Thirties, formed the pioneering independent Commodore label for which he supervised Billie Holiday's earliest sessions as well as Jimmy Yancey, Meade Lux Lewis, James P. Johnson, Jelly Roll Morton and many others. Joining Decca in 1941, Gabler was responsible for supervising the firm's 'race', jazz and hillbilly (C&W) sessions and throughout the decade he presided over a vast number of recordings by Burl Ives, Ella Fitzgerald ,the Inkspots, the Weavers, Red Foley and Louis Jordan, who became the biggest black recording star of the Forties with Gabler-supervised hits like 'Caldonia', 'Choo Choo Ch' Boogie' and 'Saturday Night Fish Fry'. In 1954, Gabler signed Bill Haley to Decca and produced such classics as 'Rock Around The Clock' and 'See You Later Alligator'. During the Sixties, Gabler gradually assumed the role of executive producer and though he still works for Decca, he is now approaching retirement age. He is one of the record industry's unsung greats.

Tommy 'Snuff' Garrett, a record producer who specializes in bubblegum and MOR music was born in Dallas, Texas, in 1939. He has been associated with the music business since the age of 15 when he began doing promotion for a distribution company in Dallas. From promotion he expanded into record sales and, at 17, he left Dallas to become a deejay at KDUB in Lubbock, Texas, where he met and befriended Buddy Holly and the Crickets. From there, he moved to Wichita Falls, Texas where he ran his own TV show and a teenage nightclub, 'Snuff's Record Hop'.

In 1958 he went to Hollywood where he took a job as local promotion man with Liberty before returning into record production. He was asked to produce the hitherto unsuccessful Johnny Burnette for Liberty, and after only two records under Garrett, Burnette achieved his first hit with 'Dreamin'', a 1960 million-seller. In 1959, Garrett signed Bobby Vee, a 17-year-old from Minnesota, and had him cover Adam Faith's 'What Do You Want?' for the American market. This flopped, but Vee's sequel, 'Devil Or Angel' reached No. 6 in America and under Garrett's masterful supervision, Vee went on to become a major American teen idol with such hits as 'Rubber Ball', 'Take Good Care Of My Baby' and 'Run To Him'. Meanwhile, Burnette registered with two more hits, 'Little Boy Sad' and 'You're Sixteen' and Garrett even managed to launch a failed jazz singer named Gene McDaniels with a series of hits including 'A Hundred Pounds Of Clay' and 'Tower Of Strength'. In the period between 1961 and 1963, Garrett was probably the most successful A&R man in America. At 22, he was made head of A&R at Liberty and hired a contemporary prodigy, named Phil Spector, to work for Liberty in New York.

Although Garrett's productions were generally aimed at America's white middle-class and epitomized the artless sterility of pop in the early Sixties, he was, nevertheless, solely responsible for Liberty's inroads into the mainstream rock market. He also launched a series of best-selling middle-of-the-road albums in the *50 Guitars Of Tommy Garrett*. During 1965–6, Garrett produced no less than ten successive American Top Ten hits by Jerry Lewis' son, Garry Lewis and the Playboys, most of which were arranged by Leon Russell.

Leaving Liberty in 1966, Garrett formed his own Viva label but, ironically, did not achieve even one hit and in 1969 he sold his assets for $2½ million and retired until 1973 when he produced a run of comeback hits by (Sonny and) Cher.

Gene and Eunice, an R&B duo of Gene Forrest and Eunice Levy, were based in California, where Forrest recorded with his orchestra for RPM and Aladdin before joining Eunice for vocal duets. Their first hit was 'Ko Ko Mo' in 1955 on Combo Records, re-recorded by Aladdin, which, when covered by Perry Como, sold a million. Further Aladdin discs failed to register, and their biggest 'pop' hit came in 1959 when 'Poco-Loco' reached the American Top Fifty on Case Records. After another disc, on Lilly, no more was heard of the duo, whose style was mellower than Shirley and Lee but harsher than Mickey and Sylvia.

Don Gibson, born in Shelby, North Carolina, on April 3, 1928, has been writing and singing country music for most of his life, but somehow he's never fulfilled his early promise of greatness. He started out as a straight honky tonk singer, but when Elvis Presley threw down his challenge to the country traditionalists he adapted his style.

In the late Fifties and early Sixties, Chet Atkins had gathered around him a group of musicians and performers at RCA Victor in Nashville, one of whom was Gibson. Atkins was doing his best to stem the flood of rock'n'roll and in Gibson he had, potentially, his greatest ally. The idea was to create a semi-rocking sound around essentially country singers, but for Gibson it was a technique that simply didn't go far enough and the result was the emasculation of a genuinely soulful voice. He had a string of hits – 'Oh Lonesome Me', 'Blue Blue Day', 'Heartache Number One', 'Legend In My Time' – but it was often left to others to reveal the true worth of his writing. Neil Young may have failed to better him on 'Oh Lonesome Me' – a Top Ten pop hit for Gibson in 1958 – but his own version of 'I Can't Stop Loving You' pales beside the Ray Charles version. His last really important record was probably his best, the archetypal country/rock single, Harlon Howard's 'Sea Of Heartbreak', a pop hit in 1961. He still works in Nashville.

Mickey Gilley, as a vocalist and pianist who lives both stylistically and commercially in the shadow of cousin Jerry Lee Lewis, he occasionally breaks into the C&W charts. Born in Louisiana, but living in Houston since 1957 when Lewis became a star, Gilley recorded rock'n'roll that year for Minor Records. A series of rock and country classics on small Southern labels followed and C&W hits with 'Is It Wrong' (1960), 'Lonely Wine' (1964), 'Now I Can Live Again' (1968) and 'Room Full Of Roses' (1974) were achieved. Gilley is currently at his most successful with Playboy Records and owns a night club in Houston.

Girl Vocal Groups were an almost purely American phenomenon of the early Sixties, although the Teen Queens, Hearts and Chordettes had made an impact. The trend started when the Shirelles had a big hit in 1960 with 'Will You Love Me Tomorrow', which led to a string of American hits. Male groups were already a part of American pop, but a consistently successful girl group was something quite new.

As audiences then tended to buy the sounds first, then look to see who was singing afterwards, images hardly counted and producers looked upon girl groups as pliable studio puppets who were even more naive than their male counterparts. By the same token, however, most of the female vocal groups were only modestly talented and were therefore only too happy to be manipulated by some whizz-kid producer if it resulted in their earning $800 a night, touring on the strength of a hit.

By 1963, most of the teenage idols of the late Fifties and early Sixties had declined in popularity and American record producers were making an increasing number of studio-contrived girl-group discs. As a consequence, many quaintly named one-hit wonders reached the American charts including the Murmaids, the Jaynetts, the Girlfriends, the Angels, the Dixiebelles, the Cookies, the Sherrys and Reparata and the Delrons – the list is endless. The majority of these records were made either by professional session-singers or by semi-pros who were coaxed into the studio with a few dollars advance. By using session-singers, a producer was able to avoid clashes of temperament with self-opinionated artists and at the same time ensure greater profits for himself, since they were only paid a standard fee.

Girl-group records became so fashionable in the States that early in 1964, Leiber and Stoller and the late George Goldner formed the legendary Red Bird label as a vehicle for instant girl-group hits. Red Bird's first releast, 'Chapel Of Love' by the Dixie Cups, topped the charts and thereafter the firm's small but shrewd writer-producer workshop gave Red Bird a hit with virtually every other release by anonymous entities like the Jelly Beans, the Shangri-Las and the Butterys, etc.

The same year, 1964, saw the emergence of a new generation of fans who, like their older brothers and sisters a decade earlier, wanted real heroes and real personalities rather than the plethora of faceless girl groups and one-hit wonders that the industry was churning out. Thus the advent of the 'British Invasion' signalled the demise of the girl-group sound.

Henry Glover was born in Manhattan, New York. After leaving college in 1943, Glover did graduate work at Wayne University, almost attaining an MA in music before joining Buddy Johnson's band on trumpet in 1944. He then played with Willie Bryant and Tiny Bradshaw before joining Lucky Millinder's band, with whom he was working when King Records boss Syd Nathan appointed him as A&R director – having first ascertained that he could write and arrange music.

Glover's duties included recording Bullmoose Jackson,

145

Lonnie Johnson and numerous R&B acts, together with Moon Mullican, Cowboy Copas and many of the company's C&W artists. He also helped Nathan design an echo-chamber, and worked on many other business projects with him. Glover became a prolific songwriter, often collaborating with Lois Mann, and was shrewd enough to get full copyright protection on his material including the now standard 'Drown In My Own Tears' and the Midnighters' infamous 'Annie Had A Baby'. He recorded acts like John Lee Hooker, Roy Brown, Little Willie John and Wynonie Harris before moving to Roulette on its inception in 1956. Here he began a further fruitful songwriting partnership with his co-director Morris Levy, also handling production/arranging duties, and was responsible for a vast amount of material by Dave Cortez, Essex, Joey Dee (he co-wrote the million-selling 'Peppermint Twist'), Sam and Dave, etc. before returning to King in 1963, where he has remained since, attaining the vice-presidency before the Leiber/Stoller/Neely combine bought the company, now Tennessee Recording and Publishing Co.

Gerry Goffin and Carole King (then his wife) were the most versatile and successful songwriting team in America during the early Sixties. Goffin was chiefly a lyricist: his flair and directness is illustrated on everything from their first big hit 'Will You Love Me Tomorrow' by the Shirelles, to songs such as 'Goin' Back', written shortly before the team split. Most of their success was under the Nevins-Kirschner-Colgems umbrella, where they worked at the Brill Building 1819 Broadway, NY 10022) together with several other contemporary writers. After their divorce, Goffin's career wavered. A couple of unsuccessful solo albums and only the odd hit (such as Gladys Knight's 'Imagination', penned with Barry Goldberg) indicated that his vast talent remained.

George Goldner, from Manhattan, was a mambo teacher with a string of dance halls in New York in the late Forties. Not unsurprisingly, Tico, his first label, specializing in Latin-

American music and had a roster which included Tito Puente and Machito. Increasing black interest in the mambo craze led Goldner to form Rama, his first R&B label, and following the success of the Orioles' 'Crying In The Chapel' in 1953, he realized that a great many black vocal groups could also 'go pop' if they were produced with the white audience in mind. Accordingly, with Joe Kolsky and, later, Richard Barrett, Goldner began to scrape groups off the street corners of New York: the Five Budds, the Valentines, the Crows, the Pretenders, the Heartbeats, the Wrens, the Rainbows – groups galore were whisked into rented studios. Their records were inevitably stereotyped, with a jaunty teenage lead tenor, a heavy drumbeat, Jimmy Wright's obligatory tenor saxophone solo and breaks in the simple arrangement where the bass singer could offer his glamorous contribution.

The Crows' recording of 'Gee', long cited as the earliest rock'n'roll record, was the first of his nationally successful discs. Its simplicity – it consisted of little more than 'Gee oh oh oh Gee' over a drumbeat – appealed to white teenagers who were just getting away from Rosemary Clooney and into Alan Freed. Similarly, the phenomenal success of 'Gee' with whites – it never got higher than No. 6 in the R&B charts – suggests that Goldner instructed the Crows to sweeten their delivery for the pop market.

Many of Goldner's acts made the Hot Hundred on the strength of New York sales alone. Others, particularly Frankie Lymon and the Teenagers, became internationally successful manfestations of New York's street-corner sound. The Teenagers – with three Top Twenty hits to their credit and well over three million records sold outside America – were a black/Puerto Rican group. Goldner never worried about creed or colour. Provided you could sing falsetto ballads or hot, impromptu scats, he would give you a chance on one of his numerous labels. Consider this list, most of whom had major hit records: on Gee – the Cleftones, the Heartbeats, the Regents; on Gone – the Channels, Jo Ann Campbell, Ral Donner; on End – the Chantels, Lewis Lymon and

147

the Teenchords, the Flamingos, Little Anthony and the Imperials; on Mark-X – the Isley Brothers, Dickie Goodman; and on Goldisc – the Temptations, the Royaltones. Juanita and Cindy were among Goldner's less successful labels. After heavy gambling, Goldner's interests were acquired by Roulette, for whom he continued to supervise many recording sessions.

In 1964, he joined Leiber and Stoller as president of the hugely successful Red Bird label, and when that was dissolved he gambled another fortune away. In December, 1969, he formed his last label, Firebird, with a view to producing hard rock with a Fifties feel. However, the dream turned sour when he signed a lot of junk, including the Crewcuts, who had had little going for them but their hairstyles in the first place. Goldner died on April 15, 1970, aged 52. Next to Atlantic, he was the most important force in New York rock'n'roll. He was the original Fifties bubblegum king, without a mind for stone blues. Nor was he entirely punctilious over royalty payments, but he cut a lot of wonderful records and did more for integration than the Supreme Court.

Jack Good. The history of British pop music cannot be written without mention of Jack Good who, almost single-handedly, brought it to the British television screen in 1957. Born in London in 1931 and educated at Balliol College, Oxford, Good joined the BBC in 1956 as a trainee. The following year, intrigued by rock'n'roll and the media's fear of it, he devised the legendary *6.5. Special* and apparently hoodwinked the Corporation into letting him produce it by pretending that it was to be a young people's magazine programme. In 1958 Good was wooed across to the commercial network, who gave him *carte blanche* to produce his own show. The result was *Oh Boy!*, arguably British television's shrewdest exploitation of rock music. He then produced, in descending order of popularity, *Boy Meets Girl* (1959) and *Wham!* (1960), but during this time introduced a wealth of

148

new talent to the screen and became a celebrity in his own right as the 'intellectual' of rock.

He saw himself as a star maker through television and, with mixed results, attempted to create images for performers like Cliff Richard and Adam Faith. He also brought a degree of critical intelligence to the British pop press through an incisive weekly column in *Disc*. In 1962, after two years in the doldrums, Good went to America 'for a year'. He stayed for eight during which time he produced *Around The Beatles*, *Shindig* and spectaculars for the Monkees and Andy Williams. He returned to Britain in 1970 to play Othello in his stage musical *Catch My Soul* and, in 1973, wrote and produced an abortive screen version. In 1974, the BBC's series of live concerts featuring the Osmonds was heavily derived from Jack Good and could almost have been produced sixteen years previously.

The Goons first emerged in a BBC radio comedy show which began in 1951 under the name *Crazy People*. The original Goons were Terence (Spike) Milligan, Peter Sellers, Harry Secombe and Michael Bentine who left before the show became *The Goons*. The show added a certain satirical attitude to an already existing tradition of surreal radio comedy. The Goon shows proper of the mid-Fifties incorporated musical interludes by Max Geldray (harmonica) and Ray Ellington's band. Two records released in 1956, 'I'm Walking Backwards For Christmas' and 'Bloodnock's Rock And Roll', reached the British Top Ten and predated later lunacy by the Bonzo Dog Band. Sellers and Secombe have both had individual record successes. In 1973, general nostalgia for things British and old met the new teenybopper market head on to give the Goons a re-issue British Top Ten hit with their 1956 recording of the 'Ying Tong Song'.

Rosco Gordon, a Memphis R&B singer and pianist, helped launch the careers of several top R&B acts besides cutting a string of hit records. During the Forties, Gordon was a popular entertainer in and around Memphis. In 1948 he helped form the Beale Streeters, which included B. B. King on guitar, Johnny Ace on Piano and Earl Forrest on drums. By 1952 the Beale Streeters were signed to Duke and issuing sides under their various names. Gordon later introduced Bobby Bland into the act, offering him encouragement and advice throughout the early years. By this time, Gordon was already recording for Sam Phillips, who leased his first record, 'Booted', to Chess in Chicago. Ike Turner was in charge of the Phillips sessions, and produced many more fine sides for Gordon including the excellent 'No More Doggin'. Gordon sang with near-fury through most of his hits, and was usually supported by a chunky backing band with a growling tenor sax. He eventually switched to Vee Jay and cut his most famous hit, 'Just A Little Bit', which was to be re-recorded by countless British R&B outfits during the early Sixties, even becoming a minor hit for the Liverpool group, the Undertakers.

Gospel Music. Stripped of their cultural heritage through slavery, the early Afro-Americans found the Church the only institution able to explain and mollify their new position. The simple life-after-death theology, delivered through parable preaching and inspirational singing, enabled the Black Churches to flourish through the 19th century. They 'Africanized' the early Anglican hymns in aural transmission, transmuting and reassembling them into the Negro Spirituals – the call and unison response of 'Swing Low, Sweet Chariot', the long sustained melody of 'Nobody Knows The Trouble' and the syncopated claprhythmic 'Shout All Over God's Heaven'.

The early 20th century upsurge of fundamental, sanctified and holiness churches in the dehumanizing industrial ghettos brought ecstatic, testifying shouts, holy dancing and musical instruments into church music. Reflecting this, the pre-depression recording boom waxed a wide range of styles of religious material, from Rev. J. M. Gates' short sermons and answering congregation, to the piano-playing evangelist singer, Arizona Dranes, to the religious blues of guitarist

150

Blind Willie Johnson and the ruggedly harmonised versions of the spirituals by Jubilee Quartets like the Golden Gate and the Norfolk Quartets.

In the Thirties, traditional spirituals were supplanted by new gospel material. Earlier, Rev. Charles A. Tindley had published 'Stand By Me' and 'Understand It Better By and By' and Lucie Campbell produced 'Something Within Me' and 'In The Upper Room', but Thomas A. Dorsey (*aka* Georgia Tom) is regarded as the Father of Gospel Music. In 1932, he co-founded the National Convention of Gospel Singers which promoted the spread of material like his own 'Precious Lord' and 'Peace In The Valley'. With performers like Sallie Martin, Roberta Martin and Mahalia Jackson pushing them, the sentimental, optimistic blue-note ridden gospel numbers swept the nation, finding white acceptance through artists like Red Foley and the Stamps-Baxter Quartet. Though Mahalia was the 'Gospel Queen', others were important. Willie Mae Ford Smith, an instructress at Dorsey's Conventions, taught many younger singers, like Brother Joe May, the improvising slurs, note bending and rephrasing techniques of gospel, while Sister Rosetta Tharpe took the gospelly blues 'This Train' into the race charts.

The golden age for gospel began in 1945. New independent recording labels like Apollo, King and Specialty prospered issuing gospel material, radio stations featured early morning and Sunday gospel shows and the gospel highway of one-night theatre stands, church benefits and anniversary programmes, was thick with travelling groups. Run by matriarch Gertrude, the Famous Ward Singers, who used daughter Clara's arrangements, Marion Williams' solos and Rev. W. Herbert Brewster's material like 'Move On Up A Little Higher' and their rivals, Albertina Walker's Caravans, who nurtured current solo stars including Shirley Caesar, Inez Andrews, Dorothy Norwood, and, more briefly, James Cleveland and Bessie Griffin, featured strong emotional lead singers in front of imaginative background harmonies, usually accompanied by simple piano or organ lines. Clara Ward exerted a considerable stylistic influence on the young

Aretha Franklin, whose first recordings were made in her father's (Rev. C. L. Franklin) New Bethel Church.

Others, like the Consolers with ethereal guitar and organ-backed versions of 'heart warming spiritual hymns' like 'Waiting For My Child' and the early Staple Singers, of the hillbilly harmony 'Will The Circle Be Unbroken', appealed more to southern audiences.

Male acappella 'quartets' were also developing. Using gospel material and a second tenor to complete the four part harmony behind the high clear tenor voice of Rebert Harris, the Soul Stirrers gave gospel and—through Sam Cooke—soul music, one of its lasting styles. Likewise, the contrast of Claude Jeter's falsetto and the harsh shouter leads of the Swan Silvertones presaged the Temptations, while the devil-demolishing ecstatic screams of the Five Blind Boys' Archie Brownlee were picked up by the young James Brown, whose stage movements could be a parody of the frenzied movement of Ira Tucker of the Dixie Hummingbirds.

The end of acappella came with the addition of guitarists, like Howard Carroll of the Dixie Hummingbirds, and in the Sixties popular groups like the Mighty Clouds Of Joy and the Violinaires used falsetto harmony behind the preaching lead voices of Joe Ligon and Robert Blair respectively. Now the instrumentation of gospel groups can be as full as soul groups, enabling the Rance Allen Group to rework secular hits, alongside the smooth jubilee hymns of the Harmonising Four or the cool sophisticated homophonic Voices-Supreme.

James Cleveland's 'Love Of God' with the Voices Of Tabernacle and 'Peace Be Still' with the Angelic Choir in the Sixties ushered in the era of choirs and soloists, with his Gospel Music Convention promoting large interdenominational choirs, and the surprising pop success of the Edwin Hawkins Singers' 'Oh Happy Day'.

Charlie Gracie, born on May 14, 1936, in Philadelphia, as Charles Graci, first recorded rockabilly for Cadillac and 20th Century in 1953–6 with limited success. In 1957, 'Butterfly' made the Top Ten on Cameo. An enormously commercial piece of rock'n'roll, it was written by Bernie Lowe and Kalmann, and credited to the producer of *American Bandstand*, Tony Mammarella, under the pseudonym of Anthony September. Other big sellers, 'Fabulous', 'I Love You So Much It Hurts' and, in Britain, 'Wanderin' Eyes', led to a part in *Disc Jockey Jamboree*. One of the few rock'n' rollers to be praised by *The Times* of London, much was made of the fact that Gracie was a proficient guitarist. He subsequently recorded for Coral, Roulette, Felsted, President, Diamond and, in 1968, Sock'n'Soul, but he has never made an album, and some sort of re-packaging of his singles is long overdue.

Billy Grammer came up through C&W as a valued lead guitarist in the bands of Clyde Moody and Jimmy Dean, and developed into a successful vocalist and songwriter. Born August 28, 1925 in Benton, Illinois, he started in C&W radio in Washington in 1949. In 1959 his Monument recording 'Gotta Travel On' became an enormous American hit (selling a million copies) and several lesser pop and C&W hits followed. He has recorded also for Decca, Rice, and Epic and gained a nationally networked TV show. Among his many successful songs are 'I Wanna Go Home', 'Jesus Was A Soul Man' and 'Bonaparte's Retreat'.

Howie Greenfield, best known for his long partnership with Neil Sedaka, was one of the original members of Don Kirschner's Brill Building organization. A lyricist with a strong penchant for the mythology of teen romance – his favourite images seemed to be of stairways-to-heaven, girl-next-door-falling-for-boy-next-door, and sixteenth birthdays – Greenfield supplied the words to sixteen hits, seven of which Sedaka himself took into the charts. Arguably his best effort, though, was 'Crying In The Rain' which he wrote in collaboration with Carole King and which became a Top Ten hit for the Everly Brothers, one of the most lucid expressions of teenage heartache ever written. In 1972, he and Sedaka parted company temporarily and wrote 'Our Last Song Together' which, with its references to 'days of devils, kings and clowns', provided an appropriate tribute to one of pop's most productive relationships.

Ellie Greenwich, born on Long Island, New York in 1940, first recorded unsuccessfully for RCA in the late Fifties, as Ellie Gay, and played local dance hops. In 1960, she majored in English at college and worked as a teacher for a short spell before breaking into the songwriting field by co-writing (with Tony Powers) 'This Is It' for Jay and the Americans and 'He's Got The Power' for the Exciters. In 1963, she began co-writing with her boyfriend, Jeff Barry, and, working in close alliance with producer Phil Spector, they notched up a series of hits by the Ronettes, the Crystals and Bob B. Soxx. Drifting away from Spector in 1964, Greenwich and Barry were responsible for 80 per cent of the Red Bird label's early output, including such hits as 'Chapel Of Love' and 'Goodnight Baby', and, during 1965–7, they performed a similar role for Bert Bern's Bang label, where they produced Neil Diamond. In the late Sixties, Greenwich and Barry were divorced and she retired temporarily before attempting a comeback as a singer-songwriter with an album on Verve in 1973.

Frank Guida, a record shop owner who branched out temporarily into record production in the early Sixties, achieved ten consecutive hits (including three million-sellers) in three years with a sound so radical that the records created attention by that virtue alone.

Born in New York of Italian heritage, Guida moved to Portsmouth, Virginia, in the early Fifties and opened 'Frankie's Birdland' which soon became Virginia's leading R&B record shop. Looking to expand, Guida formed Legrand records and recorded former Gene Vincent Bluecap, Tommy Facenda, singing 'High School USA', a novelty record which reached the Top Thirty in America in 1959. In 1960, he began recording Gary US Bonds in the back of his record shop where the poor acoustics and barely adequate equipment, combined with primitive phasing and tape-echo techniques, resulted in a synthetic 'live' effect with Bonds yelling above a muzzy, distorted background of voices and thumping rhythms. Although Guida had problems convincing his own distributor that his records were not recorded in a toilet, Bonds' hits, 'New Orleans', 'Quarter To Three', 'Twist Twist Señora' and 'School Is Out', had a great influence on English beat groups and, it is said, on Phil Spector's production techniques.

When Bonds' sound began to pall, Guida formed a subsidiary, SPQR, on which 'Twistin' Mathilda' by Jimmy Soul made the Top Thirty early in 1962. A year later, Soul scored again with the infectious 'If You Wanna' Be Happy', an American No. 1 and million-seller. Beatlemania effectively ended Guida's run of hits, but he still runs several record shops and releases occasional records on Peanut County.

Guitar Slim. Born in Greenwood, Mississippi on Dec 10, 1926, Eddie 'Guitar Slim' Jones was responsible for the biggest blues record of 1954, the passionate, soul-flecked 'The Things That I Used To Do'. A genuine blues standard, it was cut in New Orleans for Specialty, with Ray Charles on piano. Jones had previously recorded for Imperial and Bullet during 1951–2, but moved to Atco before his death in New York on Feb. 7, 1959. He was held in awe by fellow New Orleans musicians who envied his spectacular stage act.

Bill Haley, born William John Clifton Haley at Highland Park, a Detroit suburb, on July 6, 1925, spent a decade in obscurity before finally finding fame in the mid-Fifties as the first idol of the rock'n'roll era.

When Haley was four, his parents – both musical – moved to Booth-Winn, Pennsylvania, where they bought and ran a farm. As a teenager, Haley attempted to launch himself as a hillbilly act in local fairs and amusement parks. He played guitar for two years with Cousin Lee's band in Booth-Winn during the early Forties, made his first solo record, 'Candy Kisses' at 18 in 1945, and spent the next four years on the road with various obscure cowboy bands. While Haley had been on the road, a small radio station, WPWA, had been built in Chester, Pennsylvania, adjacent to Booth-Winn. In 1949, Haley returned home, worked as a deejay at WPWA and formed his own band – the Four Aces Of Western Swing – who broadcast regularly from the station. During the late Forties, he cut several more hillbilly records for small labels (including one for Atlantic) before signing, in 1950, with Essex, a small Philadelphia label owned by Dave Miller.

In 1951, Haley covered Jackie Brenston's R&B hit 'Rocket 88' in an aggressive rockabilly style. Released on an Essex subsidiary, Holiday, it sold a meagre 10,000 copies but Haley's next record, 'Rock The Joint', another cover of an R&B song, sold about 75,000 on Essex. Between these formative rock efforts, however, Haley recorded a variety of unsuccessful hillbilly songs in 1952. Finally in 1952, Bill Haley's Saddlemen – as the group was then known – dropped its hillbilly image and became Bill Haley and the Comets. Then in 1953, the group – John Grande, Billy Williamson, Rudy Pompelli, Al Reed, Francis Beecher and Don Raymond – cut the pacy 'Crazy Man Crazy', a Haley original which reached the national charts. This record crystallized the driving dance-band style for which Haley would later become famous.

Despite Haley's successes, however, Dave Miller tended to neglect him in favour of more popular orchestral recordings by another Essex artist, Monte Kelly, and in 1954 Haley's manager, Dave Myers, took him to New York following the Essex deal and accepted an attractive offer from Decca. At his first Decca session on April 12, 1954, Haley recorded 'Rock Around The Clock' as a favour to Myers who had co-written and published it some eighteen months earlier when Sunny Dae had recorded it. The Milt Gabler-produced record sold moderately well but Haley's follow-up, 'Shake, Rattle And Roll' (a dilution of Joe Turner's original) reached the Top Ten in both Britain and America and eventually sold a million. This prompted Decca to re-release 'Clock', which also sold a million and was included in the opening sequences of *The Blackboard Jungle*, a 1955 film

156

about juvenile delinquents. Partly through the film's influence and partly because public tastes were rapidly changing, 'Rock Around The Clock' turned into an instant youth anthem and Haley's Comets – at best a driving little C&W dance band – became unlikely cult figures for the new rock generation.

Between 1955 and mid-1956, Haley was the biggest rock attraction in the world and he notched up twelve hits including 'Burn That Candle', 'See You Later Alligator', 'R-O-C-K', 'Hot Dog Buddy Buddy' and 'Rudy's Rock'. It must be said, however, that in chart terms Haley was infinitely more popular in Britain where he had no opposition, than in his home country where only five of his records reached the Top Twenty. Up to March, 1957, every record released by Brunswick in Britain reached the Top Twenty and in February, 1957, Haley arrived in Britain to a tumultuous welcome. He rode from Southampton to London in state on the Bill Haley Special, a train laid on for him by the *Daily Mirror* newspaper and, at Waterloo, he was met by three thousand cheering fans, many of whom had waited all day. Someone christened the event 'The Second Battle of Waterloo'.

Despite the triumph, Haley's British tour also proved to be his undoing, for audiences saw him as he really was – chubby, married and rather sedate, not the sort of figurehead on which the new generation based their fantasies. He had starred in two Hollywood exploitation films, *Rock Around The Clock* and *Don't Knock The Rock* and they did well at the box-office but by 1958 it was over for him. He had an American comeback hit that year with 'Skinnie Minnie', but passed into the nostalgia category as an entertainer.

Always very popular in Britain, he makes periodic visits there and receives the sort of coverage in the national press which is normally reserved for contemporary stars. Although it is generally assumed that the rise of Elvis Presley and Haley's own reluctance to digress from his basic dance-hall style contributed to his demise, time has shown that Haley simply knew his limitations and stuck to them.

George Hamilton IV, born in Salem, North Carolina on July 19, 1937, became a teen idol at the age of 19 with the success of 'A Rose And A Baby Ruth' on ABC Records and continued recording in the same mode – 'Only One Love', 'High School Romance', 'Why Don't They Understand' – with declining success. However, he had always had a leaning towards country music and in 1961 he joined RCA Victor and the cast of WSM's *Grand Ole Opry* in Nashville. Never very successful with 'country' songs, he found a role for himself as Nashville's country/folk singer, recording songs by writers as different as John Hartford, John D. Loudermilk and even Leonard Cohen. He had a Top Twenty hit with 'Abilene' in 1963, but when his career sagged in the late Sixties, he came to Britain and allowed himself to be appointed 'Mr. Country Music' by the BBC for whom he fronted a series of television shows featuring local talent and the least adventurous of Nashville's performers. He now spends most of his time in Europe where he is still popular.

Roy Hamilton, born April 16, 1929, in Leesburg, Georgia, moved to Jersey City where he sang with the Searchlight Gospel Singers in 1948. Local deejay Bill Cook became his manager and obtained a contract with Epic, for whom Hamilton topped the R&B chart with 'You'll Never Walk Alone' in 1954. His fame was instantaneous, audiences regularly storming the stage when he appeared. Other Top Ten records – 'If I Loved You', 'Ebbtide', 'Hurt' and 'Unchaned Melody' (the best-selling R&B disc of 1955) – were among the vehicles for his powerful, near-operatic baritone. He strongly influenced the Righteous Brothers, who cut two of his hits. Hamilton also excelled on secularized gospel songs, enjoying hits with 'Don't Let Go' (No. 13 in 1958) and the vibrant 'You Can Have Her' (No. 12 in 1961). But chart success eluded him on later records for MGM, RCA and AGP. He died from a heart attack in 1969.

The Harptones, Willie Winfield (lead tenor), Nicky Clark, Bill Dempsey (second tenors), Bill Galloway (baritone),

Bill Brown (bass) and arranger/pianist Raoul Cita, were formed in 1953 when they recorded 14 sides from Bruce in New York. These tracks, including the classic 'Sunday Kind Of Love' and Cita compositions like 'Memories Of You' remain highly regarded in doo-wop circles despite their lack of chart success. With various changes – other members included Curtis Cherebin, Bobby Spencer and Jimmy Beckum – the group continued recording until 1964. Their discs were on Paradise ('Life Is But A Dream'), Andrea, Tip Top, Rama ('The Masquerade Is Over'), Gee, Warwick, Coed, Cub, Companion ('What Will I Tell My Heart' – their only Hot Hundred entry) and K.T.

Jet Harris and **Tony Meehan** were possibly the first example of a trend that by the end of the Sixties was to become widespread. First Jet Harris (who had some chart success on his own with 'The Theme From The Man With The Golden Arm' in 1962) and then Tony Meehan left the Shadows to develop their musical talents rather than remain in the rut of touring. They existed more as a friendly business relationship rather than a group, and released three phenomenally successful Decca singles in 1963, all in the Shadows mould – 'Diamonds', 'Scarlet O'Hara' and 'Applejack'. Meehan went on to produce records for Decca and Harris faded out of sight after a series of mishaps.

Thurston Harris, a plangent tenor, sang lead with the Lamplighters – Willie Rockwell, Alfred Frazier, Matt Nelson and himself – on a dozen singles for Federal before joining Aladdin where a cover of Bobby Day's 'Little Bitty Pretty One' – with a re-shuffled group, the Sharps – made the Top Ten in 1957. Other exceptionally good rock'n'roll singles included, 'Do What You Did' (No. 57), 'Over And Over' (No. 96), the furious 'Be Baba Leba' and 'Runk Bunk', covered in Britain by Adam Faith. Harris subsequently recorded for Cub, Dot and, in 1963, Reprise, while members of the Lamplighters/Sharps formed the nucleus of the Rivingtons.

Wynonie Harris, born in Omaha, Nebraska in 1915, started his life in music as a drummer, then became a dancer and finally, about 1940, a blues singer. He first became known as a vocalist with Lucky Millinder's band with which he recorded in 1944. By 1945, he was recording solo in Hollywood with bands led by Johnny Otis, Jack McVea, Oscar Pettiford and Illinois Jacquet. His real success started in 1947 when he joined King and made a series of records which had pop as well as jazz/R&B appeal, including 'Good Morning Judge', 'Lovin' Machine', 'All She Wants To Do Is Rock' and his fondly remembered 1955 British hit, 'Bloodshot Eyes'. By the late Fifties, however, Harris had faded from the scene and did not record again. He was a rousing, humorous, slick performer who shouted his lyrics with an infectious spirit. He died, aged 54, in Los Angeles, in 1969.

Wilbert Harrison, a truly original but often underrated R&B talent, was born on Jan. 6, 1929 in North Carolina. He first recorded on Rockin ('This Woman Of Mine') and De Luxe in Miami during the early Fifties, and followed with records on Savoy. In 1959, 'Kansas City' – a hypnotic revival of the Leiber and Stoller blues, for Fury – reached No. 1, but, as always, Harrison moved from one small uncaring label to another: Seahorn, Neptune, Doc, Port, Vest. Unable to afford sidemen, he turned eventually to a one-man band format and scored with 'Let's Work Together', a Top Forty hit on Sue in 1969. An album of the same name received critical acclaim in 1970. Harrison's work has a breadth and inventiveness at which his sporadic hits can only hint; unaffected by his limited success, he remains undeniably authentic but never tedious. Recent discs for Buddah, Hotline and Brunswick continue to couple his idiosyncratic diction with the exuberance of vintage R&B.

Dale Hawkins, born on Aug. 22, 1938 in Goldmine, Louisiana, as Delmar Allen Hawkins, was among the first group of rockabilly singers to reach the pop charts, with 'Susie Q' (Checker), which entered the Top Thirty in 1957. The fusion of a raunchy black beat (he had heard a similar blues by Howlin' Wolf), white country picking and the unorthodox use of a cowbell resulted in a fine snappy style. Other Checker singles were less popular, but no less authentic. 'My Babe', 'Class Cutter', 'Liza Jane' and 'La Do Da Da' were studded with bursts of frantic energy, often featuring innovatory guitar work from Kenny Paulsen, Roy Buchanan, Scotty Moore or James Burton. In 1961, Hawkins left Checker to record for Tilt, Zonk, Atlantic, Roulette and ABC-Paramount. In the late Sixties, he produced hits for Bruce Channel and the Five Americans.

Ronnie Hawkins, who has a not wholly unjustified reputation as the last of the original rock'n'rollers, is now a successful club owner and TV star in Canada. More important, perhaps, his band, the Hawks, once included Levon Helm and Robbie Robertson and formed the basis of the Band. Hawkins was born on Jan. 10, 1935 in Huntsville, Arkansas, and formed his first C&W band of Hawks in 1952 at the University of Arkansas. By early 1957, he was in Memphis auditioning rockabilly for Sun. Unsucessfully on this occasion, he developed an intense rock'n'roll style and was a capable rock singer with a strong voice who favoured a semi-screaming style at times. In 1957 he moved to Toronto and Quality Records, recording 'Bo Diddley', whose beat Hawkins often utilised. In 1959 he joined Roulette and enjoyed hits with 'Forty Days', 'Mary Lou' and others which were mostly powerful rockers in a soft rock era. In 1963, his classic version of Bo Diddley's 'Who Do You Love' employed almost psychedelic lead guitar work from Robertson. He recorded on his own Hawk label in the mid-Sixties before appearing on Atlantic with a tight Muscle Shoals back-up in 1969 and joining Monument in 1972.

Screamin' Jay Hawkins. With gaudy coustumes, an outlandish stage act, and a series of bizarre recordings, Hawkins achieved brief success but lasting notoriety as rock'n'roll's weirdest offspring. Born in Cleveland, Ohio, in 1929, he first worked as pianist/singer with Tiny Grimes, Lynn Hope, and other name R&B bands before launching a solo career in 1953. Records on Timely, Mercury, Wing, and Grand displayed his talent for wryly humorous lyrics, but it was 'I Put A Spell On You' (Okeh) in 1956 that became his most famous performance, completing his reputation as a voodoo man. Trapped by the image, he has spent the rest of his career label-hopping from obscure (Enrica, Providence, Queen Bee) to major (Decca, Philips, RCA) companies, trying to re-create that success. Equally powerful records, 'I Hear Voices' (1962), 'Poor Folks' (1965), 'Feast Of The Mau Mau' (1967), and several hit cover-versions of 'Spell' have so far failed to attract modern audiences to his unique brand of macabre theatre which influenced Arthur Brown.

Clarence 'Frogman' Henry was born in Algiers, New Orleans, on March 19, 1937, and after dabbling in music at high school, he became an overnight star in 1957 when his novelty rock'n'roll number, 'Aint Got No Home' (where he imitated frog noises), was a No. 30 hit on Argo. For a while it looked as if he was a one-hit wonder but he came back again in 1961 with Bobby Charles' composition 'But I Do', a compulsive slice of New Orleans R&B produced by Paul Gayten and Allen Toussaint which reached No. 4 spot in the charts. He consolidated this success with a series of minor hits in the early Sixties, and today is one of the few artists still putting down 'oldies but goodies' R&B in the clubs of New Orleans.

Al Hibbler. Born blind on Aug. 16, 1915, in Little Rock, Arkansis, he rose to fame as a vocalist with the bands of Dub Jenkins, Jay McShann and, from 1943–51, Duke Ellington who described Hibbler's unusually distorted style as 'tonal pantomime'. After R&B hits with 'Trees' (on Miracle in 1948), 'Danny Boy' (on Atlantic in 1951) and 'What Will I Tell My Heart' (on Chess in 1951), Hibbler switched to popular balladeering and remained on the pop charts until the mid-Fifties with Top Thirty hits like 'Unchained Melody' – from the film *Unchained* – 'He' and 'After The Lights

Go Down', all on Decca. He also recorded for Verve, Columbia, Argo and Score.

Jessie Hill was shot from the ghettos of New Orleans into the national spotlight when 'Ooh Poo Pah Doo' was a No. 28 hit on the Minit label in April 1960. With the use of call-and-response devices much loved by Ray Charles, the record had a raw wildness and latent power which time has not dissipated. Despite the presence of producer Allen Toussaint, Hill was unable to repeat this commercial success in a fine series of releases on Minit and in 1963 he left New Orleans for the West Coast. In California he teamed up with several exiled musicians from New Orleans including Dr. John, and cut several singles and an album for Blue Thumb in 1970.

Eddie Hodges, born on March 5, 1947, in Hattiesburg, Mississippi, moved to New York, where he appeared in the Broadway musical, *The Music Man*. Appearances in TV serials (*Name That Tune*) led to a starring role as Frank Sinatra's son in *A Hole In The Head* and a hit record, 'High Hopes'. In 1961, Hodges was signed to Cadence and his 'I'm Gonna Knock On Your Door' and 'Girls, Girls, Girls Are Made To Love' both made the Top Twenty in 1961 and 1962 respectively. His kiddie tenor delighted sub-teen listeners and infuriated others. He also cut the original version of the Brook Brothers' British hit, 'Ain't Gonna Wash For A Week' and returned to the charts for the last time with a revival of US Bonds' 'New Orleans' on Aurora in 1965.

Buddy Holly was born on Sept. 7, 1936, in Lubbock, Texas, and christened Charles Hardin Holley. Lubbock's geographical position meant that Holly would have heard hillbilly, Mexican and black music on the radio during his formative years; this cosmopolitan musical background was to prove vital to the versatility he later displayed in his own work.

As a youngster he took up the violin, but soon changed to

guitar. He showed an early interest in C&W, and while still at school had his own show on KDAV, the local radio station. He was partnered by Bob Montgomery, and in 1954 they made some hillbilly demo records which were posthumously issued as *Holly in the Hills*. Together with bass-player Larry Welborn, Buddy and Bob would sometimes fill the 'local talent' spot when travelling package shows visited the area. As a result of this exposure, and with help from KDAV disc-jockey Dave Stone, Nashville agent Eddie Crandall and publisher Jim Denny, Buddy Holly was signed to Decca in 1956 to cut some singles in Nashville. Two were released without success, and before his contract with Decca was up Holly was beginning to look elsewhere, guessing that the option would not be renewed.

Although Decca handled Holly rather insensitively (i.e. no more nor less off-handedly than any other bright young hopeful) these early sessions did produce at least two Holly classics, 'Midnight Shift' and 'Rock Around With Ollie Vee', and Holly worked with musicians like Sonny Curtis and Jerry Allison who were later to be involved in the Crickets. The tapes were eventually issued as *That'll Be The Day*. Allison and Holly had been schoolfriends, and had often played together as a drum/guitar duo. The limitations of this line-up helped forge their style; the smooth switch from rhythm to lead in Buddy's guitar-playing, the versatility of Jerry's drumming. In 1955, when the two started playing together professionally, it was still unusual to find drums in a country line-up.

Soon after his last Decca session, Holly started working at Norman Petty's studio in Clovis, New Mexico. Petty, who was also a middle-of-the-road band leader, was a pioneer of the small, independent recording studio; he was also unusual in that he charged per song rather than per hour, which put less pressure on musicians. Holly, Allison and Welborn, together with a vocal quartet which included Cricket-to-be Niki Sullivan, recorded 'That'll Be The Day' and 'I'm Looking For Someone To Love' in February, 1957. Petty first submitted the songs to Roulette in New York, since they had

164

already had hits originating from his studio with Buddy Knox and Jimmy Bowen. They weren't interested, but Holly and the Crickets were soon signed by Coral. The record made No. 3 in America and No. 1 in Britain, and was followed with almost equal success by 'Oh Boy'/'Not Fade Away'. By this time, Joe Mauldin had become the Crickets' bass-player, with Niki Sullivan on rhythm guitar.

Before long Petty, who had quickly assumed a managerial position, began to record Holly solo as well as with the Crickets, though the musicians were often the same. Holly's first hit under his own name was 'Peggy Sue', late in 1957, followed in Britain by 'Listen To Me' and in both countries by 'Rave On' and the Bobby Darin number 'Early In The Morning' (by which time, mid-1958, Holly had begun to record in New York without the Crickets as well as in Clovis).

After a British tour with the Crickets in that year, Holly married Maria Elena Santiago and moved to New York. The rest of the Crickets didn't want to make the move and so split from Holly. This was probably inevitable. Petty was trying to broaden Holly's career and one of the first results was to record him with the Dick Jacobs Orchestra (notably 'It Doesn't Matter Anymore'). Holly's backing group on live dates at this time included Tommy Allsup, whom he had brought into the Crickets earlier to play lead guitar (it is a mistake to assume that Holly fulfilled this role on all his records). Other notable musicians with whom Holly worked at this time were saxophonist King Curtis, and the young Waylon Jennings, whose first solo record, 'Jole Blon', was produced by Buddy Holly.

Early in 1959, Holly's career was at a crossroads. In spite of the significant early impact both with the Crickets and as a solo performer, in spite of his own single-minded attitude towards success and the attempts he was making to create the basis for a long career, there was little in strict commercial terms to suggest (except with hindsight) that he was any different from many other rock performers of the time. It is, of course, inconceivable that, had he lived, he would not have risen further from the pack and still be accorded the respect that his prolific few years have so justly earned for him. He died on February 3, 1959, together with Ritchie Valens and the Big Bopper soon after taking off from Mason City airport in Iowa, *en route* between package-tour concerts in Clear Lake and Fargo. His current record, 'Heartbeat', was barely making an impact on the Hot Hundred.

The first posthumous release, 'It Doesn't Matter Anymore'/'Raining In My Heart', was a huge hit in both America and Britain. And in Britain a series of processed tapes put out by Norman Petty kept him in the charts until the mid-Sixties, while an album of his best-known tracks was still in the Top Ten of the budget-price charts ten years earlier.

Buddy Holly said 'We owe it all to Elvis'. Countless stars of the Sixties owe a similar debt to Holly. He was one of the two great singer/songwriter/musicians of the pop Fifties (the other being Chuck Berry). He was a pioneer of the subsequently-standard two guitars/bass/drums line-up, and of double-tracking. Almost anything that a pop song can say was said by the twenty-two-year-old Buddy Holly nearly two decades ago.

Lightnin' Hopkins is many people's idea of what a blues-singer should be: an endlessly inventive folk-poet, whose imagination is touched by almost everything but whose singing and playing express nothing but the blues. And this, despite nearly 30 years of performing and recording, and all the pressures that might have made him something else, he unswervingly has been. But he has not, outside his own community, been very obviously influential on either American or British rock; his blues, sung by others, are not self-sustaining, as many of the Chicagoans' are.

His early recordings, in the Forties and Fifties, were characterised by thunderous amplification – as any number of reissues demonstrate – but his first ventures into a different market, with acoustic guitar, compensate in subtlety for what they lose in force (e.g. the Folkways and some Bluesville albums). Later sessions placed him with accompanying groups, rarely successfully, though his album for Jewel is an exception. Through all these records he balances slow blues with vivid boogies, occasionally leaving his guitar to essay an idiosyncratic piano style.

Born in Centerville, Texas, in 1912, he spent most of his life in Houston, and his refusal to extract himself from that milieu is the chief reason for his undiminished authenticity as an observer, through the blues, of black life.

Johnny Horton was killed in a Texas automobile crash in November, 1960, at the height of his popularity following a string of pop hits with country-based story and saga songs like 'Springtime In Alaska', 'North To Alaska', 'Battle Of New Orleans' and 'Sink The Bismarck'. Despite the wide appeal of these songs' lyrical content, he retained many elements of conventional acoustic country instrumentation and was, in retrospect, a significant artist in breaking down the rigid categorisation of country and popular singers.

Born in Tyler, Texas, April 30, 1927, Horton started his career under the title of the 'Singing Fisherman' on KLTV, Tyler, and graduated in 1948 to a starring spot on Shreveport's KWKH C&W shows with Hank Williams and Jim Reeves. He recorded first with Mercury and Dot before successfully transferring to Columbia, gaining rockabilly-influenced C&W hits on 'Honky Tonk Man' and 'Honky Tonk Hardwood Floor', prior to his success in the pop charts.

Hugo and Luigi first gained public acclaim as recording artists when 'Young Abe Lincoln' was a small pop hit on Mercury in 1955. New York Italians, Hugo Peretti and Luigi Creatore moved into exclusive circles in 1957, buying Roulette Records from George Goldner, handling producing and writing duties (they wrote under the pseudonym Mark Markwell), and scoring hits including Jimmy Rodgers' 1957 million-seller 'Falling In Love Again'. In 1959 they left Roulette to Morris Levy and Henry Glover, moving to RCA where they hit as artists ('La Plume De Ma Tante') and also produced material for such as the Isley Brothers (1959 million-seller 'Shout') and Sam Cooke. The duo remained with RCA for some years, producing much of Cooke's hit material, and came to the fore again in 1973 as vice-presidents of Avco Records, where they took over writing and producing for the Stylistics.

Ivory Joe Hunter, born at Kirbyville, Texas, in 1914, was first recorded by Alan Lomax for the Library of Congress in 1933. Moving to Los Angeles, he recorded for a number of small labels, having R&B hits with 'Blues At Sunrise' (on his own label, Ivory) and 'Pretty Mama Blues' (Pacific). In 1947, a King contract resulted in further hits : 'Guess Who', 'Landlord Blues' and 'I Quit My Pretty Mama'. Moving to MGM, Hunter's successes included 'I Almost Lost My Mind' (No. 1, in 1950) and 'I Need You So'.

Having joined Atlantic, Hunter broke into the rock'n'roll market in 1956 with a Top Twenty hit, 'Since I Met You Baby'. His own subsequent discs for Dot, Capitol and Veep sold poorly, but Nat Cole, the Five Keys, Pat Boone and Elvis Presley all did well with his songs. In recent years, Hunter based himself in Nashville where, as a member of the *Grand Ole Opry*, he had hopes of a fresh career in country music, the field with which his soulful blues ballads and understated barrelhouse piano had close affiliations. He died of cancer in a Memphis Hospital, on November 8, 1974.

Brian Hyland, born Nov. 12, 1944, in Queens, New York, was only 15 when his recording of the Paul Vance and Lee Pockriss song, 'Itsy Bitsy Teeny Weeny Yellow Polka Dot Bikini' on Leader went to the top of the Hot Hundred. A gimmick record reminiscent of Paul Evans' 'Seven Little Girls', it was followed by 'Lop-Sided, Overloaded And It Wiggled When I Rode It'. 'Let Me Belong To You' was more successful a year later and in 1962 he had two straight Top Ten entries on ABC, 'Ginny Come Lately' and 'Sealed With A Kiss' – a Top Ten hit again in Britain when re-issued in 1975 – both controlled exercises in teen *angst*. This was the high point of Hyland's career, though he has continued recording with ABC, Philips, Dot – on which he had a TopTwenty hit with the Snuff Garrett-produced and Leon Russell-arranged 'The Joker Went Wild' in 1966 – and Uni, with whom he had his last hit, 'Gypsy Woman' in 1970.

Frank Ifield, in 1962–3, was the most popular British pop balladeer. He was born in Coventry, Warwickshire (on Nov. 30, 1936), emigrated to Australia as a boy, and returned to Britain in 1959. His gimmick was his falsetto, which occasionally broke into a full-scale yodel, and was exploited on a dozen hits, most of which were re-arranged standards ('I Remember You', 'I'm Confessin' ', 'Lovesick Blues' and 'Wayward Wind' were all British No. 1s. However, his personality was weak, a fact established beyond doubt in a flop film, *Up Jumped A Swagman* (1965).

The Impalas, truly an overnight phenomenon, were propelled from a Brooklyn street corner to No. 2 on the charts with 'I'm Sorry, I Ran All The Way Home' on Cub in 1959. This bright, brash novelty, written by Gino Giosasi of Gino and Gina (who had their own hits on Mercury) qualifies as an early example of bubblegum. But black lead singer, Joe Frazier, sang with a punch that rivalled his famed namesake, while the rest of the group – white kids, Richard Wagner, Lenny Renda and Tony Calouchi – harmonised with verve. After a smaller hit, 'Oh, What A Fool', they moved to 20th Century Fox and Checker without success.

Imperial Records was formed in 1947 in Los Angeles by Lew Chudd, a university graduate who dabbled in electronics. Chudd was a businessman first and as a record man he came a poor second. So it took some time for him to get into the hit-record groove. But when he did, he guided Imperial to spectacular success in the Fifties through his vision, drive and energy, and the label became recognized as one of the top independent recording companies. 'Imperial Records promoted records well and was a very, very fine company,'

169

said producer Dave Bartholomew. 'Lew Chudd was on fire, by this I mean he was a terrific worker. He could sell more records in the world than anybody else if he wanted to.'

Chudd had started out recording the West Coast jump blues bands of Charlie Davis, Poison Gardner and King Porter but by this time these sounds were rapidly being ousted by the new rhythm and blues craze, and the early releases did not sell. His luck changed when he met up with New Orleans bandleader, Dave Bartholomew, in Houston in 1949 and talked Bartholomew into producing for him. Although De Luxe Records had been cleaning up in New Orleans the city was wide open for recording talent and the Chudd/Bartholomew team hit the jackpot first time when they signed and recorded the young Fats Domino; his initial release 'The Fat Man' shot into the R&B charts and over the next four years sold enough copies to qualify for a gold record. Domino stayed with Imperial for 14 years and his constant flow of hit platters was primarily responsible for its overall success.

Imperial enjoyed other early New Orleans R&B hits with Jewel King, Archibald and Tommy Ridgley. Lew Chudd also flirted in the hard blues, gospel and C&W markets (turning up another international star in Slim Whitman). However, when Fats Domino started to string his hits together in 1952, Chudd decided to concentrate on the more lucrative R&B field and signed Dave Bartholomew to an exclusive producing contract. Besides Domino, Smiley Lewis, Bobby Mitchell and the Topper and the Spiders were selling well – in the mid-Fifties.

Then along came rock'n'roll and those million-selling Fats Domino records, 'Ain't That A Shame', 'I'm In Love Again', 'Blueberry Hill', 'Blue Monday' and 'I'm Walkin' '; the Fat Man was doing more business than anyone except Elvis Presley. Bartholomew was also churning out further New Orleans hits by Roy Brown and Chris Kenner, and on the West Coast, Ernie Freeman had a Top Twenty hit with 'Raunchy'. By now there was no stopping Imperial and Chudd made another masterstroke when he snapped up young teen-idol, Rick Nelson, from Verve in 1957, giving him a double-headed line-up as every Domino and Nelson release careered up the Hot Hundred charts in the late Fifties.

By the early Sixties, Sandy Nelson was another big-selling star and the bulging coffers were swelled further by the acquisition of the hit-making Minit label of New Orleans. However, rock'n'roll and R&B were starting to run out of steam, and seeing gloomy prospects ahead Chudd felt it was time to cash in his chips. The sale of Imperial to Liberty in 1963 marked the end of the golden era of independent labels.

The Inkspots were once *the* group, the Brown Beatles, and more widely imitated than any other group in the world. Jerry Daniels (lead tenor), Charles Fuqua (second tenor), Deek Watson (baritone) and Orville 'Hoppy' Jones first re-corded for Victor in New York during 1935. In 1939, with Bill Kenny (Daniels' replacement) on 'If I Didn't Care', they dropped jazz'n'jive vocals to concentrate on the ballads of Tin Pan Alley sung in a fairly conventional manner which found favour among a large white audience.

The Inkspots established a pattern followed by black groups ever since. The second tenor, baritone and bass harmonize an accompaniment to the lead – in this case Kenny's ice-smooth choirboy voice. The spoken verses by Jones provide a novelty effect. His was the archetypal 'talking' bass, copied extensively by the Drifters, Coasters *et al.* Presley hoped to sound like all the Inkspots on 'Are You Lonesome Tonight', while Deek Watson's classic composition, 'I Love You For Sentimental Reasons' has been recorded by numerous R&B acts, particularly groups.

Their influence is ubiquitous, even though Jones, Watson and Fuqua are dead and Kenny records only intermittently. The rise of the Inkspots from street-corner concerts as The Percolating Puppies, to global tours and Hollywood films is related by Deek Watson in Lee Stephenson's book *The Story Of The Inkspots*.

Instrumentals in pop have always been of two kinds: dance tunes and melodic or mood pieces, often using strings and often movie themes. With the arrival of rock'n'roll, dance band records of the old kind all but disappeared from the charts, but mood music was still going strong throughout the Fifties and into the Sixties.

The bands of Percy Faith, Billy Vaughn, Don Costa, Frank Chacksfield, Perez Prado, Bert Kaempfert, Henry Mancini and Lawrence Welk all had hits with film themes like 'The Sundowners' or novelty pieces like 'Calcutta', a No. 1 for Welk in 1960. Alongside them were Ferrante and Teicher, playing their piano duets of middlebrow classical music for Middle America. But from 1957, rock'n'roll set the pace for pop instrumentals. Spearheaded by Bill Doggett's 'Honky Tonk', a whole range of boogie-based instrumentalists and groups entered the best-selling lists. The most consistent were Doggett, the two Bills from Memphis (Black and Justis), the novelty sounds of Johnny and the Hurricanes, the pounding drums of Sandy Nelson, the twangy guitar of Duane Eddy and the restrained melodic sound of the Ventures, who represented a dilution of the raw original sounds of rock just as surely as Frankie Avalon or Johnny Tillotson.

Many less successful, but often more exciting, rock'n'roll instrumentalists also made the charts between 1957 and 1962. The veteran New Orleans pianist Paul Gayten had minor hits with 'Nervous Boogie' (1957) and 'The Hunch' (1959), and his compatriot Lee Allen scored with 'Walking With Mr. Lee' in 1958 on Ember. In that year, too, the jazz drummer Cozy Cole took 'Topsy, Part 2' to No. 3 on the Love label. Then there were two raucous saxophone and guitar records, 'Weekend' by the Kingsmen (alias Haley's Comets) on East-West, and 'Poor Boy' by the Royaltones on Jubilee. The important newcomer in 1959 was Dave 'Baby' Cortez, whose record 'The Happy Organ' on Clock went to No. 1. From Detroit, his real name was David Cortez Clowney, and he was born in 1939. He had to wait until 1962 for another big hit, the classic 'Rinky Dink' on Chess. Santo and Johnny (the Farina brothers from New York) created a strange Les Paul-like sound on 'Sleep Walk' and 'Tear Drop', for Canadian-American. But the hard rockers of the year came from Preston Epps ('Bongo Rock' on Original Sound), the Wailers from Seattle ('Tall Cool One' and 'Mau Mau' on Golden Crest), and the Rock-A-Teens, with 'Woo Hoo' on Roulette. The group comprised Vic Mizell, Bill Cook, Bill Smith, Paul Evans, Boo Walker and Eddie Robinson. The record was pure New York garage band rock'n'roll. The following year, 1960, saw the arrival of Nashville-originated instrumental hits from Chet Atkins and Floyd Cramer, whose 'Last Date' on RCA got to No. 2. The Fendermen made an impact with their version of the Jimmie Rodgers classic 'Muleskinner Blues' on Soma. And the Joiner, Arkansas, High School Band got up to No. 53 with 'National City'.

Jazz instrumentals from Cannonball Adderley and the Dave Brubeck Quartet ('Take Five' and 'Unsquare Dance') were a feature of the charts in 1961, and surf music swept in with Dick Dale's 'Let's Go Trippin'' (Deltone), while 'Stick Shift' by the Duals got to No. 25. The Ramrods did the 1949 Vaughn Monroe hit 'Ghost Riders In The Sky' with a girl drummer and lots of bass strings and cattle calls. And Ferrante and Teicher were finally matched by Kokomo's 'Asia Minor', which was topped only in the Roll-Over-Beethoven stakes by B. Bumble and the Stingers 'Nut Rocker' in the following year.

Big Dee Irwin was born on August 4, 1939, in New York. Five years before his 1963 British Top Ten duet with Little Eva, 'Swinging On A Star' Irwin made the American Top Thirty as the lead singer with the Pastels – Richard Tavers, Anthony Thomas and B. J. Willingham – whose lovely ballad, 'Been So Long' was purchased from Mascot by the Chess subsidiary, Argo, in 1957. As a soul singer, Irwin recorded prolifically – with discs on Hull, Bliss, 20th Century, Fairmont, Rotate, Redd-Coach, Imperial, etc. – but he is best known as a writer – under his real name, Defosca Ervin –and more recently as a producer for Ripple.

Mahalia Jackson, though born and raised in New Orleans, her talent really blossomed in Chicago. From 1946 until 1953 she recorded a stream of gospel hits for Apollo. With tastefully simple piano accompaniment from Mildred Falls, and material like 'Move On Up A Little Higher' by Rev. Brewster, 'Prayer Changes Things' by Robert Anderson and 'Dig A Little Deeper' by Kenneth Morris, her powerful natural contralto couldn't be faulted. Moving to Columbia she continued her recording success while becoming a public figure known for her work for the civil rights movement and her reassuring 'We Shall Overcome'.

Wanda Jackson was one of the very few girl singers to achieve an energy and wildness comparable to the rock'n'roll styles of her male contemporaries, and this despite a solid C&W background. Born Wanda Goodman in Maud, Oklahoma, October 20, 1937, she worked on radio KLPR in Oklahoma City from 1952, and in 1953 began recording for Decca. She joined Hank Thompson's successful western-swing band and in 1956 joined Capitol, who saw her as a female Gene Vincent. The raw power and strangled vocalizing on singles like 'Mean Mean Man' were followed by an album *Rockin' With Wanda* and a national pop hit in 1958 with 'Let's Have A Party'. The spirited backings included Vincent's bluecaps, guitarist Roy Clark and pianist Merrill Moore, but by 1961 she had returned to C&W when the ballad 'Right Or Wrong' began a continuing series.

Etta James, born in 1938, in Los Angeles, has a career which falls into four distinct phases – phase one followed her discovery by Johnny Otis while playing San Francisco clubs in the early Fifties. Otis took her under his wing and placed her with the local Modern label, where she had two R&B Top Twenty hits in 1955, 'Roll With Me Henry', an answer-disc to the Midnighters' sexually euphemistic 'Work With Me Annie', and 'Good Rockin' Daddy'. Following these, she spent some four or five years touring with various rock'n'roll

174

shows and recording profusely, but not too successfully, for Modern.

Late 1959 saw her on a show with the Moonglows (Chess Records) in Chicago; she and the group were broke, so Harvey Fuqua (Moonglows' bass singer) recommended Leonard Chess to sign her in return for payment of hotel bills. Chess bought her contract from Modern – thus began phase two. 'All I Could Do Was Cry' was an immediate hit, followed by 18 more over the next four years, including 'At Last', 'Pushover', 'Stop The Wedding', etc., largely searing blues ballads, though 'Pushover', her biggest hit of the time, was a relatively simple teenage beat ballad.

Following a brief lull, phase three began in 1967 with a session at Rick Hall's Muscle Shoals, Alabama studio, from which 'Tell Mama' reached the American Top Thirty and four subsequent discs were progressively smaller hits. Phase four began in 1973 when, after a rehabilitation course following a drug problem, Etta began recording for Chess again, producing a series of critically-acclaimed LPs and making a welcome return to the R&B charts.

Sonny James was born on March 1, 1929 in Hackenburg, Alabama, as James Loden. After working in a dry goods store for a while, he turned to a singing career after a series of singing engagements on Southern radio stations which culminated in a residency on the *Louisiana Hayride* show in 1956, the year of his first chart success on Capitol, 'For Rent', a country Top Twenty record. His next success was 'Young Love' which, though covered by Tab Hunter whose version topped the national charts, none the less sold a million copies and reached No. 2 in the pop charts. His subsequent records for Capitol were unsuccessful in the pop charts but he was rarely out of the country charts, having a string of uninterrupted country No. 1s from 1967–71. In 1972, 'the Southern Gentleman', his voice now much deeper and smoother than the rough but lilting voice of 'Young Love', moved to Columbia with continued success.

The Jaynetts were Mary Sue Wells, Ethel Davis, Ada Ray and Yvonne Bushnell – from New York's Bronx. They first appeared on Zell Sanders J&S label in 1956. However, it wasn't until 1963 that they came to the fore with the driving, hypnotic 'Sally Go 'Round The Roses', a Top Five record on Sanders' Tuff subsidiary, that came complete with a band-track, 'sing along without . . .' flip. Sanders' daughter, Johnnie Louise Richardson – who was also half of Johnnie and Joe of 'Over The Mountain' fame – recorded but didn't perform with the group, which, after a minor hit as the Hearts, 'Dear Abby' disbanded in 1968.

The Jive Five – Eugene Pitt and the Jive Five (Billy Prophet, Richard Harris, Norma Johnson and Jerome Hanna) – made the Top Three with the Joe Rene-arranged 'My True Story' on the King-distributed Beltone label in 1961. Pitt, who wrote the song, made listeners weep with his impassioned cry of teenage *angst*. After less successful discs for Beltone and Sketch, they staged a comeback on United Artists with 'I'm A Happy Man' in 1965 and the wonderful 'Bench In The Park', that sold poorly. In the Seventies, they changed their name to the Jyve Fyve and with fresh personnel (including Casey Spencer, Webster Harris and Johnny Watson) they had some small soul hits on Avco Embassy. Eugene Pitt had previously sung with the Genies whose 'Who's That Knock-in'' was a hit on Shad in 1959.

Little Willie John was born in Camden, Arkansas on Nov. 15, 1937. His first forays into the studio are obscure, but by the age of 16 he had toured with the Paul Williams orchestra and recorded for Prize, Savoy and Rama. In 1955 he joined King, where 14 best-sellers were based on an assurance few teenage singers possessed. The ballads were overwhelmingly sad, with an intensity far deeper than the broken love affairs suggested by the lyrics. His biggest hits (all Top Thirty) included 'Fever', 'Talk To Me' and 'Sleep', all produced by Henry Glover. Few black performers from the Fifties had the authority or the long-term potential of Willie John.

Sunny and the Sunglows, Presley, Peggy Lee, Johnny Preston and many more revived his hits, faithfully copying the arrangements or his vocal inflections. His sister Mable recorded for Stax and joined the Raelettes. He died in Washington State prison on May 26, 1968.

Johnnie and Joe. In 1957, Johnnie Louise Richardson (born on June 29, 1945 in Montgomery, Alabama) and her partner, Joe Rivers (born on March 20, 1937 in Charleston, South Carolina) recorded 'Over The Mountain, Across The Sea' for J&S who leased it to Chess, the label on which it made No. 2 in the Spring of that year. This beautiful and ethereal melody also dented the charts during the oldies revival of 1960–61. It was written by Rex Garvin, a minor league soul artist – with discs on Epic, Scatt, Keynote, Chieftain, Carlton, Tower, and Zorro – chiefly remembered for the discotheque hit 'Sock It To 'Em J. B.' in 1966. Garvin and Zell Sanders, Richardson's mother, also wrote the duo's previous record, 'I'll Be Spinning' which was a minor hit. Richardson made records for Gone, Omega, J&S and Chess, before rejoining Joe Rivers to perform as Johnnie and Joe locally in the Bronx area where they now both live.

Johnny and the Hurricanes. Originally from the Toledo, Ohio area, the band – Johnny Paris (tenor sax), Paul Tesluk (organ), Dave Yorko (guitar), Lionel 'Butch' Mattice (bass) and Don Staczek (drums) – first got together at High School and then played local hops and dances behind a vocalist at Toledo's, Pearson Park. As instrumentalists, they were signed to a management contract early in 1959 by Irving Micahnik and Harry Balk, two Detroit entrepreneurs who placed them with Morty Craft's newly-formed Warwick label.

Their first record, a frantic, exciting dance-disc titled 'Crossfire', reached No. 23 in America in July, 1959, but did not feature the prominent organ-sound for which they became famous. Their follow-up 'Red River Rock' (an adaptation of the traditional 'Red River Valley') reached No. 5 in

America and the British Top Ten, establishing the group internationally. By this time, Bill 'Little Bo' Savitch from the Royaltones had replaced Staczek on drums – not that fans knew it in an era when group members were anonymous faces in photographs. Two more hits, 'Reveille Rock' and 'Beatnik Fly', followed on Warwick before the group switched to Big Top in New York where they continued their run with 'Rocking Goose' (which reached No. 1 in England but only No. 60 in America), 'Ja-Da' and 'Down Yonder' before flopping with 'Old Smokie' and 'Minnesota Fats' in 1962.

The original 1959 line-up had disbanded by 1961, and between 1962–63 the touring line-up underwent constant personnel changes with only leader Johnny Paris remaining static. While the group toured, sessionmen made the records, a precedent which had been established as early as 'Beatnik Fly' in 1959.

Johnny and the Hurricanes were the archetypal Fifties instrumental group, even if they were merely a trademark for a highly marketable sound. In all probability, the group's management profited most from the group's existence since Micahnik and Balk took writer credits (as Tom King and Ira Mack respectively) for most of their early records.

Buddy Johnson, born Woodrow Wilson Johnson on Jan. 10, 1915, in Darlington, South Carolina, moved to New York in 1938. There he recorded for Decca until 1954, and had hits with 'Stop Pretending' (1939), 'They All Say I'm The Biggest Fool' (1946) and 'Because' (1950). Moving to Mercury, his blasting big band arrangements (Johnson's orchestra was immensely popular in the South) provided further hits. Among them were 'I'm Just Your Fool' (1954), 'Upside Your Head' (1955) and 'I Don't Want Nobody' (1956) on which his sister Ella (born in Darlington on June 22, 1923) sang in a coy yet laconic manner. The duo were responsible for the original version of Johnson's blues ballad standard, 'Since I Fell For You'.

Marv Johnson, born on Oct. 15, 1938, in Detroit, first sang with the Serenaders. He went on to score nine consecutive hits between 1959 and 1961, the first rumblings of the new Detroit soul sound. Produced for United Artists by Berry Gordy Jnr., they were both crisper and more frothy than most black pop of the day: in retrospect, the sound was distinctly Motown-like. Girls sang thin, reedy 'bop shoo bops' while a bass singer hummed the kind of 'bottom' at which James Jamieson would later excel. Instantly hummable, 'Come To Me', 'You Got What It Takes', 'I Love The Way You Love' and 'More Than Mountains' (all Top Thirty) hinted at the seductive aura of later Motown classics. Johnson eventually followed his mentor to Tamla-Motown-Gordy, where he scored with 'I Miss You Baby' (1966) and 'I'll Pick A Rose For My Rose' in 1968.

Plas Johnson, the most renowned of West Coast tenor saxophonists, was born on July 21, 1931, in New Orleans, and moved to Los Angeles in the early Fifties where his name soon appeared on every studio wall. Radio Recorders, Bunny Robyn's Master Recorders and the Capitol studios used his services for most of the rock'n'roll records made there between 1955 and 1961. Abrasive and confident but rarely apoplectic, his solos can be heard on records by Thurston Harris, the Coasters, B. B. King, Johnny Otis, Gene Vincent, Duane Eddy, Larry Williams, Bobby Day, Eddie Cochran and the Piltdown Men. With the decline of authentic rock'n'roll, Johnson moved into Hollywood soundtracks – for example, *The Pink Panther* – but returned to session work in the late Sixties when he played on albums by Carole King, Shuggie Otis, Screamin' Jay Hawkins, Maria Muldaur, Marvin Gaye and many others.

Robert Johnson, often cited as the greatest, most expressive and harrowingly poetic blues singer ever to record, remains to this day a figure firmly shrouded in mystery. The only hard fact is that he cut some 29 songs during the years

1936–7. They are all gripping, magnificent performances that stand unrivalled in blues history. These recordings – Johnson's songs and the manner in which they were performed – represent the ultimate flowering of the Mississippi blues style. He died in 1938 at the age of 26, probably as the result of poisoning by a jealous girlfriend. Many rock bands have recorded Johnson's compositions including the Rolling Stones ('Love In Vain'), Cream ('Crossroads' and 'From Four Till Late') and John Mayall's Bluesbreakers ('Dust My Blues' and 'Rambling On My Mind').

Jimmy Jones, born on June 2, 1937 in Birmingham, Alabama, moved to New York in his teens, when he recorded with a number of groups including the Sparks Of Rhythm (Apollo), the Pretenders (Rama Central, Holiday, Whirlin' Disc) and the Savoys (Savoy). Despite later solo discs on Savoy, Arrow and Epic, he was poverty-stricken when Otis Blackwell took him to MGM where he recorded for the company's R&B subsidiary, Cub. 'Handy Man' and 'Good Timin'' (both in the Top Three in 1960) relied chiefly on Jones' falsetto breaks for their appeal. Despite an acrobatic stage act and lesser hits with 'That's When I Cried' and 'I Told You So', Jones was typecast as a novelty singer – and the novelty soon wore off. He later recorded for Vee Jay and Roulette before fading altogether.

Joe Jones, born in New Orleans on August 12, 1926, was an opportunist, if not a great artist, and he had a special talent for acquiring some of the best New Orleans musicians in his band for recording and live dates. He hit gold in 1960 with 'You Talk Too Much', a novelty R&B number which climbed to No. 3 in the charts on Roulette. After a minor hit with 'California Sun' and a fine album, he left New Orleans for New York to concentrate on artist management and for a time had success with two New Orleans acts, Alvin Robinson and the Dixie Cups (who had a No. 1 hit with 'Chapel Of Love' in 1964). He expanded his business interests to later include his own label (Joe Jones) and recording studios.

Louis Jordan. It is slowly becoming realized how far Jordan's popularity in the Forties was to be reflected in the R&B of the Fifties. Born in Brinkley, Arkansas, in 1908, he served a big-band apprenticeship and in 1938 formed his own combo, the Tympany Five, which he fronted as singer and alto saxophonist. For more than a decade this group produced blues, novelty blues and just novelties, making important versions of 'Caldonia' and 'Let The Good Times Roll' and sustaining the insouciance of 'Saturday Night Fish Fry'. Titles like 'School Days' and 'Blue Light Boogie' hint at an influence upon Chuck Berry, and Berry has been quick to admit his debt. Many blues and R&B artists who grew up to Jordan's music have remembered it fondly, and its effect upon early white rock'n'roll was not insignificant. The album *Let The Good Times Roll* (Decca) is a just sample of this exuberant music. Louis Jordan died in 1975.

Bill Justis. In 1957, Justis' alto-sax dominated recording 'Raunchy' was a huge hit for Phillips International, one of the first in a series of rock instrumentals which paved the way for the success of the Champs, the Ventures and Duane Eddy. Justis, born in Birmingham, Alabama on October 14, 1927, was a professional jazz musician and arranger who came to rock'n'roll production with Sun in Memphis in 1957. Besides his own recordings, he arranged hits for Johnny Cash, Jerry Lee Lewis and Charlie Rich and was active in mellowing the raw sounds of Sun rock'n'roll for a national pop audience. In 1959, he formed his own short-lived label, Play Me, and then joined Groove-RCA as an artist and producer, again working with Charlie Rich. He moved to Monument and Sound Stage 7 in Nashville, for whom he produced big hits for the Dixiebelles.

Ernie K-Doe was born Ernest Kador in New Orleans in 1937, the son of a Baptist minister. As Ernie K-Doe he was a member of that group of young black New Orleans R&B artists who turned so much national attention towards the funky Crescent City sounds in the early Sixties. In K-Doe's case, it was through that compulsive R&B novelty, 'Mother-In-Law', which rocketed to the top of the Hot Hundred charts on Minit in the spring of 1961. He had further small hits on Minit but he couldn't repeat his initial success. An extrovert showman, he's still in demand in the New Orleans clubs, singing modern soul songs to local audiences.

The Kalin Twins. Real twins, Harold and Herbie Kalin, born on Feb. 16, 1939 were discovered by Clint Ballard Jnr. Ballard who wrote 'You're No Good' for Betty Everett which later topped the American charts when Linda Ronstadt revived it in 1975 and signed them to Decca in 1958. The Paul Evans and Jack Reardon song, 'When' took them to the Top Five in America and the No. 1 spot in Britain for five weeks – on the strength of which they were among the first rock'n'rollers to visit Britain. Though their next record, 'Forget Me Not', also made the Top Twenty, they soon faded from sight. In retrospect, what was appealing about 'When' was the arrangement, not the high-pitched harmonizing of the twins.

Eden Kane, born March 29, 1942 in Delhi, India, his real name was Richard Sarstedt and he supposedly took his stage name from the Orson Welles film *Citizen Kane*. He appeared in the film *Drinks All Round* in 1960 before turning to singing and became the product of careful planning by his managers – Michael Barclay and Philip Waddilove. His first record, 'Hot Chocolate Crazy' was used to advertise a proprietary brand of drinking chocolate on Radio Luxembourg. His Decca releases 'Well I Ask You', 'Get Lost' (1961), 'Forget Me Not' and 'I Don't Know Why' (1962) all made the Top Ten in Britain and were promoted as being in the hully-gully vein – a combination of heavy beat and growl. A change in label, after 'House To Let' and 'Sounds Funny To Me' had failed, brought him back to the charts with 'Boys Cry'. In the Seventies, he re-emerged with his brothers, Clive and Peter, as the Sarstedt Brothers.

Jerry Keller, born on June 20, 1937 in Fort Smith, Arkansas, formed his first group, the Lads of Note in Tulsa. In 1959, he signed to Kapp records. The same year he wrote and recorded the quintessential 'high school' record, 'Here Comes Summer' which reached No. 14 in the Hot Hundred. He wrote Andy Williams' 1965 hit, 'Almost There'.

Chris Kenner was born on 25 December 1929 in Kenner, Louisiana, a suburb town of New Orleans. He started out as a spiritual singer with the New Orleans Harmonising Four, and it was a marriage of gospel and New Orleans R&B which gave his records such a distinctive flavour. He hit the big time in 1961 with the novelty-dance tune, 'I Like It Like That', a No. 2 record on the Instant label which was voted 'Best Rock'n'Roll Record of 1961'. He followed this with a local hit, 'Something You Got' and in 1963 'Land Of 1,000 Dances' crept into the charts at No. 77. This latter song has been covered countless times by artists like Wilson Pickett, Fats Domino and Tom Jones. Kenner has also recorded without much success as a comeback for Baton, Imperial ('Sick And Tired'), Prigan and Uptown amongst others.

Johnny Kidd was born Frederick Heath in London on Dec. 23, 1939, and has become something of a legend. At the end of the Fifties he and his band, the Pirates, featuring guitarist Mick Green, developed a form of R&B which stood in direct contrast to the careful cover jobs and polite rock of so many British artists, and predated the R&B revival by two or three years.

This reputation exceeds Kidd's actual chart successes – four British Top Twenty entries and no impression whatsoever in America. But his first hit, 'Shakin' All Over' (released on HMV and co-written by Kidd and his manager, Gus Robinson) is now a rock standard; he followed it in the same year, 1960, with 'Restless' and in 1963 scored with 'I'll Never Get Over You' and 'Hungry For Love'. 'Please Don't Touch' is another Kidd classic; his stage style, complete with gimmick eye-patch, is indicated by these titles.

Tragically, Kidd couldn't climb back to the top when R&B arrived in force, in spite of his 1963 success. His later recordings were heavily Beatle-influenced, and by the time of his death in a Lancashire car crash on Oct. 7, 1966, the Pirates had been reduced to low-priced support gigs.

Ben E. King, born Benjamin Earl Nelson in Henderson, North Carolina in 1938, first sang professionally with a New York group, the Crowns. When they were signed to Atlantic Records as the Drifters in 1959 he was brought to the attention of a mass audience as lead singer, notably on their biggest hit 'Save The Last Dance For Me' in 1960. Three months later, he had his first solo success, 'Spanish Harlem' (Atco), followed by 'Stand By Me', now considered a black music classic. Promoted as a dramatic balladeer rather than a 'soul' singer, most of King's output was aimed at a pop audience, but with the right material he was as emotionally convincing as any soul star. 'Don't Play That Song', 'Tell Daddy', 'How Can I Forget', 'It's All Over', 'Seven Letters', 'So Much Love', and 'What Is Soul' were among his most exciting performances. He left Atlantic in 1969 for the Maxwell and Mandala labels and re-signed with Atlantic in 1974, hitting the US Top Ten in 1975 with 'Supernatural'.

King Curtis, born Curtis Ousley in Fort Worth, Texas on Feb. 7, 1934, was the only rock'n'roll saxophonist to become widely known outside the recording studios. At high school, he switched from alto to tenor and – prior to returning home to take up a musical scholarship – won an amateur talent contest at Harlem's Apollo Theatre. His studies abandoned, he formed a combo to play in Texas clubs.

By 1958, when he joined Atco, he had played with Lionel Hampton, formed a jazz trio with pianist Horace Silver and drummer Osie Johnson, and recorded under his own name for many independent labels, including Gem, Crown, Apollo and Groove. Apart from the odd Prestige jazz session, Curtis did not go in for improvisation. Nor (unlike Herb Hardesty with Fats Domino, any of Little Richard's horn men or even Jimmy Wright with the Teenagers) is there any evidence that Curtis played on his back, shoulders heaving like pistons, blowing the reed from his instrument. Before becoming a full-time freelance studio player, his career had followed a mainstream path, absorbing the influence of Lester Young, Arnett Cobb and Gene Ammons. And, unlike the numerous apoplectic honkers of the period, Curtis brought a readily identifiable tone to whatever he played, whether blues (where he accompanied Roosevelt Sykes and Sunnyland Slim), R&B influenced pop (Sam Cooke, Little Eva, Bobby Darin, Sammy Turner, Bobby Lewis *et al.*) or jazz (Nat Adderley, Wynton Kelly) – the medium he preferred until the early Sixties when he discovered the warm ballad style which Southern soul men brought to Atlantic at that time.

Within each category he was not only prolific but versatile. The solos on Sammy Turner records are light years away from his tricky embellishments with the Coasters, but they are still natural, effortless and unmistakably King Curtis. He was particularly valuable to record companies who needed sessionmen to play exactly what was required of them. He was clean, note-perfect and solo breaks like those on the Coasters' records were unequalled in rock'n'roll. His tone – deep and fruity, with a characteristic burr – and his facility could combine in under twenty seconds to create a telling statement full of charm and utility. 'Charlie Brown', 'Along Came Jones', 'Shoppin' For Clothes' – all the classics have it.

In 1962, Curtis reached the Top Twenty for the first time with 'Soul Twist' (Enjoy). Nothing else released under his own name was as successful, but later records – 'Beach Party', 'Soul Serenade' (for Capitol), 'Jump Back', 'Memphis Soul Stew' and 'Ode To Billy Joe' (all three on Atco) – also made the pop charts. By the late Sixties, his soul stylings had become indispensable to the records of Aretha Franklin, Donny Hathaway and other Atlantic stars. On the verge of increased recognition for his contribution to over a decade of rock history, Curtis was stabbed to death in Harlem on Aug. 13, 1971.

Earl King. Born in New Orleans on Feb. 7, 1934, Solomon 'Earl King' Johnson was one of the major R&B artists to emerge from that city during the early Fifties. In 1954 he was featured vocalist with the legendary Huey 'Piano' Smith band, later cutting solo sides with Smith in accompaniment. By 1955 the singer/guitarist had signed with Johnny Vincent's newly-formed Ace label, scoring his biggest hit with 'Those Lonely, Lonely Nights'. King spent many years touring the Southern States, and his influence can be heard in the early work of Little Richard and Lloyd Price. King is still active today, enjoying a new lease of life on the R&B revival circuit. His composition 'Let's Make A Better World' was included on Dr John's album *Desitively Bonnaroo*.

The King Records group has included the Queen, De Luxe, Federal, Rockin', Glory, Bethlehem, Audio Lab and Starday-King labels. It was the most wide-ranging and successful independent recording operation during the Fifties.

Formed as a 'folk and country' label in Cincinnati during 1944 by Sydney Nathan, King acquired an impressive roster of artists such as the Delmore Brothers, Hawkshaw Hawkins, Moon Mullican and Cowboy Copas. Soon it launched a series of R&B/jazz/gospel issues (at first on Queen) and a 'popular' catalogue emerged in the Fifties and included Steve Lawrence and Ruby Wright. In 1947, Henry Glover began a twenty-five-year association with King as Artists and Repertoire manager and he was responsible for producing most of King's R&B artists and for mixing R&B with C&W songs, styles and singers in an era when this was almost unknown. He began working with the bands of Lucky Millinder and Bullmoose Jackson, and singers Roy Brown and Wynonie Harris, and many R&B hits were achieved. Through the Fifties, as rock'n'roll developed, King continued to be active in the full range of black music.

'Bloodshot Eyes' and 'Good Rockin' Tonight' gave way to Jack Dupree's bluesy 'Walkin' The Blues', the group sounds of Otis Williams ('Hearts Of Stone'), Hank Ballard ('Work With Me Annie'), and the instrumentals of Bill Doggett ('Honky Tonk'), Earl Bostic and Sonny Thompson.

Eventually, King found Little Willie John ('Fever' and 'All Around The World'), and James Brown ('Please, Please, Please'), who in their respective ways were important innovators of soul. In the Sixties, James Brown virtually carried the King group of labels. Something of the vital and pioneering spirit had, however, been lost although various series of repackaged hits have been successful.

The Kingsmen, a vocal/instrumental quintet from Portland, Oregon, comprised Lynn Easton (vocals), Gary Abbott, Don Gallucci, Mike Mitchell and Norman Sundholm. Formed in 1957 at high school, they developed a reputation while employing their driving, bluesy sound on TV commercials and one-nighter tours before signing with Wand in 1963. Their debut, a raw revival of Richard Berry's 'Louie Louie' delivered with virtually indecipherable diction, gained a gold disc in 1964, numerous subsequent hits following over three years, largely based on R&B songs. 'Louie Louie' enjoys a reputation as the all-time best-selling 'oldie'.

Baker Knight's success as a songwriter for Fifties teen idols such as Ray Peterson ('The Wonder Of You') and Ricky Nelson ('Lonesome Town', 'Never Be Anyone Else But You', 'I Wanna Be Loved') disguised his other life as a fine rock'n'roll singer. Under his own name, he recorded for Decca in 1956, with 'Bring My Cadillac Back' and 'Reelin' And Rockin' '. He moved on to Coral, RCA-Victor, Jubilee, Kick (where he recorded some splendid guitar instrumentals), Challenge, Checker and – as late as 1967 – Reprise.

Buddy Knox, born April 14, 1933 in a small Texas town

called Happy, was one of a wave of Southern country singers who broke into rock'n'roll in the Fifties. He formed the Rhythm Orchids locally, with Jimmy Bowen, and recorded at Norman Petty's studio in Clovis, New Mexico. Petty placed 'Party Doll' and 'Hula Love' with Roulette in 1957, and both were big hits. Knox's style on these discs was basically country-rock but it was somehow lighter than other styles and was capable of adaptation into the teen-ballad genre of the later Fifties with hits like 'Somebody Touched Me' and 'Lovey Dovey'. In this, his career was paralleled by those of Texans Jimmy Bowen, Roy Orbison and Buddy Holly. Knox was a headliner on rock'n'roll extravaganza stage shows for five years with Roulette and then Liberty Records, and he appeared in 'star-vehicle' movies like *Jamboree*, 1957. During the Sixties, he turned towards country music and has worked with minor success throughout Canada. He has recorded for Ruff, Reprise and United Artists.

Frankie Laine, a big-voiced balladeer who formed part of Mitch Miller's strategy to import a hint of Country & Western into pop during the Fifties, was born Frank LoVecchio on March 30, 1913, in Chicago. His earliest claim to fame was the setting of the all-time marathon dance record of 145 days in 1932. Laine's professional singing career began when he replaced Perry Como in Freddie Carlone's band in 1937. He moved on to Los Angeles, where Hoagy Carmichael is supposed to have discovered him singing in a night-club. He signed to Mercury Records, and the first big hit came in 1947 with 'That's My Desire'. He had thirteen million-sellers in the next decade. Most were for Columbia, to whom he was signed by Miller in 1951.

Hits like 'Jezebel' and 'High Noon' were in the muscular ballad mould favoured by Miller for his artists (Guy Mitchell was another). In the Seventies, Laine has concentrated on religious material, but still performs on the night-club circuit.

The Larks, from Durham, North Carolina, were Allen Bunn, Thermon Ruth, David McNeil, Haddie Rowe Jnr. and lead singer Eugene Mumford. They recorded for Apollo in 1951. 'My Reverie' was one of their lovliest ballads, while 'Eyesight To The Blind' and 'Little Side Car' reached the R&B Top Ten the same year, but the group disbanded in 1953. Mumford formed another group of Larks (who recorded on Apollo's subsidiary, Lloyds) and, like McNeil, subsequently joined the Dominoes. Allen Bunn (alias Tarheel Slim) went on to record blues for a great many New York companies, including Lamp, Red Robin, Fire and Fury. The Larks are not to be confused with Don Julian's Larks who made the Top Ten with 'The Jerk' in 1964.

Steve Lawrence, one of the many graduates of the famous *Arthur Godfrey Talent Scout Show*, was born Steven Leibowitz on July 8, 1935. He became a regular on the Steve Allen television show, where he teamed up with Eydie Gormé, whom he married. Lawrence recorded for King, Coral (covering Buddy Knox's 'Party Doll'), ABC, and United Artists ('Portrait Of My Love'), before gaining his first major hit with 'Go Away Little Girl', a No. 1 on Columbia in 1962. With Eydie Gormé, he recorded 'I Just Want To Stay Here And Love You', which reached No. 28 in America and No. 3 in Britain in 1963. Gormé's biggest hit was the novelty 'Blame It On The Bossa Nova' (No. 7 in 1963).

Leadbelly was born Huddie Ledbetter in Mooringsport, Louisiana, in 1885, into a family that included musicians from whom he learned the elements of playing guitar and accordion for dances and street entertainment. Discovery of his musical talent by the outside world did not come in those circumstances, however; he was serving a sentence for assault in the penitentiary at Angola, Louisiana, when, in the early Thirties, John A. Lomax, collecting prison songs for the Library of Congress Archive of Folk Song, uncovered Leadbelly's vast store of traditional music.

Throughout the Thirties and Forties, first for the Archive and (after his reprieve) for folk record companies in the East, he recorded many hundreds of blues, blues-ballads, dance songs and other specimens of black folk music, to his individual and thrusting 12-string guitar accompaniment. Though lionized by both the folk music establishment and society audiences, he died in comparative poverty in 1949.

Leadbelly's repertoire, easily the most extensive and valuable ever documented from a black folk musician, included many archaic pieces of the pre-blues era, and these – for example 'Midnight Special', 'Ella Speed', 'Pick A Bale O' Cotton', 'Rock Island Line' – became the standards of the folk revival of the Fifties, and, in Britain, of skiffle. Frequently, however, it was other artists who enjoyed success with his material; for instance the Weavers with 'Goodnight Irene'. With the coming, after his death, of a blues vogue, Leadbelly was underrated, though he was no negligible blues-singer, and his angry compositions 'Mr. Tom Hughes' Town' and 'Bourgeois Blues' are among his most powerful recordings. Gradually his uniqueness is becoming justly valued, and a good deal of his repertoire has been made available on albums, notably *The Library of Congress Recordings* (Elektra, 1966) and *Last Sessions* (Folkways, 1962). These contain many of the songs which rock musicians have continually borrowed for the last decade and more.

Brenda Lee, born in Atlanta, Georgia, on Dec. 11, 1944, was discovered by Red Foley. She made her debut at the Ozark Jubilee in 1956 and seemed set for an orthodox career as a country singer, especially when she had a minor country hit with her first record for American Decca, the standard 'Jambalaya'. However, in 1959, with Connie Francis established as the female singer of the period, Brenda Lee cut 'Sweet Nothin's'. She still had the manner and appearance of a country-singing Georgia Peach, but the song was strong – and her singing even stronger – and through extensive

190

promotion it became a huge pop hit in both Europe and America.

Before retiring from the music business in 1967, she had well over 20 chart hits, including No. 1s with 'I'm Sorry' and 'I Want To Be Wanted', and a string of Top Tens, 'Emotions', 'Dum, Dum', 'That's All You Gotta Do', 'Fool Number One', etc. Most of these were performed in a rock-ballad style, with integrated pizzicato strings and an electric rhythm section behind the voice. But if the backings were formula-ridden and the songs of a variable quality, what remained constant was Brenda Lee's voice. In complete contrast to her school-girl image, it suggested a mixture of despair, dissipation and sexual torment more often than not.

In 1971, married with two children, she returned to music and immediately gained country chart success with Kristofferson's 'Nobody Wins'. Her first return album, *Brenda*, was her biggest seller to date. She is now established as a country singer in the Nashville mainstream, along with fellow rock'n'rollers, Conway Twitty and Jerry Lee Lewis.

Curtis Lee, born on Oct. 28, 1941, in Yuma, Arizona, was poised to follow the footsteps of Fabian with whom he has been unfavourably compared. Blue-eyed and blond, his looks were his greatest asset, but his early sides on Warrior in 1960 also revealed a sweet voice with a countryish burr. The following year he was signed to Dunes by Ray Peterson. 'Pretty Little Angel Eyes', which capitalized on the Fifties trick of an over-employed bassman – Arthur Crier, who along with the rest of the Halos provided the back-up singing on the disc – and 'Under The Moon Of Love', a pounding party disc redolent of US Bonds, were produced by Phil Spector and made the Top Ten and Top Fifty respectively.

Dickey Lee. Dickey Lipscomb started out as a 'punk rockabilly' in Florida and joined Sun in Memphis in 1957, recording 'Good Lovin''. Born in Memphis on Sept. 21, 1943, he went to college at Memphis State having already cut three records. He re-emerged in the Sixties in Beaumont where he wrote, produced, played and sang along with Jack Clement at Hallway Records. He hit in the 'sob-pop' market with 'Patches', and migrated to Nashville, writing such C&W standards as 'She Thinks I Still Care' and renewing his own vocal career in 1971 with 'Never Ending Song Of Love' and other hits for Epic and RCA.

Peggy Lee. Born in Jamestown, North Dakota, on May 6, 1920, her real name was Norma Egstrom. She started professionally in 1938 and debuted with the Benny Goodman Orchestra and made her first film in 1951 – *Mr Music* – and a remake of *The Jazz Age* in 1953 for which she wrote 'This Is A Very Special Day'. It was one of many songs that she wrote and recorded – 'Mañana', 'It's A Good Day', 'Johnny Guitar' and 'Just An Old Love Of Mine'. In 1956 she co-authored the score for and sang some of the songs in *The Lady And The Tramp*. Among her chart entries were 'Mr. Wonderful' (1957) from the Broadway show and 'Fever' (1957) and the seminal 'I'm A Woman' (1963).

Jerry Leiber and Mike Stoller, the first independent producers in the history of rock, were responsible for ushering out an era when records were made by pulling groups off the street into a studio to mouth 'doowop, doowah' into a mike for three minutes. Leiber and Stoller were also the first to introduce satire and social comment into a music previously concerned with songs about a boy who just had to have a girl. They may even have been the first blue-eyed soul brothers, writing and producing records for a host of bluesmen from 1949 onwards.

It was in that year that Leiber (born in Baltimore on 25 April, 1933) met Stoller (from New York) in Los Angeles. They pooled their skills and wrote blues, usually with the first line of each verse repeated – the classic twelve-bar form. The seeds of R&B were developing in the soil of country blues and the big bands. Small independent labels relied on local talent to perform the new, hybrid music. Leiber and Stoller had no difficulty in placing their songs.

The Robins, Amos Milburn, Floyd Dixon, Peppermint Harris, Preston Love, the Flairs, Bullmoose Jackson, Jimmy Witherspoon . . . as many as twenty blues singers mopped up their compositions as fast as they were written. In 1951, Charles Brown gave them their first 'race' hit, 'Hard Times'. Shortly after, Little Willie Littlefield cut 'K.C. Lovin'' (a million seller for Wilbert Harrison as 'Kansas City' in 1959) and Willie Mae Thornton recorded 'Hound Dog' (revived by Presley in 1956).

In 1954, Leiber and Stoller founded their own label, Spark. Among the artists they signed, none were more important than the Robins, whose records – 'Framed', 'Riot In Cell Block No. 9' – were of historic importance in the development of R&B production. On the strength of this, Atlantic Records signed the pair to an independent production deal in 1955. They headed for New York, but without three of the Robins who preferred to stay in LA. Quickly augmented on the East Coast, the group was re-named the Coasters. Leiber and Stoller produced and wrote for many of Atlantic/Atco's greatest performers (Joe Turner, Lavern Baker, the Isley Brothers, Clyde McPhatter, Ruth Brown), but had they never recorded anyone else, they would be secure in rock history for their work with the Coasters, for whom they created an astonishing figure of 18 dynamic and ingenious hits.

They were also put in charge of Atlantic's other important black group, the Drifters. The liaison soon produced 'There Goes My Baby', arguably the greatest record with which Leiber and Stoller were ever involved. It combined Ben E. King's gospel-rooted voice with a Latin rhythm section and neo-classical strings. It sounded like two records playing at once and it sold a million in 1959. The combination of such eclectic ingredients unleashed a trend as significant as the invention of the electric guitar. By imposing themselves on a second black group, Leiber and Stoller had given the popular music industry entirely new ideas. After

193

'There Goes My Baby', black groups rarely recorded without strings, while Latin rhythms permeated the whole of pop from Burt Bacharach (who sat in on the Drifters' sessions) onwards. In keeping with the general softening of rock'n'roll, succeeding Drifters records were less intense and often decidedly lush. But they were extremely popular and – perhaps as important – it is probable that they inspired Phil Spector, who was 'apprenticed' to Leiber and Stoller at this time.

By maintaining their independence from Atlantic, Leiber and Stoller were able to work for many other companies during the Fifties and early Sixties. A brief list would have to include: Capitol (the Cheers), Checker (Dale Hawkins), Vee Jay (Christine Kittrell), Fabor (Larry Evans), Okeh (Screamin' Jay Hawkins), Modern (Young Jessie), MGM (Roy Hamilton), Jubilee (Betty Harris, Garnell Cooper), Big Top (Sammy Turner), United Artists (the Clovers, Jay and the Americans, Steve Lawrence, Mike Clifford, the Exciters) and RCA (June Valli, Perry Como, Julius LaRosa, David Hill). Here they also worked with Presley, who was already past his rock'n'roll peak. The urban blues satire at which they excelled would not have suited Elvis, and the atmosphere at RCA was not conducive to works of incisive wit. They were further handicapped by the need to operate within the limits of his unbearably stodgy filmscripts. But despite these restraints, they managed to write and produce some of Presley's better post-Sun records. 'Jailhouse Rock', 'Trouble' and 'Santa Claus Is Back In Town' contain magnificently earthy lines.

Few of the innumerable discs made by Leiber and Stoller with lesser artists than Presley, the Coasters and the Drifters, were of significance. Sammy Turner's 'Lavender Blue' was exceptional, as were Ben E. King's passionate, Latin-flecked soul hits, notably 'Stand By Me'. And apart from records by the Exciters and Peggy Lee, their early Sixties' productions sold only moderately. Inventive perfectionists when fired by artists of exceptional ability, they could do next to nothing with the plethora of middle-of-the-road talent with which they worked outside Atlantic.

After fresh but abortive attempts to start labels of their own, they met up with George Goldner in 1964. This led to the formation of the Red Bird and Blue Cat labels, to which they signed a host of young songwriters and producers, including Jeff Barry and Ellie Greenwich, 'Shadow' Morton and Artie Ripp. With Goldner in charge of promotion, the labels had 25 hits in two years, among which the Shangri-Las, the Dixie Cups, the Jellybeans and the Adlibs are best remembered. Leiber and Stoller took little part in the creative end of the business: to them it was bubblegum pop, for which they had no liking. Weary of administration, they sold out to Goldner.

Next, after some brilliant but poor-selling Coasters records for Columbia, Leiber and Stoller retired from studio work and invested their capital in large and durable music publishing firms. In 1970, they bought the famous Starday/King company, which would have allowed them to record, market and promote whatever they wished. But they were writers and producers first and businessmen second, and the King takeover was not a success. Soon they were back making records, and the offers flooded in. 'Stuck In The Middle With You', a worldwide hit for Stealers Wheel, marked the re-emergence of the most creative production team ever produced by rock'n'roll.

Ketty Lester, born in Hope, Arkansas, was a refined 'torch' singer who worked with Cab Calloway's Orchestra and the Ziegfeld Follies in New York before signing with Ezra on the West Coast. She enjoyed her major success on this label in 1962 with the million-selling 'Love Letters'. Especially memorable were the marvellous piano embellishments and austere but smooth arrangements showcasing her mellifluous voice and its sensuous texture. The musical charts were copied for the first Presley version of 1966, although vocally he brought even more finesse to the song. Her attempts to follow 'Love Letters' quickly in 1962 depended too much on repeating its keyboard ploys but were none the less appealing, especially 'Moscow Nights' which added words to a reworking of 'Midnight In Moscow', a traditional jazz hit for Britain's Kenny Ball the year before. Leaning towards jazz, Ketty Lester's work is the living proof that 'soul' need not be raucous.

Bobby Lewis, born on Feb. 17, 1933, in Indianapolis, Indiana, sang with the Leo Hines band and recorded for Chess, Spotlight, Mercury and Roulette in the years 1952–59. In 1961, 'Tossin' And Turnin'', his first record for Beltone, hit the No. 1 spot and stayed on the charts for 23 weeks. A throwback to the baritone jump blues singers of the early Fifties, Lewis commercialized the style by adding a chanting girl chorus (the Swanettes) who stayed with him for other hits, including 'One Track Mind' (Top Ten) and 'What A Walk'. None were as good as 'Tossin'', written by producer Joe Rene and Ritchie Adams of the Fireflies. Lewis also recorded for ABC and, although further hits were not forthcoming, a dynamic stage act has kept him in steady club work.

Jerry Lee Lewis must be counted one of the great originals of rock. Coming to the fore in 1957 with Sun Records of Memphis, he was not lost in the famous 'Sun Sound' that had by then already spawned Elvis Presley and Johnny Cash. Rather, he added his own uniquely attacking style of vocalizing and piano playing, and made the sound even better.

He hit the American national headlines in 1957 with his second and third recordings, 'Whole Lotta Shakin' Going On' and 'Great Balls Of Fire', classics of rock which have been copied by successive generations of musicians but never bettered. The Lewis style is one of the most immediately identifiable in rock. It is straightforward, powerful, even primitive, but also perfect. 'Whole Lotta Shakin'', as heard on disc, was recorded with no trial runs. The drummer makes one mistake, but otherwise a sympathetic guitar and drum backing combines with Lewis's pumping piano in a relentless rhythm that emphasizes the soaring vocals and allows full appreciation of the top-note keyboard solo gymnastics. As always, Lewis displays a swaggering self-confidence in his own ability and a full command of his material, allowing the tempo to lull before storming back for a dynamic ending.

As a showman, too, Lewis was an original. He broke pianos, he threw chairs, he swore at the band and the audience, but his arrogance was compensated by his supreme talent. His uniqueness, his originality, is in no way countered by the fact that his material is rarely his own. He has an inherent ability to mould the songs of others to his own style to such effect that the question of sameness and rigidity hardly arises. Currently, he operates in the C&W field, highly successfully, and his many interpretations of country songs are as triumphant as his rock'n'roll songs. They are all transformed, becoming Jerry Lee Lewis recordings rather than just another version of a particular song.

Lewis was born in Ferriday, Louisiana, on September 29, 1935, and learned his music from the C&W radio shows and the local black juke-joints of his teens. He claims to have no influences, and certainly his first recordings, 'Crazy Arms' and 'End Of The Road', made for Sun in 1956, show a fully developed style that he has never basically altered. However, his piano playing can be partly attributed to Texan honky-tonk pianist Moon Mullican and it is interesting that in 1954 Lewis recorded a demonstration record, in Shreveport, Louisiana, of two C&W songs that he sang and played very much in a straight country style. Between then and 1956, he acquired a driving ambition to become a success through music and he also saw the way to achieve this. Rock'n'roll had arrived, and there was room for a wildman pianist.

Following his successes of 1957 with 'Whole Lotta Shakin'' and 'Great Balls Of Fire', Lewis hit with 'Down The Line' and 'High School Confidential' and appeared in movies – *Jamboree* (1957), *High School Confidential* (1958), and later, in 1960, *Young And Deadly*. His career was booming in 1958 when his marriage to a fourteen-year-old cousin led to scandal and the string of million sellers ceased for three years. His career was shattered, but he remained with Sun Records, experimenting with pop, country and R&B songs.

In 1961, he began recording R&B songs in Nashville and 'What'd I Say' restarted him on the trail of hits. Two years later he moved to Smash Records, later Mercury, and began to find a niche in the C&W charts. Hits such as 'Another Place, Another Time', 'She Even Woke Me Up To Say Goodbye' and 'Think About It Darlin'' were identifiably country, but also unmistakably Jerry Lee Lewis and he has been able to develop his catchphrases and clichés amlost to the point of self-parody. He successfully brought off an un-believably fast rendition of Kristofferson's 'Me And Bobbie McGee' as only he could. He has recorded with soul, rock, C&W and New Orleans jazz backings, and remained in command.

Smiley Lewis, from the small town of Union, Louisiana, was born Overton Amos Lemons on July 5, 1920. His parents moved to New Orleans in 1931 and, soaked in the long musical heritage of the Crescent City, Smiley rose to become a major local R&B artist. A competent guitarist, he first recorded for De Luxe in 1947 as 'Smiling' Lewis but it was the consistent high quality of his Imperial recordings between 1950 and 1960 which established his reputation. He had two R&B hits in this time, 'The Bells Are Ringing' (1952) and 'I Hear You Knocking' (1955) but he never got the national recognition he deserved. His songs have, however, given hits to Gale Storm ('I Hear You Knocking'), Elvis Presley ('One Night') and in Britain, Dave Edmunds ('I Hear You Knocking'). After further isolated records for Okeh, Dot and Loma, he died of stomach cancer in 1966.

Stan Lewis, one of the South's leading record entrepreneurs, owns several labels, retail outlets and a distribution network spanning the South. Born of Italian heritage in

Shreveport, Louisiana, Lewis invested his small savings in five jukeboxes in black locations in Shreveport (he was 19) just after the war. Finding it difficult to re-stock these jukeboxes, he became interested in the record business itself and with his wife, Pauline, took over a struggling record shop in a black location in Shreveport. After meeting Leonard Chess, then peddling Chess's R&B discs around the South by car, Lewis increased his involvement in the lucrative R&B field and by the early Fifties had expanded into a one-stop and mail-order house, supplying virtually anything for anyone wanting records.

In 1951, Lewis decided to buy airtime on Shreveport's local radio station KWKH (home of the famed *Louisiana Hayride*) and soon found himself handling orders across 35 States. Eventually, labels like Specialty and Chess asked him to act as their local talent scout and in 1953, Lewis began recording local acts after hours at KWKH for $15 an hour and placed Slim Whitman and several lesser-known 'Louisiana Hayriders' with record companies.

In 1957, Lewis recorded two national hits, Dale Hawkins' 'Susie-Q' and TV Slim's 'Flat-Foot Sam', both sold to the Chess combine with whom he maintained close connections. In 1963, he formed his own Jewel label, followed in 1965 by the Paula and Ronn labels. In 1967, Paula achieved a million-seller with John Fred's 'Judy In Disguise'. Unlike some of his contemporaries, Lewis has never forgotten his roots and he has become America's biggest producer of authentic blues and gospel music.

John Leyton, born John Dudley Leyton in Frinton, Essex, on Feb. 17, 1939, was another actor who turned to singing by chance. He played Ginger in the ATV *Biggles* series and then Johnny St. Cyr in another TV series, *Harper's West One* which is where he got his first chance to sing 'Johnny Remember Me' and which led to the record's success in 1961. It was expertly produced by Joe Meek and featured an echo effect that masked the inadequacies of Leyton's voice. His other records were all remarkably similar and the public quickly tired of him. Written by Geoff Goddard, they were 'Wild Wind', 'Son This Is She' and 'Lonely City' in 1962. He later returned to acting and appeared in *The Great Escape* (1963), *Von Ryan's Express* (1965) and *Krakatoa* (1968). Possibly his only lasting claim to fame was that he was one of the first artists to be handled by Robert Stigwood, later to find his fortune as the producer of *Jesus Christ Superstar* and owner of RSO records.

Liberty Records formed in late 1955, in Hollywood by Si(mon) Waronker – whose son Lenny is currently a producer with Warner-Reprise – Alvin Bennett and Theodore Keep, Liberty immediately entered the rock'n'roll market with powerful acts like Eddie Cochran, Johnny Burnette and Troy Shondell. Al Bennett, originally brought in to promote the company's records, soon turned to A&R, becoming a West Coast version of George Goldner. But the company really prospered under 'Snuff' Garrett, a Texas deejay who joined the A&R department in 1958 and transformed Johnny Burnette into a successful balladeer with 'Dreamin''. He was even more successful with Bobby Vee and, in 1961, was promoted to head of Liberty's growing A&R department. The early Sixties were equally profitable, thanks to the successes of Jan and Dean, the Ventures and Gary Lewis and the Playboys. In 1967, TransAmerica, already having purchased United Artists (UA), bought Liberty (and later Imperial); later that year Liberty set up its own British organization and in the early Seventies TransAmerica merged its record interests under the UA logo.

Jimmy and Joe Liggins. Born in Oklahama on July 9, 1916, pianist Joe Liggins began recording for Exclusive in Los Angeles in 1945 with mellow 'city blues' material. His reputation grew quickly, encouraging brother Jimmy to forsake a boxing career and lead his own band, on guitar, for Specialty. Joe's rolling boogie 'Honeydripper' proved popular, and he joined his brother at Specialty in 1950 where he had an immediate million seller 'Pink Champagne'. Jimmy and his Drops of Joy recorded until 1955, latterly on Aladdin and Duplex, while Joe and his Honeydrippers remained with Specialty until 1959 before moving to Mercury, and in 1974 recorded for Johnny Otis' Blues Spectrum label.

Little Anthony and the Imperials. Anthony Gourdine's career began in Brooklyn in 1955, singing with the Duponts. However, they soon disbanded and Anthony then formed the Chesters, with Clarence Collins, Tracy Lord, Ernest Wright and Nat Rogers, who signed with End in 1958, debuting with the distinctive million seller 'Tears On My Pillow'. End renamed them Imperials, while deejay Alan Freed added the 'Little Anthony' prefix. Several hits followed, but personal problems caused them to split in 1960. Anthony, Collins, Wright and Sammy Strain re-formed the group in 1964, achieving a string of hits on DCP with plushly arranged, dramatic ballads like 'Going Out Of My Head', subsequently recording for Veep, UA, Janus and, in 1974, Avco.

Little Caesar and the Romans. From Los Angeles, the group comprised Carl Burnett (alias Little Caesar, born in Dallas, Texas in 1944), Johnny Simmons, Early Harris, Dave Johnson and Leroy Sanders. They were the first rock'n'roll revivalists with their 1961 Top Ten hit 'Those Oldies But Goodies', on Del-Fi. The Romans were rcruited from doo-wop groups of the Fifties (including the Jewels, the Cubans and the Cufflinks), and they *knew* what they were singing about. A Canadian-based group, Little Caesar and the Consuls – who had a 1965 hit on Mala with 'My Girl Sloopy', a Bert Berns song – were not related.

Little Eva, born Eva Narcissus Boyd on June 29, 1945, in Bellhaven, North Carolina, moved to New York while in her teens. Here, legend insists, she was baby-sitting for Carole King and Gerry Goffin when they asked her to record a new song they had written. The result was 'The Locomotion'. With the Cookies, of 'Chains' fame, as back-up singers, it went to No. 1 in 1962. A string of computerized dance hits followed, including 'Keep Your Hands Off My Baby', 'Let's Turkey Trot' and 'Old Smokey Locomotion', all on the Dimension label, on which Eva's sister, Idalia Boyd, recorded 'Hula Hooping'. Despite several far more soulful records (on Amy, Spring and others), Eva didn't have any more big hits.

Little Richard, of all the progenitors of rock'n'roll, still is unclassifiable. However shattering an effect Presley, Jerry Lee Lewis and Chuck Berry had on the calm of Eisenhower's America, they were ultimately assimilable. A major reason for this was colour: the first two were white and though Berry was black, his material, almost from the beginning, was oriented towards white teenagers. In contrast to these, Little Richard – for better or worse – made no concessions.

If rock'n'roll was delicious drivel, he was its epitome – 'A-Wop-Bop-A-Loo-Bop-A-Lop-Bam-Boom'; and if rock-'n'roll was a threat, it was 'the Prince of Clowns' who represented its insane vigour. Richard alone represented the crude fantasy of absolute rebellion that lay at the heart of rock'n'roll. Accordingly, it isn't surprising that his endless fascination and power over us rests on the results of scattered moments in his career.

Little Richard, it seemed, didn't develop but sprang at us fully grown. None the less, the twists and turns of his seemingly directionless career, in their own bizarre fashion, reflect the enigma that is Little Richard. Born in Macon, Georgia on Dec. 5, 1932, Richard Penniman was raised as a Seventh Day Adventist and spent his formative years singing in church choirs. He first performed professionally with a variety of itinerant medicine shows and then gained a club residency in Fitzgerald, Georgia, where his repertoire consisted primarily of Louis Jordan songs. Between 1951–2, he cut his first records for RCA, mostly blues performed very much in the shadow of Roy Brown. His first release, in 1952, was 'Every Hour' coupled with 'Taxi Blues'. The follow-up, 'Get Rich Quick' was an exuberant shouter in the tradition of Wynonie Harris. The flip was the slow, reflective 'Thinkin' About My Mother', on which Richard's stark delivery was underpinned by a loquacious saxophone. On 'Why Did You Leave Me', he aped the unearthly banshee wails of a Roy Brown or a Bobby Bland in front of an arrangement one might expect from Memphis or Houston studios, Stygian and spare, leaving the voice in splendid isolation. His final sides for RCA were 'Please Have Mercy On Me' and 'I Brought It All On Myself'.

In 1952, he joined Don Robey's Houston-based Peacock label where he was backed for the most part (instrumentally and vocally) by the Tempo Toppers – Jimmy Swan, Billy Brooks, Barry Gilmore and organist Raymond Taylor. His first session, on Feb. 25, 1953, resulted in 'Fool At The Wheel' and 'Ain't That Good News' (which bears no relation to the later Sam Cooke hit of the same title). In 1954, with the Tempo Toppers, he recorded Raymond Taylor's novelty composition 'Rice, Red Beans And Turnip Greens' and Robey's 'Always'. Richard used the Johnny Otis band next, and 'Little Richard's Boogie' – released in 1956 after he had joined Specialty – featured Otis on vibes. On the reverse was the first of several versions of 'Directly From My Heart', a plodding blues ballad bound for better days. Richard's last record for Peacock, in May 1957, coupled 'I Love My Baby' with 'Maybe I'm Right', with Otis on piano on the latter. His stay at Peacock had produced some agreeable music, but nothing that was out of the ordinary or made much improvement on the RCA sides which already saw him as an assured, if limited, singer.

A demonstration tape finally took Little Richard from Peacock to success with Art Rupe's Specialty label in 1955. None the less, it was seven months before he went to New Orleans to make his first recordings for the company. That session, produced by 'Bumps' Blackwell and engineered by Cosimo Matassa, took place at the J&M studios on Sept. 14, 1955. From this came 'Tutti Frutti', his debut Specialty release in October and the first of seven accredited million-sellers. The song was cleaned up by local writer Dorathy La Bostrie from a scurrilous ditty, while Richard's maniac swaggering was accompanied by Huey Smith on piano. Its very banality ensured its success and in some measure the disc, far from Richard's best, is nevertheless the quintessence of anarchic rock'n'roll.

In 1956, 'Long Tall Sally' was released with 'Slippin' And Slidin''. The top side, with its traditional phallic metaphor, derives from the blues, and started life as 'The Thing', when first recorded by Little Richard in New Orleans. Later the title was switched to the more likely 'Bald Headed Sally' but still was unreleased until it was finally re-cut successfully in Los Angeles. It was immediately covered by Pat Boone – who had previously covered 'Tutti Frutti' – and by Presley and Eddie Cochran after a discreet interval. Connoisseurs, however, may prefer 'Slippin' And Slidin''. A typical New Orleans number, it began life as 'I Got The Blues For You', by Al Collins on Ace, with the telling lyric 'Baby with the big box, tell me where your next stop is, I got the blues for you'. Prudently revised, but still alive with good humour, the song was next presented as 'I'm Wise' by Eddie Bocage on Apollo. Bocage's, possibly the definitive version of the song, serves as a timely reminder that there were plenty of piano playing vocalists in New Orleans who could eclipse or equal Richard on record – but never in person.

Richard's other noteworthy records for Specialty include, 'Rip It Up', 'The Girl Can't Help It' (1956), 'Lucille' (1957) and 'Good Golly Miss Molly' (1957). The sidemen on these were usually a combination of Earl Palmer, drums; Red Tyler and Lee Allen, saxes; Frank Fields, bass; Ernest McLean and Justin Adams, guitars; with Huey Smith, Edward Frank, Little Booker and Salvador Doucette as supplementary pianists. On the New Orleans recordings brass, reeds and, of course, piano dominate the sound; only 'Whole Lotta Shakin' Goin' On' (released after Richard had left the company) deviated from this pattern to feature wild guitar breaks.

Little Richard's Specialty career ended in 1959 when he

decided that religion mattered more than rock'n'roll, but releases continued up to 1964 when he re-appeared to cut 'Bama Lama Bama Loo', in Los Angeles and secure his first Hot Hundred entry since 1959. From 1957 to 1964, apart from occasional secular forays, most of Richard's studio work was gospel, frequently inspired gospel at that. With the exception of a little rock'n'roll on Little Star, his followers had to wait until the mid-Sixties and a succession of sides on Vee Jay, Okeh, Modern and Brunswick. 'Whole Lot Of Shakin' Goin' On' (Vee Jay), 'Lawdy Miss Clawdy', both in 1964, and 'Without Love' in 1965 were excellent. His work for Modern saw Richard moving into a more contemporary soul field in 1966 with 'I'm Back' while his version of Sam Cooke's 'Bring It On Home To Me' featured excellent guitar work and his 1967 duet with an un-named lady on the Jimmy Reed blues 'Baby What Want Me To Do' was compulsive. However, his Brunswick output was dire, apart from the tough-sounding 'Soul Train'.

Richard's renaissance as a performer coincided with the boom in rock festivals during the late Sixties and continued into the Seventies under the general guardianship of the rock'n'roll revival movement. However, by the mid-Seventies – as demonstrated at the 1974 Wembley Rock'n'Roll Festival in London – the increasingly self-laudatory nature of his act, in which the theatrics came at the expense of both the music and the nostalgic expectations of much of his audience, had all but closed those arenas to Little Richard. None the less, the initial success of his return to favour with the white concert and festival audience brought with it a renewed interest by record companies. He joined Reprise and 'Freedom Blues', recorded in Muscle Shoals and a Top Fifty record in 1970, gave him his first chart entry since 1965. The long instrumental jams such as 'The Rill Thing', from the album of the same name, saw him for the first time seriously adapt himself to current tastes fairly successfully. *Second Coming*, on which he was once more re-united with musicians like Earl Palmer and Lee Allen, under the guidance of 'Bumps' Blackwell, whilst exhibiting many of the hallmarks of New Orleans R&B also saw him recording, albeit a little tentatively, in the fashionable rock/soul mode of Sly Stone and the Isley Brothers.

Yet increasingly, as Little Richard has managed to come to terms with the present, his anarchic virtues are hidden – much more so than in 'live' performance, despite the hazards there of his current stage persona. Perhaps the best thing would be to record the 'King Of Rock'n'Roll' without consideration for time, in the hope that even the seen-it-all-before consciousness of the Seventies could be dented by his banshee wailings.

Little Willie Littlefield, renowned for the original version of Leiber and Stoller's 'Kansas City' (as 'K.C. Lovin'' on Federal in 1952), moved to Los Angeles from Houston, Texas, where he was born on Sept. 16, 1931. His first records, on Eddie's in 1946, caught the attention of the Bihari brothers, who signed him to their Modern label. Here, his prolific output of blues and boogies included 'It's Midnight', a Top Ten R&B hit in 1949. His Federal discs, supervised by Ralph Bass and occasionally composed by Leiber and Stoller, were often original and inventive. Subsequent records on Rhythm in 1958 were unsuccessful, but Littlefield continues to perform in the clubs of Northern California.

Jerry Lordan, born in 1933 in Paddington, London, began his career in Royal Air Force camp shows. On his demob in 1955, after failing as a professional comedian, he turned to songwriting and recording as Lee and Jerry Elvin, with a friend. The duo flopped, but one of Lordan's early songs, 'A House A Car And A Wedding Ring' was a minor hit for Mike Preston in America in 1958 and Lordan turned to songwriting fulltime. Anthony Newley's 'I've Waited So Long' came next in 1959 and on the strength of that he secured a recording contract with Parlophone. His first single, 'I'll Stay Single', flopped but 'Who Could Be Bluer' was a British Top Twenty hit for him early in 1960. Ironically, it was the instrumental 'Apache' that really established him as a writer when it topped both the British charts (by the Shadows) and the American charts (by Jorgen Ingmann) later that year. Since then he has written for Cliff Richard, Matt Monro and, of course, the Shadows.

Los Angeles. While Philadelphia and New York teemed with managers and agents looking for brooding, pudgy-faced youths to transform into teenage idols, a rather different rock'n'roll culture was developing on the West Coast. There were no big talent agencies or Svengalic managers in Los Angeles. Instead, scattered inconspicuously across LA's huge sprawl were numerous small record labels, distributors and recording studios.

This fledgling record industry began after the war when independent labels like Aladdin and Specialty sprang up to satisfy a huge demand for urban blues, created by the migration of blacks to the North and West. This R&B boom lasted until the late Fifties when white rock'n'roll caused many of the original blues labels to flounder while others like Imperial, with Ricky Nelson, quickly moved into the lucrative pop market before it was too late. From then on, the West Coast bred literally dozens of small, short-lived and often domestically-run record labels. Unlike their predecessors, few of these newer companies catered for any one market but recorded virtually anyone and anything sounding vaguely commercial (local sales alone provided adequate profit for such firms), and many companies simply made one-shot 'product' orientated records using session-singers and musicians. They had an enormous variety of struggling musicians to choose from.

Back in the late Fifties, LA's rock community was comprised of several inter-related cliques which encompassed white Southerners who had come to Hollywood to try their luck (Eddie Cochran, Johnny Burnette, Leon Russell, P. J. Proby, etc.); a variety of black artists ranging from pop singers like Bobby Day and Sam Cooke to dozens of vocal groups which changed personnel at every session; and, finally, white middle-class high school kids like Jan and Dean, Phil Spector, Herb Alpert, Terry Melcher and the Beach Boys.

With the advent of rock'n'roll, many West Coast labels began recording high school kids who were glad to be given a chance at what was basically a pastime encouraged by the rock'n'roll craze and California's sunny, recreational environment. It also became possible for an enthusiastic and latently talented college kid to squeeze into a peripheral position at one of these firms in order to learn about the record business. From this tutorial musical environment of the late Fifties and early Sixties came a new breed of youthful entrepreneurs who wrote songs, made records and even managed artists while maintaining a semi-professional status. Later-to-be-successful record producers like Herb Alpert, Frank Zappa, Shel Talmy and Terry Melcher cut their teeth on the occasional hit and many obscure failures during this period.

Until 1965, LA's record business was still searching for an identity. Unable to compete with the thriving New York scene, dozens of local labels struggled for local sales and occasionally surfaced with a national hit like the Teddy Bears', 'To Know Him Is To Love Him' and Jan & Arnie's 'Jenny Lee', two records which are acknowledged as having instigated the entire West Coast rock movement. LA's rock'n'roll future would lie in this state of frivolous apprenticeship until the mid-Sixties when the Byrds, Sonny & Cher and TV shows like *Shindig* turned the Coast into the rock industry's new focal point.

Other 'classic' West Coast-recorded hits from this period include 'Chicano' rockers such as Ritchie Valens' 'La Bamba' and Chris Montez's 'Let's Dance'; archetypal teen-ballads such as 'A Thousand Stars' by Kathy Young and the Innocents and 'Image Of A Girl' by the Safaris and one-shot novelty discs like 'Monster Mash' and 'Alley-Oop'.

John D. Loudermilk, born March 31, 1934, in Durham,

North Carolina, has usually been more successful as a song-writer than as a performer, and it was as a composer that he moved from rural North Carolina to the fast-growing centre of country music, Nashville, in the mid-Fifties. His first hit came when George Hamilton IV took 'A Rose And A Baby Ruth' to No. 6 in the American pop charts in November 1956. Subsequent hits included Stonewall Jackson's 'Water-loo' (1959) and Johnny Ferguson's 'Angela Jones' (1960), covered in Britain by Michael Cox. As 'Tommy Dee' he recorded 'Three Stars', a maudlin tribute to Buddy Holly, Ritchie Valens and the Big Bopper, in 1959.

Loudermilk's biggest period was 1961–62; Sue Thompson had successive hits with 'Sad Movies' and 'Norman', and the writer himself scored with 'The Language Of Love', 'Thou Shalt Not Steal', 'Callin' Doctor Casey' and 'Road Hog'. Mid-Sixties writing successes included 'Abilene' and 'Tobacco Road'.

Loudermilk has never sounded particularly convincing as a recording artist; even his own hits sound more like the demo records that they probably started out as, due to his light voice and simple backings. As a songwriter, though, his work has passed beyond the C&W field into the pop and 'novelty pop' categories. He continues to prosper as a live entertainer, armed with guitar, harmonica, and plenty of patter.

Jim Lowe, born in Springfield, Missouri, May 7, 1927, worked in Chicago and New York as a deejay after gradu-ating from the University of Missouri. He retained a liking for country music, writing songs such as 'Gambler's Guitar' for Rusty Draper. He recorded country for Mercury and joined Dot from 1955 till 1960. In 1956, 'The Green Door' became a national rock'n'roll hit and was even covered by Bill Haley. Other recordings included 'Blue Suede Shoes' and 'Talkin' To The Blues', and two minor hits, 'Rock A Chicka' and 'He'll Have To Go'. Currently, he is a deejay with WNEW New York.

Bob Luman started with Imperial Records in 1957 as their answer to Presley, a role later filled more successfully by Ricky Nelson. Born April 15, 1938, in Nacogdoches, Texas, he was working for radio KWKH and turned from C&W to rockabilly, a style for which he had great aptitude. Singles like 'Red Hot' and 'Red Cadillac And A Black Moustache' failed commercially, but he appeared in the 1957 movie *Carnival Rock* and gained radio and TV work. Returning to C&W with Capitol, Warner Brothers, Hickory and Epic, he has been moderately successful since; 'Let's Think About Living' (written by Boudleaux Bryant) in 1960 and 'The File' in 1964 became C&W and popular hits.

Frankie Lymon, born in Washington Heights on Sept. 30, 1942, fronted the accurately named Teenagers who, with Little Anthony's Imperials, were prototypes for contemporary soul groups like the Jackson Five. Apart from Lymon the group comprised Sherman Garnes (born June 8, 1940), Joe Negroni (Sept. 9, 1940), Herman Santiago (Feb. 18, 1941), and Jimmy Merchant (Feb. 10, 1940). Hy Weiss, owner of New York's Old Town label passed Lymon on to rival George Goldner of Gee Records. In 1955, the group sold two million copies of 'Why Do Fools Fall In Love'. In 1956 came the mawkish 'I'm Not A Juvenile Delinquent', an apologia for rock'n'roll that was both ghastly and ironic, though the sound was undeniably attractive if you discounted Goldner's lyric. Finally, there was Lymon's exultantly youthful voice, almost feminine, tackling the standard 'Goody Goody' to full orchestral accompaniment.

The same year, 1957, the group disintegrated. Theirs had been the typical saga of exploitation of blacks and teenagers in the first rock'n'roll boom – a handful of calculated and rather bland hits, some film appearances, then fade. Frankie Lymon went solo on Roulette in 1957 and soldiered into oblivion in the early Sixties. Totally forgotten, he died of drug abuse in February 1968.

Willie Mabon, a singer and pianist born in Memphis on Oct.

24, 1925, was a major presence in the R&B charts between 1952 and 1954. His hits for Chess included 'I Don't Know' (originally on Parrot), 'I'm Mad' and 'Poison Ivy'. The first two both reached the Top Ten. He had previously recorded for Apollo as Big Willie.

A suave and sophisticated performer, Mabon's singing was laconic and dry, leaning more towards the urban blues of the West Coast than the style of the Chicago musicians with whom he often worked. His 'Got To Have Some' was released on Sue in Britain and was included in the repertoire of white R&B performers, like Georgie Fame, in the early Sixties. Mabon's economical blues piano and occasional harmonica playing – also heard on subsequent records for Delta, Mad, Formal and USA – now delights audiences in France where he has cut several albums.

Barry Mann was born on Feb. 9, 1939 in Brooklyn, New York. A would-be architect, he became a songwriter when Paul Case, the general manager of the Aberbach family-owned Hill and Range Music, put one of Mann's first songs on the flip of Bobby Pedrick's 'White Bucks and Saddle Shoes' on Big Top – which was affiliated to Hill and Range – in 1958.

In 1961, Mann married Cynthia Weil, with whom he was to write most of his hits, and turned briefly to recording when his own 'Who Put The Bomp' – with the bomp supplied by New York session singer, Ronald Bright – became a Top Ten hit on ABC in the summer of that year. Further records failed, as did his return to recording when, in the wake of the success of his fellow Brill Building songwriter, Carole King, he attempted a comeback as a singer/songwriter with solo albums in 1971 and 1975.

However, if Mann's recording career was unspectacular, he and Cynthia Weil were one of the most successful non-performing American songwriting teams of the Sixties. In the years 1959–70 – on his own, with Cynthia Weil and with others – Mann wrote nearly 50 Hot Hundred records – only failing to score in 1967. Moreover, as a list of these songs makes clear, Mann and Weil wrote in a variety of styles, though they were most successful with their urban protest songs. 1959: Mann's first hit, 'She Say (Oom Dooby Doom)' (the Diamonds, No. 18). 1960: 'Footsteps' (Steve Lawrence, No. 7) and 'The Way Of A Clown' (Teddy Randazzo, No. 44). 1961: among others two Top Twenty records, 'Bless You' (Tony Orlando) and (with Larry Kobler) 'I Love How You Love Me' (the Paris Sisters). 1962: six Top Twenty records, including 'Come Back Silly Girl' (the Lettermen), 'He's Sure The Boy I Love' and 'Uptown' (the Crystals), 'I'll Never Dance Again' (Bobby Rydell), 'My Dad' (Ray Peterson) and 'Patches' (Dicky Lee). 1963: ten Hot Hundred entries, including four Top Twenty records, 'Blame It On The Bossa Nova' (Eydie Gormé), 'I'll Take You Home' and 'On Broadway' (the Drifters) and 'The Grass Is Greener' (Brenda Lee). 1964: three Top Ten records, 'I'm Gonna Be Strong' (Gene Pitney), 'Saturday Night At The Movies' (the Drifters) and (with Phil Spector) the chart-topping 'You've Lost That Lovin' Feeling' (the Righteous Brothers). 1965: seven Hot Hundred entries, including 'We Gotta Get Out Of This Place' (the Animals) and 'Home Of The Brave' (Bonnie and the Treasures and Jody Miller). 1966: another No. 1, '(You're My) Soul And Inspiration' (the Righteous Brothers) and a Top Ten, 'Kicks' (Paul Revere and the Raiders). 1968: eight Hot Hundred entries, including a Top Ten revival of 'I Love How You Love Me' (Bobby Vinton) and possibly Mann's strangest song 'The Shape Of Things To Come' (Max Frost and the Troopers). 1969: two Hot Hundred entries, including a Top Twenty revival of the Ronettes' 'Walking In The Rain' (Jay and the Americans). 1970: four Hot Hundred entries, including 'New World Coming' (Mama Cass) and 'I Just Can't Help Believing' (B. J. Thomas).

Carl Mann, in a brief recording career, produced a series of rock adaptations of standard tunes and one top national hit with 'Mona Lisa' in 1960. Born in Jackson, Tennessee, in 1941, Mann recorded first for Jaxon in Memphis in 1958 before transferring to Philips International. He recorded several fine soft rock sides, including the original version of Charlie Rich's 'I'm Comin' Home' which Presley copied for RCA. Mann's vocal and piano style was his own, although the legacy of Jerry Lee Lewis's rock hits was evident. In 1963, Mann recorded for Monument before retiring from the music scene.

The Marcels – Cornelius Harp (lead), Ronald Mundy (first tenor), Gene Bricker (second tenor), Dick Knauss (baritone) and Fred Johnson (bass) – were a racially mixed group from Pittsburgh who hit the No. 1 spot in both Britain and America in 1961 with 'Blue Moon'. The goofy 'bom, ba ba bom' introduction was effective in restoring the much-neglected bassman to respectability, and the Marcels, named after a wavy hair style, were much copied. They applied the same novelty treatment to other standards, including 'Summertime', 'Heartaches' – a No. 7 hit by the then all-black group, Allen Johnson and Walt Maddox replacing Knauss and Bricker – and 'My Melancholy Baby', all Col-pix records arranged by Stu Phillips and Bert Keyes.

Ernie Maresca, born on April 21, 1939, reached the Top Ten on Seville in 1962 with 'Shout Shout (Knock Yourself Out)', which has claims to being one of the first punk rock records. The chaotic cacophony of the disc contained echoes of Dion, for whom Maresca had written 'Runaround Sue', 'The Wanderer' and others. A minor league figure in the doo-wop revival of the early Sixties, he also provided songs for the Belmonts ('No One Knows', 'Come On Little Angel'), the Regents ('Runaround'), Nino and the Ebbtides, the Five Discs, the Del-Satins and other New York groups. The Del-Satins, in return, backed him on 'Shout Shout' and worked with Dion on his solo records for Laurie. In the Seventies, Maresca moved to an executive post with Laurie.

Dean Martin, born Dino Crocetti in Ohio on June 7, 1917, began as a singer although his earliest success was as a comedian in partnership with Jerry Lewis. His recording career with Capitol began as a by-product of his movies with Lewis, and took off in 1955 when 'Memories Are Made Of This' reached No. 1. A crooner with an engaging, slurred delivery which managed to suggest his popular image as a tippler without over-emphasizing it, he moved to his chum Frank Sinatra's label Reprise. There he had a series of hits in the early and mid-Sixties with songs such as 'Everybody Loves Somebody' and 'Send Me The Pillow You Dream On'.

Al Martino, a singer of the old school with an almost operatic tenor, was born Alfred Cini in Philadelphia on Oct. 7, 1927. A former bricklayer, he was encouraged to take up singing by Mario Lanza, and the melodramatic 'Here In My Heart' was a hit in 1952 on BBS. He has recorded with varying success for Capitol ever since. 'Spanish Eyes' (originally recorded in 1955) was recently a hit when re-released in Britain. His career took another upward turn following his association with the film *The Godfather*.

Johnny Mathis, born on Sept. 30, 1935, is said to have been the first black American to become a millionaire. Ironically, his success came through his adoption of a white pop ballad approach. He was signed to Columbia in 1956, and at first recorded in a jazz style. Then Mitch Miller decided that Mathis should switch to ballad singing, with the result that he immediately made the charts. Ever since, his ethereal but schmaltzy voice has haunted the hit parade on both sides of the Atlantic. Principally choosing conventional ballads ('The Shadow Of Your Smile', 'The Twelfth Of Never'), in 1974 he had a big hit with a re-make of the Stylistics' Philly-soul song 'Stone In Love With You'. In a sense, Mathis is the natural successor to Nat 'King' Cole, though he lacks the depth of Cole's best work.

Percy Mayfield, from Minden, Louisiana, recorded for Supreme in Los Angeles before joining Specialty, the label on

214

which he hit No. 1 on the R&B charts in 1950 with his own blues ballad, 'Please Send Me Someone To Love'. Other R&B hits included 'Lost Love', 'What A Fool I Was', 'Cry Baby' and 'The Big Question'. His gentle Creole phrasing and urbane style returned to the R&B charts with 'River's Invitation' on Tangerine in 1963, and 'To Live In The Past' on RCA in 1970. Mayfield wrote 'Hit The Road Jack' for Ray Charles.

Jimmy McCracklin, perhaps the most prolific if uneven R&B singer/pianist that the American West Coast has produced, is still active after thirty years of recording. During that time he has worked his way through just about every popular form of R&B. He has sung to piano accompaniment, has played piano and harmonica simultaneously, and led lively bands featuring jump music, blues, R&B, rock'n'roll and soul.

Born in St Louis in 1931, he first recorded in the mid-Forties for the Los Angeles-based Globe label, eventually signing to Modern in 1949 and Swingtime in 1951. He cut his best sides over this period, usually hard-rocking blues highlighted by the nimble guitar work of Lafayette Thomas. As the Fifties progressed, McCracklin began to alter his style to suit the rock'n'roll market. The trick worked, for while at Chess he cut his biggest ever hit, 'The Walk', now regarded as a rock'n'roll classic. Apart from 'Just Got To Know', an R&B No. 2 in 1961 (Art-Tone) his record sales dropped off during the Sixties, culminating in an all-time low with Imperial where he cut dire material like 'These Boots Are Made For Walking'. Fortunately, Stax Records salvaged him in the Seventies, teaming him up with the Memphis Horns for an excellent album, *Yesterday Is Gone*, produced by Al Jackson and Willie Mitchell.

Gene McDaniels, born on Feb. 12, 1935, in Kansas City, and a gospel singer from Omaha University and Conservatory of Music, joined Liberty in 1960. His stay there produced a string of melodic pop hits in the early Sixties including 'A

Hundred Pounds Of Clay' (a No. 3 in 1961, covered in Britain by Craig Douglas), 'A Tear', 'A Tower Of Strength' (an American Top Five record, covered in Britain by Frankie Vaughan), 'Chip Chip' (Top Ten in 1962), 'Point Of No Return' and 'Spanish Lace', both Top Forty records in 1962. These songs, produced by Snuff Garrett, were provided by, among others, Bacharach and David, Goffin and King and Pomus and Shuman. His moody version of 'Another Tear Falls' was the undoubted highspot of Dick Lester's *It's Trad, Dad*. With the dawn of the new black consciousness in the Seventies, McDaniels spurned the synthetic pop trappings of his past, and his records for Atlantic as Eugene McDaniels – including the album, *Outlaw* – dealt frankly and angrily with America's social problems.

Brownie McGhee and Sonny Terry formed a 35-year partnership which has had an incalculable effect on blues appreciation, its interplay of harmonica (Terry) and guitar (McGhee) having left strong impressions on skiffle and every subsequent phase of blues revivalism. McGhee was born in Knoxville, Tennessee, in 1914; Terry in Georgia in 1911. After recording prolifically for black audiences in the Forties and Fifties, they discovered the white market and a new future which they were temperamentally suited to handle. McGhee's personable and articulate manner, coupled with Terry's virtuosity, has clarified the blues for many non-American listeners at concerts and, more recently, on film. Inevitably their repertoire has become somewhat settled, but in performance they have retained a remarkable and communicative vivacity.

Big Jay McNeely's fame as a rock'n'roll contortionist – he was one of the first to play tenor sax lying on his back – went hand in hand with his brash, swinging, coarse-toned style. Born Cecil McNeely on April 29, 1928, he recorded for Exclusive in 1946 and for Savoy in 1949, when 'Deacon's Hop' made the R&B charts. His best-known composition was 'There Is Something On Your Mind', a No. 5 R&B hit in 1959, which also reached the national pop charts. This often revived soul ballad was an even bigger hit for New Orleans singer, Bobby Marchan, in 1960. The original version featured Little Sonny Warner, the McNeely band's vocalist, and was released on Hunter Hancock's Swingin' label. McNeely has also recorded for Aladdin, Federal and Warner Bros, but now makes a living as a post office worker in Los Angeles.

Clyde McPhatter, born on Nov. 15, 1933, in Durham, North Carolina, the son of a Baptist minister, formed a gospel group, the Mount Lebanon Singers, at the age of 14. In 1950, he entered the secular field, joining Billy Ward's Dominoes as lead tenor, recording successfully for Federal. Leaving in 1953, he formed the Drifters and his distinctive high-tenor lead is evident on such hits as 'Money Honey' and 'White Christmas'. Drafted into the USAF in 1954, Clyde embarked on a solo career with Atlantic on discharge in 1956, enjoying a string of R&B best-sellers including 'Treasure Of Love' (also a British hit), 'Without Love', and the million-selling 'A Lover's Question'.

He signed with MGM in 1959, but one year and four minor hits later moved to Mercury, soon finding himself in the upper reaches of the charts with 'Ta Ta'. In 1962 the jumping, percussive 'Lover Please' was an American Top Ten hit. Two more smaller hits followed – Mercury also released seven McPhatter albums over three years – before he switched to Amy in 1966, recording five pleasant but unsuccessful singles. The following year Clyde moved to London, but two 1968 Decca sessions failed to find a winning formula: 'Denver', a solitary 1969 disc on B&C, was well-received but flopped, and he was obliged to return to America in 1970 when his work-permit expired. Clyde Otis persuaded American Decca to record him, and a fine but unsuccessful album resulted. He died in June 1972. Jerry Wexler's was the best epitaph: 'The great, unique soul singer of all time.'

Joe Meek. Meek came from Gloucester and did his National Service in the RAF as a radio technician in the early Fifties. In 1953, he came out and went to work as an engineer at the IBC studio, at that time one of only two independent studios in London. There he engineered records by Frankie Vaughan ('Green Door'), Denis Lotis, Lita Roza, Shirley Bassey, Anne Shelton, Harry Secombe and Petula Clark.

In 1956, Meek went to work for Denis Preston at Lansdowne Studios, where he was engineer on several of Lonnie Donegan's early hits, including 'Cumberland Gap' and 'Don't You Rock Me Daddy-O' as well as trad jazz records by Humphrey Lyttelton and Chris Barber. He also began dabbling in songwriting and in 1958 wrote Tommy Steele's 'Put A Ring On Her Finger'.

Leaving Lansdowne in 1960, Meek built his own studio in a flat above a shop in Holloway, North London, equipping it with £3,000 worth of second-hand equipment. He called it RGM Sound and simultaneously activated his own label, Triumph, going against all odds at a time when British pop was monopolized by the three major labels. A cover version of an American hit, 'Angela Jones' by Michael Cox, reached the Top Ten in June, 1960 but none of Triumph's other releases were successful and Meek discontinued the label in favour of tape-lease deals with the majors. He scored the following year with John Leyton's eerie, futuristic 'Johnny Remember Me' and 'Wild Wind', Mike Berry's poignant 'Tribute to Buddy Holly' and several smaller hits by the Outlaws (with Richie Blackmore) who backed many of Meek's artists on record.

In 1962, a combination of Meek's session musicians recorded an instrumental he wrote titled 'Telstar', under the name of the Tornados, which proved his biggest selling hit, reaching No. 1 in both Britain and America. In production terms, it still remains far ahead of contemporary records. The Tornados followed up with several slightly less successful records including 'Robot', 'Globetrotter' and 'Ice Cream Man' before being swamped in the ensuing Merseybeat craze. Nevertheless, Meek scored early in 1963 with Mike Berry's 'Don't

You Think It's Time' and in 1964 with the Honeycomb's 'Have I The Right', but found the going hard in the mid-Sixties. He had no hits in 1966 and faced with increasing anxiety through personal problems, blew his brains out with a shotgun on February 3, 1967.

Memphis is traditionally the first stop for anyone from the rural Mississippi Delta on their way to find work in the industrial North. White and black musicians from Louisiana and Arkansas, Mississippi and Tennessee, heard each other's music in person and on the radio, and the results were sounds which inspired musicians far beyond the city limits. Thus the recording history of Memphis reveals an amazing range of styles and a series of complex developments.

It was first known as a blues town, with a number of field recording sessions held there in the Twenties and Thirties. But there was no Memphis recording studio as such until after World War II, and much of the jazz, hillbilly, gospel and blues tradition of the town went unrecorded. Sam Phillips was the post-war pioneer. In 1950, he set up the Memphis Recording Service and in 1952, Sun Records. Soon, other labels like Flair (with Elmore James), Meteor, Blues Boy, Buster, Wasco and OJ began to record R&B and C&W. Meanwhile, Sun launched the careers of Rufus Thomas, Junior Parker, Elvis Presley, Carl Perkins, Johnny Cash, Jerry Lee Lewis, Charlie Rich, Roy Orbison and Billy Lee Riley.

In the wake of Sun's success with blues and especially rockabilly, a new clutch of labels emerged. Hi, founded by local record distributor Bill Coughi, had consistent success with the Bill Black Combo ('Smokie', 'White Silver Sands') and occasional hits from Gene Simmons ('Haunted House') and Ace Cannon ('Tuff'). Fernwood scored with Thomas Wayne's 'Tragedy' and Rita Records had Harold Dorman's 'Mountain Of Love'.

Even smaller labels had to lease successful records to larger companies, as Renay did with the Matt Lucas rocker 'I'm Movin' On' (to Smash), and Penn with Sam the

Sham's 'Woolly Bully' (to MGM). The enterprise of Sam Phillips and the success of rockabilly had established Memphis as a major recording centre by the early Sixties. During the soul era, the mantle of Sun would be picked up by a new company, Stax Records.

Memphis Slim. The barrelhouses of Beale Street in Memphis, Tennessee, where he was born Peter Chatman in 1916, probably gave Memphis Slim his declamatory vocal and pianistic style, which was introduced to the blues market in 1940 with the hit 'Beer Drinking Woman'. He continued to record for this audience through the Forties and Fifties, but by the Sixties had discovered a second role as blues and boogie interpreter for whites, a part he developed in cafés, concerts and a series of Folkways albums. For the past 20 years he has lived in France, dividing his recording activity between somewhat sentimental commemorations of the past and somewhat undirected sessions with European (or, occasionally, visiting American) blues, jazz and rock musicians. Though rarely recapturing the unassuming vitality of his small-group recordings in the Fifties he has had a significant influence as an *émigré* bluesman.

Mercury Records, formed in 1947 in Chicago by Irving B. Green, Berle Adams and Art Talmadge as an independent, quickly became a major, setting up its own pressing facilities and national distribution network in its first year. The company had immediate hits by Frankie Laine (which helped it buy up Majestic Records in 1948), Vic Damone and Patti Page, under the supervision of Mitch Miller (who later joined Columbia) and Talmadge (who later left to set up Musicor Records).

Mercury's R&B division was headed by Clyde Otis – the first black A&R man in a major company – and Nat Tarnapol and included Eddie Vinson, Dinah Washington, Brook Benton, Damita Jo and Roy Byrd. However, it was in the mid-Fifties when the company entered the rock'n'roll field that it really prospered, first with white covers of R&B songs

– 'Sh-Boom' (the Crewcuts), 'Tweedle Dee' and 'Dance With Me Henry' (Georgia Gibbs) and 'Little Darlin'' and 'Silhouettes' (the Diamonds), all of which were gold records – and then with originals by the Platters, the Big Bopper and others. The Platters provided Mercury with their biggest hits of the rock'n'roll years and came to the company almost by accident – Mercury signed the Penguins whose 'Earth Angel' had been covered by the Crewcuts and as part of the contract got Buck Ram's other group, the Platters.

With this success behind them Mercury continued to search out rock'n'roll talent, signing up Freddie Bell and the Bellboys and employing Shelby Singleton as a free, floating Southern A&R man. Singleton's signings were the most interesting – Johnny Preston, Bruce Channel, the Big Bopper and, possibly even more important, Jerry Kennedy who was later to produce a string of hits for Mercury with Tom T. Hall, Charlie Rich, Jerry Lee Lewis and others.

Smash, originally a pop subsidiary, was set up in 1959 and in 1962 the company was bought up by North American Phillips bringing Mercury into the worldwide Phonogram set-up and creating another pair of labels, Philips-Fontana. Through its British organisation Fontana became an important source of new talent – the Troggs and the Mindbenders – while Philips had success with acts as varied as Paul and Paula, the Singing Nun and the Four Seasons.

MGM Records was formed in Hollywood in 1946 as an outlet for the company's movie scores. A C&W series was launched with Hank Williams, whose recordings had a profound influence on most country-oriented rock'n'rollers. Although the label recorded jazz-blues artists like Billy Eckstine and Ivory Joe Hunter, occasionally in an R&B vein, it did not have success in the rock field until 1958.

Producers like Jim Vienneau began experimenting with country singers and writers and Marvin Rainwater and Conway Twitty brought considerable success to the label with 'Whole Lotta Woman' and 'It's Only Make Believe' respectively. MGM followed up with Connie Francis whose

'Stupid Cupid' began a lengthy series of hits. An R&B group, the Impalas, was recorded and also Jimmy Jones' successful pop-rock 'Handy Man' and 'Good Timin''.

Mickey and Sylvia. McHouston 'Mickey' Baker, born Oct. 15, 1925 in Lexington, Kentucky, and Sylvia Robinson (née Vanderpool), born March 6, 1936 in New York, met in 1955 when Mickey gave Sylvia guitar lessons. Both had previously recorded solo, and their partnership was some two years old when their fifth disc, 'Love Is Strange', became a 1956 million-seller on Groove. The next five years yielded a string of smaller hits on Vik, RCA and Willow, and the duo remained active as such until 1965. Mickey is now esteemed as a blues solo artist, while Sylvia is co-owner/performer with All Platinum Records.

Amos Milburn, born in Houston, Texas, on April 1, 1927, played an important role in the development of West Coast R&B. His husky blues voice and sophisticated jazz-tinged piano identified the club-style blues of Los Angeles and San Francisco. In 1946 he signed with newly-formed Aladdin records, whose roster was later to boast Charles Brown, Shirley and Lee and the Five Keys. A year later, Milburn cut his most famous hit, the million-selling 'Chicken Shack Boogie'. Other huge sellers included 'One Scotch, One Bourbon, One Beer' and 'Bad, Bad Whiskey'. As the Fifties progressed, Milburn's records veered more and more towards rock'n'roll, but with only the minimum of chart success. In later years he cut one album for Motown. Milburn now resides in Cincinnati, playing club dates and working the occasional studio session.

Ned Miller, born April 12, 1925, at Raines, Utah, is best known for the multi-million selling single 'From A Jack To A King'. This song topped the charts in 1962 but was written when Miller was starting out as a C&W singer with Fabor Records in 1956. He has registered many C&W hits and some minor national successes with Fabor, Challenge,

Capitol and Republic, but has been more successful as a songwriter in the country-pop styles with 'Do What You Do, Do Well', 'Southbound' and 'Invisible Tears'.

Roy Milton, a drummer and vocalist from Wynnewood, Oklahoma, moved to Los Angeles where he and his group, the Solid Senders – Ben Waters (tenor sax), John Kelson (alto), Arthur Walker (trumpet), Camille Howard (piano), Johnny Rodgers (guitar) and Dallas Bartley (drums) – monopolized the R&B charts through 1946 to 1952 with a series of gutty and repetitive jazz-based blues. His Top Ten hits included 'RM Blues' and 'Milton Boogie' (on Jukebox in 1946) and 'True Blues', 'Thrill Me', 'The Hucklebuck', 'Oh Baby', 'T-Town Twist' and 'So Tired' on Specialty. As city blues waned in popularity, Milton recorded less successfully for Cenco, Warwick, Thunderbird and Kent.

Guy Mitchell, born on Feb. 27, 1927, of Yugoslavian parents as Al Cernik, was a child actor in the Thirties, then joined the Navy and set about becoming a singer when he was de-mobbed in 1946. In 1949, he won an Arthur Godfrey Talent show and was signed to Columbia by Mitch Miller the following year. He immediately scored with a series of million-sellers – 'My Heart Cries For You' (1950), 'The Roving Kind', a cover of the Weavers' original version and 'My Truly Truly Fair', another dilution of a folk song by Bob Merrill – who wrote most of Mitchell's hits – both in 1951. But it was 1956 that produced his best known record, 'Singing The Blues' – covered in Britain, as was its follow-up, 'Knee Deep In The Blues', by Tommy Steele. Despite the overly cheerful backing provided by Mitch Miller, Mitchell somehow suggested he really was singing the blues. That song, however, was the exception; and when he recorded 'Heartaches By The Number', another No. 1 in 1959, Mitchell was in complete accord with Miller's backing.

Modern Records stands as one of the great R&B/blues labels of the postwar era. It was formed in April, 1945, in Los

Angeles by white American businessman Jules Bihari and his three brothers Saul, Joe and Lester. In a matter of a few years the brothers had achieved one of the most streamlined distribution networks in the country, with a regional office in New York and contacts throughout the South.

In 1948, a deal was arranged to distribute the Texas-based Gold Star label, thus bringing the talents of country blues singer Lightnin' Hopkins to a mass public. That same year, Modern discovered and signed John Lee Hooker, one of the best and most prolific postwar bluesmen. His debut single, 'Boogie Chillen' became a nationwide R&B hit. It was B. B. King's records that established the RPM label which got underway in Sept. 1950 and became the longest surviving Modern subsidiary. King recorded literally hundreds of sides for the Biharis including his first big seller, 'Three O'Clock Blues'.

At about this time, Ike Turner (band leader) joined Modern as a talent scout. Josea, Taub and Ling, credited writing much of Modern's output were in fact Joe, Saul and Florette Bihari. During this period the company issued product by Howlin' Wolf, Bobby Bland, Junior Parker, Etta James, Rosco Gordon, Jimmy Witherspoon, Smokey Hogg, Saunders King, Floyd Dixon, the Cadets, Johnny Moore's Three Blazers and dozens more. In 1954, Modern signed Mississippi bluesman, Elmore James, to another of its subsidiaries, Flair. In 1956, the brothers decided to slacken off production of singles and concentrate on the growing market in albums via a low-budget line on Crown. Artists like Hooker and James were dropped, only B. B. King being retained. In 1957 production of all labels ceased bar Crown and Modern's present-day successor, Kent.

The Monotones' 'Book of Love' – on Argo – soared into the Top Five of both the R&B and pop charts early in 1958. Founded in Newark, New Jersey in 1954, the group comprised Charles Patrick (lead vocal, born Sept. 11, 1938), Warren Davis (March 1, 1939), George Malone (Jan. 5, 1940), Warren Ryanes (Dec. 14, 1937), John Smith (May

224

13, 1938) and John Ryanes (Nov. 16, 1940). Based on a Pepsodent commercial, the arrangement – featuring a snappy drumbeat – occurred to the group when kids outside threw a ball against the window of the room in which they were practising: 'That ball hit the window, "boom", so we kept it in as the drum part.' Other discs for Argo (leased from Hull) were unsuccessful and the group disbanded when several members were conscripted.

Chris Montez, born Jan. 17, 1943, in Los Angeles, attended the same school in Hawthorne, California, as the Beach Boys. He made his first record, 'She's My Rocking Baby' at 17, in 1960. After graduating in 1961, he met Jim Lee, a young writer-producer working at Indigo Records in Hollywood. Leaving Indigo, Lee formed Monogram Records around Montez, whose first record for the label, 'All You Had To Do Was Tell Me' (a duet with Kathy Young) became a local hit. The sequel, 'Let's Dance', sold a million late in 1962, as did the follow-up, 'Some Kinda Fun' (although it only reached No. 43 in America), and Montez toured Britain with Tommy Roe early in 1963, headlining over newcomers the Beatles. Montez's subsequent releases flopped and in 1964, Jim Lee abandoned the label to pursue a singing career. Montez came back on AM in 1966 with 'Call Me' and 'The More I See You', both sung in the coy middle-of-the-road style he still practises today.

The Moonglows – Bobby Lester (born Jan. 13, 1930), Harvey Fuqua (1924), Alexander Graves (April 17, 1930) and Prentis Barnes (1921) with Billy Johnson (1924) on guitar – emerged from Louisville, Kentucky, in 1952 and recorded briefly on Champagne before Alan Freed had them signed by Chance. Chance folded in 1955 and they joined Chess, debuting with the Fuqua–Freed ballad 'Sincerely', an R&B hit covered by the McGuire Sisters for the pop market. The group led a schizoid career for a while, recording occasionally as Bobby Lester and the Moonlighters on Checker, and as the Moonglows on Chess, who scored a national Top

Thirty hit in 1955 with a jump tune, 'See Saw', featured in the *Rock Rock Rock* movie. Their peak came in 1958 when 'Ten Commandments Of Love' featuring Fuqua made No. 22 in the Top Hundred. The original personnel split shortly after this, and though Moonglows discs appeared on Chess in 1960, no original members were in this group, who subsequently became Motown's Spinners. Fuqua re-formed the group in 1970 for 'revival' concerts, and the Moonglows, featuring Harvey and unspecified others, recorded for RCA in 1972.

Merrill Moore, born 1923 in Algona, Iowa, was part of a small school of country-boogie pianists whose style pre-dated rock'n'roll. His pounding right-hand improvisations, chopped rhythms and steady drum backings on titles such as 'House Of Blue Lights', 'Rock Rockola' and 'Down The Road Apiece' were an important link between boogie-woogie and Western-swing of the Forties and the early rock styles. Moore moved to San Diego in the late Forties and has worked the club scene steadily, recording for Capitol 1952–8 and B&C in 1969. He was employed, too, as a session pianist, backing Tommy Sands' and Wanda Jackson's Capitol hits.

Scotty Moore, born Dec., 1931, in Gadsden, Tennessee, served a musical apprenticeship in conventional country music on radio WBRO Washington and in Nashville session work. Moving to Memphis in 1954, he formed Elvis Presley's first group and was his first manager. Moore's guitar style developed out of R&B and C&W and his contribution to Presley's Sun and RCA rockabilly recordings was crucial to their sound. He toured with Presley, and appeared in movies such as *Loving You* before buying into Fernwood Records in Memphis and producing Thomas Wayne's hit 'Tragedy'. His style has inspired a wide range of guitarists from James Burton through Lonnie Mack to Amos Garrett.

Moon Mullican, born in Corrigan, Texas, in 1909, gained experience as a pianist in the clubs of Houston, Beaumont and Nashville before recording for Decca in the Thirties and appearing in several western movies. He earned the title 'King of the Hillbilly Piano Players' with C&W hits for King such as 'Jole Blon' in 1947 and 'I'll Sail My Ship Alone' in 1951. His pumping left hand and 'two-finger' right hand style influenced Jerry Lee Lewis and in 1956-7 Mullican recorded several rock songs himself, including 'Seven Nights To Rock' with Boyd Bennett's band, whose 'Seventeen' had been a rock hit in 1955.

Nashville, Tennessee, is often called 'Music City USA'. It boasts a multi-million dollar recording industry which developed in the first instance from country music. In 1925, radio WSM started a *Barn Dance* programme which became known as the *Grand Ole Opry*, a country music institution which continues to this day.

No record labels were based there until Bullet was formed in 1945 and recorded C&W, R&B, gospel and popular music in the WSM studios. Nashville quickly became the C&W capital after radio engineers Aaron Shelton and Carl Jenkins had set up their Castle Recording Studio in the Tulane Hotel, providing facilities for major companies like Decca, while Acuff-Rose and Hill And Range Publishers were formed in 1942 and 1945 respectively, opening the way for a thriving recording and business network. The Tennessee and Republic labels were formed locally, and soon all the major companies followed Decca in establishing an office in the city. The music itself had not substantially altered at this time, however, being mainly traditional and played on acoustic instruments.

Ironically, the catalyst in the development of the 'Nashville Sound' was rock'n'roll. C&W took a battering from the sales of rock records and many labels based in Nashville began to record the style. Elvis Presley was imported from nearby Memphis, the Everly Brothers recorded there, and the session musicians learned to adapt. By now, amplified guitars were the rule and the piano also came to the fore while the traditional country fiddle and banjo were in decline. By the late Fifties ,a group of musicians including Chet Atkins, Floyd Cramer, Grady Martin, Bob Moore, Buddy Harman and Boots Randolph had evolved a sound that became known as the most slick, professional studio back-up in popular music. The guitar was rock, but smooth, and vocal choruses added sophistication to the sound of Patsy Cline, Don Gibson, Jim Reeves and Faron Young. Very soon the full range of orchestral and choral effects were being utilized in the Nashville studios.

In 1958, the Country Music Association was formed and in 1960 the town grossed thirty-five million dollars through music. Studios, such as RCA and Bradleys, became renowned, and the producers and A&R men provided hit after hit. They recorded popular singers like Connie Francis and Petula Clark as well as country-based artists. Men like Steve Sholes, Don Law, Ken Nelson, Shelby Singleton and Jim Vienneau had transformed the C&W industry until, by 1963, half the recordings made in America came out of Nashville.

Ken Nelson, born in Minnesota in 1915, but brought up in Chicago, played pop in the Thirties with a trio led by Lee Gillette, who later activated Capitol's C&W division. In the early Forties, Nelson became one of Chicago's top classical radio announcers but became enamoured with the C&W music also being broadcast from his station. In 1948, he followed Lee Gillette to Capitol where Gillette gave him a job as a C&W A&R man.

In the early Fifties, Nelson found he had to travel all over the country, recording artists in radio stations and local studios, but gradually, as the Nashville scene developed, he began to commute between Hollywood and Nashville. Among his earliest hits were Hank Thompson's 'The Wild Side Of Life' and Jean Shepard's 'Dear John Letter'.

Nelson, it is claimed, was the first A&R man to use drums on a country session – by white gospel singer, Martha Carson, in 1952 – several years before drums were formally accepted by country music. He recorded Ferlin Husky, Tennessee Ernie Ford and Merle Travis in the early Fifties before instigating Capitol's inroads into rock'n'roll in 1956 by signing Gene Vincent, who scored immediately with 'Be-Bop-A-Lula'. However, Capitol's initial lack of success in this field must be attributed to Nelson's lack of sympathy for the idiom and although Vincent, Tommy Sands and Sonny James all achieved million-sellers in the pop market in 1956–7, the uniformly unsuccessful follow-up material Nelson picked for them was merely a Tin Pan Alley caricature of true rock'n'roll.

In the Sixties, Nelson built up an impressive roster of country talent for Capitol, including Buck Owens, Merle Haggard and a revitalized Sonny James, three of the era's biggest stars. He retired in 1973.

Rick Nelson was born in Teaneck, New Jersey, on May 8, 1940, into a showbusiness family. His parents, Ozzie and Harriet, had a popular radio show and Ricky joined the cast in 1948, making his film debut the following year.

In the Fifties, the show moved onto television, and as a result of his nationwide popularity Ricky gained a recording contract with Verve in 1956. In May of the following year he scored a double-sided hit with 'A Teenager's Romance' and the Fats Domino cover 'I'm Walkin'' and followed this three months later with 'You're My One And Only Love'. He was then signed to Imperial, and stayed with the label through 36 Hot Hundred titles (usually double-sided hits) until 1963 – among them were 'Stood Up' (No. 5 in 1957), 'Believe What You Say' (No. 8 in 1958), 'Poor Little Fool' (No. 1 the same year), 'Never Be Anyone Else But You/It's Late' (No. 6 and 9 respectively in 1959) and 'Travellin' Man'/'Hello Mary Lou' (No. 1 and 9 in 1961).

Having changed his name to 'Rick' in 1961, Nelson moved to Decca and the hits continued for a couple of years.

Although the late Sixties were a lean time as far as chart success was concerned, Nelson's growing interest in country music resulted in a maturing of his style and more satisfactory albums than many of his 'teen idol' years. He returned to the Hot Hundred in 1969 with a version of Dylan's 'She Belongs To Me', and in 1972 reached the Top Ten with his classic autobiographical song 'Garden Party'. This describes his reception at a Madison Square Garden 'rock'n' roll revival' show and his difficulty in getting over his new work in the face of his long list of teenage hits. During the previous year, Nelson had formed his Stone Canyon Band, the unit with whom he continues to work today.

Nelson had his first hit at the age of sixteen, and he was carefully packaged to appeal to a young audience; greased hair, lop-sided grin and slightly rebellious (but not dangerous) stance. His voice, though distinctive, was rather weak and limited in range, and was bolstered up by double-tracking. The songs he was given were carefully tailored to suit his image, and above all he was provided with first-rate musicians. The most notable was guitarist James Burton, whose innovative guitar solos were central to the success of Rick's records until well into the Sixties. In spite of his stature, Burton has never been particularly successful as a front-man but seems to revel in a supporting role, most recently for Elvis. In the Stone Canyon Band, Nelson derives similar support from steel-player Tom Brumley, late of Buck Owens' band.

It was the albums *Bright Lights and Country Music* (1966) and *Country Fever* (1967) which showed Nelson's determined attempt to find a new direction now that he had slipped past the age of twenty-five. His progress has so far taken him to an individual position in 'country rock'; and although one will always wish that he could put a bit of edge onto his voice, the maturity and professionalism of Nelson and his band currently produce albums of a high standard. Unfortunately, there will always be people, particularly those who suffered the corn of the *Ozzie and Harriet* show, who will never be able to take early Ricky Nelson at any price. But songs like 'Stood Up', 'Poor Little Fool' and 'It's Late' are a worthy part of pop history.

Sandy Nelson, born Sander Nelson in Santa Monica, California, on Dec. 1, 1938, attained considerable popularity in the early Sixties with a series of instrumentals which pitched his monotonous drumming against a solitary guitar playing menacing riffs. Originally a member of the same West Coast high school clique with Jan and Dean, Phil Spector and Nancy Sinatra, Nelson first played drums in an obscure local band called Kip Tyler and the Flips, which recorded for the Ebb and Challenge labels (ex-Beach Boy Bruce Johnston played piano). In 1958, he played drums on the million-seller 'To Know Him Is To Love Him', by the Teddy Bears, with whom he also travelled during a cash-in tour. Turning to session work, he played on Gene Vincent's *Crazy Times* album (1959), shortly before recording 'Teenbeat' for the small Original Sound label. The record sold a million worldwide and Nelson immediately moved to the larger Imperial label where he had to wait two years for his second hit 'Let There Be Drums'. Shortly before recording it, Nelson lost his left foot in a car crash but his drumming was unimpaired.

During the Sixties, he recorded a series of near-Muzak instrumental albums covering a variety of contemporary themes but has not been active recently.

Art Neville, born Arthur Lanon Neville in New Orleans on Dec. 17, 1937, has a career spanning all the phases of New Orleans music-mambo, rock'n'roll, soul and modern funk. Heavily influenced by Professor Longhair, Neville joined the Hawketts – Carol Joseph (trombone), August Fleury and Israel Bell (trumpets), George Davis (alto), Maurice Bashman (tenor), Alfred August (guitar) and John Boudreaux (drums) – in 1955. Their record of 'Mardi Gras Mambo', with Neville on piano and vocals, is released annually by Chess to coincide with the local celebrations. Neville went solo on Specialty in 1958 with several rocking singles, all made with the assistance of Cosimo Matassa's finest studio sessionmen. Jerry Byrne's 'Lights Out', also on Specialty, features Neville's brain-bending piano solo. In 1961,

Neville followed his brother Aaron to Minit where he recorded under Allen Toussaint. Later he formed the Meters.

New Orleans. The good-time, happy-go-lucky New Orleans R&B sound was a contributory factor to the rise of rock'n' roll music in the Fifties, and many rocking classics were cut at Cosimo Matassa's tiny studios in the French Quarter with the best sessionmen in support. It was a sound which Mac Rebennack has described as 'strong drums, heavy bass, light piano, heavy guitar and light horn sound, and a strong lead vocal'.

With a long and colourful musical heritage to fall back on, the present scene really started in the immediate post-war years when David and Julian Braund of De Luxe Records, New Jersey, were the first record men to realize the vast potential that New Orleans and its artists offered. They recorded everybody in town between 1947–9, and got the big hit they were looking for with Roy Brown and 'Good Rockin' Tonight'. It was Lew Chudd and Imperial Records who struck real gold when they signed first Dave Bartholomew, as A&R man, and then Fats Domino as artist in 1949. Fats' first record, 'The Fat Man', was an immediate success and it started an almost unbroken sequence of hits until 1963 when Chudd sold Imperial to Liberty; 'Ain't That A Shame', 'Blueberry Hill', 'Blue Monday', 'I'm Walkin'', 'Walking To New Orleans', all familiar million-sellers which helped put New Orleans well and truly on the record map.

The success of Fats Domino inspired other labels to make the long trip down to Louisiana to seek out further talent. Aladdin scored with Shirley and Lee, Atlantic with Ray Charles and Professor Longhair, Specialty with Lloyd Price, Guitar Slim and Little Richard, Chess with Sugar Boy Crawford, the Hawketts, Bobby Charles and Clarence Henry, and of course Imperial with Smiley Lewis, Tommy Ridgley, the Spiders, Bobby Mitchell and Roy Brown. Most also made use of the talents of the famous Studio Band of New Orleans session musicians, including Earl Palmer (drums), later replaced by Charles 'Hungry' Williams, Frank Fields (bass), Red Tyler and Mel Lastie (horns), and Harold Battiste (with, later, Allen Toussaint) on piano. Regrettably, most companies were only on a get-rich-quick exercise, and the artists and indeed the city's overall music scene were the last to profit. So when sales of R&B records dipped in the late Fifties, the independents dropped New Orleans like a hot potato, leaving the locals to their own devices.

Johnny Vincent's Ace label had been the first local company to operate in New Orleans in 1955 and with a star-studded roster of Huey Smith and the Clowns, Earl King, Frankie Ford and Jimmy Clanton they could hardly fail. Ace had several national successes which inspired other local operators to start their own labels – men like Joe Ruffino (Ric and Ron), Joe Banashak and Larry McKinley (Minit), and Irvine Smith (Instant). By 1960 the heavier rock'n'roll sounds of the Fifties were falling out of favour, and it was Minit, and producer Allen Toussaint in particular, who directed the new trend towards a softer, mellower yet funkier R&B approach. This policy paid handsome dividends when Jessie Hill, Ernie K-Doe, Irma Thomas, Benny Spellman and Aaron Neville all had hit records along with Instant's Chris Kenner. Several outside labels came back, and Chess scored again with Clarence Henry, Fire/Fury with Lee Dorsey and Bobby Marchan, while Imperial were still going strong with Earl King, Ford Eaglin and, of course, Fats Domino. In 1962 Harold Battiste, frustrated by so many bad record deals, set up AFO Records on a co-operative basis and although Barbara George had an immediate hit, the label soon crumbled in chaos and disillusionment. The demise of AFO effectively marked the end of the classic New Orleans R&B era.

New York Record Companies. The first New York independents to start up were Apollo and Savoy – both in 1942 – although the latter was, strictly speaking, in New Jersey. Apollo was formed by Ike and Bess Berman and its artists included Wynonie Harris, the Five Royales and gospel singer Mahalia Jackson. Savoy, formed by Herman Lubinsky, had a wide range of R&B artists that included Nappy Brown, Big Maybelle, Paul Williams and Johnny Otis, who in 1950 had eight Top Ten R&B hits. However, the company became less and less successful through the Fifties and increasingly relied on gospel singer James Cleveland. While both labels brought out some excellent songs that foreshadowed what was to come, neither had a rock'n'roll hit and either lost their artists (Johnny Otis, for example, had hits for Capitol in 1958) or succumbed to cover versions.

Similarly, many labels, such as the various ones put out since 1953 by Bobby Robinson, were not hugely successful – despite a No. 1 on Fury with Wilbert Harrison's 'Kansas City' in Robinson's case – due to copyright and distribution problems, always the bugbear of 'indies'.

National, the most successful independent up to 1950, was formed by Al Green in 1946, at a time when the New York record scene was becoming much more localized with the boom of the West Coast 'indies'. They had hits from Dusty Fletcher and the Ravens, plus million-selling records from Eileen Barton and crooner Billy Eckstine. But by the birth of rock'n'roll, they had folded – they had their own record plant but never made the transition from 78s to 45s.

Jubilee, with its subsidiary Josie, was founded in 1948 by Jerry Blaine, a distributor for lots of local labels who was therefore regularly in contact with managers. Jubilee was one of the first independents to achieve success with a black group, the Orioles, who had their first hit with the rhythm and blues song 'It's Too Soon To Know'. By 1953 they had moved towards a more sentimental style, with 'Crying In The Chapel', that other black groups like the Four Tunes (also on Jubilee) adopted. Other hits the label had were 'Speedoo' by the Cadillacs (1956) and Bobby Freeman's 'Do You Wanna Dance' (1958) but after they veered towards minority tastes that included 'party' records.

Archie Bleyer's Cadence (1950) differed from the rest of the 'indies' in that it catered for commercial rather than specialist tastes, with artists like the Chordettes, Eddie Hodges and the Everly Brothers (though they were not recorded in New York). Yet it was Herald/Ember, formed in 1952 by Al Silver, that had the most hits, specializing in group records with the Nutmegs, the Turbans, Charlie and Ray and the Silhouettes.

The disc jockey's role in making more people aware of black music was considerable. Jocko Henderson, for example, on a so-called black station, oriented his programmes to the whites who began listening in, and Alan Freed's role in particular on white stations was of paramount importance. Thus more 'indies' signed up black musicians in the hope of success; Rama, a subsidiary of Tico, founded by George Goldner in 1953, had many black groups that included the Crows ('Gee'), the Cleftones, the Valentines and the Harptones, as did Red Robin, also formed in 1953 by Bobby Robinson and Old Town (1955 by Hy Weiss) with Arthur Prysock.

With the continuing spread of audience taste, new 'indies' emerged. Roulette, the largest apart from Atlantic, was formed in 1956 by Phil Kahl and Maurice Levy, and George Goldner, who came in later, set up the subsidiaries Gone and End the following year.

The establishment of Scepter/Wand by Florence Greenburg in 1959 brought the first important rival to Atlantic. They had Luther Dixon to produce Goffin and King, and Bacharach and David material for people like the Shirelles, Chuck Jackson and Dionne Warwick and in a sense it was Dixon's work that heralded Spector's era.

Anthony Newley, the child actor who became the darling of the Las Vegas night-club circuit, flirted very briefly with rock'n'roll during his transition period. Born in Hackney, London, in 1931, his most famous juvenile role was that of the Artful Dodger in *Oliver Twist* (1948). In 1959, having successfully bridged the gap to adult parts, he played a conscripted rock'n'roll singer in the film *Idle on Parade* and also sang and co-wrote the title song. An infectious rock number despite the fact that it was primarily intended as parody (note the amount of voice echo) it entered the charts and launched Newley on a recording career. His follow-ups, however, were plaintive ballads ('Why?', 'Do You Mind?', 'D-Darling' etc.) and three more of these ('Gonna Build A Mountain', 'Once In A Lifetime' and 'What Kind Of Fool Am I?') were the mainstays of *Stop the World, I Want to Get Off!*, the new-wave stage musical he wrote with Leslie Bricusse in 1961. The show not only broadened and revitalized the regimented structure of the musical, but also established the public image that Newley maintains today of the dynamic, but tortured, all-round entertainer.

Novelty Records. Early in 1956, when rock'n'roll was itself a novelty, two young songwriters named Dick Goodman and Bill Buchanan conceived 'The Flying Saucer', a record which preserved in almost documentary form the impact of rock'n'roll on the media. It gave a phoney account of an invasion from outer-space, integrating snatches of then popular rock records into the dizzy narrative. A record which deejayed itself was destined for heavy airplay and by late August, 1956, was an American hit.

From then on, novelty items were seen as part and parcel of rock'n'roll. Indeed, reflecting the industry's ambiguous attitude to rock'n'roll, it often became the subject of novelty records. Examples of this are Stan Freberg's 'version' of 'Heartbreak Hotel' and, more obviously, his 'The Old Payola Roll Blues' in America and Peter Sellers' minor British hit, 'I'm So Ashamed', in which the singer is eight and worried if he's not too old since he hasn't had a Top Twenty record for a whole three weeks.

But not all novelty records were inspired by rock'n'roll. One particular zany slice of humour in 1956 was 'Transfusion' by Nervous Norvus, actually Jimmy Drake, a 44-year-old truck driver living in San Francisco. Musically, it was a very quiet folksy record but the lyrics were about a speed-crazed driver who crashed repeatedly and required countless pints of blood. The grizzly narrative, sung nonchalantly in an adenoidal tenor, was punctuated at intervals by the screech of tires, a deafening crash and choruses ending with lines like 'Hey Daddy-O, Make That Type O' and 'Pour The Crimson In Me, Jimson'.

In 1958, Ross Bagdasarian, an American actor turned songwriter, discovered that by speeding up tape, funny voices resulted and he made 'The Witchdoctor' ('Ooh-ee-ooh-aah-aah' etc.) a children's favourite in the late Fifties. Changing his name to David Seville, Bagdasarian then developed the sound into multiplicity by creating the Chipmunks, a ghastly figment of the electronic imagination which helped establish Liberty as a major label.

The record industry apes itself with witless intensity and Sheb Wooley, another actor-songwriter, capitalized on 'The Witchdoctor' by recording 'The Purple People Eater' for MGM. It was the fastest-selling novelty record for five years, and manufacturers rushed on the market with Purple People Eater hats, T-shirts, buttons, 'The Cuban Purple People Eater' (in cha-cha rhythm) and 'The Purple Herring Fresser', a Yiddish version.

One of the better records to emerge from Philadelphia during the late Fifties was John Zacherle's 'Dinner With Drac', a rock'n'roll instrumental punctuated by horrific limericks which Zacherle clumsily related like a businessman telling a tasteless joke at a party, bursting into laughter at the offence he has caused. 'Drac' made America's Top Twenty but was castigated for its tastelessness when issued in Britain.

Dozens more obscure novelty discs were made by black vocal groups who often featured vocal gimmickry on the up-tempo sides of their records. 'Alley-Oop' by the Hollywood Argyles, released in 1960, featured Gary Paxton (one half of Skip and Flip) croaking out contrived comic-book jargon backed by what sounded like a drunken Salvation Army choir playing a heavy walking beat. Two years later, Paxton, as a producer, snatched Bobby 'Boris' Pickett from a local bar-band and had him perform his Boris Karloff imitation on 'Monster Mash' for Paxton's small Garpax label.

237

Hoping for local sales, Paxton found he had an American No. 1 which has since become timeless in its appeal – re-released in 1974, it made No. 1 again.

In 1963, Jeff Wayne, currently David Essex's producer, and two friends doctored up their voices electronically to produce the Dalek-like 'Martian Hop' which they released as by the Ran-Dells. Over the years we've had the insipid Napoleon XIV, the Goons, and crown-prince of novelty, Ray Stevens, whose successes over ten years, which include 'Ahab The Arab', 'Gitarzan', 'Harry The Hairy Ape', 'Bridget The Midget' and 'The Streaker', have kept the novelty record tradition alive beyond the era of rock'n'roll.

The Nutmegs. In 1955 Leroy and James Griffin, Wiliam Emery, James Tyson and Thomas McNeil, from New Haven, Connecticut, formed a group and borrowed their State's 'nutmeg' emblem for themselves. Lead singer Leroy Griffin was a talented writer; thus the group were able to perform original material, arousing the interest of a local publisher who took them to Herald Records. Their first disc was 'Story Untold', a ballad of lost love featuring Leroy's mournful lead and wailing harmony – a massive R&B hit. The follow-up, 'Ship of Love', also sold well but further success eluded them. Leroy was killed in a smelting furnace accident in 1969 and replaced by nephew Harold Jaynes when the group re-formed in 1974 and recorded a fresh version of 'Story Untold'.

The Orioles – Sonny Til (born Earlington Tilghman), George Nelson, Alexander Sharp and Johnny Reed – were singing together in 1947 as the Vibra-Naires in local Baltimore clubs when they were spotted by Deborah Chessler, who booked them onto Arthur Godfrey's *Talent Scout* show. They lost to George Shearing, but Godfrey was sufficiently impressed to invite them onto his daytime radio show.

In 1948, they met Jerry Blaine of Natural Records and cut 'It's Too Soon To Know', changing their name to Orioles after the Maryland State bird. Natural then became Jubilee, for whom the group recorded until 1956, scoring many R&B hits including chart-toppers 'Tell Me So' (1949) and 'Crying In The Chapel' (1953), characteristic sentimental love ballads with subtle instrumental accompaniment. Nelson quit in 1953, to be replaced by Gregory Carroll, but a year later the original group disbanded. Of the founder-members, Nelson died of asthma in 1959 and Sharp, of a heart attack, in 1970. Meanwhile Til 'adopted' the Regals (Albert Russell, Paul Griffin, Billy Adams and Jerry Rodriguez) as new Orioles, recording for Jubilee until early 1956 when, following problems with royalties and material, they moved to Vee Jay where they cut a further series of mellow love-songs before disbanding in 1957.

In 1962 Til put together a third 'Orioles' (Delton McCall, Billy Taylor and Gerald Gregory), cutting an album for Charlie Parker Records, and with personnel variations the group have subsequently recorded for Lana, Sutton and, in 1971, RCA.

Tony Orlando, born in New York, on April 3, 1944, first worked as a singer on demonstration discs for Don Kirshner's famous Brill Building music publishing operation. Orlando cut the originals of 'Will You Still Love Me Tomorrow' and 'Some Kind Of Wonderful' (hits for the Shirelles and the Drifters) before Kirshner realized his potential as a singer in his own right.

He specialized in the perfectly organized pop single and had three hits on Epic during 1961: 'Halfway To Paradise' (a British hit for Billy Fury), 'Bless You' (Top Twenty) and 'Happy Times'. As a vocalist, he was one of the first 'blue-eyed soul' singers and the productions – by Kirshner and Al Nevins – were almost symphonic. But despite the rich strings, Spanish guitars, castanets and girl choruses, it was Orlando that you heard. Hours of practice in acappella groups had helped to perfect a distinctive voice which often outshone the Goffin-King songs he was given. Machine-tooled, market-tested pop can be fine when you hum like

239

Ben E. King. Although the Orlando voice disappeared later in the Sixties, he re-appeared in the next decade with a string of equally successful records with Dawn.

The Orlons comprised Shirley Brickley, Rosetta Hightower, Steve Caldwell and Marlena Davis. They had a string of weak and watery dance hits on Cameo-Parkway between 1962 and 1964. Not the best black singers around, they owed much of their success to frequent exposure on Philadelphia's *Bandstand* TV show. 'The Wah Watusi' (No. 2), 'Don't Hang Up' (No. 4), 'South Street' (No. 3), 'Not Me' (No. 12) and 'Cross Fire' (No. 19) were the biggest hits, while the girls also sang on records by Dee Dee Sharp and Bobby Rydell.

In 1964, Caldwell left and Audrey Birchley replaced Davis. After further discs for ABC and Calla as a trio, the group split up when Hightower left for a solo career in Britain, where the Searchers had enjoyed a big hit with an Orlons original, 'Don't Throw Your Love Away'.

Johnny Otis, now billed as the Godfather of Rhythm and Blues, was born in Vallejo, California, on Dec. 28, 1921, to Greek immigrant parents, Alexander and Irene Veliotes. By 1940, the big band jazz of Count Basie and Duke Ellington had inspired him to start learning drums, later progressing to piano and vibes. In 1946 he switched from a small boogie-blues outfit to a 16-piece jazz-swing band, signed a contract with Excelsior Records and scored his first hit, 'Harlem Nocturne'. The band took off on a nationwide tour with Louis Jordan, Nat 'King' Cole and the Inkspots. They were later to record with such jazz greats as Lester Young, Illinois Jacquet and Jimmy Rushing.

In 1948, Otis opened the Barrelhouse Club in Los Angeles, thus launching the very first nightspot to feature R&B music exclusively. While at the Barrelhouse, he discovered 13-year-old Little Esther (Philips). Throughout 1950, the pair cut numerous hits for Savoy records, usually billed as Little Esther with Johnny Otis and the Robins (who were another Otis find). Their first recording, 'Double Crossing Blues', was a No. 1 R&B seller throughout the nation. This was followed by 'Mistrustin' Blues', 'Wedding Boogie' and 'Deceivin' Blues'.

At about the same time, Otis saw the potential of a touring R&B review, and so 'The Johnny Otis R&B Caravan' took to the road – again the first of its kind. The package featured several Otis discoveries, including Big Mama Thornton, who was later to cut the original version of Leiber and Stoller's 'Hound Dog,' with Otis in accompaniment. Even with lengthy tours to contend with, Otis found time to search out new talent. While in Detroit in 1951, he discovered Jackie Wilson, Little Willie John and Hank Ballard. A few years later the legendary Johnny Ace joined the Otis package, and quickly became the star of the show. Otis went on to arrange and produce most of Ace's recordings for the Texas-based Duke-Peacock label, including his smash hit of 1954, 'Pledging My Love'. Little Richard, Etta James, Charles Brown, Johnny 'Guitar' Watson and Sugarcane Harris are just a few of the other artists he has been associated with over the years.

As the Fifties progressed, Otis became more and more aware of the changing public taste in R&B, notably with the introduction of rock'n'roll styles into the music. By 1957 he had signed a contract with Capitol records in LA, and later that year cut 'Ma (He's Makin' Eyes At Me)', sung by Marie Adams & The Three Tons Of Joy. Shortly after he recorded what was to become his best remembered hit, 'Willie And The Hand Jive'. It was a novelty rock song aimed straight at the teenage market, and the Top Ten, that exploited to the full the now famous 'Bo Diddley' beat. Whether the arrangement was inspired Diddley is open to debate, although Otis insists that he first played by this rhythm – know as 'shave-and-a-haircut, six-bits' – during the early Forties. The song was later covered in Britain by Cliff Richard.

Otis spent most of the Sixties working in a producer-arranger capacity, until 1968 when he and his son, Shuggie, collaborated on a progressive album called *Cold Shot*. It was a surprise hit and led to a producer-recording contract with Columbia-Epic. By 1970, however, Otis had decided to re-form his original touring show of the Fifties, and has since played a string of successful concert dates throughout America and Europe.

Earl Palmer. Born in New Orleans in 1925, his career as a drummer literally spans the entire history of rock. As a child during the Thirties, he tap-danced on his parents' vaudeville shows and played toy drums in local street groups. After leaving the US Army in 1945, Palmer sought a new vocation in drumming and joined Dave Bartholomew's band which backed Fats Domino, Little Richard, Shirley and Lee and a host of other R&B artists on record sessions during the mid-Fifties. Leaving New Orleans in 1957, Palmer went to work as an A&R man for Aladdin in Los Angeles, but soon reverted to session drumming for Larry Williams, Don and Dewey, Bobby Vee, Eddie Cochran and countless others. He remains one of LA's foremost sessions musicians.

Bobby Parker. Parker's 'Watch Your Step', his own fierce, pounding, gospel-charged composition, reached No. 51 on V-Tone in 1961. The seminal guitar introduction influenced the Beatles ('I Feel Fine'), while the flip-side, 'Steal Your Heart Away', was revived by the Moody Blues. A club tour of Britain in 1968 revealed a dynamic modern blues performer, but in America Parker was restricted to the chitlin' circuit with his band, the Silver Kings. He recorded unsuccessfully for Josie, Vee Jay, Amanda, Sabu and Gama, until August 1973, when he died in Tunica, Mississippi.

Colonel Tom Parker, born on June 29, 1910, in West Virginia, went to work for his uncle's 'The Great Parker Pony Circus' as a child, before setting up on his own on the carnival circuit. In the mid-Thirties he did press publicity for carnivals and circuses and by the Forties was promoting country acts on a tie-in basis with various Southern commodities, before signing Eddy Arnold to a management contract. By 1950, Parker had helped to make Arnold *the* country star. In 1953 – despite Arnold's having left him – he secured his famous honorary title in the Tennessee Militia and in 1954 he took control of Hank Snow's career, for one of whose tours he booked Elvis Presley, still managed then by Bob Neal.

Parker, who knew Steve Sholes through his dealings with him on behalf of Arnold and Snow, organized the RCA contract for Presley, helped set up Elvis Presley Music with Hill and Range and became Presley's manager – all at once. He had taken complete control of the careers of Arnold and Snow – except for their music – and did the same with Presley, this time with an artist whose appeal was universal. Once Presley's success was assured, Parker set about making him a superstar, refusing to display Presley to the world, creating a mystique about the singer, and – coincidentally – making himself a legendary character.

Though he has never interfered with the musical decisions made for and on behalf of Presley, Parker's essentially hucksterish attitude to his charge must take some of the blame for the series of career decisions that led to Presley's awful film career of the Sixties and then to the way Presley's revival turned sour in the Seventies.

Larry Parnes, known as 'Mr Parnes, Shillings and Pence', was *the* British rock'n'roll manager of the late Fifties. He first became involved in management through a partnership with publicist John Kennedy to promote Kennedy's discovery, Tommy Steele. They billed Steele as 'Britain's first rock and roller' and invented a name to match. Despite the fact that Steele's metallic qualities were hardly apparent, Parnes lost no faith in the power of naming. The year following the Steele breakthrough, 1957, saw Parnes grooming singer Reginald Smith for stardom. He changed his name to Marty Wilde, booked him in to BBC TV's *6.5 Special* and got him a record contract with Philips.

Parnes put all his performers on a rising yearly wage –

employing them under the terms of a five-year contract rather than taking a percentage. Another of Parnes' innovations was to promote shows using up to ten performers from the 'stable' – in many ways his operation provided a model for future managers, agents and promoters.

Of all the Parnes stable only Wilde, Steele, Billy Fury and Joe Brown were to make any significant impact during their time with him. Georgie Fame and Duffy Power (sticking with their Parnes names) became established – the latter only in a small way – after leaving the stable. Among the names consigned to the margins of rock history are Dickie Pride, Johnny Gentle, Nelson Keene, Peter Wynne, Davy Jones, Johnny Goode and Vince Eager. In 1961, the Silver Beetles auditioned for him to back another Liverpudlian, Billy Fury. Parnes booked them to back Johnny Gentle (also from Liverpool). But when they became the Beatles he turned down a deal with Brian Epstein, and as his contracts expired he slowly moved out of the business leaving Epstein to shoulder his mantle.

Patience and Prudence, an early example of the Osmonds syndrome, were sisters 'discovered' by their father, songwriter Mark McIntyre, in 1956. Aged 11 and 14 they had two novelty hits in that year on Liberty. 'Tonight You Belong To Me' reached No. 6, and 'Gonna Get Along Without You Now' No. 12.

Les Paul and Mary Ford. Born on Jan. 9, 1916, in Waykesha, Wisconsin, as Lester Polfuss, Paul started out playing guitar in hillbilly bands and then moved on to jazz combos, first with the Les Paul Trio in the late Thirties, before becoming the guitarist with first Fred Waring and later Bing Crosby. He had always been interested in electronics and in 1941, while in hospital after a car crash, he had the idea of making a solid body electric guitar – the 'log' – which he eventually sold to Gibson as the 'Les Paul Guitar'. It was finally issued by the company, complete with its famous sustaining pick-ups, in 1952.

In the late Forties, he met Mary Ford – born on July 7, 1928, as Colleen Summer, in Pasadena, California – and they began performing and recording as a duo, unsuccessfully, for Decca and Columbia. After their marriage, they moved to Capitol and almost immediately had a series of million-sellers – 'Mockin' Bird Hill', 'How High The Moon' and 'The World Is Waiting For The Sunrise', records which are remembered more for their originality. Mary Ford's voice complementing Les Paul's 'talking guitar' – than anything else. Their hits ceased in 1961, but by then Les Paul, who had built the first eight-track recorder in 1954, was far more interested in experimenting with guitars than playing them. Since his divorce from Mary Ford in 1963, he has devoted himself to 're-inventing the guitar'.

Paul and Paula. In the time of Kennedy optimism, America's dream of what her youth should be was symbolized by young duos like Paul and Paula and Dick and Deedee. Paul (born in 1940 as Ray Hildebrand) and Paula (born Jill Jackson in 1942) took the cute 'Hey Paula' to the top of the American charts in 1962, and followed it up with 'Young Lovers' which made the Top Ten in both Britain and America the next year. Their unisex sweaters, with 'P' embroidered on them, started a national craze. Their following releases, 'First Quarrel', 'Something Old, Something New' and 'First Day Back At School', never recaptured their initial success.

The Penguins' 'Earth Angel' was reputed to have sold two million copies on Dootone in 1954. The song was written by Jesse Belvin and recorded by Cleveland Duncan (lead vocal, born July 23, 1935), Curtis Williams (1935), Dexter Tisby (1936) and Bruce Tate (1935). Gently rock-inflected, the record distilled the feeling of adolescent uncertainty perfectly. It remains America's favourite oldie. Subsequently managed by Buck Ram, the Penguins had no comparable success, but recorded a series of fine discs for Mercury, Wing, Atlantic, Dooto, Sunstate and Original Sound, where

Frank Zappa wrote and produced 'Memories Of El Monte' for them in 1963. During this period, Teddy Harper and Randolph Jones replaced Williams and Tate.

Carl Perkins. The original fusion of musical strands that produced the first rock'n'roll sounds was the product of a particular environment at a particular moment in time. If, from the white standpoint, Elvis Presley was the best interpreter of that moment, then it ought to be conceded that Carl Perkins, his stablemate at Sun Records, Memphis, was the best chronicler.

Like Elvis, Johnny Cash and Jerry Lee Lewis, Carl Perkins was born into poverty in the South – on April 9, 1932, in Lake City, Tennessee. Like them, his principal musical influences were black blues and white country: 'The man who taught me guitar was an old coloured man. See, I was raised on a plantation in Lake County, Tennessee, and we were the only white people on it. White music, I liked Bill Monroe, his black stuff; for coloured, I liked John Lee Hooker, Muddy Waters, their electric stuff. Even then, I liked to do Hooker songs Bill Monroe-style, blues with a country beat.'

Perkins was a restless teenager, and it wasn't until Elvis Presley made his mammoth psychological breakthrough with 'That's All Right Mama' that he decided to enter the music business seriously. With the release of 'That's All Right', the secret was out – the poor young whites in the South had absorbed the music of the local black communities of places like Beale Street in Memphis – there had been a crucial shift in attitudes since the heyday of Hank Williams, and Sam Phillips and Elvis Presley had spotlighted this changeover.

Perkins differed from Presley in that he was primarily a guitarist, and his lead playing on his early Sun tracks acted as an inspiration for a whole generation of guitarists – the sound of his records was closer to the feel of the new generation than that provided by Bill Black and Scotty Moore on Presley's contemporary recordings. Moreover, Perkins' material was usually self-composed, and again his material has, in retrospect, more lasting value than Presley's – it was written from a better vantage point, from within the communal change itself. Carl Perkins wrote and sang about things that mattered – about 'the cat bug' biting him (in 'Boppin' The Blues'), about brawls in bars ('Dixie Fried'), about the importance of his clothes and his style ('Blue Suede Shoes'). He sensed the release inherent in the new music for the poor ('All Mama's Children') and he wrote about the wild young girls of the local area ('Put Your Cat Clothes On'). In short, he wrote about life for the young hepcats in Tennessee in the mid-Fifties – and, in doing so, he captured the sense of fun, and at the same time the sense of urgency of that moment in time.

Perkins was a brilliant chronicler, and his records with Sun will remain as works of sheer magic for all time – but he was never a real star. Maybe his preoccupation with the development of his musical form prevented him from seeing the possibilities open to a talent like his. Maybe, as others have suggested, he was simply too modest and too honest to want to make the steps that his friends at Sun made. It is difficult to imagine the rawness of Carl Perkins attaining the heights of the Ed Sullivan TV show, though he was invited and but for a car crash at Wilmington, Delaware, on March 21, 1956, he would at least have had his chance to try and become a teenage idol.

Since the mid-Fifties, Carl Perkins has continued playing – latterly as a member of the Johnny Cash extravaganza – and recording. He has made little impact in those years since his heyday at Sun: but the impact he made then was enormously important. He was, and always will be, the King of the style he created on his guitar – rockabilly.

Paul Peterson, born in Glendale, California, on Sept. 23, 1945, received a classic apprenticeship for a teenage heart-throb, moving from Walt Disney's Mouseketeers to various television series, notably a role as the son in *The Donna Reed Show*. His brief recording career with Colpix included such adolescent epics as 'She Can't Find Her Keys' (No. 19 in 1962), 'My Dad' (No. 6 in the same year), and 'The Cheer Leader'. On occasion, he also duetted with Shelley Fabares.

Ray Peterson, born on April 23, 1939, in Denton, Texas, moved to Los Angeles where he was discovered by Stan Shulman, who signed him to RCA-Victor in 1958. His early discs, which included 'Let's Try Romance' (his very first record), 'Tail Light', a cover of 'Fever' and the bright rocker 'Shirley Purley', all failed to make the charts. 'The Wonder Of You', a Baker Knight song, gave Peterson his first Top Twenty hit in 1959. His emotional and petulant voice, with its range of four-and-a-half octaves, was ideally suited to such classic death discs as 'Tell Laura I Love Her' (a No. 7 in 1960) and 'Give Us Your Blessing' (a Hot Hundred entry in 1963). Between the two, he scored with the Phil Spector-produced 'Corinna, Corinna' and one of the finest Goffin-Mann ballads, 'I Could Have Loved You So Well', both on his own label, Dunes, to which he also signed Curtis Lee. After less successful records on MGM, Peterson tried to establish himself as a country singer.

Norman Petty and his wife ran a cocktail lounge trio which recorded fairly successfully for Columbia and ABC in the mid-Fifties. Growing tired of being bundled in and out of recording studios under record-company pressure, they decided to build their own studio in their home town of Clovis, New Mexico. Completed in 1955, Petty discovered that he had unwittingly built the only *bona fide* studio in the area and before long began hiring it out to local talent for demo recording.

First to record there was Roy Orbison who made his first disc, 'Ooby Dooby', for the local Jewel label under Petty's supervision before leaving for Memphis and re-recording it for Sun. Next came Buddy Knox and Jimmy Bowen (from Dumas, Texas) who recorded 'Party Doll' and 'I'm Stickin' With You' for their own Triple D label in 1956. These tracks were sold to Blue Moon, before the giant Roulette combine in New York bought the rights and released each title separately. Both songs became hits – 'Party Doll' made No. 1 in America – and these early successes prompted Buddy Holly, a hitherto unsuccessful Decca artist from Lubbock, Texas, to visit Petty's studio and record some demos.

Sensing Holly's potential, Petty secured Holly's group, the Crickets, a new contract with Decca and released 'That'll Be The Day' which sold a million in 1957. Under Petty, Holly also began recording as a solo artist. More hits followed ('Oh Boy', 'Maybe Baby') and by 1958, Petty, who not only produced but often co-wrote the Crickets records, headed a thriving concern. A shrewd businessman, Petty did not lease out his studio at an hourly rate but simply charged a standard fee for each song recorded and offered to publish it.

When Holly moved to New York late in 1958, his relationship with Petty grew strained and Petty was about to sue when Holly was killed in a plane crash. Petty spent the next decade processing and patching together remnants of Holly's considerable recording legacy and several of these songs became English hits in the early Sixties.

Although Petty never again discovered a talent comparable to Holly, he produced several more million-sellers including 'Wheels' by the Stringalongs in 1961, and 'Sugar Shack' by Jimmy Gilmer and the Fireballs in 1963. Petty still resides in Clovis where he runs a radio station and a larger, more lavish, studio.

Esther Phillips (Little Esther) was born on Dec. 23, 1935, in Galveston, Texas, as Esther May Jones and modelled her style around Dinah Washington's gritty jazz-blues. As Little Esther, she won a talent contest at Johnny Otis' Los Angeles Barrelhouse Club in 1949 and recorded a number of ballad and jump-blues sides in distinctive, almost nasal tones for Savoy, Modern and Federal Records, backed by Otis's usually mellow 'city blues' orchestra, sometimes duetting with Mel Walker from the Otis troupe. Her discs enjoyed fair success – 'Double Crossing Blues' was an R&B No. 1 in 1950.

She joined King Records, of Cincinnati, in 1951, where she stayed for two years, using the Johnny Otis Orchestra and recording in Cincinnati, New York, and Los Angeles. She even duetted with Clyde McPhatter, of the Dominoes, before her final fling with Decca in New York and her retirement in 1954. In 1960 she emerged to work with Warwick in New York and was rediscovered by Lelan Rogers who signed her to Lenox Records, Nashville. Her hard-edged style, very much an acquired taste, finally broke through in 1962 with a Top Ten hit in 'Release Me', one of the few C&W songs she had recorded under Rogers' supervision. When Lenox folded, Esther Phillips (she took her surname from a gas station hoarding) signed with Atlantic, and from 1963 through 1970 recorded an assortment of blues, pop, jazz and soul songs (excepting a further brief retirement in 1966 and a 1969 Roulette jazz-blues session), making little impression on the charts apart from a moderate 1965 hit 'And I Love Him'. In 1971 she signed with Kudu and has produced a series of artistically excellent, critically acclaimed jazz-blues albums.

Phil Phillips, born on March 14, 1931, in Lake Charles, Louisiana, as the archetypal one-hit wonder, although his 'Sea Of Love' was preferable to a dozen hits by lesser talents. Previously a bell-hop and a member of the Gateway Quartet, he co-wrote the song with George Khoury, who originated the record with its producer, his fellow Louisiana record man Eddie Shuler. It was leased to Mercury and got to No. 2 in 1959. The British cover version (also a hit) was by Marty Wilde. On subsequent records (seven for Mercury and one for Clique) Phillips strove in vain to recapture the perfect simplicity of his nonchalant, conversational singing set against the muzzy, rudimentary back-up by the Twilights. He is now a disc-jockey in Louisiana.

Bobby 'Boris' Pickett was born on Feb. 11, 1940 in Somer-

250

ville, Massachusetts. After an unsuccessful attempt to become an actor and comedian, he joined a vocal group, the Cordials. In 1961, Gary Paxton (the lead singer with the Hollywood Argyles of 'Alley Oop' fame) produced Pickett's novelty narrative, 'Monster Mash'. It went to No. 1 and was another big hit when revived in the early Seventies. 'Mash' and other gory slices from the same cadaver – 'Monster's Holiday' and 'Monster Motion' – depended more on Pickett's ability to imitate Boris Karloff than on musical content for their success.

The Piltdown Men were an anonymous group of Capitol sessionmen, produced by Ed Cobb and Lincoln Mayorga, who doubled as the Link-Eddy Combo. While 'Brontosaurus Stomp' was a small hit in America in 1960, the unit were much more popular in Britain, having Top Twenty hits with 'McDonald's Cave', 'Piltdown Rides Again' and 'Goodnight Mrs Flintstone'. Symphonic arrangements (Mayorga was an accomplished classical pianist) and fat, walloping saxes combined to create a series of epic instrumentals meant to be played really loud. The flips were equally good, particularly 'Bubbles In The Tar', Mayorga's neanderthal workout on a Jack Dupree-Fats Domino theme. Cobb, at one time a member of the Four Preps, wrote 'Every Little Bit Hurts' (Brenda Holloway), 'Dirty Water' (the Standells), and produced various San José rock groups for Tower, Uptown and his own label, Sunburst. Mayorga played piano on many hits including 'Love Letters' (Ketty Lester).

The Platters. In 1953, Tony Williams, David Lynch, Alex Hodge and Herb Reed met Buck Ram in Los Angeles and signed with Federal Records. Their discs were unsuccessful, so Ram replaced Hodges with Paul Robi, added a female voice, Zola Taylor, and placed the group with Mercury in a package-deal including the Penguins, the hottest group at that time.

They recorded for Mercury from 1955 until 1964,

managing to combine a prodigious output with a vast quantity of hits, ranging in style from the virtual acappella of 'Only You' and the piano triplets of 'Great Pretender' to the vast, orchestral arrangement of 'Smoke Gets In Your Eyes' as Ram steered them towards the lucrative cabaret circuits. Sonny Turner took over as lead tenor when Tony Williams quit in 1961, and more changes followed when the group moved to Musicor in 1966: Sandra Dawn replaced Taylor and soon afterwards Nate Nelson supplanted Robi. The Platters regained chart status with such contemporary soul songs as 'I Love You 1,000 Times' and 'With This Ring', which became transatlantic discotheque favourites, and also re-recorded most of their Mercury hits.

Following dwindling singles sales and changing personnel, they moved to UA in 1973 where a dismal year yielded but one 45, and returned to Mercury (now Phonogram) in 1974 as the Buck Ram Platters, now featuring the neo-operatic lead tenor of Monroe Powell.

Pomus and Shuman. 'Doc' Jerome Pomus, confined to a wheelchair from his early youth, and Mort Shuman – born Nov. 12, 1936, in New York City – had their first hit when Dion and the Belmonts took their classic expression of teenage anguish, 'A Teenager In Love' to the No. 5 spot in 1959. In the Forties and early Fifties, Pomus recorded blues, in a Mose Allison vein, unsuccessfully for numerous record companies, including Apollo, Coral and Groove, before turning to songwriting. On his own he wrote 'Still In Love' (1951) and (with Reginald Ashby) the classic 'Boogie Woogie Country Girl' (1955) for Joe Turner and 'Lonely Avenue' for Ray Charles. Before joining forces with Pomus, Shuman wrote (with Garson) more pop-oriented songs for Charlie Gracie and others, such as 'Angel Of Love' and 'Doodlebug'.

In 1956, Pomus, already closely associated with Atlantic, gave Leiber and Stoller the title 'Young Blood' to a song they were writing for the Coasters. That song was a Top Ten hit for the group in 1957, and Leiber and Stoller secured

Pomus's services for Aberbach, the music publishing company they were associated with. There, Pomus met and began writing with Shuman. One of their first collaborations was 'A Teenager In Love', closely followed by 'Save The Last Dance For Me' which provided the Drifters with their first No. 1 in 1960. This double success established them – with Leiber and Stoller – as *the* rock'n'roll songwriters; while 'Save The Last Dance For Me', in particular, was the model and inspiration not only for the Drifters' and Ben E. King's subsequent records, but also for the budding writers of the Brill Building – Goffin, King, Mann, Weil, Sedaka, Greenfield, etc. – who were to write many of those songs.

If Pomus and Shuman were successful in America, in Britain they were respected, too: British managers and A&R men queued outside their door for their songs – British rock'n'roll at that time consisting almost entirely of (usually less successful) cover versions of American hits – and Jack Good devoted a whole programme of his *Oh Boy!* TV show to their songs.

It was quite easy to do this because, in the early Sixties, Pomus and Shuman's output was phenomenal and generally very successful. For Presley they wrote 'A Mess Of Blues' (No. 32 as the flip of 'It's Now Or Never 'in 1960), 'Surrender' (No. 1 in 1961), 'She's Not You' (No. 5 in 1962) and 'Viva Las Vegas' (No. 29 in 1964) among others. For the Drifters, 'This Magic Moment' (No. 16 in 1960) and 'I Count The Tears' (No. 17 in 1961); as well as writing for Ral Donner, Gene McDaniels ('Spanish Lace' in 1962) and Gary U. S. Bonds ('Seven Day Weekend' in 1962). For Ben E. King, they wrote both together ('Here Comes The Night') and individually with Spector – e.g. 'Ecstasy' (Pomus and Spector) and 'Young Boy Blues' (Shuman and Spector).

By 1965 their string of hits was coming to a close – in the new atmosphere generated by the Beatles, there was less demand for their songs and what demand there was was for middle-of-the-road material which they weren't very interested in producing. They more or less retired as an active partnership. In 1966, Shuman wrote a few songs with Jerry

Ragovoy for Howard Tate – including the classic 'Get It While You Can' and Tate's minor 1966 hit, 'Look At Granny Run, Run' – before emigrating to Paris where he revealed another aspect of his talents, by writing, performing and producing his own one-man show.

Elvis Presley was the biggest symbol of, and idol within, rock'n'roll during the late Fifties. In the Sixties, under the astute guidance of his manager, Colonel Tom Parker, he gave up live performances for a prolific but uninspired career as a film star. Records became little more than a spin-off from the movies. His popularity scarcely waned, though, and when, in 1968, he returned to live appearances in Las Vegas with his image modified to fit the changing times, his legendary status was reaffirmed. His immense popularity was borne out by a 1971 survey that reckoned his record sales to be 155 million singles, 25 million albums and 15 million EPs, figures bettered only by Bing Crosby and the Beatles.

Born Elvis Aaron Presley in Tupelo, Mississippi on Jan. 8, 1935, the son of a poor white farmworker, his earliest musical experiences were of the gospel singing at the First Assembly Of God church, where the impassioned swaying of preacher and congregation formed the basis of the notorious pelvic gyrations that would horrify/delight nationwide television audiences.

In 1948, having already made his first public appearance at the age of ten when he sang the tear-jerking country song 'Old Shep' at the Mississippi-Alabama Fair, Presley moved with his parents Vernon and Gladys to the city of Memphis. Here, he came into contact with professional musicians for the first time, sitting in occasionally with the Blackwood Brothers gospel quartet, and at one point nearly joining them. However his own career began almost accidentally as a result of a visit to the Memphis Recording Service studio, where he paid four dollars to cut a record as a birthday present for his mother.

The studio was owned by Sam Phillips, who had only

recently started his Sun record label. His assistant, Marion Keisker, thought Elvis had potential and noted down his address. Nearly a year later, in June 1954, Phillips called him in to record a song he had received from Nashville. He also brought in local musicians Scotty Moore (guitar) and Bill Black (bass). However, the session didn't go well until Elvis began singing Arthur (Big Boy) Crudup's R&B song, 'That's All Right Mama'. The result was his first Sun single, which quickly became a local hit.

Other records followed, and soon Elvis was touring as 'The Hillbilly Cat' and 'The King Of Western Bop', names which reflected the combination of country and R&B music in his style. His popularity grew rapidly and in November 1955 he was named the most promising Country & Western artist in a disc-jockey's poll. The same week Col. Parker became Presley's manager Phillips sold his contract to the RCA-Victor label for $35,000. RCA had the national promotion and distribution facilities which Sun lacked, and those facilities coupled with Parker's masterminding of selected television appearances soon made Presley a national star, with each successive record moving automatically into the upper reaches of the charts.

Sam Phillips had foreseen that a young white singer who sounded black would be a sensation. Presley was that singer, and offered a highly personal and experimental fusion of white and black music, at once fluid and brash. His Sun recordings were characterized by light, yet restless, vocal phrasing over a country-based instrumentation that veered towards black rhythms and the distinctive 'Sun sound' which derived from that studio's primitive recording facilities and Phillips' constant use of echo.

The Sun singles (issued on HMV in Britain) featured a blues song on one side and a country song on the other, each performed in a radically different manner. They were: 'Thats' All Right Mama' and Bill Monroe's 'Blue Moon Of Kentucky'; 'Good Rocking Tonight'/'I Don't Care If The Sun Don't Shine'; 'Milk Cow Blues Boogie'/'You're A Heartbreaker'; 'Baby Let's Play House'/'I'm Left, You're

Right, She's Gone'; and 'Mystery Train'/'I Forgot to Remember To Forget'. Material recorded at Sun but purchased by RCA before it was released included two versions of 'I Love You Because' (one of which – recorded in July 1954 – wasn't issued until the 1974 album *Elvis – A Legendary Performer:* Vol. 1) plus 'Blue Moon', 'I'll Never Let You Go (Little Darlin')', 'Just Because' and the magnificent 'Trying To Get To You'. Further unissued material from this period is contained on a bootleg album, *Good Rocking Tonight*.

The vast majority of white rock'n'roll singers who tackled R&B material diluted the power of the original – for example, Pat Boone, Presley's arch-rival for the allegiance of the teenage audience. In contrast to Boone Elvis showed a deep understanding of many black artists' styles in his Sun recordings. Presley didn't make cover versions; with the aid of Bill Black, Scotty Moore and D. J. Fontana (on drums), he created the songs anew.

His first recording sessions for RCA took place in Nashville, in Jan. 1956 with Chet Atkins and the Jordanaires among the backing musicians. (Later sides were mainly cut in the company's main studios in New York.) The critical consensus has been that the move to RCA heralded an immediate deterioration in the quality of Presley's work, and that it's gone downhill ever since. But though the records made up until his Army call-up in 1958 saw a considerable change in Elvis' style and type of material, they also produced a body of work which in retrospect can be seen as the cream of mainstream Fifties rock'n'roll.

Songs like 'Don't Be Cruel' and 'One-Sided Love Affair' saw Presley halfway between the light, frenetic Sun style and the smouldering, ominous, heavy recordings which came soon after. The latter, although more calculatedly commercial, were no less exciting or sexually-charged. Moreover, these were the songs which, principally through his traumatic appearances on prime-time TV, introduced so many white teenagers to rock'n'roll: 'Heartbreak Hotel' and 'Hound Dog'. And the same qualities were present on the material recorded earlier but only issued while Elvis was serving as a GI in Germany: 'One Night', 'I Got Stung', 'A Fool Such As I' and 'Big Hunk O' Love'.

By the late Fifties Elvis' career was worth millions and was being handled with exceptional acumen. In September 1956, RCA had taken the unprecedented step of releasing seven Presley singles simultaneously, and he was at No. 1 every week between August and December. Meanwhile Colonel Parker was busily exploiting the Elvis image – through the first of many films (*Love Me Tender*) and by licensing the manufacturers of everything from key-rings to pillow-slips to produce official Elvis souvenirs. Similarly Presley's recorded output was an astute mixture of ballads ('Old Shep', 'Loving You', 'Don't') and rock'n'roll songs, with the added bonus of the mixture of religious ballads, carols and popular seasonal standards that made up the original *Elvis' Christmas Album*, released in 1957. None the less it was as much a testament to the quality of the music as to Parker's marketing skills that two years in the Army away from recording studios made no difference to the level of Presley's popularity.

In March, 1960 Elvis returned to civilian life and a much changed music scene. Classic rock'n'roll of the kind he had pioneered had all but disappeared to be replaced by the softer and more conventional sounds of the Philadelphia school of 'Soda-Pop'. His first release, 'Stuck On You'/ 'Fame And Fortune', was firmly in the tough, don't-mess-with-me style he had perfected in 1958. But the album, *Elvis Is Back* hovered between what seemed to be a renewed commitment to R&B and country music, and an entirely new softness of vocal delivery. This softness, however, did not involve any new sensitivity. Rather, it indicated a loss of intensity and of focus. The drama of his earlier work had become mere melodrama and with spasmodic exceptions, this would be true of all Presley's subsequent work.

Between 'Stuck On You' and the rise of Beatlemania in America, Presley still functioned primarily as a singles artist, though only the occasional record – 'A Mess Of Blues' and 'His Latest Flame'/'Little Sister', for example – echoed the fire of his Fifties work. Now at the peak of his success in terms of worldwide record sales, his image was far less forceful than it had been in the Fifties. The majority of his hits were smooth ballads like 'It's Now Or Never', 'Are You Lonesome Tonight' and 'Surrender', or singles taken from the movies: 'Wooden Heart' and 'Wild In The Country'. Also many albums were released, a considerable proportion of which were soundtracks from the seemingly endless series of Hollywood musicals he was beginning to make.

In the early Sixties he settled down to a career which relied on making three films a year, each revealing a more tired and timid Hollywood orthodoxy than the last, in which he sang whatever third-rate songs had been chosen to fill out their plotless vapidity. The records which ushered in this era began with 'Good Luck Charm' and continued through 'She's Not For You', 'Return To Sender' and 'One Broken Heart For Sale'.

The earliest Presley movies – *Love Me Tender* (1956), *Loving You* (1957), *Jailhouse Rock* (1958) and *King Creole* (1958) – had made use of songs and songwriters of the same standard as the singles of the period. But after attempts to provide Elvis with scripts in which he could act – *Flaming Star* (1960), *Wild In The Country* (1961) – there followed a series of over twenty films notable only for their stunning anonymity.

By 1968, Presley was widely regarded as the epitome of all that was cynical, flaccid and regressive within pop. Moreover, the films were by now making less and less money (for a long time they had contributed significantly to his income of about $4m. a year). They were also getting worse and worse, with even Elvis apparently as bored with them as everyone else.

Then he made his first TV appearance since 1960 when he had appeared, dressed in a dinner-suit – arm in arm with Frank Sinatra. This time, he had his own *TV Special* and dressed in black leather. He performed on a small stage surrounded by an audience. Presley was charismatic, lithe and ominous; it seemed as though he had been reborn.

258

The show's success presented Elvis with a difficult choice. He could either use it as a starting-point for a renewal of musical application and risk-taking, or else return to the production-line procedures that had seen him through previous years, with merely a new formula. At first, the issue seemed in the balance. The single taken from the TV show, 'If I Can Dream', was especially powerful, seeming to show the sheer effort it took him to shake off the plasticity of the Sixties. Then early in 1969 he returned to Memphis to cut *From Elvis In Memphis* at Chips Moman's American Recording Studio, and using the cream of the local session musicians, he produced his most exciting album for some time.

However, he next opened in Las Vegas, giving his first live performances since 1961. But despite the quality of his band (led by guitarist James Burton) and the strength of his material, Elvis' live act failed to live up to the expectations aroused by the *TV Special*. Rapidly his career became as safe a showbiz routine as the films had been, a fact attested to by the various album releases of 'live shows' – from New York, Hawaii and Las Vegas. All involved half-hearted, vulgarly scored renditions of his earlier hit songs, none of which bear comparison with the original. None the less, when the Hawaii albbum reached the top of the American charts in 1973 it came as a reminder – along with his hit singles of the Seventies – that Presley's career as a top-selling recording artist was by no means over.

The irony is that the generally downward trend of his work since 1960 suggests Presley's choice of material shows a continuing interest in less calculatedly commercial music than he himself has produced. His early policy of recording black material has been maintained right into the Seventies. He cut Ivory Joe Hunter songs in 1958 *and* 1973, while the post-Army records have included songs drawn from Chuck Jackson, Little Walter, O. C. Smith, the Coasters, Jerry Butler, Ketty Lester, Chuck Berry, the Clovers, the Drifters, Rufus Thomas, Willie Dixon and many others. In addition, Elvis has turned to the newer breed of Southern writers, such as Jerry Reed ('Guitar Man'), Mac Davis ('In The Ghetto'), Tony Joe White ('Polk Salad Annie') and Dennis Linde ('Burning Love').

This enterprise in choice of material makes the frequently poor standard of execution all the more inexplicable. The exceptions in Presley's work since 1960 have been few. The religious album, *His Hand In Mine* (1960), had a particular delicacy and purity of vocal tone, and on the B-side of 'Kissin' Cousins', 'It Hurts Me' (1965) there are sudden flashes of a Fifties brand of Elvis excitement and risk, with even that drawled Southern pronunciation. Also notable are the *From Elvis In Memphis* and *Elvis Country* (1971) albums, and the evocative 'live' version of 'American Trilogy' on the album, *Elvis: Aloha From Hawaii Via Satellite* (1973).

By the mid-Seventies though, Presley was firmly stuck in his latest rut. He appeared once more to have given up any attempt to win respect as an artist. His voice was often less focused than ever – rougher at the peaks of volume, more inaccurately wavering on the lower notes, and altogether without the subtlety, or vitality, of which he had once been a master.

Twenty years after the first Sun recordings, it is a measure of the impact of the Fifties Elvis on at least one generation of listeners that there is a widespread fantasy that the 40-year-old Presley could be restored to his pristine glory if only he were removed from his Las Vegas/Hollywood lifestyle and shut in a room with a jukebox full of the early records, thus forcing him to recognize how great a singer he once was and goading him into a renewed effort to emulate his former self. The extreme improbability of this ever happening in no way diminishes Presley's importance to rock'n'roll. The rare and innovative talent he displayed in the Fifties (and intermittently thereafter) remains unaffected by any subsequent activity (or inactivity). Presley's work determined the shape rock'n'roll was to take more than any other single factor in its history. He gave teenagers their own musical identity for the first time. In short, he was to the Fifties what Dylan, the Beatles and the Stones were to the Sixties.

Johnny Preston, born in Port Arthur, Texas on Aug. 18, 1930, sang with the Shades before going solo in 1959. Then, with the aid of the Big Bopper, who produced the 'oom-pah-pah' sounds, Preston made 'Running Bear', a No. 1 hit on both sides of the Atlantic. Other hits for Mercury (produced by Jack Clement at Bill Hall's Beaumont studio), included the crassly commercial follow-up 'Cradle Of Love' (written by Wayne Grey and Jack Fautheree of the C&W duo Johnny and Jack), 'Feel So Fine' (previously made by Shirley and Lee as 'Feel So Good') and a rocking version of Little Willie John's 'Leave My Kitten Alone'. Preston's East Texas vocals transformed these otherwise undistinguished pop novelty records. He was, however, a poor live performer, and despite other discs for Southern labels, he was soon forced out of music to work as a garage-hand, an obscurity from which he has not re-emerged.

Lloyd Price was born in New Orleans on March 9, 1934, and after failing several recording auditions managed to land a contract with Specialty in 1952. Armed with a little tune called 'Lawdy Miss Clawdy' and backed by Dave Bartholomew's band – with Fats Domino on piano – Price's first record became the No. 1 R&B Record of the Year on the *Billboard* and *Cashbox* charts, earning a gold record in the process. More important, it was one of the first 'race' records to break out into the white markets, and it was this cross-fertilization which soon led to the new sound of rock'n'roll.

Price's recording career was hindered by a spell in the Army between 1954–6 but on his return he had an immediate hit with the ballad, 'Just Because' on ABC Paramount in 1957. After dabbling with his own label, KRC Records, with Harold Logan and Bill Boskent, he went back to ABC Paramount and his brash version of the old New Orleans folk song, 'Stagger Lee', crashed through to No. 1 in early

1959, giving Price another gold record. It seemed he could do no wrong in 1959 and he had further smashes with 'Personality' and 'I'm Gonna Get Married'. With the New Orleans content of his material almost extinguished, his later records, on Double and Turntable, had little distinction, artistically or commercially. However, he has invested his cash wisely and is one of the few New Orleans R&B men who has profited from his music.

Professor Longhair, next to Fats Domino, must rank as New Orleans' most influential musician. Born Henry Roeland Byrd in Bogalusa, Louisiana, on Dec. 18, 1918, his family moved to New Orleans when he was still a child. He soon picked up the wonderfully diverse styles of the old pianists who used to play the clubs and clip joints, and moulded them into his unique way of playing, with Spanish and rhumba accents predominating. He made his first record in 1949 for Star Talent as Professor Longhair and the Shuffling Hungarians and in 1950 'Bald Head' on Mercury was his one and only record to dent the R&B charts. Records for Atlantic, Federal, Wasco, Ebb, Rip and Watch flopped badly although his 1959 Ron recording of 'Go To The Mardi Gras' still sells well every year at New Orleans' annual blow-out. He was out of work for much of the Sixties, but there has been a welcome revival of interest in his music of late, which has led to many live appearances and a visit to Europe.

Arthur Prysock, a vastly underrated jazz vocalist whose urbane stylings belong with Billy Eckstine, Brook Benton, and the grittier Jimmy Witherspoon, his prolific but commercially unspectacular output has emerged on Verve, Bethlehem, Old Town and King. He can handle blues like 'It's Too Late' with complete conviction, provide a tricky jazz rendition of 'You Had Better Change Your Ways', dramatize 'pop' with 'Mama' or 'A Working Man's Prayer', and intelligently explore standards such as 'I'm Gonna Sit Right Down' or Gershwin's 'Unforgettable'. His accompaniments are invariably restrained and involve some combination of sax, guitar, piano or vibes in an orchestral setting. His recordings are resolutely in that tradition established in American supper clubs of the late Forties and Fifties.

Red Prysock, born in Greensboro, North Carolina, the brother of balladeer Arthur Prysock, didn't actually blow a serious note on the tenor saxophone until he was in the Occupation Army in Germany, but soon starred in a GI band and upon his discharge joined Cootie Williams' band in New York. He later played with Tiny Grimes and Tiny Bradshaw before forming his own band in 1953, recording for Red Robin then signing with Mercury, where he made a string of storming rock'n'roll instrumentals in the mid-Fifties, including the frantic 'Foot Stomping' which culminated in an archetypal honking single-note climax. He subsequently recorded for King in 1961 and resurfaced briefly on Chess in 1968.

RCA Victor. The Radio Corporation of America was formed in Camden, New Jersey, in 1901, and operated record labels under the Victor (Talking Machine Co) and Bluebird logos. Bluebird issued mainly 'race' and 'folk' music while RCA Victor issued popular material. By the Fifties, Perry Como headed the RCA roster but there was a strong interest in R&B and C&W, fostered by Chet Atkins in Nashville and Steve Sholes, the Southern area representative. Sholes was promoted to head RCA's A&R department – after his signing of Presley proved a success – in place of Joe Carlton, who left in 1957 to join ABC. There he discovered Jack Scott – before setting up his own Carlton label with Scott and Anita Bryant as his major artists.

The C&W representation was headed by Eddy Arnold, Hank Snow and, later, Jim Reeves, which Arthur Crudup was most successful in the black market. The subsidiary label, Groove, formed in 1953, also carried strong R&B singers such as Varetta Dillard and Piano Red. Through 1951–2, RCA recorded Little Richard but the style he used

263

then was big band R&B; and RCA's first *bona fide* rock singer did not appear until 1955. This, of course, was Elvis Presley, acquired from Sun in October for a then record fee of $35,000 – and a Cadillac for Presley himself – which turned out to be the best investment ever made in rock music. Earlier, Perry Como had covered R&B hits like 'Ko Ko Mo' for RCA, but Presley came through 1956 with monumental hits such as 'Heartbreak Hotel' and 'Hound Dog' and as a result RCA's interest in R&B and in re-moulding crooners was ended – Sam Cooke and Della Reese being left in the hands of independent producers Hugo and Luigi. The company issued records by several other rock'n' rollers, such as Jean Chapel (also from Sun), Janis Martin, the Rhythm Rockers and Joe Clay (on the short-lived sub-subsidiary, Vik). As rock'n'roll merged into 'pop' they developed a strong country-pop roster under Atkins, with Jim Reeves and Don Gibson among others, and achieved the occasional hit by lesser-known artists like Mickey and Sylvia with 'Love Is Strange'. Other successes came from Harry Belafonte and various sound-track albums.

Radio in America was the ideal medium for the dissemination of rock'n'roll. It was not accidental that a discjockey, Alan Freed, was responsible for giving the new music its name, and his shows, plus those of other radio men, built up its youthful audience in the Fifties.

As early as the Thirties, though, discjockeys had begun to assume an essential role in the process by which new songs were brought to the attention of the public, and became hits. They had superseded the 'boomers' or promotion men of the pre-wireless, sheet music era, whose job was to pitch songs to singers or bandleaders to perform in live shows. As records replaced sheet music, juke boxes and radio stations became central to the pop process. By the end of the Thirties, programmes like Al Jarvis' *Make Believe Ballroom* and the American Tobacco Co-sponsored *Lucky Strike Hit Parade* (which introduced the notion of a ranking of records) were the targets of record men who wanted to get their new discs across. Discjockeys became privileged beings. In the late Forties, Capitol Records hit on the idea of giving them special promotional copies of new singles, pressed on expensive vinyl. The other companies quickly followed suit.

Radio stations had played a large part in the upsurge of the country and R&B music which predated rock'n'roll's emergence. The older school of Tin Pan Alley songwriters and publishers, with vested interests in sheet music, distrusted the medium. In 1939, a dispute between their monojolistic organization ASCAP (the American Society of Composers, Authors and Publishers) and the radio men led to the formation of Broadcast Music Inc. (BMI). BMI primarily represented C&W and R&B interests, which provided most of the material used by stations in the South and West of the country. And it was the discjockeys on those stations who championed the new sounds of the Fifties. Radio had also played a part in shaping rock'n'roll itself, for while it was not possible in the segregationist South for white kids to watch black musicians perform, they could tune in to R&B stations and absorb the music that way.

As the Fifties progressed, discjockeys became more and more crucial to the fate of a new record. This was quickly recognized by the record companies and the practice of payola became endemic. On one level, the payment of cash to deejays to ensure airtime for particular discs was 'the industry's abortive attempt to control its market in a manner similar to its non-entertainment counterparts listed on the New York Stock Exchange' (R. S. Denisoff). But Congress didn't see it that way. After a lengthy investigation into payola in 1960, it was outlawed and a maximum fine of $10,000 introduced.

It was, in any case, being made less significant by the growth of the Top 40 radio format. Under this system, first introduced in 1955 by Todd Storz on his chain of stations in the Midwest, a rigid playlist based on the *Billboard* Hot Hundred chart was enforced. There was no room for individual discjockeys to exercise personal choice. Just as rock'n'roll itself had given way to formula pop, by the start of the Sixties the idiosyncrasies and personal influence of jockeys like Freed had all but disappeared.

Marvin Rainwater, an American Indian born in Wichita, Kansas, July 2, 1925, who is best known for the 1958 rock'n'-roll hit, 'Whole Lotta Woman', has usually recorded in straight country styles. A country songwriter and singer-guitarist of some originality, Rainwater has had major successes in that field with 'Gonna Find Me A Bluebird', 'Half Breed' and 'I Miss You Already'. He has recorded for MGM, United Artists, Warner Brothers and Philips (Britain), and has also contributed several songs in more traditional country styles, such as 'Tennessee Hound Dog Yodel' and 'Tea Bag Romeo'.

Buck Ram, born in Chicago in 1908, first came to the fore as a writer and arranger for the bands of Duke Ellington, Count Basie and the Dorsey brothers in the Thirties. During the Fifties, he moved to the business side of music, handling the Platters and composing many of their hits.

He founded Personality Promotions in 1954, and the agency grew quickly, attracting many of the young Los Angeles R&B stars, including the Flairs, Dolly Cooper, the Harris Sisters, the Penguins and Linda Hayes. A talented lawyer, Ram was able to place the Penguins and the Platters with a major record company, Mercury. When the Platters' 'Only You' took off, demand for Ram's services trebled: the Teen Queens, Joe Houston, the Empires and the Colts (who had the original of the Drifters' hit 'Adorable') flocked to his stable. Ram worked with them on his own labels – Antler, Discovery and Personality – or through other companies which employed him as an arranger: Mercury, Capitol, Modern, Felsted, Press. By 1967, when the Platters had their last big hit, Ram had taken a back seat. 'I'm out of it now,' he said, 'the companies are going with the kids themselves.'

Teddy Randazzo formed the Three Chuckles – Tom

Romano, Russ Giliberto and himself – in Brooklyn in 1955. Small hits, like 'Times Two I Love You' (1955) and 'And The Angels Sing' (1956) on RCA's X and Vik subsidiaries led to appearances in rock'n'roll movies, notably *The Girl Can't Help It*. In 1958, Randazzo, a skillful singer parading a multitude of styles embracing black R&B, Presley slurs and Latin choppiness, went solo but the hits were infrequent: 'Little Serenade' (Vik, 1958), 'The Way Of A Clown' (ABC, 1960) and 'Big Wide World' (Colpix, 1963). In 1962, he cut 'Dance To The Locomotion', a wild sequel to the Little Eva hit. Other sides included 'Broken Bell', featuring some Italianate crooning, and a relaxed version of the traditional 'Cotton Fields'. Though he still records occasionally, Randazzo has moved into writing and production, most recently with Little Anthony and the Imperials.

Boots Randolph is – and always was – the top saxophone player on the Nashville recording scene. The Western-swing element in C&W had always admitted wind instruments, but the country-pop revolution of the 'Nashville Sound' in the late Fifties saw Boots rise to the top as a session musician and then wade into the pop charts in 1963 with the instrumental 'Yakety Sax'. He has produced a string of solo recordings for RCA and Monument and interjected sax statements behind almost everyone who ever recorded in Nashville, memorably on *Elvis Is Back*.

The Ravens were formed in 1945 when Warren Suttles and Jimmy Ricks, waiters in a Harlem club, contacted Leonard Puzey and Ollie Jones through a booking agency. After recording for Hub, Jones was replaced by Maithe Marshall and the group appeared at the Apollo Theatre with Stan Kenton and Nat Cole in 1947, gaining an incredible reaction to their bass lead voice, Ricks. They signed with National and immediately hit with a distinctive revival of 'Old Man River' – bass lead, gentle harmony support and sparse rhythm accompaniment. The Ravens recorded prolifically, with various personnel changes, for Columbia, Okeh, Mercury,

Jubilee and Argo until 1956, rarely attaining chart status. Ricks died in 1974.

James Ray, a black New Yorker (born in 1941) with a gospel music background recorded for Galliant in 1959, and moved to Caprice, where he made the charts with the Rudy Clark songs 'If You Gotta Make A Fool Of Somebody' (No. 22) and 'Itty Bitty Pieces' (No. 41), in 1961–2. Both records owed as much to Hutch Davies' scintillating band arrangements as to Ray's vocals, but the songs themselves – singalong R&B at its very best – abounded with catchy hooks. While Ray went to make obscure discs for Congress Barr and Dynamic Sound, Freddie and the Dreamers' insipid version of 'If You Gotta Make A Fool Of Somebody' reached Britain's Top Ten in 1963.

Johnnie Ray, born on Jan. 10, 1927, in Dallas, Oregon, of part Blackfoot ancestry, has been partially deaf since the age of nine as the result of an accident, but the need to use a hearing aid didn't inhibit his musical progress. For his first professional engagement, aged 15, he shared the billing with Jane Powell on a child talent radio show in Portland, Oregon. He headed for the West Coast two years later, finding work in Hollywood and Los Angeles, where he became a resident night-club pianist. Moving to Detroit in 1951, he was spotted singing at the Flame Club by deejay Robin Seymour, who persuaded Columbia to sign him. Placed on the newly re-activated R&B/pop Okeh label, his second release, 'Cry'/'Little White Cloud That Cried' became a double-sided million seller, topping the American charts for 11 weeks in 1952. 'Cry', with simple rhythm accompaniment to Ray's dynamic, emotional vocal and subtle harmony support also from the Four Lads topped the R&B chart. Not surprisingly, he was subsequently switched to Columbia and his follow-up, 'Brokenhearted', also went gold, as did 'Just Walking In The Rain' in 1956, while he enjoyed numerous other hits to the end of the decade.

Johnnie's popularity increased through reaction to his emotionally histrionic stage act – he put so much feeling into the sad songs that he literally cried the words, being variously nicknamed the 'Cry Guy', 'Prince of Wails', etc. Although no longer a chart artist, Ray still records sporadically and tours regularly.

The Rays – Hal Miller, Davy Jones and Harry James, from Brooklyn, New York, and Walter Ford, from Lexington, Kentucky – were formed in 1955 and quickly became a very competent vehicle for the composing and production talents of Bob Crewe and Frank Slay. They recorded a handful of ballads and novelty-rockers for Chess in 1956 before moving to Cameo, where 'Silhouettes', a strikingly original beat-ballad tale of 'right number, wrong block' mistaken identity, became a 1957 million-seller. After two smaller hits on XYZ in 1960–61, the Rays faded into obscurity as Slay and Crewe switched their attention to the Four Seasons.

Della Reese, among the few black woman singers to make an impact on the pop charts in the Fifties, was born Dellareese Taliafano on July 6, 1932. She began as a gospel singer, at first with Mahalia Jackson's troupe and later with the Clara Ward Singers. On signing with Jubilee in 1957, she moved into the pop field. Her biggest hit came in 1959, with 'Don't You Know', which climbed to No. 2 on RCA. Later records were on ABC and Avco.

Jim Reeves' death in a plane crash in Tennessee on July 31, 1964 resulted in the growth of a dedicated 'cult' following. His influence in spreading pop-country music internationally has been considerable. Reeves, nevertheless, came from a pure C&W background. Born August 20, 1924, in Galloway, Texas, he became a pro baseball player and then a radio station manager before succeeding as a C&W singer. He recorded locally for Macy's Records, in 1949, and Abbott, in 1952, achieving success with 'Mexican Joe'. On joining RCA, his already smoother-than-usual vocal style was moulded into the 'Nashville Sound', blending with lyrical pop instrumentation and vocal choruses. His C&W roots were maintained only marginally in such giant hits as 'Four Walls', 'He'll Have To Go' and 'Distant Drums'. In the year of his death, he starred in the Embassy movie *Kimberley Jim*.

Debbie Reynolds, born May Frances Reynolds on April 1, 1932 in El Paso, Texas, made her way to the screen through winning a beauty contest and made her first film, *The Daughter Of Rosie O'Grady*, in 1950. Her only No. 1 record came in 1957 with 'Tammy', from the film of the same name, which also led to the naming of Berry Gordy's Tamla label. She was married for a time to Eddie Fisher and made the film *Bundle Of Joy* (1956) with him. Her other films include *How The West Was Won* (1962) and *Divorce American Style* (1968). She had her own TV series in 1969.

Cliff Richard, born Harry Rodger Webb in Lucknow, India, on Oct. 14, 1940, came to Britain with his family at the age of eight. After settling in Cheshunt, Hertfordshire, the young Webb went to Cheshunt Secondary Modern School where he sang with a vocal group called the Quintones – two boys and three girls. In 1957, Webb saw Bill Haley when he played at Edmonton, London, and after leaving school that year he joined a skiffle group run by Dick Teague.

Webb's ambition to form his own rock'n'roll group led him to leave the Dick Teague Skiffle Group, taking with him his neighbour and the group's drummer, Terry Smart. While with Dick Teague, Webb had picked up a little guitar playing and with Smart on drums and another local boy, Ken Pavey, he started the Drifters. The group became quite popular around their home town and occasionally played at the legendary Two I's coffee bar in Soho, London. While playing there one night they met up with Ian 'Sammy' Samwell, who joined the group. As bookings became more regular and Webb concentrated on singing, a change of name for the group seemed desirable. John Foster, who acted as a booking agent for London gigs suggested that Harry Webb become Cliff Richard – without an s – and the group was billed from then on as Cliff Richard and the Drifters. A performance at a Carroll Levis audition at the Shepherd's Bush Gaumont led to the group being taken up by agent George Ganjou. Ganjou booked them into Butlin's Holiday Camp at Clacton for a four-week season and arranged for a demo disc ('Breathless' b/w 'Lawdy Miss Clawdy' to be sent to Norrie Paramor, label manager at EMI's Columbia label. Paramor decided to record the group doing a cover of Bobby Helms' 'Schoolboy Crush'. The B-side was an up-tempo number written by Ian Samwell, called 'Move It'. The publisher of 'Schoolboy Crush' took the record to Jack Good who was preparing his *Oh Boy!* TV show and Good decided to use the group, but insisted that Richard abandon his sub-Presley image – shaving his sideburns and getting rid of the guitar he carried but rarely played. On Sept. 15, 1958, Cliff Richard and the Drifters made their first appearance on *Oh Boy!* and two weeks later 'Move It', now the A-side, entered the British charts, and eventually made No. 2.

By 1959, the line-up of the Shadows – the Drifters changed their name to avoid conflict with the American vocal group – had altered to become Bruce Welch, Jet Harris, Tony Meehan and Hank B. Marvin, Samwell having left to concentrate on writing and (later) production.

From the start, Richard was compared to Presley, and while the comparisons were invidious, Richard's early records were genuinely exciting: 'Move It', 'High Class Baby' and his first album, *Cliff* (recorded in a studio in front of an audience) showed that unlike, say, Tommy Steele, Richard understood rock'n'roll. In 1959 he was given a supporting role in the film *Serious Charge*, singing three numbers. One of the songs from the film, 'Livin' Doll' (written by Lionel Bart), was released as a single. A medium tempo number in an almost C&W vein, it became a million-seller, reaching No. 1 in Britain and No. 30 in America –

his highest chart place there – and from then on Richard's style as a pop ballad singer was set, each record bringing him closer and closer to 'showbiz'.

In 1960, he toured America with little impact and appeared in the film *Expresso Bongo*, in a major role. Richard topped polls as the best British male singer from 1959 to 1965, has received four gold discs and 21 silver discs and has had eight British chart-toppers ('Livin' Doll', 'Travellin' Light', 'Please Don't Tease', 'The Young Ones', 'The Next Time'/'Bachelor Boy', 'Summer Holiday', 'The Minute You're Gone' and 'Congratulations' – between 1959 and 1968). With his own TV series, Royal Variety performances and a string of film musicals beginning with *The Young Ones* (1961), *Summer Holiday* (1962) and *Wonderful Life* (1964), Cliff Richard has become one of Britain's entertainment institutions. But he has always been, and will remain, essentially a British star.

Billy Lee Riley, launched by Sun in 1957 as a successor to Elvis Presley, is a talented multi-instrumentalist who has recorded vocal and instrumental discs in virtually every rock style related to C&W and blues. A prolific sessionman in Nashville, Memphis and Hollywood, he was born on October 5, 1933, in Pocohontas, Arkansas, and left Sun in 1960 to form a label, Rita, which had several hits. He has recorded country for Sun, Mojo, Pen, Hip, Sun Int., Entrance, backwoods blues for Rita, R&B for Dodge, Checker and Hip, rock for Brunswick and Home of the Blues, and soul for Smash, Fire, Fury, Mojo and Myrl. His best-selling rocker was 'Red Hot' on Sun, and lately 'Thing About You Baby' made the American charts.

The Rivingtons and 'Papa-Oom-Mow-Mow', the craziest of all novelty vocal group records, made the Top Fifty on Liberty in 1962. Al Frazier, Carl White, Rocky Wilson and Sonny Harris had already worked together as the Sharps for various labels including Jamie, where they sang behind Duane Eddy's twangy guitar. Individual members of the

Rivingtons had also sung with the Lamplighters and the Tenderfoots on Federal.

Their other Liberty discs – 'Mama-Oom-Mow-Mow' and 'The Bird's The Word' (Top Fifty in 1963) were as wild as their hilarious predecessor. The group also recorded unsuccessfully for Reprise, Vee Jay, Columbia, RCA and Wand, while the Trashmen of 'Surfin' Bird' fame based their brief career entirely on the Rivingtons' sound.

Marty Robbins' career effectively illustrates the development of C&W in relation to rock. Born in Glendale, Arizona, on Sept. 26, 1925, Robbins began his country career in Phoenix at Radio KTYL in 1948. In 1952, he joined Columbia, recording singly and duetting with manager Lee Emerson. Through 1954–6 he recorded several rockabilly songs, easily outselling Presley's version of 'That's All Right'. Through 1956–8, Robbins' country-based rock stylings on 'Singin' The Blues', 'White Sport Coat' and 'Story Of My Life' provided national hits, the vocal choruses and pop arrangements of these songs being later accentuated in a string of ballad recordings when Robbins was known as 'Mr Teardrop'.

Robbins also became known for gunfighter ballads following his recording of 'El Paso' and the inclusion of 'The Hanging Tree' in the movie of the same name. He appeared in several westerns, like *Buffalo Guns* in 1958, but operates today mainly in C&W music with Capitol and through films like *Music City USA*.

Abe 'Bunny' Robyn was the recording engineer who pioneered today's multi-microphone techniques in Los Angeles during the Fifties. Working as engineer at Universal Studios, Hollywood, in the late Forties, Robyn, a former classical violinist, became popular with the area's newly-formed independent R&B labels because he produced quality records despite the era's primitive lacquer recording techniques. In 1952, with the guaranteed patronage of labels like Imperial and Specialty, Robyn built his own independent studio in Hollywood – Master Recorders – which he specially designed to record the era's boisterous R&B combos. Utilizing as many as twelve microphones and acoustically separating each instrument, Robyn engineered some of the era's outstanding records, including 'Searchin', 'Long Tall Sally' and 'Willie And The Hand Jive'. In 1959, Robyn demolished Master Recorders and built LA's then largest studio, United, before retiring in 1962.

Rockabilly was, simply, the white Southerner's rock'n'roll. It derived from honky-tonk and juke-joint music of the early Fifties' South. From the Western-swing, country-boogie and Hank Williams-influenced hillbilly music of the whites came the basic instrumentation of acoustic guitar and bass with their chopped rhythms, while black R&B and boogie provided the drum styles and – most importantly – the electric lead guitar styles. Sometimes the piano, steel guitar, fiddle or saxophone would be added, but basically rockabilly was a raw acoustic rhythm with a heavy backbeat and cutting electric guitar solos. Throughout the South, this music developed with young bands using the traditional C&W booking circuits. It was dance music, it was wild, it was fun, but it was not quite rock'n'roll.

The catalyst that transformed rockabilly was the emergence of Sun Records in Memphis, and in particular Elvis Presley's first record, 'That's All Right'. The enthusiastic high-pitched vocals, the slapping bass rhythm of Bill Black and the violent guitar runs of Scotty Moore caused a stir among deejays, but Presley's attitude, sex-appeal and downright outrageousness drew attention to the music even more. When Presley was transferred to RCA Victor, he became a national phenomenon, and for two years, at least, rockabilly was the music of most white kids.

Sun took off with Carl Perkins and others whose music typified and exemplified the style. Perkins' 'Blue Suede Shoes' topped all charts and the music of 1956 became the basis for the careers of Ricky Nelson, the Everly Brothers, Roy Orbison, Conway Twitty, Buddy Holly, Buddy Knox,

Johnny Burnette and a host of others. Most of them forsook rockabilly with the demise of rock'n'roll in the late Fifties, but the style has remained embedded in the rock tradition. Its influence has been of prime importance, on the early Beatles, on West-Coast country-rock and on Creedence Clearwater Revival.

During the heyday of rockabilly – between 1954 and 1958 – small and major companies alike recorded the style profusely. In Nashville, the larger labels recorded Gene Vincent, Eddie Bond, Johnny Carroll, the Everly Brothers, Charlie Feathers and Mac Curtis, and Sanford Clark. These labels (Capitol, Mercury, Decca, Cadence, King, Dot, and Columbia) were joined in a dozen other recording centres by independent companies who recorded almost anyone who would attempt the style. Fine regional variations were sometimes achieved. In Beaumont, Starday were one of the first and the songs of Sonny Fisher and guitar style of Hal Harris were as near perfect as Perkins and Presley. The output from the studios at Houston-Fort Worth, the Lowery studios of Atlanta, the Louisiana sounds of Goldband, Feature, Zynn and others, the Shreveport sound of Dale Hawkins, the Clovis studio of Norman Petty, the Al Casey sound from Phoenix, Westport in Kansas City, Imperial in New Orleans and Hollywood and a dozen other labels and studios – all provide evidence of the grass-roots appeal of rockabilly and its influence on later developments in rock.

Rock'n'Roll Movies. The music could not have arrived at a more opportune moment for a cinema fighting TV for survival and using films, such as *Rebel Without A Cause* and *Blackboard Jungle* in an effort to cling to the youth market. To Hollywood executives, therefore, rock music was just another means of getting arses on seats, and since the fans never complained, rock films were thrown together on low budgets, and invariably revolved around the same plot – a teenager is prevented from rocking by an older figure of authority, who is eventually won round. Musical content was variable, many acts being cheap and talentless, while others were plainly inhibited by having to mime play-back. Exceptions to these rules were few.

One was the first rock film, *Rock Around the Clock*, a piece of pure corn that magically captured the high-octane emotion that surrounded Bill Haley in 1956. The film started the seat-slashing craze, was banned in many cities and still incites a desire to misbehave today. Also unique was *The Girl Can't Help It* (1956), the only film of the period in colour and the only one to sandwich its obligatory seventeen musical numbers in between a witty satire of the contemporary rock scene (Tom Ewell is given the task of turning Jayne Mansfield, who can't sing, into a rock star). Otherwise the many films of 1956–9 served only to record the acts of pioneer rock stars, many of whom (the Platters, Chuck Berry, Fats Domino, Jerry Lee Lewis, Little Richard and Alan Freed in particular) made regular appearances.

Some rock idols were also called upon to act. The first and most successful was Elvis Presley, a natural. His early films (from *Love Me Tender*, 1956) creaked with sentimentality, but had guts – more than could be said for the soulless glossies to which he progressed. In 1960, Hollywood bowed out of rock movies and moved into Beat Generation dramas. When the Twist attacked in 1961, it was briefly exploited (*Rock Around the Clock* was re-made as *Twist Around the Clock*), but there was no further activity until a wave of beach musicals began in 1963.

In Britain, meanwhile, some American trends were reflected, while others were not. During 1956 Wardour Street felt that the kids would be content with *It's A Wonderful World* featuring Dennis Lotis and Ted Heath and his Orchestra. The first British rock film, a tatty variety bill called *Rock You Sinners*, arrived in 1957, the same year producers realized the potential of Tommy Steele. It was through his films that Steele gradually extended himself into the all-round entertainer he had always aspired to be. There was only one equivalent (*6.5 Special*, 1958) of the American rock movie and only one British rocker who was regularly expected to act: Cliff Richard. Tried out in *Expresso*

Bongo, Richard was given his head in *The Young Ones* (1961) and the string of all-singing, all-dancing musicals that ensued were acclaimed (in the absence of American counterparts) as major achievements.

Unfortunately, the later additions to the series did not move with the times. There were no other musical developments in the British cinema until 1962 when *It's Trad, Dad*, a mixture of pop music and the Goonish humour of director Dick Lester, showed the shape of things to come.

Jimmie Rodgers, though not the first white country singer to draw on the blues, nor the first to employ the yodel, 'America's Blue Yodeler' – born in Meridian, Mississippi, in 1897 – was unquestionably the initiator of an important and enduring idiom. His blue yodels, blues songs couched in rural black phrasing and imagery with yodelled refrains, were inspirations for countless singers after him. His influence, however, resides in his whole output, which included railroad songs, parlour balladry, novelty songs and rearranged fragments of traditional Southern themes. He performed these in a warm, relaxed vocal style, to a highly characteristic guitar accompaniment (sometimes augmented), on a series of recordings between 1927 and 1933, the year of his death from tuberculosis.

The massive popularity of his records, which sold in tens of thousands, established Rodgers as the first rural artist to attain the commercial status of the Northern popular singers. The image of personal success he generated was tempered by his retention of Southern homeliness, humour and unaffectedness; and despite his easy command of his market, he made few changes in the presentation of his music, so that his last recordings were little more sophisticated than his first.

Among his most typical pieces were the first of the blue yodels, also known as 'T For Texas'; the railroad songs 'Waitin' For A Train' and 'Hobo Bill's Last Ride'; and many evocations of Southern locales, such as 'Peach Picking Time In Georgia' and 'Mississippi River Blues'. These and their companion pieces have been both specifically and generally recalled in the work of such later singers as Ernest Tubb, Webb Pierce, Lefty Frizzell, Merle Haggard and Hank Snow. (Tubb, Frizzell, Haggard and Snow have all recorded album-length tributes to Rodgers). Western swing and bluegrass repertoires also reflect very sharply the impact of Rodgers' work. It has become commonplace to refer to Rodgers as the father of country music, and, unlike some such tributees, he has maintained this role through the continued currency of his songs.

Jimmy Rodgers, the son of veteran country singer Hank Snow, was named after the great 'Singing Brakesman' and was born on Sept. 18, 1933, in Camus, Washington. Rodgers was the most successful folk-pop (not folk-rock) performer of the late Fifties and early Sixties. Although his material was folksy, he sounded more like the contemporary, soft-voiced teenage singers than the Kingston Trio. His Roulette recording career began with three hits in 1958: 'Honeycomb' (No. 1), 'Kisses Sweeter Than Wine' (No. 7) and 'Oh, Oh, I'm Falling In Love Again' (No. 22). After that, he began to fade, though an album-track, 'English Country Garden' was a British hit in 1962. He later recorded for Dot and A&M, but a severe accident in 1967 curtailed his career.

Tommy Roe, born Thomas David Roe in Atlanta, Georgia on May 9, 1942, formed his own group, the Satins, at Brown High School when he was 16. They played local dances and school hops and began recording in 1960 for the local Judd label. As Tommy Roe and the Satins, he first recorded 'Sheila' for Judd that year, but without success. He switched to ABC-Paramount in 1962 where, under the supervision of Felton Jarvis (currently Elvis Presley's producer), he recorded 'Save Your Kisses'. Unexpectedly, however, it was the flip, a re-recording of 'Sheila' which registed internationally, topping both the British and American charts late in 1962.

Unlike many of his contemporaries, Roe proved durable.

His follow-up, a revival of Robin Luke's 'Susie Darlin'' flopped but his third ABC disc, 'The Folk Singer' reached No. 4 in England, despite flopping in America. Roe made a solid comeback when his fourth release, the futuristic 'Everybody' reached No. 3 and No. 8 in Britain and eventually sold a million. Three relatively barren years followed until Roe began his career anew with a series of huge 'bubblegum' hits, beginning with 'Sweet Pea' and 'Hooray For Hazel' in 1966, followed by 'Dizzy' (a British and American No. 1 in 1969) and 'Jam Up Jelly Tight'.

Since 1970, however, little has been heard of Roe but it seems possible that he will re-emerge as a successful country-pop singer in the same mould as Freddy Weller and Mark Lindsay.

Chan Romero, born in Billings, Montana, on July 27, 1941, was a 'chicano' rock'n'roller best remembered for his original rendition of 'Hippy Hippy Shake'. He was first discovered in 1957 by Specialty A&R man 'Bumps' Blackwell but Specialty's boss, Art Rupe, automatically shunned white artists and Romero had to wait until 1959, when Los Angeles deejay Don Redfield took him to Bob Keene's Del-Fi label who were urgently seeking a Latin-styled singer to fill a spot vacated by the recently killed Ritchie Valens. Using the same studio and musicians as Valens, Romero recorded his own frantic 'Hippy Hippy Shake' on which he demonstrated a lusty, hiccoughing vigour untypical of the late, more restrained Valens. Although popular on the West Coast, 'Shake' failed to register nationally, nor did his follow-up, the even more pulsating 'My Little Ruby. Before recording gospel music for his own Warrior label he cut discs on Challenge and Philips. In 1963 the Swinging Blue Jeans took an exact facsimile of 'Hippy Hippy Shake' to No. 2 in Britain.

Doctor Ross is an energetic bluesman whose style of blues and boogie demonstrates the traditions of the Memphis and Mississippi Delta area. Working usually as a left-handed one-man-band, he has recorded for Sun, Chess, Fortune and Testament and has contributed indirectly to the development of Memphis rock. Born Isiah Ross on October 21, 1925, in Tunica, Mississippi, he first recorded in 1951 and the derivative but infectious boogie-styled 'Chicago Breakdown' and 'Cat Squirrel' are his best-known songs. Since 1954, he has lived near Detroit and recent visits to Europe have enhanced his popularity and stimulated interest in Fifties blues among rock audiences.

Roulette Records was formed in 1956 by Morris Levy and Phil Khals, an adjunct to their music publishing operations, with George Goldner, into whose Rama and Tico organisation it was slotted. In 1957, Hugo and Luigi more or less took over the company, leaving Goldner to concentrate on his new enterprises, Gone and End, which were distributed through Roulette. Roulette itself had limited success with a variety of acts ranging from Buddy Knox, through Jimmy Rodgers (of 'English Country Garden' fame) to Ronnie Hawkins whose 'Forty Days' in 1959 with the Rock-A-Teens' 'Woo Hoo', was the label's only hard piece of Fifties rock'n'roll. By 1962, however, the company was concentrating on repackaging its own oldies and, later, oldies in general, as well as signing new talent.

Otis Rush was born on April 29, 1934, in Philadelphia, Mississippi, and moved to Chicago to record modern blues for Cobra. In 1956, he cut sixteen sides of exceptionally high quality, one of which – 'I Can't Quit You Baby' – made the R&B Top Ten. An important, but often unremarked, influence on the more 'purist' of the British R&B musicians, he is a left-handed guitarist with an unparalleled sustained note technique. The superb 'So Many Roads' heralded Rush's move to Chess in 1960 and he has recorded for Duke, Vanguard and, in 1969, Cotillion, with Mike Bloomfield and Nick Gravenites producing. He remains one of the few younger bluesmen whose work is comparable with that of the older generation.

Bobby Rydell, born Robert Ridarelli in Philadelphia on April 26, 1942, he became a regular on Paul Whiteman's local Teen Club TV show in Philadelphia, singing and doing impersonations, at the age of nine. In 1957, he joined a local rock'n'roll group, Rocco and his Saints, but went solo under the close guidance of manager Frankie Day. Rydell recorded two flops for Day's Veko label – formed after Capitol, Decca and RCA had turned Rydell down – then joined Cameo, recording three more flops before registering with 'Kissin' Time' in 1959. Clean-cut Rydell went on to become an American teen-idol of gigantic proportions and between 1959–63 he notched up a further 16 American hits, including 'Volare', 'Sway', 'Swingin' School', 'Wild One' and 'Forget Him', until Beatlemania caused his fortunes to wane rapidly in 1964. He appeared with Ann-Margret in the film version of *Bye Bye Birdie*.

Mike Sarne, born in Paddington, London, in 1939, has been a jack-of-all-arts and began, in 1957, as a bit part actor. In 1962, he and actress Wendy Richard recorded a comic song for Parlophone called 'Come Outside' and its success, coupled with the well-publicized fact that he was simultaneously studying Russian at the University of London, briefly took him to semi-stardom. His subsequent records ('Will I What?' with Billie Davis, 'Just For Kicks' and 'Code Of Love') attempted to mine the same vein of Cockney humour, but failed. The acting roles his pop status brought him were equally banal. Declaring that his recording career had been 'mismanaged', Sarne faded out rapidly and, by the mid-Sixties, was compèring a children's TV quiz and dabbling with film criticism and photography. These pursuits eventually led to his emergence as a film director, although his films *Joanna* and *Myra Breckinridge* both had very hostile critical receptions. Recently, he has been directing TV commercials and experimental stage plays in London.

Jack Scott appeared on the rock'n'roll scene in 1957 and, while he recorded several powerful rockers in a Southern style, he found that a career as a rock balladeer was more acceptable to the late Fifties public. Born Jack Scafone on January 24, 1938, in Windsor, Ontario, he was living in Detroit when he joined ABC Paramount in 1957, having first gained a writing contract with Southern Music. Rockers like 'Two Timin' Woman' and 'Baby She's Gone' saw some deejay action, but in 1958 producer Joe Carlton left ABC to form Carlton Records and took Scott with him. A rockabilly tune about a buddy named 'Leroy' who had been sent to jail was a hit, but the ballad flip 'My True Love' was bigger. It was followed into the charts by 'With Your Love', 'Goodbye Baby' and a latter-day rockabilly song that fought off the vocal choruses, 'The Way I Walk'. Scott joined Rank and then Capitol in 1960–61, scoring with the ballads 'What In The World's Come Over You' and 'Burning Bridges'. He recorded unsuccessfully for Jubilee and more recently has re-emerged as a country singer on Dot.

Linda Scott, born on June 1, 1945, in New York, first sang in public at the age of four, and used a 'little girl' voice on her three hits for Canadian-American in 1961–2. The first was the Oscar Hammerstein and Jerome Kern standard 'I've Told Every Little Star', which reached No. 3 in America and No. 9 in Britain, where it was released on EMI's Columbia label. 'Don't Bet Money Honey' and 'I Don't Know Why' made less impact, although they both reached the American Top Twenty. Later records on Canadian-American and Congress were unsuccessful.

Screen Stars. Two full years before the rise of Fabian, Tab Hunter – born July 11, 1931 – proved that an image could sell records as well, if not better, than a sound, with his watered-down version of Sonny James' 'Young Love'. By 1957, the year of Hunter's 21-week run in the charts, the one thing that was clear about rock'n'roll to the record industry was that it had defined a totally new market – the teenager – that would buy almost anything specifically aimed at it. Thus began the real exploitation of rock'n'roll with a slew of shoddy films and shoddy records, held together only by the common image of youth.

Eddie 'Kookie' Byrnes – born July 30, 1938 – the mandatory teenager of TV's *77 Sunset Strip*, had possibly the most bizarre Top Ten hit ever with 'Kookie, Kookie Lend Me Your Comb' (Warner Bros) in 1959 on which he did little but listen to Connie Stevens plead with him. When he eventually returned to the small screen in the early Seventies after an up-and-down film career, it was in a commercial for combs.

The recording career of the 'teenager' of *Hawaiian Eye*, Connie Stevens – born on April 18, 1938 as Concetta Ann Ingolia – continued beyond 'Kookie, Kookie' with a No. 3 hit, 'Sixteen Reasons' (also on Warner Bros), in 1960. After a series of minor hits up to 1965, she finally dropped her 'teen' image and turned to acting proper. The first chart success of three times Academy Award winner, Walter Brennan – born July 25, 1894, died 1974 – came in 1960 with the monologue, 'Dutchman's Gold', on Dot. Two years later, he reached the Top Five with the tear-jerking 'Old Rivers' on Liberty – the flip of which was the equally bizarre 'The Epic Ride Of John H. Glenn'. But perhaps the strangest case of misrepresentation was that of Lorne Greene – born in 1914 and known to the world as 'Pa Cartwright' of *Bonanza* – and 'Ringo', a No. 1 record on RCA in 1964. Supposedly a narrative based on the life of the notorious gunfighter Johnny Ringo, the record's success can be attributed to a mixture of reasons, not least of which was the fact that it was released at the height of American Beatlemania. After the Beatles, a few screen stars still scored in the charts – notably Richard Harris, Lee Marvin and more recently Telly Savalas – but it was more common for rock stars to become screen stars than *vice versa*.

Neil Sedaka. Although trained as a classical pianist, Brooklyn-born Sedaka (March 13, 1939) initially won fame as composer of 'Stupid Cupid', one of Connie Francis' biggest hits. In 1960, he joined Don Kirschner's stable of young writer/performers based at the Brill Building on New York's Broadway and teamed up with lyricist Howie Greenfield to write over 500 songs, many of which Sedaka himself recorded for RCA whose intention was to groom him as yet another teen idol in the style of Frankie Avalon and Ricky Nelson. Far too tubby to be taken seriously in that role, he none the less had a string of hits in America – over 15 before 1964, some of which, in retrospect, catch the flavour of the early Sixties almost better than any other records: 'Oh Carol' (written to Carole King who replied with 'Oh Neil'), 'Calendar Girl', 'Happy Birthday Sweet Sixteen' (all Top Ten records) and his 1962 chart topper, 'Breaking Up Is Hard To Do'. Although less successful in the British charts, he was more respected as both a writer and a singer.

With the coming of the Beatles and the new cult of self-sufficiency, demand for songs of such engaging cuteness declined and, though he continued writing material for the Monkees, Tom Jones and others, Sedaka stopped recording. The success of Carole King's *Tapestry* encouraged him to try again, but, significantly, it was in Britain that his revival started. First caught up in the rock'n'roll revival with songs like 'Standing On The Inside' and 'Laughter In The Rain' – his first American Top Ten record for over ten years – and albums like *The Tra La Days Are Over*, he managed to distance himself from the revival. His present appeal lies in the innate tunefulness of his songs and his ability to maintain a careful balance between the nostalgia of his early work and his newer, more recognizably adult material.

Ronnie Self, born Springfield, Missouri, in 1939. Self has been a prolific country-oriented songwriter, following a career during the late Fifties as a rockabilly singer. In 1957, he recorded twice for ABC Paramount, 'Pretty Bad Blues' being a good harsh-voiced rocker. In 1958, he moved to Columbia, adapting Bill Monroe's bluegrass tune 'Rocky Road Blues', and making the popular charts with a violent screaming rocker 'Bop A Lena'. He also recorded unsuccessfully for Decca, Kapp and Amy while writing hits for Brenda Lee and Jerry Lee Lewis.

The Sensations were one of the few black male groups with a female lead singer. They first recorded for Atco – 'Yes Sir That's My Baby' was an R&B hit in 1956 – but enjoyed their greatest success on Argo in the early Sixties. The hits from that period included 'Music Music Music', 'Let Me In' (No. 4) and 'That's My Desire'.

The group – Yvonne Baker (lead), Richard Curtain (tenor), Tommy Cooke (baritone) and Alfonso Howell (bass) came from Philadelphia where they were discovered by disc-jockey Kae Williams. Baker, who wrote 'Let Me In' and was influenced by Dinah Washington, left to start an undistinguished solo career in 1963 and the group was not heard of again.

The Shadows, originally the Drifters, consisted of Hank Marvin, Bruce Welch, Ian Samwell and Terry Smart in 1958, when they became Cliff Richard's backing group for his first hit, 'Move It'. Samwell and Smart were replaced by Jet Harris (bass) and Tony Meehan (drums) and the Drifters began recording in their own right early in 1959. After three non-chart singles (only one an instrumental) they changed their name to avoid confusion with the American Drifters, began to concentrate on instrumental A-sides, and reached the British No. 1 spot with 'Apache' on Columbia in summer 1960.

From then on they pursued parallel careers as the country's most successful pre-Beatles group, and as the backing unit for Richard. Hits followed in unbroken succession, including four more chart-toppers – 'Kon-Tiki', 'Wonderful Land', 'Dance On' and 'Foottapper'. The Shadows survived various personnel changes and the Merseybeat onslaught, and even though the hits ceased by 1965, they were by then part of the rock establishment. After all, the new generation of British guitar heroes had all started by copying Hank Marvin's clean, melodic instrumental style – and his heavy spectacles. They had no impact at all in America, where the Dane, Jorgen Ingmann, had the hit with 'Apache'.

Brian Bennett replaced Meehan late in 1961, and the following March Jet Harris left and was replaced by Brian Locking. Locking lasted a year, and his successor, John Rostill, was the band's bassist until they formally disbanded in 1969. Since then Marvin and Welch have played in a group with John Farrar, and the final Shadows line-up occasionally re-form for short-term projects. They were also associated with the launching of Olivia Newton-John's career, and Farrar still produces her and contributes songs.

The Shadows' instrumental sound was cleanly-recorded, simple and dramatic, with clear separation between the lead and rhythm guitars. They had twenty British Top Twenty entries apart from their success with Cliff Richard.

Del Shannon, born Charles Westover at Grand Rapids, Michigan, on Dec. 30, 1939, began playing guitar and singing at 14. In 1957, he entered the US Army and made his first public appearance in 1958 in Germany in the Army show *Get Up And Go*. On his discharge in 1959, he returned home to Battle Creek, Michigan, and took up a dayjob while playing nights in a local dive with a pianist friend, Max Crook. In 1960 he came to the notice of a local black entrepreneur and deejay, Ollie McLaughlin, who took Shannon to Detroit to sign a management contract with Harry Balk of Talent Artists Management, who also managed Johnny and the Hurricanes. Shannon's first session in New York followed soon after, but nothing was released and he returned to Battle Creek where he composed 'Runaway' with Crook one afternoon while jamming in a small club.

Recorded late 1960 and leased to Big Top in New York, 'Runaway' went on to become one of 1961's biggest hits. Shannon followed up with another million-seller, 'Hats Off To Larry', and a series of international hits including 'So Long Baby', 'Hey Little Girl', 'Swiss Maid' and 'Little Town Flirt', all of which reached Britain's Top Ten, although they were less popular in Shannon's home country.

Leaving Big Top in 1963, he formed his own Berlee label and recorded 'Sue's Gotta Be Mine' but it flopped and in 1964 he signed with Amy records and made a comeback with 'Handy Man' and the excellent 'Keep Searchin' ', which sold a million.

In an era when pop music was dominated by malleable teenage idols who were told how and what to sing in the studio, Shannon was a genuine self-contained talent who not only wrote his own material, but took an active interest in the production of his records. They remain classic pop productions, combining barnstorming arrangements (usually featuring pipe-organ) with Shannon's aggressive falsetto.

During the late Sixties, after joining Liberty Shannon went into a decline as an artist but took up production and supervised Brian Hyland's 'Gypsy Woman', a Top Three American hit in 1970. Now semi-retired, Shannon still makes annual visits to Britain, earning up to £2,000 a week playing cabaret in the North where he still maintains a loyal following. In 1972, he sold a piece of land in California, bought with early income, for more than he had made in a decade in show business.

Helen Shapiro was born on Sept. 28, 1946, in Bethnal Green, London. A protégé of voice coach Maurice Burman and EMI's Norrie Paramor, she emerged in 1961 as a 14-year-old schoolgirl with a rich, booming voice and an artfully aimed John Schroeder song 'Please Don't Treat Me Like A Child'. Later that year, 'You Don't Know' and 'Walking Back To Happiness' both went to No. 1.

Two more hits followed in 1962, as well as an appearance in the film, *It's Trad Dad*, but Shapiro was elbowed aside by Merseybeat, having decided to concentrate on 'quality' material. She continues to appear in cabaret and has recently recorded for DJM.

Dee Dee Sharp, born on Sept. 9, 1945, in Philadelphia, as Dione LaRue, she began her rise to stardom at the age of 15 by answering a newspaper advertisement for a 'girl singer'.

After singing backgrounds on various Philadelphia recording sessions, she signed with Cameo and was featured on Chubby Checker's 'Slow Twistin'' hit, recording her first solo disc, the 1962 million-seller 'Mashed Potato Time', at the same session. 'Gravy' was a natural follow-up, and 'Ride' won another gold disc the same year. Further hits followed until Cameo folded in 1967, when she joined Atco briefly before retiring to housewife chores for her renowned husband, Kenny Gamble.

Shep and The Limelites – James 'Shep' Sheppard, Clarence Bassett and Charles Baskerville – was formed by Sheppard in 1960 when 'A Thousand Miles Away' by his previous group, the Heartbeats, was successfully reissued. Employing a unique lead/two-part harmony style, they recorded an answer-song 'Daddy's Home' (Hull), a 1961 American smash hit and five follow-ups (progressively smaller hits) continued the story sequence – 'Three Steps From The Altar', 'Our Anniversary', etc., until the group split in 1963. They re-formed for a revival concert in 1969. On Jan. 24, 1970 Shep was found battered to death in an automobile on the Long Island Expressway.

The Shirelles were Addie Harris (born Jan. 22, 1940), Shirley Alston (June 10, 1941), Beverly Lee (August 3, 1941) and Doris Kenner (August 2, 1941). After recording briefly for Tiara, the group gained their first success with the buoyant 'Met Him On A Sunday', one of four releases on Decca. In 1960, their manager Florence Greenberg founded Scepter Records and the girls had their first million seller on the label with a haunting ballad, 'Tonight's The Night'. The same year saw 'Will You Still Love Me Tomorrow' and 'Dedicated To The One I Love', written by Lowman Pauling and previously recorded by his group, the Five Royales, followed in 1962 by 'Soldier Boy', all gold records. Among the best New York girl groups, they utilized excellent material from Goffin and King, Bacharach and David, and Luther Dixon. They sang mostly adolescent R&B ballads, with fragilely naive conviction and that slightly nasal suggestion of flatness common to black groups of the period. In 1968, Doris Kenner left the group.

Shirley and Lee, born Shirley Goodman (1937) and Leonard Lee (1935) in New Orleans, cut their first record 'I'm Gone' (1952) for Atlantic, soon a No. 2 R&B hit. They were just neighbourhood kids of 14 and 15 but as 'The Sweethearts of the Blues' they influenced many male/female rock'n'roll duos. For a while they were stuck with a series of sentimental boy-meets-girl love songs, but they dropped these shackles when the rollicking classic 'Let The Good Times Roll', written by Lee, became a million-selling hit in 1956. Backed by the best New Orleans sessionmen, and with Shirley's shrill, theatrical vocals and Lee's lovely blues voice, their records were certainly distinctive and deceptively good. After Aladdin folded, the couple recorded for Warwick and Imperial in the early Sixties before going their separate ways, occasionally reuniting for rock'n'roll revival shows. Then, in 1974, Shirley had a major hit with 'Shame Shame Shame' on Vibration. The duo have been very influential on Jamaican girl singers such as Millie Small.

Troy Shondell, born Gary Shelton in Indiana on May 14, 1940, first recorded Presley-ish rock'n'roll in the late Fifties under his real name for Mercury ('Kissin' At The Drive-in') and the local Regis label before adopting his new name. 'This Time' (written by Chips Moman) had already been recorded as a flip-side in 1958 by Thomas Wayne, on Mercury. Shondell's revival on the Gold Crest label began selling in the Chicago area, prompting Liberty in Hollywood to buy the master for national distribution and make it a national hit in 1961. Shondell was unable to follow-up, however, despite the efforts of producers like Phil Spector and Snuff Garrett. He moved to Nashville in the late Sixties where he recorded for TRX and worked as a producer.

The Showmen, from Norfolk, Virginia, were General Norman Johnson (lead vocal), Dorsey and Gene Knight, Milton Wills and Leslie Felton. They had recorded for Atlantic in the mid-Fifties, but the tracks were never released. They were managed by Noel Biggs who took them down to New Orleans in 1961 and recorded their classic rock'n'roll anthem, 'It Will Stand', for Allen Toussaint and Minit Records. It reached No. 61 in the charts and made a surprise reappearance at No. 80 in the summer of 1964. Despite their excellent 'Country Fool', the group were unable to capitalize on this good start and after further records on Minit and Swan, they disbanded. However, Johnson persevered and made it again in the Seventies in a far more substantial way as lead singer with the hit soul group, Chairmen Of The Board.

The Silhouettes – four Philadelphians, Earl Beal, Raymond Edwards, Billy Horton and Richard Lewis–formed the Gospel Tornados in 1955, but it wasn't until 1958, as the Silhouettes, that they turned the charts upside-down when the startling sound of 'Get A Job' sold a million copies within three weeks of release – its bass chant, 'Sha-na-na-na', is now infamous in the annals of rock'n'roll. Released initially on deejay Kae Williams' Junior label and leased to Ember, the Silhouettes' song was strong social comment for its time, but was obscured by the lead singer's barely intelligible diction. The group recorded for Ember and Ace until 1961 without further success.

D 14/5/98

Frank Sinatra, born on Dec. 12, 1915, in Hoboken, New Jersey, of Italian extraction, blended big band vocalizing with Bing Crosby-like personal projection to become one of the outstanding singers and charismatic entertainers of the twentieth century. He organized and sang in a quartet called the Hoboken Four from 1936 on. After some minor success, he was hired as a solo singer by Harry James, and then by Tommy Dorsey. He recorded as a soloist, eventually getting his own CBS radio show and causing near riots at performances at major venues. In 1943, he started an important acting career with a role in the film *Higher And Higher*. Known as 'The Voice' because of his unmistakable jazz-inflected vocal style, he joined the other side of the record business by starting the Reprise label in 1962.

Skiffle was the term originally applied to the Chicago jug bands of the Twenties, in which 'found' instruments replaced the rhythm section of the traditional jazz band and voices replaced the front line instruments. However, the British skiffle boom of 1956–58 bore little relation to such music.

Skiffle had its origins in the first British trad boom of the early Fifties – Lonnie Donegan's 'Rock Island Line', for example, was recorded by Donegan when he was part of the skiffle unit in Chris Barber's Jazz Band (Donegan on guitar and vocals, Barber on bass and Beryl Bryden on washboard) – when it was played as the interval music. But it soon burst beyond these confines to become Britain's first do-it-yourself music. Donegan opened the door to the skiffle boom, but it was the ease with which skiffle could be played more than anything that ensured the movement's success. In contrast to rock'n'roll which demanded electric guitars, saxophones and an American accent, skiffle required only a basic guitarist (three chords and a capo), somebody with a good sense of rhythm (on washboard), a stand-up bass (or tea chest) player and a lot of energy – even the ever-present American accent wasn't a strict necessity. In the wake of Donegan's success, various skiffle aggregations had hits, including Chas McDevitt and Nancy Whiskey ('Freight Train') Johnny Duncan ('Last Train To San Fernando') and the Vipers ('Cumberland Gap'). But the real importance of the movement lay outside the charts; in the church cellars and coffee bars of Britain – the Two Is, where all Britain's rock'n'-rollers were supposed to have been discovered was originally the skiffle club – where thousands of young people formed skiffle groups, including John Lennon's Quarrymen.

Skiffle had no lasting impact. By 1958, if not earlier, the would-be skifflers were hunting out electric guitars and forming rock'n'roll groups. Yet it was skiffle more than anything else that laid the foundations of British rock.

Skip and Flip, fairly lightweight American pop duo who achieved moderate American success in 1959–60 with 'It Was I' and 'Cherry Pie' were Gary (Flip) Paxton and Clyde (Skip) Battin. The duo independently recorded 'It Was I' in Phoenix, Arizona, and leased the tape of the L. A. Brent label. The record reached No. 11 in July, 1959, precipitating a national tour. By 1960, Battin had been replaced as Skip by an ex-dishwasher from Phoenix, Dave Martinez, who was in turn replaced by Rod Marshall. The duo registered again with 'Cherry Pie' (No. 11 in May, 1960) but disbanded that year when Paxton became lead singer of the Hollywood Argyles of 'Alley-Oop' fame. He later became a producer ('Monster Mash') while Skip Battin joined the Byrds in 1969 and then the New Riders of the Purple Sage in 1973.

The Skyliners, perhaps the finest of all white R&B vocal groups, were based in Pittsburgh and were renowned for the stunning lead singing of Jimmy Beaumont (born Oct. 21, 1940) and for the much-revived Top Twenty hit, 'Since I Don't Have You', recorded for Calico in 1959. Their manager, Joe Rock, produced other hits for Al Capozzi's label: 'This I Swear', 'It Happened Today' and 'Pennies From Heaven'.

When the group – Janet Vogel Rapp (born June 10, 1942), Joe Verscharen (1940), Wally Lester (Oct. 5, 1941) and Jackie Taylor (1941) – split up, Beaumont made solo records for May, Colpix, Scepter and Bang. Taylor formed his own Skyliners in 1965 and cut 'The Loser', a minor hit on Jubilee. In 1969, the original members re-formed to appear at rock revival shows and cut an album for Buddah.

Slim Harpo, born James Moore on Jan. 11, 1924, in Lobdell, Louisiana, made his initial public appearances as 'Harmonica Slim' before meeting Excello Records boss, Jay D. Miller, in 1957, who signed and recorded him as Slim Harpo. His first disc, 'I'm A King Bee'/'I've Got Love If You Want

It', meant little commercially, but both sides were later revived by British R&B groups. Slim's first taste of success came in 1961 when 'Raining In My Heart' was a substantial pop and R&B hit in America. Little different to his preceding material, it was a relatively simple song with drawled vocal backed by harmonica and a small rhythm section. Further discs in the same vein sold only locally until 'Baby Scratch My Back' soared into the Top Twenty in 1966, but succeeding years saw just two small R&B hits, and Slim died of a heart attack in February 1970.

Bessie Smith, if not the greatest woman ever to sing the blues, will do until that person comes along. It is difficult to find secure ground for disagreeing with this assessment; no other singer has possessed her expressive range, her capability with material of extremely variable quality and style, and at the same time her subtlety of inflection and beauty of tone.

Born in Knoxville, Tennessee, in 1898, she developed her music in travelling shows, a life vividly described in the biography *Bessie* by Chris Albertson. Between 1923 and 1933 she recorded more than 100 blues, quasi-blues and popular songs with accompanists sometimes apt (Louis Armstrong, cornettist Joe Smith, pianist James P. Johnson), sometimes mundane. Her contemporaries were undoubtedly affected by her work, but it was the jazz musicians perhaps more than the blues singers who learned from her phrasing and delivery. Nevertheless, all the important women singers since her time, from Billie Holiday to Janis Joplin, have acknowledged her achievements, and her most famous performances, such as 'St Louis Blues', 'Nobody Knows You When You're Down And Out' or the rumbustious 'Gimme A Pigfoot And A Bottle Of Beer', are plainly immortal components of the jazz/blues canon.

Bessie Smith died in a motor accident in 1937; her recordings have rarely been out of catalogue since then, and were reissued in their entirety on five double albums by Columbia in 1971–73.

Huey 'Piano' Smith, born in New Orleans on Jan. 26, 1934, was one of the brightest and biggest New Orleans R&B stars of the Fifties. He started out playing piano with Guitar Slim and Earl King, and did session work for Smiley Lewis, Little Richard and Lloyd Price before recording on his own for Savoy. An impeccable pianist whose style was a refined development of Professor Longhair's and an unusually talented songwriter, his voice was not strong and this led to the formation of his famous vocal group, the Clowns. It was with the Clowns, and Bobby Marchan in particular, that Huey Smith had his biggest hits for Ace – 'Rockin' Pneumonia And The Boogie Woogie Flu' (1957), 'Don't You Just Know It' (1958) and 'Pop-Eye' (1962), showing all that was good in New Orleans R&B. He was able to make the adjustment from R&B to soul with comparative ease, but his later records never sold well and after a lot of financial problems, he gave up music in favour of religion when still in his thirties.

Hank Snow has been in the forefront of C&W artists for forty years, but his impact on rock has been unusual, and unintentional. Born May 9, 1914, in Liverpool, Nova Scotia, he gained fame as the 'Singing Ranger' before moving to the States in the Forties. Recording for RCA since 1936, he is known for 'The Lonesome Blue Yodel', 'The Golden Rocket' and 'Nobody's Child'. His best-known song 'I'm Movin' On' was recorded in 1950 with his usual pure C&W sound, but became popular with rockabilly artists, whose emergence Snow disliked. In 1954 he refused to complete a tour with Elvis Presley. His son recorded under the name Jimmy Rodgers and had hits with 'Honeycomb' and 'Kisses Sweeter Than Wine' in 1958.

The Solitaires were a black vocal group from Harlem, comprising Buzz Willis, Pat Gaston, Bobby Baylor, Monte Owens and Herman Curtis. They were signed by Hy Weiss for his Old Town label in 1954 and remained on it until 1963. Cecil Holmes from the Fi-Tones replaced Willis in 1960.

The group cut about twenty records for Old Town and others for Roulette and MGM, spanning all the styles of R&B. Their most famous disc, a gimmicky foot-stomper, 'Walking Along', was outsold by a cover version by the Diamonds in 1958. Willis and Holmes later held various executive posts with major record companies, becoming head of Polydor R&B operations and vice-president of Buddah respectively.

Jimmy Soul, born James McCleese in New York in 1942, was a boy preacher who was taken to North Carolina by his parents at the age of seven, where he became a circuit minister. On moving to Portsmouth, Virginia, he joined the Nightingales gospel group for a while before forming a secular group and touring Virginia clubs. He was spotted by Gary Bonds and introduced to Frank Guida, who signed him to his new SPQR label as Jimmy Soul. His debut, 'Twisting Mathilda', was a Top Thirty hit in 1962, and the following year 'If You Wanna Be Happy', a rocking, calypso-like number, was a million-selling No. 1.

The Soul Stirrers, incorporating the amazing high tenor of Rebert Harris, pioneered the use of dual lead singers, and changed from a jubilee quartet into *the* gospel quintet of the post-1945 era. Their unique sound promulgated by recordings for Aladdin and then Specialty, enabled Sam Cooke who succeeded Harris in 1951, to establish a reputation as a black teenage idol even before he secularized their style, when he turned to popular music. Despite adding instrumentation, including songwriting guitarist, Leroy Crume, the Texan group maintained their sound with first Johnnie Taylor and later Willie Rogers filling Cooke's role.

The Spaniels. In May, 1953, James 'Pookie' Hudson, Gerald Gregory, Opal Courtney, Ernest Warren and Willis Jackson started their recording career with Chance, who soon folded. They were signed to Vee Jay and started a period of seven years' prolific, often successful, recording. The personnel changed in 1954 – Donald Porter, Carl Rainge and James Cochran joining Hudson and Gregory when the others left – and this team recorded a diverse selection of love ballads, standards and jumping rockers for Vee Jay until 1960, their *forte* being contrasting tenor/bass parts on material like 'Stormy Weather', 'Red Sails In The Sunset' and their original 'Goodnight Sweetheart Goodnight'. The group made one disc for Neptune in 1961 before disbanding. Hudson reformed the outfit in 1969 for a revival concert, and they enjoyed further success recording for Calla ('Fairy Tales') and Buddah (an updating of 'Goodnight Sweetheart').

Otis Spann is remembered as an impressive and markedly individual solo pianist, and by far the most responsive and sensitive of accompanying musicians in the whole modern blues idiom. Born in Mississippi on March 21, 1930, he moved to Chicago at 17 and joined forces with his half-brother, Muddy Waters. The Spann–Waters partnership proved to be one of the most enduring and perhaps the most fruitful in the entire history of the blues, the two men working together for over 20 years. Spann's powerful rolling piano style has graced most of Waters' hit records, as well as those by Chuck Berry, Bo Diddley, Howlin' Wolf, Sonny Boy Williamson and Little Walter. In 1964, he came to London and recorded with Eric Clapton and Jimmy Page for Decca. In later years he worked with Fleetwood Mac, gaining American chart action with the British recorded 'Hungry Country Girl'. Spann died on April 25, 1970.

Specialty Records was a top-selling R&B independent label in the Fifties thanks to massive hits by Lloyd Price, Guitar Slim, Little Richard and Larry Williams, but the company's influence went back even further. It was founded by Art Rupe in Los Angeles in 1946 out of the remnants of his original label, Juke Box. Specialty had an early R&B hit with Roy Milton's 'RM Blues', one of the most important city blues records of the Forties. The success inspired Rupe to record more big bands doing ballads, jump and boogie numbers, a policy which paid off with a string of good-selling hits by Jimmy Liggins, Joe Liggins and, of course, Roy Milton. Percy Mayfield's smoky blues ballad, 'Please Send Me Someone To Love' opened the Fifties in fine style but Art Rupe, ever astute, felt his West Coast recordings were getting stale.

He therefore went down South on a field trip looking for new blues and R&B material. He came back with the master of Lloyd Price's 'Lawdy Miss Cawdy' made in New Orleans, and the result was the biggest R&B record of 1952, which sold over a million. It was also in New Orleans that he signed the extrovert showman, Guitar Slim, and Slim's first record for Specialty, the archetypal 'The Things That I Used To Do', was another million-seller and No. 2 R&B record of 1954. Rupe's raid on New Orleans was complete when the Crescent City gave Little Richard that distinctive sound to make 'Tutti Frutti' a national hit in 1955.

By then the R&B market was being encroached on by rock'n'roll and Art Rupe cashed in on the new craze with a constant stream of hits from Little Richard between 1956–8 and Larry Williams chipped in with 'Short Fat Fannie' and 'Bony Moronie' in 1957. Don and Dewey, Jerry Byrne and Art Neville had regional hits, and it was only when rock'n'-roll stopped dead in its tracks in 1959 that Specialty came to a grinding halt. Art Rupe didn't seem too concerned. All along he had preferred gospel music to R&B (Specialty released many such records). He refused to get involved in payola (which he could ignore with immunity when Little Richard was selling) and in the end he was having problems with his producers, Bumps Blackwell, Sonny Bono and Harold Battiste in New Orleans. He invested all his earnings from Specialty in other profitable business enterprises, but revived the label in the Sixties and, thanks to researcher Barrett Hansen, a large and intelligent reissue programme was initiated as a reminder of past glories.

Benny Spellman, born in Pensacola, Florida in 1938, briefly flirted with fame when his infectious song, 'Lipstick Traces' backed with 'Fortune Teller' on Minit brushed the Hot Hundred charts in the summer of 1962. Before this, Spellman had been a background singer on many New Orleans sessions for Allen Toussaint and was responsible for the deep, rich vocal responses on Ernie K-Doe's 'Mother-In-Law.' He continued to record for Watch, Alon and Sansu and had a minor R&B hit with 'The Word Game' on Atlantic in 1965. Now working as a beer salesman, he has recently been brought out of musical retirement to play the occasional gig in New Orleans.

The Springfields originally consisted of Tom and Mary O'Brien (Dusty Springfield) and Tim Field, who left in 1962 and was replaced by Mike Pickworth (*aka* Mike Hurst, who went on to produce Cat Stevens). According to their publicist, they got their name from practising in a field on a Spring day. Their first chart entry in Britain was 'Bambino', an old Neapolitan carol that exemplified their commercial approach to folk music, as did their later hits 'Island Of Dreams' and 'Say I Won't Be There' which was adapted from 'Au Clair De La Lune'. They were one of the first British artists to record in Nashville and 'Silver Threads And Golden Needles', a failure in Britain, was a Top Twenty hit in both the country and pop charts in America. In 1963, the group split up when Dusty went solo.

Kay Starr, an adept in most styles of popular song, was born on an Oklahoma Indian reservation on July 21, 1922. As a jazz singer, she performed with Joe Venuti, Bob Crosby, Glenn Miller and Charlie Barnett. In 1950, she turned up on the country charts with Tennessee Ernie Ford singing 'I'll Never Be Free', on Capitol. In 1956, she swam with the stream and reached No. 1 in both America and Britain with 'Rock 'n' Roll Waltz'. She is said to have studied practical psychology as an aid to her career.

Tommy Steele, born Thomas Hicks in Bermondsey, London on Dec. 17, 1936, was Britain's first rock'n'roll star. Discovered singing Hank Williams material and calypsos – learnt while working on a cruiser based on New York – he became a teenage idol almost literally overnight. His first record, 'Rock With The Caveman', was made just two days after his recording test in September, 1956. Within a month it was a British Top Ten hit. Steele's first tour began in November, 1956, and introduced the amplifier to the British stage.

With Lionel Bart and Mike Pratt, Steele wrote some of his British hits of the Fifties, including 'Rock With The Caveman' and 'A Handful Of Songs' and he had further hits with cover versions of American records, 'Singing The Blues' (Guy Mitchell), 1957, and 'Tallahassee Lassie' (Freddie Cannon), 1959. The latter showed Steele in unfamiliar guise as a tough, heavy rocker. Heavy rocker he was not, however, and it was inevitable that Steele would leave rock'n'roll. His personality was that of the archetypal cheery Cockney, and clearly stemmed more from the vaudeville tradition than from an imported rock'n'roll milieu.

By the beginning of the Sixties, Steele had begun to succeed in All-Round Entertainment, at which he has since triumphed. Steele's importance to British rock'n'roll simply derives from his having been there first, rather than from any subsequent creative contribution.

Jesse Stone was the arranger who brought a coherent rock'n'roll backbeat to the R&B of the Fifties. He had worked with big bands and recorded for RCA and MGM before moving to Atlantic. There, he accompanied the label's executives on early field trips, introduced King Curtis to session work, and wrote, rehearsed and arranged many classics, often under his real name, Charles Calhoun. They included 'Cole Slaw' (Frank Culley), 'Money Honey' (the Drifters), 'Shake, Rattle And Roll' (Joe Turner) and 'Your Cash Ain't Nothin' But Trash' (the Clovers).

Stone's success led to work for other companies, notably Aladdin, Capitol and Epic, where he wrote Roy Hamilton's 'Don't Let Go'.

Barrett Strong was born in Mississippi on Feb. 5, 1941, and moved with his family to Detroit where his cousin, Nolan, was singing with the Diablos. In 1960, Barrett was signed to Gwen Gordy's Anna label. Soon afterwards, he reached the Top Thirty with the original version of the Janie Bradford–Berry Gordy classic 'Money'. The gospel-charged riff and unadorned message ('Money – that's what I want') were perhaps the basic ingredients on which Gordy (the producer of the record) founded the Tamla-Motown empire later the same year. The song was equally influential during the British group boom, when it was recorded by the Beatles on their second album and a version by Bern Elliott and the Fenmen made the Top Twenty in 1963.

After less exciting records on Tamla, Atlantic and Tollie, Strong returned to Tamla-Motown-Gordy, where he worked as a producer and writer alongside Norman Whitfield, turning out hits for the Temptations and Undisputed Truth in the Seventies.

'Big' Jim Sullivan, one of Britain's leading session guitarists – and thought by Les Paul to be one of the world's great guitarists – made his first impact playing lead in Marty Wilde's Wildcats. Session work – with artists as varied as Crispian St Peters and P. J. Proby – kept Sullivan busy after the Wildcats disbanded in the early Sixties, with the occasional outing under the name of Big Jim's Combo, until he joined Tom Jones as featured guitarist in Jones's touring band for five years (he'd already played on Jones's records). In between tours he began arranging music (for Dave Dee, Dozy Beaky Mick and Tich and Three Dog Night among others) and this led to his quitting Jones and doing the arrangements for Lou Reisner's version of *Tommy*. In 1974 he formed his own label, Pacific Eardrum, and released a solo album, *Big Jim's Back*.

Sun Records, of Memphis, Tennessee, is the label which more than any other has become identified with the emergence of white rock'n'roll. The label was formed late in 1952 by Sam Phillips, a former radio announcer who had set up the first permanent studio in Memphis, in 1950, to record the myriad local blues, R&B and C&W performers.

For two years he leased successful recordings to labels like Chess and his recordings of Howlin' Wolf, B. B. King and Jackie Brenston formed the basis of the Sun R&B sound of Rufus Thomas and Junior Parker, which in turn provided the inspiration for the rhythm of Elvis Presley and Carl Perkins.

The Sun label had scored several R&B hits by July, 1954, when Presley's 'That's All Right' was issued. Less than two years later, Carl Perkins' record of 'Blue Suede Shoes' became a monumental hit and those two records defined a new area in the repertoire of Southern music, and eventually in the whole development of rock. The music was called 'rockabilly' and it drew together the many styles of Southern music. It became the local form of rock'n'roll and the success of Presley, whose contract was sold to RCA in October 1955, and Carl Perkins was added to by a string of artists who have now emerged as top-selling stars – Roy Orbison, Johnny Cash, Jerry Lee Lewis and Charlie Rich were among them. The Sun catalogue was filled with the new music for around four years, during which time Sam Phillips became a millionaire.

Among the rockabilly artists were Warren Smith and Billy Riley – two performers whose records were unjustly neglected in their heyday – Sonny Burgess, Conway Twitty, Dickey Lee and Ray Smith. Their music came from country roots, and in this style Sun recorded fine artists like Charlie Feathers, Mack Self and Malcolm Yelvington. Bluesmen Rosco Gordon, Little Milton, Walter Horton and Frank Frost started here, too, and during the Sixties several fine country and soul singers recorded at Sun.

By the Sixties, the musical climate had changed and Sun was no longer a leader on the charts. It was financially stable, but musically it had already made its biggest contribution to rock. It continued until 1968, in the main reflecting local trends and providing a school of experimentation for musicians like Steve Cropper, Booker T., and the new Memphis

Sound. The very existence of Sun in the Fifties and its sub-sequent success enabled a tremendous number of talented performers to find their entry into recording. Sun was the foundation of the new massive music industry in Memphis.

Swamp-Pop, known locally as South Louisiana Rock'n'Roll, came out of the bayou lands of South Western Louisiana and was a rich hybrid of New Orleans R&B, Cajun and Hillbilly music. It hit its peak at the end of the Fifties with a series of national hits – Rod Bernard's 'This Should Go On Forever' (Argo), Cookie and His Cupcakes' 'Mathilda' (Judd), Jivin' Gene's 'Breakin' Up Is Hard To Do' (Mercury) and Phil Phillips's' 'Sea Of Love' (Mercury) and came back strongly in 1961 with Joe Barry's 'I'm A Fool To Care' (Mercury) and Cookie and His Cupcakes' 'Got You On My Mind' (Chess) in 1962.

The overall influence was Fats Domino and both black and white artists easily absorbed his lazy Creole vocals to such an extent that it was often difficult to tell a singer's race. There was a two-way flow of acts in and out of New Orleans and the Louisiana country towns which increased this musical cross-fertilization. The sound was nurtured by local Southern record men like George Khoury (Khoury's), Lee Lavergne (Lanor), Huey Meaux (Tribe), Jay Miller (Zynn), Sam Montel (Montel), Eddie Shuler (Goldband) and Floyd Soileau (Jin). Today, only Soileau, Meaux and, to a lesser extent Shuler are actively recording and promoting the infectious Swamp-Pop sound.

The Swan Silvertones, a smooth jubilee quartet in the Thirties, evolved a gospel style around the silky falsetto of Claude Jeter and a succession of harsh, shouting lead singers including Rev. Percell Perkins, for King, and Rev. Robert Crenshaw, for Specialty. Their greatest success was for Vee Jay in the early Sixties when the rhythmic harmonies organized by Paul Owens provided the ideal foil for Jeter and gravel-voiced shouter, Louis Johnson. Jeter's influence

302

spread into the secular field with hit versions of 'Oh Mary, Don't You Weep' and 'The Lord's Prayer'.

The Teddy Bears, a white vocal group from Los Angeles, were the launching pad for the career of master-producer Phil Spector. He formed the group while still a student at the Fairfax High Schoool, LA, with Annette Kleinbard (born 1940) and Marshall Lieb (Jan. 26, 1939).

Spector had already written a song, 'To Know Him Is To Love Him', apparently inspired by an inscription on his father's grave. He booked a local studio and cut the record, with Annette Kleinbard's high-pitched, 'little girl' voice taking the lead vocal. The disc was leased to Dore and by the end of 1958 it was No. 1 on the Hot Hundred.

A follow-up on Dore made no impact, and the trio moved to Imperial, where 'Oh Why' crept in at the bottom of the charts for two weeks. Other Imperial singles were less successful and soon after Kleinbard changed her name to Carol Connors, the group split up. Later, the Fleetwoods had a massive hit with 'Come Softly To Me', which utilized the Teddy Bears' formula of girlish lead vocal backed by cooing male harmonies.

TV, American. One of the great changes implicit in the rise of rock'n'roll was the end of the-song-not-the-singer adage, the central precept of Tin Pan Alley. By 1960, pop would have its own Tin Pan Alley (in the form of the Brill Building) but in the formative years of rock'n'roll it was the singer, not the song, that mattered – hence the demise of the cover version syndrome once the originals were readily accessible.

For American TV, this meant that the format of *Lucky Strike Hit Parade*, which saw 'Snooky' Lanson and the other regulars weekly perform their interpretations of the hits of the day, could not survive the arrival of the raucous R&B and rock'n'roll songs of the Fifties. Essentially hostile to rock'n' roll, yet fully aware of the increased viewing figures that a Presley could make to a TV programme, the networks were in a quandary, especially as putting Presley on TV was to make even more accessible a music they hated. TV's brief encounter with Presley in 1956 was, to say the least, an electrifying experience. His six appearances on Jimmy and Tommy Dorsey's *Stage Show* (starting on Jan. 6, 1956) showing him from head to toe, gyrations and all, attracted a record mail for the programme, and ensured that 'Heartbreak Hotel' was a *national* hit. His chart success assured, Presley became a willing pawn in the ratings battle between Steve Allen and Ed Sullivan. They tried to deaden his impact – Allen, by dressing Presley in a tuxedo and then putting him in a comedy sketch, and Sullivan by showing Presley only from the waist up. The result was even more controversy. TV could control neither Presley's image nor his impact, and the next time he appeared on TV, after his discharge from the Army it was by choice that he remained stationary and sang a duet with Frank Sinatra.

If Presley couldn't be contained, in Dick Clark TV found someone who could tame rock'n'roll. *Bandstand* had been running since 1952 in Philadelphia, with Bob Horn as its presenter. In 1957, a year after local deejay Dick Clark took over its presentation, it went national as *American Bandstand* on Saturday afternoons. The show's success – it inspired innumerable local dance shows – depended on its concentration on records and teenagers dancing to them, with the odd guest now and then, in an atmosphere of good, clean fun to which parents couldn't object. Having weathered the payola hearings of 1960, Clark and *American Bandstand* continued, but the show, reflecting the mood of the times, was becoming less interesting. Fittingly, it was Ed Sullivan, the would-be castrator of Presley, who introduced the Beatles to America and – on the basis of the phenomenal ratings his British Invasion shows got – paved the way for TV's next battle with rock, Jack Good's *Shindig* in 1964 and *Hullabaloo* in 1965.

TV, British. The first British series to cater specifically for the 'under twenty-ones' was *Teleclub*, a magazine programme with 'modern music', first broadcast on Oct. 9, 1953. It faced stiff opposition from the BBC hierarchy who were staunchly opposed to any form of youthful expression and suffered *Teleclub* only on the understanding that the noise be interspersed with features on sport and hobbies. On March 24, 1955, just as advance warnings of rock'n'roll were crossing the Atlantic, they took the show off the air and for the next two years both BBC and the commercial network steadfastly ignored the emergence of the new music. Finally, on New Year's Day, 1957, the commercial channel (which had begun in 1955) timidly offered its 'intimate record programme' *Cool for Cats*, which featured a group of Beat Generation dancers interpreting the week's new releases. This may well have prompted the BBC to unveil – on Saturday, Feb. 16, 1957 – *6.5 Special*, the first programme to fill the previously vacant six–seven p.m. slot.

Justly famous as the innovation of Jack Good, the programme is remembered today more for its style than its content, which was too often bogged down in sport, comedy and general interest items. Before very long Good was tempted over to commercial ITV to set up his masterpiece, *Oh Boy!*, the first unadulterated rock show. He did away with the jiving teenagers of *6.5*, relegated his audience to the auditorium of a former music hall and focused attention on the stage, where he organized superb choreographed action between Lord Rockingham's XI, the Dallas Boys, the John Barry Seven, Marty Wilde, organist Cherry Wainer and the Vernons Girls. The show had an enormously successful run from June 15, 1958 to May 30, 1959 and bit so deeply into the BBC's viewing figures that on Dec. 27, 1958, *6.5 Special* was replaced by the *Oh Boy!*-inspired *Dig This!* A pale imitation and, after only three months, the programme was succeeded by *Drumbeat*. Produced by Stewart Morris, later to become associated with *Top Of The Pops*, it also failed to steal Jack Good's thunder. Meanwhile, the BBC had introduced its pop panel game, *Juke Box Jury*, and for most of its eight year run (1959–67) the stupidity of most of the guests made compulsive viewing.

Drumbeat was the BBC's last serious attempt to combat their rival's superiority in the pop field until hitting back with

Top Of The Pops in 1963. ITV followed *Oh Boy!* with *Boy Meets Girl* (1959), in turn replaced by Jack Good's last British TV series, *Wham!* (1960). During the summer of 1960, the BBC's Josephine Douglas switched channels to produce *The Tin Pan Alley Show*, a series which accurately reflected the blandness of pop music at the turn of the Sixties. It was aimed at 'teenagers and their mums and dads'. In 1961, the BBC cashed in with *The Trad Fad* for a few weeks, and on Sept. 9, *Thank Your Lucky Stars* (ITV) started a new trend when it became the first programme to dispense with 'regulars' and present a completely different bill every week. *Lucky Stars* developed into an invaluable showcase for artists and, despite its conveyor belt approach, enjoyed great popularity until it was axed during the death throes of the British pop boom in 1966.

In 1963 the Beatles made their TV debut on the Feb. 23 edition of *Lucky Stars*. A BBC appearance followed on April 16, when they were four of the 'artists of the future' to be presented on Jimmy Young's *625 Show*. One of the countless side-effects of the Beatles' success was the creation by the end of the year of *Ready Steady Go!*, *Top Of The Pops* and a dozen other programmes to accommodate the new-found enthusiasm for rock music.

The Temperance Seven – there were actually nine of them – were a tongue-in-the-cheek attempt to recreate Twenties white dance band music. Often lumped in with the trad scene, the Seven were camp nostalgia rather than jazz. The Seven were formed in 1955 and settled down with a line-up of Captain Cephas Howard (trumpet, euphonium); Alan Swainston Cooper (soprano sax, clarinets, phonofiddle and Swanee whistle); Sheik Haroun Wadi el John R. T. Davies (trombone, alto-sax, trumpet); Ray Whittam (replacing Phillip Harrison on bass and tenor sax and clarinet); Dr John Gieves Watson (banjo, spoons); Martin Fry (sousaphone); Brian Innes (percussion); Clifford de Bevan (replacing Colin Bowles on piano); and Whispering Paul McDowell (vocals). They had two British Top Ten hits in 1961 with

'You're Driving Me Crazy' – a No. 1 – and 'Pasadena', which came complete with a series of false endings. When they disbanded, McDowell had a try at being a satirist – very fashionable then. They re-formed in the early Seventies with Ted Wood, older brother of the Faces' guitarist, as the vocalist.

Nino Tempo and April Stevens were a brother-and-sister duo from Niagara Falls. Nino was born on Jan. 6, 1937 and April on April 29, 1936. After playing sax on Bobby Darin sessions on the West Coast, Tempo won a recording contract with Atco in 1962. The lines of hits which followed featured re-workings of pop standards through their unusual vocal harmonies. The most successful were 'Deep Purple' (No. 1 in 1963) and 'Whispering' (No. 11 in the same year). They re-emerged briefly on White Whate in 1968, and Tempo is now working as an arranger in Los Angeles. He is credited on Cher's 1974 record 'Dark Lady', which was produced by Snuff Garrett.

Sue Thompson, whose distinctively light vocal style made 'Sad Movies' a huge popular hit in 1961, was born Eva Sue McKee, in Nevada, on July 19, 1926. Having moved to California and won her quota of local talent contests, she began to record with Mercury and Columbia. Moving to the country-oriented Hickory label she gained a string of popular hits between 1961–5 with 'Norman', 'James (Hold The Ladder Steady)' and 'Paper Tiger'. Many of her songs were by the prolific John D. Loudermilk. She still records for Hickory, often duetting with Don Gibson.

Willie Mae ('Big Mama') Thornton, born in Montgomery, Alabama on Dec. 11, 1926, recorded for Peacock between 1951 and 1957. Her version of the Leiber and Stoller composition 'Hound Dog' topped the R&B charts in 1953, selling the then phenomenal figure of 500,000 copies in the process. This classic song, featuring a guttural vocal and a tough guitar solo from Pete Lewis of the Johnny Otis band, was revived by Elvis Presley in 1956. Big Mama also recorded for Baytone and Sotoplay, and toured Europe with the 1965 Blues Festival, when she cut some of her finest sides for Arhoolie. More recently she has recorded for Mercury.

Johnny Tillotson was born in Jacksonville, Florida on April 20, 1939. Originally a country singer, the baby-faced singer was discovered at the Nashville Pet Milk talent show and signed to Cadence Records. Between 1958 and 1966, he was rarely out of the pop charts and had over 25 records in the Hot Hundred. 'Poetry In Motion' (No. 2), 'Without You' (No. 7) and 'It Keeps Right On A-Hurtin' ' (No. 3) were the most successful. Some of his hits had a stupendous beat, but he was clear-voiced with no rough edges, and parents liked him. He left Cadence for MGM in 1963, and again reached the Top Ten with 'Talk Back Trembling Lips'. Similarly melancholic country songs (he claimed Hank Williams as his greatest influence) still keep him busy today.

The Tokens. Various musicians including Neil Sedaka, Carole King and Neil Diamond played and recorded with Jay Siegel (born Oct. 20, 1939) and Hank Medress (Nov. 19, 1938) before Phil (April 1, 1942) and Mitch Margo (May 25, 1947) joined to make up the Tokens proper. Their first record 'Tonight I Fell In Love', which they produced, made the Top Twenty. After a dispute with their record company, Warwick, they moved on to RCA and had further hits with 'When I Go To Sleep', 'Sincerely' and their American No. 1 'The Lion Sleeps Tonight'. While their material made them the first folk rock group, their early harmonies and arrangements were influenced by the style of the Skyliners and Dion and the Belmonts. After leaving RCA they recorded with little success on B.T. Puppy, Warner Bros, Buddah and Atco. Hank Medress now works with Dave Appell, producing Tony Orlando, while the other members of the Tokens recorded as Cross Country.

Rudolph Toombs provided a steady stream of material for

their earliest successful R&B artists when Atlantic Records began in 1948. 'Teardrops From My Eyes' and '5-10-15 Hours' were No. 1 R&B hits for Ruth Brown in 1950 and 1952 – both love songs of extraordinary depth for their time. But Toombs' *forte* was songs about drinking and its ill-effects – 'One Mint Julep' is perhaps his best-known, while others in this vein include 'Nip Sip', 'In The Morning' (Clovers), and Amos Milburn's 'One Scotch, One Bourbon, One Beer'. Whatever the subject, though, his songs were generally raunchy, bluesy numbers.

The Tornados – George Bellamy (born Oct. 8, 1941), Heinz Burt (July 24, 1942), Alan Caddy (Feb. 2, 1940) Clem Cattini (August 28, 1939) and Roger Laverne Jackson (Nov. 11, 1938) – came together in 1960 to do session work for Joe Meek. Dubbed the Tornados when they became Billy Fury's backing group. In 1962, they had an enormous hit with a solo record, 'Telstar'. Others followed, virtually indistinguishable from the first and, as the group's popularity waned, Heinz left and had an erratic career singing eulogies to Eddie Cochran. The others eventually drifted into other branches of the music business. Momentarily the Tornados' up-tempo, organ-dominated instrumentals succeeded in stealing some of the Shadows' thunder.

Ed Townsend, born in Memphis, Tennessee, the son of a Methodist minister, had a church upbringing and was a choir member. Before becoming a professional singer, initially with Horace Heidt's band, he studied law in Memphis. A prolific songwriter, his ballad 'For Your Love' was a 1958 American Top Twenty hit on Capitol, sung in a sophisticated, mellow baritone style akin to Brook Benton. Ed married Theola Kilgore, for whom he wrote and produced the 1963 hit, 'The Love Of My Man'. Owner of KT and Tru-Glo Town Records, he was latterly involved in writing and producing Marvin Gaye discs before starting a fresh company, Century City Records, in Los Angeles.

Traditional ('Trad') Jazz came to Britain during the Second World War when many British musicians were granted their first contact with real recorded New Orleans jazz – courtesy of some thousands of American servicemen. Probably the first and most influential British traditional jazz band was George Webb's Dixielanders, formed around 1944 by George Webb. The band broadcast in 1945 with a line-up borrowed fom King Oliver's Creole Jazz Band – piano, two cornets, clarinet, trombone, banjo, tuba and drums. By 1947, Humphrey Lyttelton had joined the band and they had reverted to the traditional Hot Seven line-up using only Lyttelton's cornet. The Dixielanders broke up in 1948, leaving Lyttelton fronting a band composed mainly of ex-Dixielanders. In 1951 he and clarinetist Wally Fawkes reorganized the band using a rhythm section of piano, guitar and banjo, bass and drums, and in 1953 they added the alto saxophone of Bruce Turner to the front line. To the disgust of the most purist fans, the sacrosanct tradition of New Orleans marching bands was giving way.

In 1951, the National Federation of Jazz Organisations put on a traditional jazz concert at the Festival Hall in London, graced by the presence of the then Princess Elizabeth, future Queen of England. By this time the number of working 'trad' bands had enormously proliferated. Among the best remembered pioneers are Chris Barber (whose band included Lonnie Donegan and Monty Sunshine), Ken Colyer (whose important influence fell on musicians such as Barber, Acker Bilk, Alexis Korner and Micky Ashman), Mike Daniels (who used Cy Laurie, Charlie Galbraith and Micky Ashman in his Delta Jazzmen), Mick Mulligan (whose vocalist was blues shouter George Melly), and Alex Welsh.

Trad quickly became associated with radical politics and the bohemian image of the music attracted a sizeable following in the record buying public. In some ways the world of trad jazz (clubs, beatniks and beer rather than coffee) became a symbol of rebellion in Britain. However, as the music grew in popularity it lost most of its purist connota-

tions and the biggest hit records associated with trad –
Acker Bilk's 'Stranger On The Shore' (1961) and Chris
Barber's 'Petite Fleur' (1959) emphasised that trad had
been merged with Tin Pan Alley. Nevertheless, the skiffle
movement flourished within trad itself, and the Chris Barber and Ken Colyer skiffle groups had earlier provided the
motor for a new resurgence in British pop – leading directly
to the success of Lonnie Donegan, an increasing interest in
the blues and small-group music, indirectly to the successes
of a host of British pop stars (culminating with the Beatles)
who all started in skiffle groups, and to the development of
the British R&B of the Sixties.

Bobby Lee Trammell, like many singers of his generation,
started recording rockabilly and migrated to country afterwards. Trammell was never a successful artist, but his recordings show great range and feeling. In 1956, he wrote
and recorded 'Shirley Lee' which was later cut by Ricky
Nelson and encouraged him to continue recording with
several mid-South labels. His recordings for the Jonesboro, Arkansas label Atlanta are among his best, amalga-
mating various rock and blues styles in songs like 'I Love
'Em All'. Recently, he has been more successful in C&W,
recording for his own label, Souncot, and for Cinammon in
Nashville.

Joe Turner, born in Kansas City on May 18, 1911, proved
the most experienced of all the singers on the R&B charts
in the early Fifties. He was also a prominent part of the
Kansas City jazz scene of the Thirties, often teaming up
with boogie pianist Pete Johnson. Coming to New York in
1938, he made his first record, the very popular 'Roll 'Em
Pete' (with Johnson on piano) for Vocalion, and became a
major figure in the boogie-woogie revival of 1938–41
(sparked off by his appearance on John Hammond's legendary Spirituals To Swing concert at Carnegie Hall, one of the
first instances of authentic black blues and jazz musicians
winning a large white audience). By 1951, Atlantic records

had signed him to a recording contract and released 'Chains Of Love', the first of a string of Turner hits that lasted well into the rock'n'roll era. Of these, probably his most influential was the 1954 recording of 'Shake, Rattle And Roll', a Jesse Stone composition – written under the pseudonym of Charles Calhoun – that was to form the basis of Bill Haley's bowdlerized version. Whether Turner is strictly a rock'n'roll singer is debatable; he never changed his style from the way it was in 1938. But then, he didn't have to. He even sounded great singing 'Teenage Letter' at the age of 46. No other artist from the Swing era became anywhere near as vital a force in the R&B music of the Fifties as Joe Turner.

Sammy Turner. Born Samuel Black in Paterson, New Jersey on June 2, 1932, Turner's sinuous, smoky tenor was one of the most underrated voices in pop. All his records shared an inimitable, highly stylised approach, while the accompaniment – a blend of violins, cellos and King Curtis' stuttering sax – produced some diverting and unusual sounds. Masterminded by Leiber and Stoller, 'Lavender Blue' made No. 3 in 1959, and three other discs – 'Always', 'Symphony' and 'Paradise' (all on Big Top) – entered the charts during that year. The highly regarded 'Raincoat In The River' missed out, however. Turner also recorded, unsuccessfully, for Motown, 20th Century Fox, Verve, and Singers Studio International.

Titus Turner is one of a number of black R&B artists who have been recording steadily over many years, but is best remembered for penning such standards as 'All Around The World'. Beginning with Okeh in 1951, he has dabbled in a vast spectrum of styles – ballad and jump-blues, rock'n'roll, novelty songs, standards, soul ballads and funky discotheque dancers – on Wing, Atlantic, King, Glover, Jamie, Enjoy, Josie, Columbia, Atco, Philips and Mala, achieving chart status with only three discs. He sings in a slightly flat-pitched baritone style, not unlike Lloyd Price.

Conway Twitty, born in backwoods Mississippi at Friars Point on Sept. 1, 1933, developed through country and rockabilly into an extremely successful rock ballad singer in the late Fifties. 'It's Only Make Believe' was one of the turning points in white rock'n'roll, highlighting the move of Southern artists away from rockabilly.

Twitty took his professional name in 1957 from towns in Arkansas and Texas that he passed through while touring under his real name, Harold Jenkins. His group, the Rockhousers, was first formed in Helena, Arkansas, in 1947 as the Phillips County Ramblers and was then strictly downhome country. In 1956, they worked in Memphis as the Rockhousers and demo tapes were made for Sun. In 1957, Mercury released rock'n'roll singles that had been based on Twitty's ability to sound like Presley. 'I Need Your Lovin'' was a minor hit.

His first real contribution to rock'n'roll came after he signed with MGM in 1958 and 'It's Only Make Believe' was rivalled for success by 'Mona Lisa' and several other ballad hits. An intense, deep, throbbing vocal style that was more or less his own was the keynote to success. Top media exposure and several 'college' and 'teen' movies followed. By 1963, after a brief association with ABC-Paramount, Twitty was in decline as a pop singer. He joined Decca and made a successful return to his roots – and to the music he had always wanted to sing – as a country singer. By the Seventies he had established himself as one of Nashville's foremost artists, singing (often with Loretta Lynn) hard-bitten songs of love and marriage in a pleading and mournful manner.

Ritchie Valens, born Richard Valenzuela of Mexican-Indian lineage in Los Angeles, on May 13, 1941, took up the guitar as a child and had written songs and formed his own group, the Silhouettes, while still at Pacoima High School. In the Spring of 1958, Valens signed a recording contract with Bob Keene's Del-Fi label in L.A., and after considerable coaching recorded the quasi-Latin rocker,

'Come On Let's Go' which reached No. 42 in America in October, 1958, and was covered in Britain by Tommy Steele. Valens consolidated his success in December that year when both sides of his follow-up, 'Donna'/'La Bamba', reached America's Top Ten. Valens subsequently appeared on the Perry Como TV show, toured Hawaii and featured on package shows. He also filmed a cameo spot in *Go Johnny Go*. After an appearance at the Surf Ballroom in Clear Lake, Iowa, Valens and co-stars Buddy Holly and the Big Bopper were killed while travelling to their next gig in a private plane on February 3, 1959. Valens was the prototype chicano rocker and forerunner in the style of Chris Montez, Chan Romero, Eddie Quinteros, Sunny and the Sunglows and Cannibal and the Headhunters.

The Valentinos, formerly a gospel group called the Womack Brothers, they recorded for Sam Cooke's Sar Records. In 1962, they sold half a million copies of 'Lookin' For A Love', written by Cooke's manager, J. W. Alexander, together with Zelda Samuels. Lead singer and session guitarist Bobby Womack subsequently made a vastly superior recording in Muscle Shoals, Alabama, in 1974. Born in Cleveland, Ohio, he often contrived to sound like his mentor Cooke in vocal style and texture, especially on limpidly austere ballads like 'Somewhere There's A Girl'. The Valentinos recorded Cooke's composition 'Tired Of Livin' In The Country', a fall-apart blues ballad, but are best remembered for 'It's All Over Now', a raunchy up-tempo item they wrote themselves. It was covered by the Rolling Stones in 1964.

Leroy Van Dyke, born on Oct. 24, 1929, in Spring Forks, Mississippi, began singing and playing the guitar in the Army. On his discharge he became a livestock auctioneer, and in 1956 had the idea of writing a novelty song around the auctioneers' cry. The result, 'The Auctioneer', recorded by him and leased to Dot later that year was his first national hit. It was covered in Britain by Don Lang, but surprisingly didn't sell well in the country market. Further chart success eluded him until 'Walk On By', the apotheosis of country-pop, a country No. 1 and a pop Top Five record in the autumn of 1961 on Mercury. 'If A Woman Answers', another song of illicit love sung by Van Dyke's strangely warm voice, was his last pop hit in 1962. From that point on his only (minor) successes were in the country charts. Though he has switched labels at regular intervals – to Warner Bros in 1966, to Kapp in 1969 and to Decca in 1970 – further national success has eluded him.

Bobby Vee was both the luckiest and prettiest of a generation of American 'college boy' soloists who jockeyed for precedence in 1959 and then fell back against the opposition of the beat groups in 1963. He was born Robert Velline in Fargo, North Dakota, on April 30, 1943, and his first claim to fame was that he and his brother were members of the group (the Shadows) who deputized for air crash victim Buddy Holly at a gig in Mason City, Iowa, in 1959. Producer Snuff Garrett heard their disc, 'Suzie Baby', and took the group to Liberty Records, where Vee was groomed for a solo career.

Supervised by Garrett, it flourished. After four American releases, 'Rubber Ball' took off on both sides of the Atlantic in 1960 and, for the next three years, Vee extolled the pain and pleasure of chaste romance in a series of slick, bouncy hits that included 'Take Good Care Of My Baby', 'Run To Him', 'Sharing You', 'A Forever Kind Of Love', 'The Night Has A Thousand Eyes' and 'Bobby Tomorrow'. His popularity in Britain was immense and he seemed to be forever either touring with the Crickets or making guest appearances in British films and TV shows.

After the bubble burst, he continued to record but was fighting a losing battle and bowed out in 1969, a wealthy family man. He returned in 1972 and, under his real name, recorded an LP, *Nothin' Like A Sunny Day*, that included a dull new arrangement of 'Take Good Care Of My

Baby'. Response was slight and left his future somewhat open to question.

Vee Jay Records. Vivian Carter, from Tunica, Mississippi, and Jimmy Bracken, from Kansas City, Missouri, (actually Mr and Mrs Bracken) owned Vivian's Record Shop in Chicago when they launched a record company in 1953. Their first two acts, Jimmy Reed and the Spaniels, literally walked in off the street and asked to record. The Brackens remodelled a garage into a studio where they rehearsed local artists before sessions at Chicago's Universal Recording Studio. Initially distributed by Chance Records, who soon folded, Vee Jay found their feet when the Spaniels' 'Goodnight Sweetheart Goodnight' hit in Spring, 1954, providing finance to establish the label, and Ewart Abner and Vivian's brother Calvin joined the A&R staff.

In 1957, the Falcon subsidiary was formed, later renamed Abner, scoring hits with the Impressions and Dee Clark, while Vee Jay secured a stream of hits over the years with Jimmy Reed, El Dorados and Dells among others. These were Chicago artists, but a fair proportion of the label's output comprised masters leased from small companies all over the country, while there was also a substantial catalogue of gospel material. Randy Wood became a director in 1960, joined by Bill Shepherd. Bill brought in Gene Chandler, whose 'Duke Of Earl' was a 1962 million-seller and further success followed – the Four Seasons' 'Sherry', plus two follow-ups, each sold a million in 1962–3. Then the Beatles broke in 1964 with their first half-dozen hits on Vee Jay and its new Tollie subsidiary. But for every hit there were 20 flops, and the company hit financial trouble. They moved to Hollywood and back to Chicago before suspending operations in May, 1966. Vivian Carter is now a Chicago radio personality, but James Bracken died in 1974.

The Ventures were formed in 1959 by Bob Bogle (born June 16, 1937) and Don Wilson (Feb. 10, 1937) on guitars and

Nokie Edwards (May 9, 1939) on bass, with Howie Johnston as the first of many drummers. Their first single, 'Walk Don't Run' was issued in June of that year on Dolton. Its distinctive features were the cleanness of the instrumental sound and liberal doses of the tremolo arm – a technique the Shadows used in their 1960 hit, 'Apache'. 'Walk Don't Run' and its follow-up made the Top Ten in both Britain and America, but as an instrumental group the Ventures had little fire or imagination, depending for their popularity on simple and melodious arrangements of other people's hits. With the advent of the Beatles, the Ventures turned their attention away from America and Britain towards Japan, where they have been rewarded by a fistful of golden albums.

The Vernons Girls were a troupe of singers and dancers whose matchless raw enthusiasm perfectly suited the late Fifties. They were formed in 1957 by the Liverpool-based Vernon Pools, who wanted to encourage an interest in choral singing among their employees. Sixteen of the original 70 turned professional and made their TV debut in *6.5 Special*, but it was *Oh Boy!* (1958) that fully exploited their athletic and sexual potential. Subsequently no TV pop show was complete without them.

During the sweet music era of 1961, they disbanded and later re-emerged in smaller units. One girl (Lyn Cornell) went solo; three (Maureen Kennedy, Frances Lee and Jean Owen (later known as Samantha Jones) retained the name the Vernons Girls and had some minor hits ('You Know What I Mean', 'Lover Please' and 'Funny All Over') while the Twist raged. A further trio (Vicki Brown, Margo Quantrell and Jean Hawker) became the Breakaways, an invaluable backing group. Much later, the most popular member of the original line-up, bespectacled Margaret Stredder, joined Gloria George and Marion Davis as the Ladybirds, whose background harmonies are to British TV's *Top Of The Pops* what the original Vernons Girls' short shorts were to *Oh Boy!*

317

Gene Vincent, born Vincent Eugene Craddock of a poor family in Norfolk, Virginia, on Feb. 11, 1935, left school at 16 and joined the Merchant Navy as a boiler-tender, fully intending to pursue a lifelong career on the seas. In 1955, while riding motorcycle despatch on the Naval base in Norfolk, Vincent suffered severe injuries to his left leg in a crash and was permanently disabled. During several months of convalescence in the Naval hospital, Vincent began devoting more time to his favourite recreation – singing. Late in 1955, he began sitting in with a country band affiliated to Norfolk's C&W radio station, WCMS, and by 1956 was appearing regularly on the station's *Country Showtime* talent show. At WCMS, Vincent ment 'Sheriff' Tex Davis, a local deejay who took Vincent under his wing and had him record some demos (including 'Be-Bop-A-Lula') with a hand-picked band of local musicians. These tapes were submitted to Capitol, in Hollywood, who were urgently seeking an answer to RCA's Elvis Presley and signed Vincent as their man.

Vincent and his band of ingenuous but adept country musicians – Cliff Gallup, lead guitar; Jack Neal, bass; Willie Williams, guitar and Dickie Harrell, drums – by now called the Bluecaps, were flown to Nashville to record 'Be-Bop-A-Lula' and 'Woman Love' on May 4, 1957. So closely were Capitol treading in RCA's footsteps, they had the single in the shops within two weeks. Promoted as a double A-side, it was 'Be-Bop-A-Lula' which took off and launched one of the most erratic and traumatic careers in the history of rock. The excitement generated on 'Be-Bop-A-Lula' came primarily from Gallup's startling, dipping and swirling guitar runs behind Vincent's distorted soft voice – he had to be recorded in another room to be heard at all, so loud were the Bluecaps playing.

However, through appalling mismanagement and a series of much weaker follow-ups chosen by his elderly Capitol A&R man, Ken Nelson, Vincent's career lost its original impetus. He came back, none the less, in 1957 with a new band – Harrell, Paul Peek, Tommy 'Bubba' Facenda,

Bobby Lee Jones and Johnny Meeks on lead guitar – and a second million-seller, 'Lotta Lovin' '. Despite the hit, however, Vincent's greasy working-class viciousness was unacceptable to an American media geared to middle-class respectability. By 1958, he was a virtual outcast in an American rock scene now dominated by younger boy-next-door types like Fabian and Ricky Nelson.

Vincent came to Britain and entered a new phase in his career as a European idol, renowned for his newly-adopted all-leather stage gear. In his heyday, he was the most extraordinary and unique spectacle on stage and although major hits eluded him he was by far the most popular live draw in the country. By 1964, Beatlemania, combined with his alcoholism, had taken their toll on both his health and his audiences and he returned to America a year later. When he re-emerged in 1969 to tour England, it was hard to equate his portly appearance with that of the erstwhile wild rocker – and his Kim Fowley-produced re-recording of 'Be-Bop-A-Lula' didn't help matters.

Later that year, he appeared at the Toronto Rock Festival but found work hard to come by in America and returned to Britain in 1971 only to be involved in alimony proceedings with his English former wife. He fled to the States and died a fortnight later after a seizure attributed to a bleeding ulcer.

Eddie 'Cleanhead' Vinson, the singer and alto-saxophonist, born on Dec. 18, 1917, in Houston, Texas. His career began with the bands of Milt Larkins and Floyd Ray. In 1942 he joined the Cootie Williams band, with whom he gained recognition as a rich and powerful blues singer. His hits for Mercury in 1945–7 included 'Cherry Red Blues', 'Kidney Stew Blues' and 'Old Maid Boogie'. His 1949 records on King, including the R&B hit 'Somebody Stole My Cherry Red', demonstrated his humorous style.

Although Vinson's popularity has waned, his expressive singing – laced with the curious squeal characteristic of Texas bluesmen – and rugged alto playing have graced many labels, including Riverside, Black & White, Bluesway and Bluestime.

T-Bone Walker, born Aaron in Linden, Texas, in 1910, entered music as a country bluesman and medicine-show artist in the Dallas area. Joining a territory band in the Thirties, he began to use electric guitar (which he first heard played by Les Paul) and moved to the West Coast, where he played with Les Hite's orchestra. During the Forties, he recorded for both Chicago and Los Angeles independents, having particular success with 'Call It Stormy Monday' (Black & White); in the Fifties he recorded chiefly for Imperial, and then made a variety of albums for different companies.

Walker's experiments with electric guitar in a small blues-band format were profoundly influential, and the whole school of postwar guitar-playing that centres about B. B. King owes its existence (whether it knows it or not) to Walker's early demonstrations of the medium's potential. An unremarkable but pleasant blues-singer, temperamentally he never seemed inclined to reach out for the status to which his influence clearly entitled him. He died in March, 1975.

Dinah Washington, born Ruth Jones on August 29, 1924, was a pianist in a Baptist church as a child. A spell singing with Lionel Hampton followed, setting her on a career as a jazz singer. She recorded a wide range of material for Mercury from the late Forties onwards. There were blues ('Trouble In Mind'), pop songs and even a Hank Williams number ('Cold Cold Heart' in 1951). Dinah Washington's biggest hits were 'What A Difference A Day Makes' (No. 10 in 1959) and a duet with Brook Benton, 'Baby You Got What It Takes' which got to No. 5 in 1960. She moved to Roulette in 1962, but died of an overdose of sleeping pills on Dec. 14, 1963.

Johnny 'Guitar' Watson, acknowledged as a leading

rock'n'roll accompanist, is also an impressive singer and a pioneer who experimented with the electronic characteristics of the guitar during the early Fifties.

Born February 3, 1935, in Houston, Texas, Watson was inspired by blues guitarists T-Bone Walker, Gatemouth Brown and Lowell Fulson. He moved to Los Angeles while in his teens, and worked with the bands of Big Jay McNeely and Chuck Higgins. Watson signed with King Records in 1952 and cut the futuristic instrumental 'Space Guitar' and the rock'n'roll-styled 'Motor Head Baby'. In 1955, he scored a huge hit with 'Those Lonely, Lonely Nights', a blues cut for RPM records. Watson went on to tour with Sam Cooke, Jackie Wilson, the Drifters, Ruth Brown and Louis Jordan. During this time he developed his showmanship with the guitar, even playing it with his teeth while doing a handstand, pre-dating Jimi Hendrix by a decade. More hits followed, including the atmospheric 'Three Hours Past Midnight' and 'Cuttin' In'. In the early Sixties, Watson teamed up with veteran rocker Larry Williams. The duo came to England and cut a live album produced by Guy Stevens. Watson's blistering guitar work can also be heard on Little Richard's 'Whole Lotta Shakin' Goin' On', which he recut in 1964.

Watson is today signed to Fantasy, and working in a producer/arranger capacity with such names as Betty Everett and Percy Mayfield. His guitar style has been absorbed by several white rock musicians, including James Burton and Roy Buchanan.

Bert Weedon, the British session-gutarist, was already a little too old to be a pop idol when his cover version of 'Guitar Boogie Shuffle' (an American Top Ten hit for the Virtues) put him in the limelight in 1959. He had another instrumental hit the following year with 'Sorry Robbie', and it is reputed that his version of Jerry Lordan's 'Apache', which made No. 1 for the Shadows, was the first. Bert then returned to session work, occasionally making an album under his own name, and had a surprise success in 1970 with *Rockin' At The Roundhouse*, a budget-price album recorded at a rock'n'roll revival gig.

Western Swing. At the beginning of the Thirties, the Texas fiddle-band tradition spawned a curious new music: Western Swing. It began as an elaboration of the fiddle band, uniting the fiddler and guitarist with pianist and other stringed-instrument players, and developed into a form of hillbilly jazz, played by five- to eight-piece bands in a fashion that owed much to contemporary jazz, swing and blues.

In most groups there was a core of fiddler(s), steel guitarist and, in time, brass and reed players, supported by a rhythm section of piano, rhythm guitar, tenor banjo and string bass that laid down a brisk 2/4 time. The repertoire embraced traditional fiddle breakdowns and waltzes, jazz standards, Thirties blues and a wide range of Tin Pan Alley songs, and numerous writers within the genre proved capable of imitating virtually all these idioms.

The leading band, and the first to expand into a substantial group with brass and reed sections, was Bob Wills' ffTexas Playboys. Wills, the son of an old-time fiddler, began in 1935 the creation of a very diverse record output, including such hits as 'San Antonio Rose' and 'Steel Guitar Rag'. A somewhat more local reputation was enjoyed by Milton Brown's Brownies, who included the highly creative steel guitarist, Bob Dunn. Other leading bands were Bill Boyd's Cowboy Ramblers, the Light Crust Doughboys (most jazz-influenced and versatile of the groups) and Cliff Bruner's Texas Wanderers. All Western Swing bands were primarily dance bands, and toured incessantly through the small towns of Texas and Oklahoma. A couple of thousand recordings, by 50-odd bands, formed the body of documented Western Swing in the Thirties and early Forties.

After World War II, small bands were less common, and the style was maintained by the large orchestras of Wills, Spade Cooley and Ted Daffan. By the Fifties, there was little left of the original sound, but the lessons of Western

Swing had been learned by C&W musicians all over; both in instrumentation and in repertoire the format of country music had been vastly expanded.

Marty Wilde, born Reginald Smith in Blackheath, London, in 1939, had only two years at the top but his voice, appearance and style made him a major British sex symbol. After a series of odd jobs, he was singing at London's Condor Club in 1957 when he was discovered by Larry Parnes. His height (6′ 3″) and Presleyish sullenness were novelties, but it was his fourth record, a cover version of 'Endless Sleep,' that brought him stardom. He was a resident on *Oh Boy!*, the host of *Boy Meets Girls*, had a girls' magazine named after him and, in 1959, had four big hits in a row: 'Donna', 'Teenager in Love', 'Sea of Love' and 'Bad Boy'. Only the last (which he wrote) was not a cover version. In the years that followed, he failed to adapt to the changing climate as well as his Larry Parnes stablemate, Billy Fury. He lost fans through touring America for too long and getting married and, by 1962, he was more an actor than a musician. The Seventies have seen Wilde pursuing a variety of occupations within showbusiness, although he has had less success in promoting his son, Ricky, as Britain's answer to Little Jimmy Osmond.

Andy Williams is a master at updating himself, and retaining his devoted middle-of-the-road following by adapting just enough of the latest rock trend to suit his soothing tenor voice. The 1974 album *Solitaire*, produced by the fashionable Richard Perry, is only the most recent example of this process. He was born in 1931 and started on a radio show in Iowa and then moved on to LA and Chicago. He accompanied Kay Thompson for a while and became associated with Steve Allen on NBC's *Tonight* where he both sang and acted. His first No. 1 (in both America and Britain) was 'Butterfly' (1957). Other classics included 'Canadian Sunset', 'Moon River', 'Almost There' and 'Can't Take My

Eyes Off You'. He won an Emmy TV award in 1962–3 for the best variety show. His films include *55 Days To Peking*.

Hank Williams was to country music in the Forties what Jimmie Rodgers was to it in the Twenties, and more; and it is appropriate that, in his rise, he followed much the same track as Rodgers, from a poor family through local popularity to a sudden elevation. Born in Mt Olive, Alabama, in 1923, he was close to neither the Southeastern harmony style of the Thirties nor its Southwestern contemporary, Western Swing; if he was influenced by what he heard, it was by such bands as Roy Acuff's. From Acuff, too, he may have derived the elements of his grieved yet resolute singing, which implied a commitment previously uncommon in country music.

When he emerged on record in 1946, he did so as a singer and bandleader of the honky tonk school, yet capable of an emotional range that swept up audiences far from the honky tonk environment. First among country singers, he impinged upon a nationwide pop market with such recordings as 'Lovesick Blues', 'There'll Be No Teardrops Tonight', 'Your Cheatin' Heart' and 'You Win Again': lovesongs of despair phrased with a succinctness that few Tin Pan Alley songwriters could emulate.

Other songs belonged to a more recognizable tradition of good-time music – 'Honky Tonkin' ', 'Rootie Tootie', 'Jambalaya' – and there were occasional novelties like 'Kawliga'. More in keeping with the melancholy of his best-known hits was a group of blues-derived songs, ingeniously distinct from the blues as such: '(I Heard That) Lonesome Whistle' is a supremely affecting example. Williams preserved, too (as Rodgers had never sought to do), his responses to old-time religion, which produced a number of powerful renderings of traditional and newly-composed gospel songs. Finally, in a series of recordings under the name 'Luke the Drifter', he delivered monologues on the right life and its wrong paths, such as 'Too Many Parties and Too Many Pals'.

Williams died of a drug overdose in the back of a car on New Year's Day, 1953, possessed of a remarkable past and an incalculable future. Few C&W singers since his day have been entirely unaffected by his music, and the standard country repertoire contains perhaps more of his songs than anyone else's.

Larry Williams, although born in New Orleans in 1935, learned to play piano on the West Coast. He started out singing and playing in the bands of R&B greats like Lloyd Price, Roy Brown and Percy Mayfield and it was while accompanying Price on a recording session that he was discovered by Art Rupe of Specialty Records. His first record was an unsuccessful cover of Price's 'Just Because', but he made it next time out with the R&B classic, 'Short Fat Fannie', which climbed to No. 6 in the Hot Hundred in 1957. 'Bony Moronie' and 'Dizzy Miss Lizzy' completed a rocking hat-trick for Williams, who for a time looked like rivalling Specialty's label star, Little Richard. Despite a succession of records for many labels and a good British tour in 1964, Williams has turned to record production in recent times.

Maurice Williams and the Zodiacs – including Henry Gasten, Willie Bennet and Charles Thomas – hailed from Lancaster, South Carolina, where they won a talent contest in 1955 and travelled south to Nashville in the hope of recording. There they signed with Excello Records as the Gladiolas, and their first disc was the mambo-styled 'Little Darling', written by Williams, an American Top Fifty hit in 1957, while the Diamonds' cover-version was a transatlantic million-seller. Subsequent discs failed to register and in 1959 the group moved to New York where they signed with Herald Records as the Zodiacs. They struck gold immediately when the distinctive falsetto wail of 'Stay' sold a million in 1960, topping the American charts and just missing the British Top Ten. Similar sounding follow-ups, 'I Remember' and 'Come Along', were minor American hits, but by 1963 the Zodiacs' fortunes had expired, though Williams – composer of most of the group's material – subsequently recorded solo for Atco, Scepter and Veep.

Otis Williams and the Charms – Roland Bradley, Joe Penn, Richard Parker and Donald Peak – were based in Cincinnati, Ohio, signed with local King Records in 1954 and immediately shot to fame when 'Hearts of Stone' sold a million in 1955. Next year, 'Ivory Tower' repeated the feat, and the group issued a prodigious quantity of discs featuring Williams' fine lead vocals on De Luxe and King until splitting up in 1964. Williams then went solo on Okeh and later on Stop, where he began a fresh career recording country material as Otis Williams and the Midnight Cowboys.

Chuck Willis, born in Atlanta, Georgia on Jan. 31, 1928, first sang with Red McAllister's band. In 1951, he was signed to Columbia's 'race' subsidiary, Okeh, where under the astute management of the famed Atlanta R&B discjockey Zena Sears, his success was immediate. 'My Story', 'Going To The River', 'Don't Deceive Me', 'You're Still My Baby' and 'I Feel So Bad' – all Top Ten R&B entries in 1952–4 – were among his many hits. In 1956, Willis was signed to Atlantic, whose superb production transformed the R&B veteran into a major rock'n'roll artist. 'It's Too Late', 'Whatcha Gonna Do When Your Baby Leaves You', 'CC Rider' (No. 12 in 1957), 'Betty And Dupree', 'Hang Up My Rock'n'Roll Shoes', and 'What Am I Living For' (No. 15 in 1958) were classics of their period. A fine songwriter, his compositions were recorded by Elvis Presley, the Drifters and Buddy Holly. After collapsing with a stomach ulcer, Willis died on April 10, 1958.

Jackie Wilson, born in Detroit, Michigan on June 9, 1936, was discovered by Johnny Otis at a talent show in 1951. An admirer of Clyde McPhatter, he replaced him as lead singer with Billy Ward's Dominoes in 1953. His solo career took off in 1957 when he recorded 'Reet Petite', written in part by Berry Gordy Jr of Motown fame, for Brunswick. It's said that Elvis Presley derived some of his singing style and presentation from watching Wilson's dynamic stage act.

In October, 1958, Wilson had his first million seller in 'Lonely Teardrops', an unexceptional side after the initial shock of his suitably jerking, sobbing style. Once again, Gordy had a hand in the composition. His second million seller came in March, 1960, with his double-sided hit 'Night' and 'Doggin' Around'. The first was an adaptation of Camille Saint-Saens' 'My Heart At Thy Sweet Voice' from *Samson and Delilah*, a hugely swelling ballad ambitiously standing in a direct line from Tauber, Mario Lanza, and other operatic popularizers of the immediate post-war years. But perhaps 'Doggin' Around' was more characteristic of the R&B artist, replete with sanctified organ strains and unbelievable, wailing vocal peaks.

Wilson's best sides were less successful commercially. 'Reet Petite' represents him at his finest with a truly joyous performance pulling every local stop possible as he rolls and stutters and screams over the band. Equally wild were 'Baby Work Out', released in March, 1963, a tough dance exhortation in that familiar, crying blues style to heavy brass accompaniment and an earlier recording, the greasily sliding 'Woman A Lover A Friend' from July, 1960. This was copied later by Otis Redding. Impressive ballad performances include 'To Be Loved', a semi-operatic styling from February, 1958, and 'Alone At Last', based on Tchaikovsky's Piano Concerto in B Flat Minor and sung with barely contained power.

Jackie Wilson is a masterly 'live' performer and an artist of astonishing range, technically and generically. Unfortunately, his unique blend of big voice, gospel fervour and rock'n'roll rhythm gave way to the first soul boom of the Sixties. The girls stopped screaming although he continued to haunt the Hot Hundred. He saw some action on 'Whispers' in Sept. 1966. 'Higher And Higher' made No. 6 in 1967 and later that year he had a modest disco success with 'Since You Showed Me How To Be Happy.' His last noteworthy outing was 'I Get The Sweetest Feeling' released in July 1968, re-released British hit in 1975.

Jackie Wilson is one of the greatest popular R&B exponents to emerge from the Fifties and he has suffered shameful critical neglect. Unique and without parallel, only a handful of singers can come near him. If his influence has been limited, it is because the standard he set has proved too high.

Jimmy Witherspoon, born in Gurdon, Arkansas, on August 8, 1923, is one of the big names in hard-driving blues shouting which developed in the Thirties (and on which R&B grew) particularly in and around Kansas City. In 1945, he teamed up with boogie pianist, Jay McShann, who led an earthy jump band on America's West Coast. Rapidly gaining experience, he went solo in 1952 and soon became established as an international name on the jazz and blues circuit. His biggest hits include 'Big Fine Girl', 'Ain't Nobody's Business' and 'No Rollin' Blues'. For the last 20 years, Witherspoon has travelled widely, increasing his reputation all the time. His musical activities have been diverse, ranging from straight jazz to a rock album with Eric Burdon.

Kathy Young and the Innocents. Kathy was born in Santa Ana, California on 21 Oct., 1945, and signed to Indigo Records at the suggestion of singer Wink Martindale. The Innocents – white teenagers Jim West, Al Candaleria and Darron Stankey – backed her on a haunting and sensual revival of the Rivileers' R&B ballad, 'A Thousand Stars', which reached No. 3 in 1959. Kathy followed that with two minor hits, while the Innocents had Top Thirty entries with 'Honest I Do' and 'Gee Whiz'. Kathy Young subsequently married one of the Walker Brothers, while Jim West became one of Gary Lewis's Playboys.

Timi Yuro, born Rosemarie, in Chicago on August 4, 1940, enjoyed a brief vogue in the early Sixties, coming closer than any other white female singer to the deep, raw and soulful sounds of authentic R&B balladeering. Her only rival in this respect was Brenda Lee. In timbre, texture and mannerisms Timi Yuro sounded very like blues vocalist Esther Phillips. Her biggest success was a throbbing, sobbing ballad entitled 'Hurt' on Liberty in 1961. Her powerful, cracked tones were recorded effectively up front and the rapping, talking passage continued a tradition developed in the Forties by Inkspot Orville Jones, enlarged by Presley, and brought into full fashion by today's soul singers. The reverse was 'What's A Matter Baby', this time 'putting the hurt' on the man and evincing even more black mannerisms. Both sides were arranged by Bert Keyes and produced by Clyde Otis.

Her best single was her arrangement of 'Down In The Valley', a song generally associated with Solomon Burke and, later, Otis Redding, but here taken at a slower, bluesier pace with plenty of piano and brass. Coupled with it was a superb rendition of the standard 'Gotta Travel On'. Much of her subsequent material veered towards the supper club style.

INDEX

331

332

335

336

337

Glover, Henry, 101, **145–6**, 167, 176, 186
Goddard, Geoff, 200
Godfrey, Arthur, 58, 75, 78, 135, 223, 238
Goffin, Gerry, 44, 74, 92, 118, **146**, 201, 216, 235, 239, 253, 288
Goldberg, Barry, 146
Golden Gate Quartet, The, 151
Goldner, George, 28, 69, 92, 145, **146–8**, 167, 195, 200, 210, 235, 280
Good, Jack, 54, 129, **148–9**, 253, 271, 305
Goode, Johnny, 244
Goodees, The, 99
Goodman, Benny, 192
Goodman, Dickie, **57–8**, 148, 236
Goodman, Shirley, 288–9
Goodman, Steve, 18
Goons, The, **149**
Gordon, Rosco, 43, 71, 119, **149–50**, 224, 301
Gordy, Berry, 179, 270, 300, 327
Gordy, Gwen, 300
Gorham, Jimmy, 106
Goring, Sonia, 69
Gormé, Eydie, 189, 212
Gospel Tornados, 290
Gough, Tommy, 90
Grace, 'Daddy', 27
Gracie, Charlie, 64, **152–3**, 252
Grammer, Billy, **153**
Grand Funk Railroad, 67
Grande, John, 156
Grant, Julie, 52
Gravenites, Nick, 280
Graves, Alexander, 225
Grech, Ric, 92
Green, Al, 234
Green, 'Doc', 117
Green, Irving B., 220
Green, Jerome, 44
Green, Lee, 47
Green, Mick, 183
Greenaway, Roger, 119
Greenberg, Florence, 235, 288
Greene, Lorne, 283
Greenfield, Howie, **153–4**, 253, 284
Greenwich, Ellie, **154**, 195
Gregory, Gerald, 239, 295
Greig, Stan, 41
Grey, Wayne, 261
Griffen, Bessie, 151
Griffin Bros, 115
Griffin, James, 238
Griffin, Leroy, 238
Griffin, Paul, 239

Grimes, Tiny, 162, 263
Gross, Leon T., 108
Guida, Frank, 27, 46, 128, **154–5**, 295
Guitar Slim, 30, **155**, 232, 293, 296
Gummoe, John, 68
Gunter, Arthur, 127
Gunter, Cornel, 80, 81
Gunter, Cornelius, 133
Guthrie, Woody, 38
Guy, Billy, 80
Guy, Buddy, 72, 106

Hackberry Ramblers, The, 63
Hagans, Buddy, 110
Haggard, Merle, 67, 229, 278
Halcox, Pat, 26
Haley, Bill, 31, 32, 46, 51, 87, 99, 100, 101, 126, 141, **156–7**, 209, 270, 276, 312
Hall, Bill, 261
Hall, Rick, 18, 175
Hall, Roy, 99
Hall, Tom T., 221
Hambone, Kids, The, 76
Hamilton, George IV, **158**, 209
Hamilton, Gerald, 92
Hamilton, Roy, **158**, 194, 299
Hamilton, Russ, 51
Hammerstein, Oscar, 282
Hammond, John, 311
Hampton, Lionel, 184, 320
Hancock, Hunter, 217
Hanna, Jerome, 176
Hansen, Barrett, 297
Hardesty, Herb, 110, 184–5
Hardin, Tim, 95
Hare, Pat, 121
Harman, Buddy, 228
Harmonising Four, The, 152
Harp, Cornelius, 213
Harper, Teddy, 246
Harpo, Slim, 127
Harptones, The, **158–9**, 235
Harrell, Dickie, 318
Harris, Addie, 288
Harris, Betty, 194
Harris, Bill, 79
Harris, Don 'Sugarcane', 111
Harris, Early, 201
Harris, Hal, 275
Harrie, Jet, **159**, 271, 286
Harris, Lois, 69
Harris, Peppermint, 16, 193
Harris, Richard, 283
Harris Richard (Jive Five), 176
Harris, Rebert, 152, 295
Harris Sisters, The, 266

338

340

344

345

347